The Essence of Islamist Extremism

This book provides a critical and a conceptual analysis of radical Islamist rhetoric drawn from temporally and contextually varied Islamist extremist groups, challenging the popular understanding of Islamist extremism as a product of a "clash of civilizations."

The author argues that the essence of Islamist extremism can only be accurately understood by drawing a distinction between the radical Islamist explanations of violence and the radical Islamist justifications of violence more significantly, the posits that despite the radical Islamist contextualization of violence within Islamic religious tenets, there is nothing conceptually or distinctly Islamic about Islamist extremism. To this end, she engages in a critical analysis of the nature of reason in radical Islamist rhetoric, asserting that the radical Islamist explanations of violence are conceptually reasoned in terms of existential Hegelian struggles for recognition (as fundamentally struggles against oppression), and the radical Islamist justifications of violence are conceptually reasoned in terms of moral consequentialism.

With a detailed analysis of Islamist extremist discourse spanning a wide range of contexts, this book has a broad relevance for scholars and students working in the field of Islamic studies, religious violence, philosophy and political theory.

Irm Haleem holds a PhD in Political Science from Boston University. She has taught at Fisher College, Northeastern University and Seton Hall University. Her published works have focused on political violence and Islamist extremism in South Asia and Central Asia. Her current research focuses on a conceptual and a philosophical analysis of violence, as well as the narratives of the justifications of violence.

Routledge Studies in Political Islam

The Essence of Islamist Extremism

Recognition through violence, freedom through death

Irm Haleem

Routledge
Taylor & Francis Group

LONDON AND NEW YORK

First published 2012
by Routledge
2 Park Square, Milton Park, Abingdon, Oxon OX14 4RN

Simultaneously published in the USA and Canada
by Routledge
711 Third Avenue, New York, NY 10017

Routledge is an imprint of the Taylor & Francis Group, an informa business

British Library Cataloguing in Publication Data
A catalogue record for this book is available from the British Library

Library of Congress Cataloging in Publication Data
Haleem, Irm.
The essence of Islamist extremism : recognition through violence, freedom
through death / Irm Haleem.
    p. cm. – (Routledge studies in political Islam)
    Includes bibliographical references and index.
    1. Violence–Religious aspects–Islam. 2. Political violence–Religious
aspects–Islam. 3. Islam and politics. 4. Islamic fundamentalism. I. Title.
BP190.5.V56H35 2011
320.5'57–dc23

                                                                    2011024837

ISBN: 978-0-415-78298-2 (hbk)
ISBN: 978-0-203-80927-3 (ebk)

Typeset in Times
by Wearset Ltd, Boldon, Tyne and Wear

For My Parents:
Abdul Haleem
For being my role model of intellectual inquiry
For being my role model of humanism
For all the wisdom, guidance and support you have always offered
Saleema Haleem
For showing me grace
For teaching me courage

For My Husband:
Itai Boublil
For giving me wings when I could not fly
For being my beacon in rough waters
For showing me hope when I could not see any
For believing in me
For being the reason I was able to finish this book

Contents

Preface

The arguments forwarded in this book are based on my critical analysis of radical Islamist reason as found in the many different communiqués of radical Islamist groups from temporally and contextually varied settings. This book is a philosophical and a conceptual analysis of the essence of violence and brutality. This analysis is based in part on the arguments forwarded by Georg Wilhelm Friedrich Hegel, Friedrich Nietzsche, Axel Honneth and Hannah Arendt. What I have chosen as significant in the works of these philosophers, and how I have interpreted their arguments in terms of their broader contemporary significance, may very well be a matter of contention, but this in itself is nothing new to academic work.[1] Nonetheless, I have found the works of these philosophers particularly instructive in shedding light on the essence Islamist extremism.

In terms of Hegel's philosophy, this book draws upon Hegel's notion of the life-and-death struggles for recognition and its related notion of the master–slave dialectic, as found in his work *The Phenomenology of Spirit* (*Phänomenologie des Geistes,* 1807). The analysis in this book is not, however, a hermeneutical study of Hegel's *Phenomenology* as I do not concern myself with questions of what Hegel intended to demonstrate with the use of his concepts, nor with the context of Hegel's own writings or the implications of the trajectory of his writings. The analysis in this book is instead an application of one infamous notion in Hegel's *Phenomenology*, namely, the life-and-death struggles for recognition and the subsequent inevitability of the master–slave dialectic. In relation to Hegel's notion of struggles for recognition, I engage Axel Honneth's arguments, particularly as they relate to his assertion of the moral grammar of struggles for recognition, as presented in his work *The Struggle for Recognition: The Moral Grammar of Social Conflicts* (1995).

In terms of Nietzsche's philosophy, this book draws upon three of his most popular works: *Beyond Good and Evil,* published in 1886, in his *On the Genealogy of Morals* (also known as *On the Genealogy of Morality*) published in 1887, and *The Will to Power* (notes written by Nietzsche during 1883–1888 and published after his death in 1901). Of particular interest to me in these works is Nietzsche's view of the essence of morality itself and his related view of the instrumentality of religion, in terms of how both play a critical role in struggles for self-assertion, what Nietzsche calls the 'will to power.'

Finally, in terms of Hannah Arendt's philosophy, this book draws exclusively on her notion of the 'banality of evil' as it is presented in her infamous publication *Eichmann in Jerusalem: A Report on the Banality of Evil* (1963). Although many of my references to Arendt's notion of 'banality' are parenthetical and footnoted, their significance cannot be understated; this is particularly so, I argue, in terms of how this notion sheds light on the uncritical acceptance by individuals of the notions of morality that are dictated to them. This applies to the uncritical acceptance of radical Islamist rhetoric by audiences receptive to its reason, or the uncritical acceptance of notions of 'Just War' by broader international audiences receptive to its dichotomous and contradictory reason.

In terms of *conceptual* analysis, this book addresses the question of the 'what is' (not the 'why' or causes) of Islamist extremism. The question of the 'what is' is a question of the essential nature—the essence—of Islamist extremism. The notion of an 'essence' is necessarily abstract since an essence "cannot be seen in any ordinary sense of that term."[2] However, the 'essence' of a phenomenon refers to those characteristics that remain the same despite the existence of many other variations of the phenomenon (see the *Appendix on Essence*). To the extent that I argue in this book that the *nature of reason* in radical Islamist rhetoric from temporally and contextually varied Islamist extremist groups displays common *themes,* such reason can be understood as the *essence* (the 'what is') of Islamist extremism, since such reason remains the same despite the many temporal and contextual variations of Islamist extremist groups.

My method of conceptual analysis in this book draws upon the sociological and linguistic method of *critical discourse analysis.* In the *Appendix on Essence* at the end of this book, I argue that critical discourse analysis is an effective method to make tangible what is otherwise intangible: the essence of a thing (in this case, the 'thing' being Islamist extremism). The radical Islamist discourse that I examine critically in order to delineate the essence of Islamist extremism comes in the form of declarations (*fatwas*), speeches, charters and statements. Of course, discourse of any kind is rich with multiple implications, and in this radical Islamist discourse is no exception. To account for the varied nature of reason in radical Islamist discourse, some of the quotes from radical Islamist communiqués are repeated in the various chapters in this book. I have found this repetition necessary since each quote often yields insights into both the radical Islamist *explanations* of violence and the radical Islamist *justifications* of violence, making such repetition almost unavoidable.

Finally, it should also be noted that while this book engages in a critical analysis of *radical Islamist* rhetoric, this book is by no means a study in Islamic jurisprudence. Islamic jurisprudence comprises a rich literature on the matters of the interpretations, implications, and dimensions of Islamic law and its genealogy and comprises work beyond the *radical* Islamist interpretations of Islamic religious tenets. This book does not engage any such scholarly and theological debates. Indeed, such debates are not relevant to the nature of the study in this book, which concerns itself with *radical* Islamist reason, *not* Islamic reason; the former implies a manipulation of Islamic tenets for the interests of recruitment for violent and self-destructive missions, while the latter implies a study of Islam (as religion) and Islamic reason (as in Islamic jurisprudence) for the purposes of a theological understanding alone.

Acknowledgments

A book is never done; so say the sages. There comes a point, however, when years of writing must be presented to one's audiences, lest in the futile search for perfection, the writing never sees the light of day. In the words of many an author, this book has been a long time in the making. And while many more years could have been spent in substantiating the arguments that I forward in this book, I offer this book to you in the hopes that the discourse it might generate may benefit humanity in the long run.

The writing of this book started one summer afternoon in 2004, in the annals of the philosophy section of the 'Pusey' basement level stacks at Harvard University's Widener Library (where I had a 'special borrower' visitor access at the time). At Widener Library, I would like to thank Linda for all the moral support she offered in the many chance conversations we had as she checked my books upon my many exits from the library; I would also like to thank Cheryl LaGuardia (Research Librarian, Research Services) and Michael C. Currier (Library Privileges and Access Services) for their encouragement and most reliable assistance.

At Routledge, I would like to thank James (Joe) Whiting (Acquisitions Editor, Middle Eastern, Islamic and Jewish Studies, Routledge, UK) for his enthusiasm in my project, from the time I introduced the ideas to him in an informal conversation during the Middle East Studies Associations conference in 2009, to the time I submitted the manuscript to him for external review. Joe's professionalism, efficiency and reliability were remarkable indeed; I was very lucky to have come across such a great editor. I would also like to thank Suzanne Richardson (Senior Editorial Assistant, Middle Eastern, Islamic and Jewish Studies, Routledge, UK), with whom I had most of the interactions after Routledge offered a contract for this book. Suzanne's expedient responses to my email inquiries were priceless at the latter stages of the writing of this book. It was indeed a pleasure working with both Joe and Suzanne. I would also like to acknowledge my two anonymous reviewers' your appraisal of my work was more flattering than I could have imagined, your critical comments were more constructive than you may have imagined. Thank you!

At Princeton University, I would like to thank Miguel Centeno (Professor of Sociology and International Affair) for allowing me the use of his study carrel in

Princeton University's Firestone library during the last three years of the writing of this book. The carrel space in Firestone library was most instrumental in keeping me focused (particularly in the last year of the writing of this book) by providing me the excluded environment that I needed. And for this, I am truly grateful to Miguel for his generosity; quite possibly, the book may still have not been finished had it not been for this valuable space. I would also like to thank Miguel Centeno, along with Deborah Kaple (Associate Professor of Sociology), Amany Jamal (Associate Professor of Politics) and Charlie Westoff (Professor Emeritus, Center for Demographic Studies) for their willingness to be my audience in a 'mock talk' where I presented the ideas in my book; their critical comments helped me refine some of my arguments in this book.

At Tufts University, I would like to acknowledge Ayesha Jalal (Mary Richardson Professor of History and Director of the Center for South Asian and Indian Ocean Studies) for being my role model of academic rigor and for the support she has offered me over the years.

At Seton Hall University, I would like to thank King Mott (Associate Professor of Political Science and Public Policy) for always being an enthusiastic audience for my ideas and arguments. King always understood the reason behind my arguments in a manner quite unprecedented. His encouragement alone made the years I spent as an Assistant Professor in the department enjoyable. I would also like to thank Lesile Bunnage (Assistant Professor of Sociology) for her tireless moral support, especially during the academic year 2010–2011.

Finally, I would like to acknowledge those friends that played a supportive role during the writing of this book. Dimitri Apsotolitis (PhD, Boston University) for so graciously allowing me space in his Boston apartment during August 2008 in order to facilitate my research. Paul B. Wilkinson (Major, United States military) for being my role model of 'grace under pressure,' and for his constant inquiries about the status of my writing and the expected date of its completion. Mila Dragojevic (Assistant Professor, University of the South) for sharing with me her knowledge of methodological frameworks early on in this project which helped me conceptualize the method I had employed as that of critical discourse analysis. Mila's moral support, particularly in the last year of the writing of this book, was most critical. And, perhaps most significantly, I would like to thank Edan Johna, for being my biggest critic and my biggest fan. The conceptual distinction that I draw in this book between 'explanations' and 'justifications' have to be attributed to the many conversations I had with Edan where he challenged my arguments and forced me to rethink the very basis of my reason.

If it were not for the love and support of my parents and of my husband, Itai Boublil, this book would *never* have been finished. My parents' consistent enthusiasm for all the different endeavors in my life has been critical to my success; and Itai's steadfast moral support over *all the years* of the writing of this book was critical in the finishing of this book. This book is thus dedicated, wholeheartedly, to these three very special gems in my life.

Preliminary note

The analysis in this book does not claim to know the motivations of the recruiters of radical Islamist groups. Scholarly analysis of this subject hypothesizes that the motivations of the leaders of Islamist extremist groups may have little to do with the manner in which they present their cause in their recruiting rhetoric. The question of the motivations of the recruiters of radical Islamist groups is not, therefore, the focus of this book.

This book concerns itself instead with the question of 'why do they do this' by analyzing the *manner in which* radical Islamists *themselves present their cause* in their recruiting rhetoric, since such reason in rhetoric shapes the motivations of those individuals that voluntarily join Islamist extremist groups. This is not to ignore that motivations are multi-faceted, but to emphasize the importance of epistemological assumptions and logical deductions in understanding the motivations of individuals based on the reason given to them. The 'essence' of Islamist extremism that this book seeks to delineate, then, is delineated through a critical analysis of the *nature of reason* in radical Islamist rhetoric, since such reason shapes the *nature of the motivations* of its voluntary recruits. The 'what is' of Islamist extremism, then, is that which its voluntary recruits understand it to be. And this insight sheds important light on the *resonance* of radical Islamist rhetoric and thus the *resilience* of Islamist extremist groups. It also sheds light on the kind of policies that are likely to combat its threat as opposed to those that are likely only to exacerbate its threat.

It must be stated at the outset that the analysis in this book is not in any way as a promotion or a justification of violence; nothing would be farther from the purposes of this book. It should also be noted at the outset that while in Chapter 4 of this book I analyze the radical Islamist justifications of violence by juxtaposing them onto the justifications of violence found in the internationally accepted Just War doctrine, this is not to suggest that radical Islamists themselves refer to the Just War doctrine to justify their violence. Nothing could be farther from the reality since, I argue, radical Islamists fundamentally *reject* western reason. My aim in comparing radical Islamist justifications of violence with the Just War doctrinal justifications of violence is instead to highlight their *conceptual* similarity, so as to emphasize that radical Islamists utilize the same notions as justifications of their violence as do proponents of the Just War doctrine. And this highlights the fact that the moral algorithm used by radical Islamists to justify their violence is the same as the moral algorithm used by western and non-western states in justifying their violence and wars.

Introduction

Radical Islamist rhetoric makes frequent references to violence as 'jihad,' 'jihad' as duty, self-destruction as imperative, 'killing the infidels' as aim, the 'return of the caliphate' as desire, '72 virgins in heaven' as reward, and 'loving death' as the description of the self. But while such references are popularly understood as indicative of the distinctly *Islamic* nature of Islamist extremism, I argue in this book that there is nothing distinctly *Islamic* about Islamist extremism.[1] Through a critical analysis of the nature of reason in radical Islamist rhetoric drawn from contextually and temporally varied Islamist extremist groups, I argue that the radical Islamist explanations of violence and self-destruction are existential in essence, while their justifications—despite their contextualization within Islamic religious tenets—are consequentialist in essence. More specifically, I argue that the radical Islamist explanations of violence are reasoned in terms of Hegelian struggles for recognition while their justifications are reasoned in terms of moral consequentialist arguments.

Struggles for recognition in the Hegelian sense are struggles for the autonomy of the self, and as such are struggles against the negation of the self. In this way, they are fundamentally struggles against oppression (whether actual or perceived). The references to struggles for recognition in this book, therefore, should *not* be understood in terms of a desire for an international acknowledgement of a sovereign statehood. Struggles for recognition in this book refer to struggles for the recognition of the 'self' (defined either as an individual or the collective the individual belongs to) as at once distinct (autonomous) and equally significant to the other (independent). To the extent that Hegelian struggles for recognition are at once struggles against the negation of the self as well as struggles for the demarcation of the autonomy of the self, these struggles are argued to be fundamentally existential in essence; that is, such struggles are viewed as being based on the common human *fears* of negation and enslavement and the common human *desires* for autonomy and independence.[2] With violence explained in such a way, the radical Islamist references to religious tenets, I argue, are intended to provide a 'moral' guise to otherwise consequentialist reason. In this way, radical Islamist references to Islamic religious tenets create a justification for violence that is fundamentally a struggle for recognition and, as such, these justifications are consequentialist and not theological in essence.

Given that struggles for recognition, as well as their moral consequentialist justifications, are not unique to the radical Islamist context and are in fact universal in nature, I argue that there is nothing distinctly *Islamic* about Islamist extremism.[3]

My assertion that the radical Islamist explanations of violence are Hegelian in nature and that the radical Islamist justifications of violence are consequentialist in nature is premised on my related assertion that there is a *conceptual distinction* between 'explanations' of violence and 'justifications' of violence. This distinction can be simply understood as thus: 'explanations' consist of references to grievances (such as to oppression and occupations) that offer reasons *why* an action is necessary, while 'justifications' consist of references to notions of 'morality' that offer an *urgency*—a moral imperative if you may—for those actions which have already been described as necessary. In this way, 'explanations' logically *precede* 'justifications' since without explanations, the justifications would be vacuous. And if this is so, then to understand Islamist extremism in terms only of its justifications—which are Islamic in rhetoric—is to misunderstand the essence of Islamist extremism. This blurring of distinction between 'explanations' and the 'justifications' has led many scholars to conclude that Islamist extremism is uniquely *Islamic* (theological) in essence. This only takes us farther away from an understanding of the possible nature of the motivations of individuals that voluntarily join Islamist extremist groups and leads further to misguided policies intended to combat its threat.

Contending theories, meta-narratives, perplexing paradoxes

The existing literature on Islamist extremism can perhaps be categorized in the following manner: context-specific and causal explanations; theological explanations; ideological explanations. These studies have yielded as many hypotheses as they have yielded paradoxes. The paradoxes created by such studies are linked to the weakness of the hypotheses in explaining contradictions and anomalies *within* the particular context-specific, temporally defined cases of Islamist extremism. In the category of context-specific and causal explanations, I include all those analyses that focus on a variety of causes that are argued to create and consolidate Islamist extremist groups in a particular context (country or region) such as: historical struggles; government oppression; hatred and revenge based on foreign occupations; and dire poverty. See, for example, Crenshaw (1978), Ajami (1986), Norton (1987), Nasr (1994), Moghadam (2003), Abbas (2005), Gerges (2005), Jalal (2008).[4]

One of the most popular paradoxes that challenge the context-specific causal explanations is the motivations of voluntary recruits far removed from causes such as oppression, occupations, or economic drudgery. Indeed, in challenging the poverty–terrorism nexus arguments, Robert Pape (2005) observes that "suicide attackers are rarely ... economically destitute individuals, but are most often educated, socially integrated, and highly capable people who could be expected to have a good future."[5] Similarly, Luca Ricolfi (2005) observes that the new generations of Palestinian Islamist extremists have tended to come from higher economic, wealth and educational background as compared to the rest of their society.[6] Alan B. Krueger (2007) goes as far as dispelling the poverty–terrorism nexus explanations as a myth by arguing instead that incidences of terrorism correlate more to the demographics of a society, such as accessibility to groups dispensing rhetoric espousing violence, accessibility to targets and so on, and not to poverty levels. As such, Krueger considers the poverty–terrorism nexus argument to be "myth."[7]

In the category of theological explanations, I include all those analyses that focus on religious scriptures as both the explanations and the motivations for violence, thereby understanding extremism justified with reference to religious tenets as 'religious violence.'[8] Among many studies in this category, some notable ones are Bonney (2004), Juergensmeyer (2003), Cook (2005).[9] One of the most popular paradoxes that challenge the scriptural violence explanations is that a number of voluntary recruits of Islamist extremist groups have secular worldviews, a fact that directly contradicts the scriptural violence thesis. Indeed, in challenging the scriptural violence hypothesis for Islamist extremism, prominent Pakistani journalist Azmat Abbas notes that "a vast number of recruits [of Islamist extremist groups] ... lack any real religious knowledge or [any religious] motivation."[10] Indeed, in a report profiling eight known members of Pakistan's most notorious Islamist extremist group, *Jaish-e-Mohammad,* it was revealed that *only* four of the eight men had any specialized religious training, and the remaining half had either very little or no formal religious knowledge or training.[11] Scriptural violence explanations of Islamist violence thus inadequately explain the new breed of Islamist extremists that are decidedly secular and outwardly modern in their worldviews, such as those individuals that took part in the September 2001 terrorist attacks on the United States, or the British-born Pakistanis that took part in 'suicide bombings' in Britain on July 7, 2005.[12]

In his study of Palestinian Islamist extremists, Christoph Reuter argues that contrary to popular beliefs, religious convictions do *not* form the bases of the motivations of Palestinian suicide bombers.[13] The central motivations of Palestinian Islamist extremists, argues Reuter, are their rejection of Western policies.[14] Similarly, Mia Bloom notes that "there is nothing inherently dysfunctional about the Islamic faith per se that predisposes its adherents towards violence ... suicide terrorism has mistakenly been associated with this one religion in particular."[15] In his comparison of the various radical Islamist suicide bombers (from Palestinian to Lebanese to members of al-Qaeda) with the suicide bombers from non-Islamic groups (such as the Tamil Tigers in Sri Lanka and the radical Sikhs movement in India), Robert Pape argues that Islamist suicide operations are fundamentally motivated by struggles against colonial occupations and territorial disputes and *not* by fanatic *Islamic* fundamentalism.[16] The popularity of al-Qaeda, argues Pape, can be explained in terms of its espoused struggle against the "Crusader–Zionist alliance" (namely western powers and its allies such as Israel) which it sees as seeking to dominate the Muslim world.[17]

Finally, in the category of ideological explanations, I include all those western-centric, neoconservative explanations of Islamist extremism that point to what they claim is a uniquely barbaric Islamic religious and cultural milieu. Such narratives are encapsulated in the notion of a 'clash of civilizations'; indeed, so popular is this notion amongst the western and non-western neoconservatives that it has in fact become a metanarrative. Consider, for example, the remarks made by Italian Prime Minister Silvio Berlusconi in the immediate aftermath of the terrorist attacks on the United States in 2001: "We must be aware of the *superiority* of [western] civilization ... *in contrast* to the Islamic countries."[18] As well, Marvin Perry and Howard E. Negrin explain Islamist extremism in terms of a phenomenon reflective of an intrinsically violent 'Muslim civilization' which is at war with the more civilized western 'Judeo-Christian civilization.'[19] Islamist violence, according to them, is a manifestation of "an abhorrence of Western civilization" with aims that are purely "theological" and as thus a movement that "threatens Western civilization's core values."[20] Shmuel Bar explains the motivations of Islamist extremists as being grounded in a "religious culture" that is argued to be distinct from its more civilized Judeo-Christian culture.[21] Mary R. Habeck explains radical Islamist violence as "systematic" and fundamentally based on "precedents set by Muhammad."[22] Melanie Phillips, in reacting to the July 2005 bombing of the London transit system by a group of radical British Islamists, argues that Islamist extremism can only be understood in terms of a religion (Islam) that is intrinsically violent and distinctly brutal compared to its Judeo-Christian counterparts.[23] Raphael Israeli blames not only "Islamic ideology" but Muslim society "as a whole" for Islamist extremism, with an analysis that basically turns into "a condemnation of the [entire] Muslim world."[24]

Since the analysis in this book directly challenges the central tenets of the clash-of-civilizations explanation of Islamist extremism, a more detailed look at this western-centric metanarrative is in order here. Adherents of the clash-of-civilizations school of thought base their arguments on the theological rhetoric of Islamist extremist groups and anchor their conclusions in dichotomous views of the self (the Judeo-Christian world) as 'rational' and 'civilized' and the other (the Muslim world) as 'irrational' and 'brutal.' Indeed, this narrative of 'us' versus 'them' has shaped popular Western understanding not only of violence and brutality, rationality and irrationality, but also of 'just' and 'unjust' wars. The most critical assumption in such a metanarrative is that Islam, as a religion and a cultural milieu, is *in essence* violent, in contrast to the more civilized Judeo-Christian religious and cultural milieus. This assumption leads to three other damaging assumptions: (1) Islamist extremism is *Islamic* in essence and thus an unavoidable manifestation of an apocalyptic religious culture; (2) the violence unleashed by Islamist extremists is preemptive and not reactionary; and (3) Muslims, by the very fact of subscribing to Islam, are tacitly supportive of violence and brutality. The first assumption leads to a critical misunderstanding of the essence of Islamist extremism. This, together with the second assumption, leads to misguided policies that are overly aggressive and militaristic so that while they are intended to combat the threat of Islamist extremism they only exacerbate its threat. The third assumption leads to the homogenization of an entire people—the Muslims in this case—which leads to what history has become all too familiar with: the demonization of an entire people that then justifies any and all actions taken against *all* such people, thereby not distinguishing between the innocents (non-combatants) and extremists (combatants).

The origin of the metanarrative of a 'clash of civilizations' can be traced to the works of Bernard Lewis who, in a 1964 publication, proclaimed that "we shall be better able to understand this situation [namely, the conflict in the Middle East] if we view the present discontents of the Middle East *not* as a conflict between states or nations but as a *clash between civilizations*."[25] In a later article entitled *The Roots of Muslim Rage*, Lewis reiterated his explanation of Islamist violence in terms of a movement that is "no less than a clash of civilizations."[26] Lewis' notion was later carried through to popularity by Samuel Huntington's infamous article *The Clash of Civilizations?*[27]

Interestingly, proponents of such a metanarrative tend to absolve themselves of any responsibility—in terms of the consequences of their actions and their foreign policies—in the perpetuation of Islamist violence. Aggressive militaristic policies such as the American occupation of Iraq, the US–NATO occupation of Afghanistan, the American CIA-controlled use of predator drones that target suspected terrorists but that also destroy the lives of many innocent civilians in the process, the American military's employment—and indeed deployment—of private American contractors that serve as de facto paramilitary forces and engage in extrajudicial killings in Iraq, Afghanistan and Pakistan are just a few examples of the consequences of accepting dichotomous narratives as explanations of Islamist violence. This is because dichotomous narratives—such as the 'clash of civilizations'—create a sense that the self (in this case the Judeo-Christian world) is necessarily and perpetually at war with the other (in this case the Muslim world) and this fuels the dehumanization of the other. Ironically, this very dehumanization of the other as an indivisible collective (where extremists and non-extremists are one and the same) reinforces the radical Islamist explanations and justifications of violence.[28] Terrorism then becomes, in the words of Joseba Zulaika, a self-fulfilling prophecy.[29]

Of course, the very clash-of-civilizations narrative that portrays Islam as a religion with a unique and distinct propensity towards violence and brutality casts a veil on those cases of violence and brutality that are justified within the context of other religious. For example, as Qureshi and Sells point out, "Christianity's history of inquisition, pogrom, conquest, enslavement, and genocide offers little support for assertions that Islam's sacred text or its prophet entails a propensity for violence *greater* in degree or different in kind."[30] As well, Qureshi and Sells argue that "the destruction of the African civilization in South Africa, the taking of the land, and the placing of the remnant populations in shrinking reservations and ultimately state apartheid were carried out with Bibles open, by Christians executing what they viewed as their divinely ordained right and duty."[31]

In his landmark publication *Orientalism* (1978), Edward Said argued that the tendency to 'other the other' was situated in the need to portray the self (the westerner) as superior to the other (the non-westerner). This, argued Said, served a number of purposes. First, it legitimized imperialistic and colonial rule on grounds that the other was in need of such directing and direction, consistent with the notion of 'white man's burden.'[32] Second, western imperialists' distinctions between the 'civilized' and the 'enlightened,' the 'primitive' and the 'primordial,' served to create a necessary contrast between the self (the westerner) and the other which was necessary to present the self as superior. This portrayal of the self as the superior master and the other as the inferior slave then served to justify the imperialist control of the other since such a portrayal created a justification for paternalism, and indeed racism. While Said drew primarily on Foucault, the understanding of the need to negate the other in order to present the self as superior to the other has a distinct Hegelian flavor.[33] In his analysis of the existential struggles for recognition, Hegel argued that recognition for the autonomy and independence of the self necessarily takes place through the negation of the other.

Edward Said's critical work opened the door to a rich scholarly tradition that challenged, and challenges, the clash-of-civilizations narrative; or, if you may, Said's critical work has created a counter-narrative to the neo-conservative metanarratives of non-western world. This counter-narrative comprises of the works of a number of prominent contemporary scholars and journalists researching the Middle East and Islamist extremism in particular. A most thought provoking critique of the neo-conservative metanarratives comes from Talal Asad.[34] Asad criticizes the assumptions of the clash-of-civilizations narrative by challenging its exclusive focus on Islam as *the* explanation of Islamist extremism. His arguments, however, are premised less on 'what is' the nature of Islamist violence and more on the question of why violence and brutality are presented as the exclusive domain of Islamist extremists in popular western media. Violence and brutality, he argues, are universal phenomena, committed as much by transnational and supranational groups as by official (legitimate) governments, both in the West and in the Muslim world. In addressing the selective focus in western media on the violence emanating from Islamist extremists while downplaying the violence—often on a significantly larger scale—initiated by powerful western hegemonic states, Asad argues that *the essence* of modern terrorism cannot be understood in the context of any one religious tradition; if Islam is to be blamed for its sanctions of violence and brutality then Judaism and Christianity might also join its ranks.[35]

In addition, Assad's criticism of the western neo-conservative metanarratives rests in his observation that the determination of what is considered repugnant and inhumane in popular western media is *not* based on the actual cruelty and human destruction of actions but on the manner in which such actions are taken as well as the identity (state or non-state, western or non-western) of the perpetrators of such actions. And so, a government's decision to engage in a bombing campaign of another state does not get as much attention in the media as does a suicide bomber of Muslim descent even though the former unleashes human destruction of a much larger scale. It appears, argues Asad, that violence and brutality unleashed by formal governments through unilateral or international sanctions is considered 'legal' while violence and brutality unleashed by Islamist extremist groups is considered 'illegal.' Asad thus criticizes the 'moral justifications' of 'fighting evil' behind which western conservatives and liberal politicians hide as it creates a banner that takes away from the spotlight its subsequent horror and destruction on the victim (which since September 2001, he argues, has tended to be the collective Muslim populations of certain Middle Eastern states). The labeling of an act as 'terrorism,' concludes Asad, should not be determined by its source—western or non-western—but by the violence, destruction and horror it generates.

Conceptualizing Islamist extremism, re-addressing paradoxes

This book extends the traditional parameters of analysis of Islamist extremism, from context-specific and temporally confined causal analysis of Islamist extremism to a broader non-context-specific and temporally fluid *conceptual* analysis of Islamist extremism. Robert Goodin and Charles Tilly define a conceptual analysis as an endeavor which seeks to understand the 'general laws' that are characteristic of a thing. General laws may be understood as the essence of a thing—in this case, the 'thing' is Islamist extremism—or the very nature of a thing. A conceptual analysis thus yields an explanation that is descriptive in nature, as opposed to causal analysis that yield context-specific linear hypotheses of the sort that argue that 'A' leads to 'B.'[36] To put it simply, a conceptual analysis is an analysis of the concepts that describe a phenomenon and that are critical in understanding the phenomenon.

The conceptual analysis of Islamist extremism in this book focuses not only on the concepts that are invoked in radical Islamist discourse, but also the *genealogy* of the concepts that are invoked—that is, their sequence and how they are presented as related to each other. The analysis in this book thus examines the significance, as well as the sequence, of the oft-repeated concepts in radical Islamist rhetoric such as injustice, servitude, mastery, slavery, humiliation, respect, independence, freedom, duty, and morality. Such an analysis is, I argue, critical to understanding the essence of Islamist extremism.[37] In conceptualizing Islamist extremism, I draw upon the linguistic and sociological tradition of Critical Discourse Analysis (CDA) to analyze radical Islamist rhetoric drawn from temporally and contextually varied Islamist extremist groups.[38] I use the term 'radical Islamist rhetoric' to refer to the speeches, declarations, pamphlets and other such publications of Islamist extremist groups. This method allows for a more accurate understanding of the *essence* of Islamist extremism as it sheds light on *how* radical Islamists *themselves* explain, and then justify, their calls for violence and self-destruction to their audiences.

In arguing that radical Islamist explanations of violence are Hegelian in nature and that radical Islamist justifications of violence are consequentialist in nature, I forward an alternative framework of explanation for the success and resilience of Islamist extremist groups. This framework of explanation combines Hegelian recognition-theoretic framework with moral consequentialist arguments of ethics to offer a dual-theoretic framework of explanation for Islamist extremism. Broadly speaking, in drawing upon Hegelian recognition-theoretic framework, I argue that reason in radical Islamist explanations of violence can be understood in terms of a *deconstructive reason*; that is, reason that challenges the master's grand narratives and offers instead a counter-narrative. The aim of the radical Islamist counter-narrative—as is the aim of any counter-narrative— then becomes the challenging of the common wisdoms, particularly those of the masters that legitimize the oppression of the self. The logic in such a rejection is, I argue, Hegelian dialectical. That is, the acceptance by the slaves of the master's narratives legitimizes the subjugation of the slaves by the master. But if the slaves come to challenge the master's narratives, then the bases of the master's mastery become immediately challenged. And it is such a challenging of reason that is at the heart of self-assertion, both in the Hegelian theoretical sense and in the reason in radical Islamist rhetoric.

The critical significance of Hegel's master–slave dialectic in understanding the nature of radical Islamist explanations of violence can be seen, I argue, in the radical Islamist *rejection* of the self as the slave (the negated and the oppressed) through the rejection of the grand narratives imposed on the self by the masters (the 'other' broadly speaking). I argue further that the radical Islamist rejection of the 'West' as well as its rejection of the 'sectarian other' (the Shia or the Sunni) is based on such dialectical reason, a reason based on the realization of a *reciprocal causality* between the self (the slave) and the dominating other (the master).[39] That is, the status of the self as the slave (the oppressed) is presented in radical Islamist rhetoric as linked to the *acceptance* of the other as the master (the oppressor), so that the existence of the master is linked to the acceptance of the self as the slave. In this way, radical Islamist rhetoric seeks to counter the grand narratives of the master that present the master as the master and the self as the helpless slave. In so doing, radical Islamist rhetoric rejects the position of the self as the slave by challenging the master's mastery through the promotion of sporadic violence intended to catch the master off-guard and thus to challenge his mastery over his environment and over the self. Self-destruction is thus promoted in radical Islamist rhetoric as an alternative method to challenging the master's mastery through challenging the master's control over the self since the decision to take one's life is completely independent of the master, thereby making impotent the master's control over the self (the slave).

A deconstructive reason as this, that challenges the constructs of the established norms, thus presents a distinctly *radical* Islamist narrative (an antithesis of the grand narratives) as a guide for domestic and international relations. It is within such deconstructive reason that violence and self-destruction become *justified* in radical Islamist rhetoric as a 'morality' while the tacit and passive acceptance of oppression becomes presented as an 'immorality.' Moral consequentialism, thus, becomes an integral component of the deconstructive reason that forms the bases of struggles for recognition. The conceptual analysis of Islamist extremism in this book thereby sheds light on some of the most popular paradoxes associated with the study of Islamist extremism.

Re-addressing paradoxes

The analysis in this book readdresses the following popular paradoxes:

- If Islamist extremism is linked to poverty, then how might we explain the motivations of individuals from privileged socioeconomic backgrounds?[40]
- If Islamist extremism is *Islamic* in nature, then how might we explain the motivations of its secular recruits?
- If Islamist extremism is fundamentally motivated by a hatred for the Judeo-Christian world, then how might we explain radical Islamist sectarian violence (violence that targets the sectarian other, the Muslim Shia or the Muslim Sunni)?
- If 'suicide missions' are a way to escape a life of drudgery, then why do radical Islamists kill the other?[41]
- If 'suicide missions' are a tool for exacting revenge, then why do radical Islamists kill themselves?[42]

Chapter contents

This book is divided into five chapters. Chapter 1 outlines the dual-theoretic framework of explanation that I forward in this book in order to shed light on the essence of Islamist extremism. This framework combines the following: Georg Wilhelm Friedrich Hegel's argument of the existential nature of struggles for recognition; Axel Honneth's argument of the inevitability of moral consequentialist justifications for struggles for recognition; Friedrich Nietzsche's argument of the consequentialist nature of morality and his related argument of the instrumentality of religion in creating notions of 'morality.' The framework of explanation presented in this book is thus a combination of the recognition-theoretic framework in the discipline of philosophy and the moral consequentialist framework in its sub-discipline of ethics.

In explaining the notion of struggles for recognition, the chapter includes an analysis of the meaning of 'recognition' and 'self-consciousness' in Hegel's notion of struggles for recognition. I argue that the Hegelian notion of self-consciousness is compatible with the Islamic notion of the *ummah,* thereby making Hegel's explanations of violence in terms of struggles for recognition particularly insightful in understanding the essence of radical Islamist explanations of violence. Within this framework, the chapter examines the relationship between life-and-death struggles for recognition and the master–slave dialectic in Hegel's analysis, with particular attention to the dynamics of the master–slave dialectic that ultimately lead to self-recognition. The notion of self-recognition is most critical, I argue, in understanding the nature of reason in the radical Islamist explanations of violence since such explanations are fundamentally premised on the perception of the self—the radical Islamists—as the Hegelian slaves.

Chapters 2 and 3 examine the nature of reason in the radical Islamist *explanations* of violence and self-destruction. Chapter 2 focuses specifically on the Hegelian self-recognition nature of the radical Islamist explanations of *violence,* while Chapter 3 focuses specifically on Hegelian dialectical nature of the radical Islamist explanations of self-destruction. My analysis in Chapter 2 sheds light on how radical Islamist reason is consistent with the Hegelian logic of struggles for recognition in its following emphasis: the fear of the other (where the other is seen as a threat to the self); and the desire for the recognition of one's autonomy (or the desire for honor and prestige). Since I argue that radical Islamist violence is reasoned in terms of a self-recognition—which in Hegel's analysis and in the radical Islamist reasoning does not expect a recognition from the other but values instead its own recognition of its own self—this chapter analyzes the dialectical logic in Hegel's notion of self-recognition in terms of how such logic appears in the radical Islamist explanations and promotions of violence. Dialectical logic that challenges the master's mastery and the servitude of the self in the process of a self-recognition ultimately challenges the master's reason upon which the mastery rests. I show in this chapter that radical Islamist reason not only challenges the master's reason but also promotes the use of sporadic violence (to which the master's conventional means of defense and recourses are useless) in order to render the master impotent and to thereby display the façade of the master's mastery. Chapter 3 takes the analysis of this Hegelian dialectical logic further in order to explain how such logic can be used to understand the radical Islamist promotion of self-destruction (martyrdom) in terms of an act that (a) negates the masters (since there can be no master without a slave) and thus (b) leads to a self-transcendent recognition (since there can be no slave without a master).

Chapter 4 examines the nature of reason in the radical Islamist *justifications* for violence and self-destruction. In so doing, the analysis in this chapter readdresses the popular assertion that the radical Islamist justifications of violence, contextualized as they are within Islamic religious tenets, is a reflection of a uniquely barbaric religious and cultural milieu. In addressing this question, I argue that the references to religious tenets in radical Islamist rhetoric are a reflection of the *instrumentality of religion* and not of a religious context uniquely disposed to violence. Historical examples of the instrumentality of religion include the religious justifications of the medieval Christian Crusades as well as the religious rhetoric of the German World War I mobilization for violence and war. Given the instrumentality of religion, and the nature of reason in the radical Islamist *explanations* of violence (struggles for recognition), I argue that the religious rhetoric of Islamist extremist groups is fundamentally a deontological guise for otherwise consequentialist reason. That the nature of the radical Islamist justifications of violence is consequentialist in nature is illustrated by the fact that such justifications revolve around notions of self-defense, extreme emergency, and the last resort stipulations; stipulations that are the same as those offered as justifications for wars and violence in the internationally accepted Just War doctrine.

Chapter 5 analyzes epistemological assumptions to argue that knowledge of reality can be gained through reason in addition to experience. In fact, in drawing upon Kant's notion of transcendental idealism, I argue that reason—as for example, reason in radical Islamist rhetoric—can add something new to the knowledge _____ extent that reason systemizes and categorizes expe_____ experience is understood. In the case of radical Isl_____ at is, the radical Islamist explanations of violence a_____ is of violence—is used not only to understand reali_____ an understanding of reality to its audiences. Most criti_____ the recruits of radical Islamist groups need not thems_____ ocities in order to be motivated for violent action ag_____ latter assertion combines epistemological assumptio_____ perience shape knowledge of reality) with logical de_____ dge of reality (such as that gained through reason in_____ ith motivations for action (of the voluntary recruits)._____ I argue in this chapter that misunderstanding the essence of Islamist extremism as *Islamic* in nature (by not distinguishing between the radical Islamist *explanations* and *justifications* of violence) leads to a misunderstanding of the nature of the motivations of individuals that voluntarily join such groups. In other words, using epistemological assumptions and logical deductions, one can assume that the nature of reason in radical Islamist rhetoric equals the nature of the motivations of its voluntary recruits. And if this nature of reason is existential and consequentialist then so will be the nature of the motivations of voluntarily recruits based on such reason. In light of this, I argue that the current US–NATO policy of counterinsurgency through the occupation of Afghanistan, its previous presentation of the occupation of Iraq as a 'counterinsurgency,' and its current overly aggressive militaristic tactics in the tribal and northern territories of Pakistan is bound to only exacerbate the threat of Islamist extremism in the long term.

1 Struggles for recognition and moral consequentialism

The essence of Islamist extremism can be most accurately understood, I argue, in dual-theoretic terms: as a struggle for recognition in its explanations, and as moral consequentialist in its justifications (see Figure 1.1).[1] That resort to violence may be explained in terms of struggles for recognition is an argument that draws Wilhelm Friedrich Hegel's notion of life-and-death struggles for recognition, as outlined in his infamous book *The Phenomenology of Spirit* (*Phänomenologie des Geistes,* 1807). The related argument that links struggles for recognition to moral consequentialist reason draws upon Axel Honneth's work *The Struggle for Recognition: The Moral Grammar of Social Conflicts* (1995). Even more critically, however, the theoretical and philosophical framework that I present in this chapter not only links struggles for recognition to moral consequentialism but also links struggles for recognition to the *inevitability* of moral consequentialism. In arguing the latter, I draw upon Friedrich Nietzsche's various works wherein he argues not only that moral consequentialism is inevitable, but that such consequentialism reflects the *very nature* of the notions of 'morality.' But even more provocative is Nietzsche's assertion that such consequentialist morality is typically contextualized within religion. The critical implication here is that 'religious notions' of morality are intrinsically consequentialist notions of morality, despite their presentation as 'divine' and thus beyond question. Nietzsche's notions of morality as well as his assertion of the instrumentality of religion can be seen in his following works that I draw upon in this chapter: *Beyond Good and Evil,* published in 1886, *On the Genealogy of Morals* (also known as *On the Genealogy of* Morality) published in 1887, and most explicitly in his *The Will-to-Power,* which comprises of notes written by Nietzsche during 1883–1888 and published after his death in 1901.[2]

The questions that arise at the onset of such a theoretical and philosophical discussion are, of course, the following: 'What are struggles for recognition?'; 'Why are struggles for recognition important?'; 'Can one understand Hegel's notion of struggles for recognition beyond his eighteenth century European context?' Since I have devoted the first subsection of this chapter to answering the first question posed here, I shall leave this aside for now and address the latter two questions. Hegel argued that life-and-death struggles for recognition were an integral component of *human existence*; that is, that they were *existential* in nature. Violence, then, was not *only* an integral part of struggles for recognition but it was the very definition of struggles for recognition. To Hegel, the nature—or motivation, if you may—of these struggles could be explained in the following sequence: the development of human consciousness (a sense of self) to self-consciousness (a sense of identity), and the inevitable desire of self-consciousness to be *recognized* as such (as distinct and unique). In this chapter I argue that the Hegelian notion of self-consciousness is compatible with the Islamic notion of the *ummah* in the sense that both refer to a sense of identity that defines the self; the critical difference is that the Hegelian notion is individualistic while the Islamic notion is collective. Despite this difference, I argue that a sense of identity—whether in the sense of the individual's self-consciousness as in Hegelian analysis or in the sense of a collective consciousness of a group in the Islamic sense—remains critical in the desire for recognition since struggles for recognition are struggles for the acknowledgment of the worth of one's identity (one's very being); the acknowledgement of autonomy of the self from the other (from all others). Or, to put it in terms familiar to Hegelians, struggle for recognition is the struggle for the recognition of one's identity *as at once* distinct and equally significant to the other. The latter implies that the self is not a slave to the other; and, as such, struggles for recognition fundamentally challenge any master–slave relationship. Even more critical in this is Hegel's discussion of the *master–slave dialectic* which describes the realization, by the slave, of a cyclical causality between the master and the slave. This realization of the existence of a dialectic at once challenges the master's mastery and the slave's servitude, and it is this logic, I argue, that sheds the most critical light on the *nature of reason* in radical Islamist explanations of violence and self-destruction.[3]

The master–slave dialectic takes shape when the slave, over time, comes to see the master's mastery as rhetorical and thus tenuous. This is the point where the Hegelian slave is argued to achieve an awakening of his distinct self-consciousness, his sense of an absolute autonomy from his master (in the metaphysical sense even if not in the physical sense). In other words, while the master may continue to use force and intimidation on the one he treats as a slave, the slave no longer accepts this as the natural order of things. This is a point where the slave achieves a *self-recognition,* a point where the slave comes to recognize his own worthiness despite the lack of recognition from the master. It is at this point that the master losses *absolute* control over the slave. To put it in contemporary terms, while the slave may remain militarily inferior to the master, the slave no longer accepts the master's military superiority as an indication of his metaphysical or spiritual superiority; at this time, the master looses the rhetorical war against the slave, even if the master may try to compensate by using excessive force to create an illusion of his mastery.[4] Once a slave reaches a self-recognition, he is empowered, not only because he sees the tenuous nature of the master's mastery but also because he no longer depends on the master for the recognition of his distinct and autonomous sense of self. At this point, the slave then becomes the master, and the master the slave.[5]

It has been argued that struggles for recognition are based on the *fears* of negation and *desires* for recognition. In this way also, struggles for recognition have
been argued to be existential; that is, not merely a component of human existence
but a common tendency of all human existence.[6] Thus, the central presumption in
this theory of struggles for recognition is that such struggles are universal and
fundamentally against the negation of the self.[7] And so, struggles for recognition
are 'life-and-death' struggles since the fear of enslavement is terrifying enough to
warrant putting your life at risk in order to avoid such an eventuality.

But if struggles for recognition are existential in their explanations, then they
are also moral consequentialist in their justifications. The connection between
desires for recognition and consequentialist notions of morality is also found in
Axel Honneth's analysis of what he refers to as the 'moral grammar of struggles
for recognition' in his work *The Struggle for Recognition* (1995). As temporally
varied as these works are, the central argument in these works is that notions of
morality are *constructed* to give legitimacy (or a moral license if you may) to
struggles for recognition. Still, argues Honneth, the connection between struggles for recognition and consequentialist morality is typically overlooked, if not
ignored all together, in studies of social conflicts (whether violent or non-
violent). To illustrate this point, Honneth notes that even Emile Durkheim and
Ferdinand Tonnies who "both approached the development of empirical sociology with the intention of critically diagnosing the *moral* crisis of modern societies" failed to give dialogue over morality a "systematic role in their basic
concepts."[8] Thus, notes Honneth, "however many insights they may have had
into the *moral* preconditions for social integration [or disintegration for that
matter], they drew few theoretical conclusions from this for the category of
social conflict."[9] Honneth adds to this list the works of Max Weber, "who sees
the process of socialization as virtually geared towards a conflict of social
groups, [but] *excludes* every aspect of *moral motivation* from his conceptual definition of 'struggle'."[10] In contrast to such oversight, Honneth argues that struggles for recognition necessarily become presented in moral consequentialist
terms, where morality becomes re-defined in terms of actions that seek a justice
for the self (however 'justice' may be defined and however it may manifest
itself).[11] Or, in other words, morality becomes defined in consequentialist terms,
as anything that seeks respect, dignity and honor for the self (the 'self' defined
in collective terms as a particular ethnic or socioeconomic group in his analysis).

The link between moral consequentialism and religious rhetoric can be seen in
Nietzsche's arguments of the instrumentality of religion. Nietzsche's 'denial' of
morality and his rejection of what he called 'Christian morality' can be understood in this context. For Nietzsche, notions of morality were shaped and defined
(and even re-shaped and re-defined) by the desires for self-assertion; the desire
for self-assertion, of course, can be understood in terms of the Hegelian desires
for recognition.[12] Thus, notions of morality for Nietzsche were necessarily consequentialist since such notions defined all the actions taken towards self-assertion
as justified and presented as the 'right' over the 'wrong.' And in this, references
to religion played a crucial facilitating role in Nietzsche's analysis. It is within

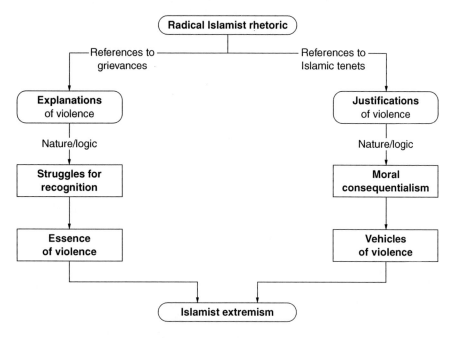

Figure 1.1 A conceptual analysis of Islamist extremism.

this context that one must understand Nietzsche's critique of 'morality,' since notions of 'morality' to Nietzsche were nothing more than constructions designed to legitimize the self in a given social order or to challenge an existing social order in which the self is not dominant. And it is also within this context that one should understand his critique of 'Christian morality,' since to him the references to Christianity (particularly in terms of its tenets) in framing something as a morality were consequentialist in motivation (consequence intended being self-assertion).[13] As such, religion to Nietzsche was instrumentalist; an instrument used to legitimize or promote the self.

The meaning, significance and universality of struggles for recognition

It has already been noted that struggles for recognition in the Hegelian sense are struggles for the demarcation of one's autonomy and independence; desires for recognition are thus desires for autonomy and independence from the other, desires for the recognition of the *self* as an autonomous being at once distinct and equally significant to the other. In his *Phenomenology of Spirit*, Hegel argued that "violent combat is not an accidental occurrence in human affairs, but a *necessary* element in the process of proving oneself a person."[14] Proving oneself a person, argued Hegel, requires the *recognition* of one's distinct self-consciousness (one's distinct identity, one's sense of self), and thus the recognition of one's independence and autonomy from the other. Hegel's definition of 'self-consciousness' asserts that "to be self-conscious or a PERSON is to be aware of oneself as an I, in contrast to one's bodily and psychological states."[15] In other words, to be self-conscious is to have a *sense* of one's identity, the 'I' as distinct from 'you' and the 'other.' Or, in the words of Jean-Paul Sartre's analysis of Hegel's *Phenomenology of Spirit*, "self-consciousness is pure *self-identity*."[16] The development of one's self-consciousness, notes Hegel, take a dialectical form. Consciousness begins with the basic sensory knowledge (primitive consciousness), progresses to perceptual knowledge (more developed consciousness) and ultimately to knowledge based on understanding of the self and the environment (most developed consciousness). The progression from this primordial consciousness (sensory consciousness) to *self-consciousness*—the consciousness of the self as distinct from the other—translates into the development of one's distinct identity. And it is this distinct identity that Hegel argues requires recognition from the other.

Interestingly, the notion of the *ummah* in radical Islamist discourse—especially its presentation as a distinct 'Muslim identity' and/or a collective 'Muslim mentality'—is, I argue, similar to the notion of self-consciousness in Hegelian analysis to the extent that in both the distinctness of the self is both emphasized and valued.[17] Radical Islamist explanations of violence are based on thE defense of this *ummah,* which appears strikingly similar to the Hegelian life-and-death struggles for the recognition of one's self-consciousness. Such primordial struggles for recognition, argues Hegel, are necessarily zero sum struggles where one emerges the master and the other the slave. The knowledge of this makes such struggles matters of life and death. Thus, one finds in both Hegel's ethics of recognition and, I argue, in radical Islamist rhetoric the framing of the other as a threat to the self.

Given that self-consciousness is a sense of one's identity, two questions arise. First, what does the recognition of such self-consciousness seek? And why is such recognition important?[18] On the first question of what recognition seeks, it is useful to understand what Michael Inwood labels as the dual meaning of 'recognition' in the Hegelian sense. Recognition means at once the *identification* (acknowledgment) of one's distinct self-consciousness as well as the *approval* (respect) of that distinct self-consciousness.[19] The concept of recognition can be further understood, argues Inwood, by appreciating the dual meaning of the word self-consciousness in German, which means both self-confidence and self-respect.[20] So in desiring recognition of one's self-consciousness from the other, one desires both an *identification* of one's distinct self-consciousness as well as a *respect* for that distinctness. So it is not enough that the other acknowledges the distinctness of the self if such an acknowledgment is not accompanied by a respect of differences. So if the other acknowledges one's distinctness but relegates it an inferior status, that is not the recognition that is sought in struggles for recognition for in such a case one is not considered equal to the other but only distinct from the other. Critically then, the desire for recognition seeks an acknowledgment of the self as *at once* distinct and equally significant to the other. In other words, the acknowledgment of the difference between a Muslim Palestinian and an Israeli Jew for example does *not* imply a respect for that difference, much less an acknowledgment of the other as equally significant to the self. And if one is not considered equally significant to the other one is considered inferior to the other which implies, in turn, that one is not considered deserving of the same stature as the other. And so, as Robert Williams notes, "what each seeks is not the recognition of the mere fact of his existence but the *recognition of his freedom.*"[21]

This brings us to the second question posed earlier: why is recognition of self-consciousness important? Here, Solomon's analysis of Hegel's ethnics of recognition is particularly insightful; Solomon argues that "self-consciousness in Hegel carries with it a sense of dignity, pride, autonomy."[22] And thus, recognition (acknowledgement) of one's self-consciousness is in turn an acknowledgment of one's dignity, pride and autonomy. The acknowledgment of one's autonomy is critically significant here as it implies the acknowledgment of one's independence from the other, or an acknowledgment of his freedom. And so, for Hegel, it is the recognition from the other of one's self-consciousness—in all the senses of such a recognition as discussed above—that epitomizes one's *independence* as it at once demarcates the *distinctness* as well as the *equal significance* of one compared to the other and, by extension, demarcates the purgative of one's actions. Understanding recognition in the context of the demarcation of one's freedom and independence is most critical in understanding why recognition of one's self-consciousness is relegated such a heavy weight in the theory of desires for recognition.

If we can understand what recognition seeks (acknowledgment and respect) and why it is important (as a demarcation of one's freedom) we can understand why the other is so critical in the achievement of both objectives. Quite simply, Hegel argues that the other is *needed* for a contrast to the self. To put it in another way, the entire notion of distinctness of the self is based on the *existence* of the other from whom one is distinct and who thus is a contrast to the self. If there were no contracting beings, with their distinct self-consciousnesses, we would not need recognition of our distinctness from the other. To put it quite simply, without recognition of our distinctness are we really free? After all, it is because the Hegelian masters do not recognize the slave as distinct but as mere extensions of their selves that the slave lacks a sense of self-consciousness and comes to believe his non-worth. This dynamic change only after the slave become aware of the existence a dialectical relationship and thus comes to realize the contingent nature of the master's mastery. I shall address Hegel's master–slave dialectic later in this chapter. For now let us return to the argument that one depends on the other for recognition, and that the other is thus needed in the fulfillment of desires for recognition.

A critical qualification is in order here. Terry Pinkard explains that this dependence is "a matter of conceptual necessity; it is not the kind of contingent dependence on other that is, for example, constituted by the dependence on others to produce certain goods."[23] In other words, the dependence on the other for recognition is *not* an economic or political dependence, it is worse, it is, if you may, an *existential dependence*—that is, a dependence that is intrinsic to human existence and its desires for recognition and freedom. Pinkard further underscores the point of the dependence of the self on the other for recognition as thus:

> the agent takes himself to be an *independent* agent only in taking himself to be *recognized* by another *as* independent. In being recognized as *independent,* his self-understanding (his being-for-self) is *affirmed for him* as being true, as being in line with what he really is (his being-in-itself).[24]

This underscores an important point in Hegel's ethics of recognition. While the desire for recognition culminates into *life-and-death* struggles for recognition (given the importance attached to recognition), the life of the other from whom recognition is sought *must be preserved* for the other is *needed as a contrast* to the self. It is important to understand, however, that this imperative is the concern of the incumbent master who wouldn't be a master if there was not a slave to demarcate the master's superiority and contrast to the slave. In other words, since the other is needed for the recognition of self, the other *cannot* be physically eliminated for Pinkard argues that the struggles for recognition "can have a resolution only when the lives of *each* [the masters and the slaves] are preserved."[25] The importance of this statement comes to light only when we appreciate the critical assumption in Hegel's analysis that the other is needed to assert one's distinctness and thus for the recognition of the self as *superior* to the other. In other words, the other is needed as a contrast to the self, the superior, the master. So the life of the slave is preserved during struggles for recognition *precisely* because the slave is *needed* by the master as the *object* to demarcate his mastery. In other words, struggles for recognition *not only* assume a contrast in identity between the self and the other that form the bases of such a struggle but, even more critically, struggles for recognition seek to *maintain* this contrast between the victors (masters) and the losers (slaves). Kojeve explains the master's need for a slave, and for the slave's recognition of his mastery as thus:

> what he [the master] wanted by engaging in the fight was to be recognized by *another*—that is, by someone *other* than himself but who is *like him,* by *another man.* But in fact, at the end of the Fight, he is recognized only by a Slave. To be a *man,* he wanted to be recognized by another man. But if to be a man is to be Master, the Slave is not a man, and to be recognized by a Slave is not to be recognized by *man.* He would have to be recognized by another Master. But this is impossible, since—by definition—*the Master prefers death to slavish recognition of another's superiority.*[26]

In other words, while the recognition from the slave is deemed unsatisfactory to the master, the acceptance by the master of another master is deemed a worse alternative. That is, the master cannot accept the existence of another master, or, given another master, cannot accept servitude to another master manifest in the recognition of the other's superiority, the other master. Thus the recognition by the slave is not only *needed* by the master but also reluctantly accepted by the master to demarcate and maintain his mastery, or his hegemony. It is in this way that Kojeve argues that *the truth of the master is the slave*. This means, significantly, that the perpetuation of the master–slave relationship is *utilitarian* for the incumbent master who is *unwilling* to abandon his position of power and whose position of power depends on there being a slave to put in servitude.[27] This is why, argues Hegel, the master goes to great lengths to spare the life of the slave during the life-and-death struggles for recognition as he realizes that the death of the slave would take away from the master the very object the master needs to demarcate his supremacy. In other words, the elimination of the slave *negates* the master.

But there is yet another complexity to the Hegelian rubric of desires for recognition. The desire for recognition from the other does *not* grant significance to the other (in the sense of acknowledging the superiority of the other) *despite* the fact that recognition is *dependent* on the other for its realization. Instead, the desire for recognition is a desire for the other to *affirm* one's *significance* in contrast to the other and is thus *narcissistic*. This may make more sense in light of Jean Hyppolite's analysis of Hegel's ethics of recognition:

> [t]he end point of desire is not, as one might think superficially, the sensuous object—that is only a means—but the unity of the I with itself. Self-consciousness is desire, but what it desires … is itself.[28]

The inevitable struggle that Hegel expects will ensue from the desire for recognition takes shape when we remind ourselves that in the struggles for recognition, it is *not only* the self but *all other selves* that desire recognition and it is not only the self but all other selves that reject the idea of a 'slavish recognition of the other.' It is little wonder than it that desires for recognition should culminate into violent life-and-death struggles for recognition for it is this fear of slavery that, argues Hegel, converts struggles for recognition into struggles viewed in zero-sum terms: *the recognition for the other is seen as negating the self, and the pursuit of the recognition from the other seeks to negate the other*.[29] It is in this sense that the other is seen as a threat to the self as it is assumed that the other is no more willing to grant recognition to the self than is the self willing to grant recognition to the other. It is the realization of this existential dynamic that, I argue, forms the bases of radical Islamist explanations of violence. Let us turn now to perhaps the most interesting component in Hegel's examination of self-consciousness, namely the master–slave dialectic.

The master–slave dialectic and the critical logic in self-awakening and self-recognition

I had noted in the Introduction of this book that reason in radical Islamist rhetoric may be understood as a deconstructive reason, that is, reason that challenges the hegemonic narratives imposed on the self by the dominating other. That grand narratives are challenged implies three critical things. First, it implies the awareness that the narratives that have been imposed on the self are not absolute but subjective. Second, and related to the first, it implies the awareness that narratives are changeable. And third, perhaps most critically, it implies that the hegemony of the grand narratives is directly related to the uncritical acceptance by the self of these narratives. Deconstructive reason thus seeks to dismantle the existing narratives, and the relationships that are based on the existing narratives, by presenting counter-narratives as legitimate. Deconstructive reason thus rejects the position of the self as the passive observer, the slave, and the other as the dominating entity, the master. In so doing, deconstructive reason challenges the mastery of the other (who purported the grand narratives) and the servility of the self (the passive observer). It is in this way that I argue that reason in radical Islamist rhetoric can be understood in terms of a dialectical reason that challenges the master's mastery. It is dialectical in the sense that it is reasoned in terms of an awareness of the existence of master–slave dialectic.[30]

Edward Ballard defines a 'dialectic' as a relationship based on a "cyclical (or continuous reciprocal) causality."[31] In other words, in contrast to the more familiar linear causal relationships where causality is unidirectional, in a cyclical causal relationship the causality is circular. So, in a linear causality, X (say, drought) leads to Y (say, bad harvest), but Y (bad harvest) cannot lead to X (drought). On the other hand, in a circular causality, X (say, the existence of a master) leads to Y (say, the existence of a slave), but Y (the existence of a slave) also leads to X (the existence of a master).[32] Even more importantly, Ballard argues that a cyclical causality (a dialectical relationship between X and Y) implies a *dynamic* relationship that is not only ever-changing but that in which each round of momentum affects (or alters) the nature of the other entity involved in the relationship.[33] To put it simply, a dialectical relationship is one that is dynamic and mutually reinforcing *by its very nature* (as opposed to by choice). Let us more specifically understand such a relationship in terms of the Hegelian master–slave dialectic. Here, the master's mastery is contingent on the slave's acceptance of the mastery and the slave's slavery is contingent both on the existence of the master and the slave's acceptance of his slavery. Significantly, then, not only is this relationship based on a circular causality but, most importantly, based on a momentum that creates a dynamic. The critical implication in the latter is that *if* the momentum is altered, the dynamic changes.

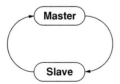

Figure 1.2 Cyclical (non-linear, multidirectional) causality in Hegel's master–slave dialectic.

To put it simply, if the slave suddenly realizes the contingent nature of the master's mastery (contingent on the slave's acceptance of the mastery), then the slave would suddenly feel empowered as he realizes that his slavery was based on his willingness to acceptance of the master's mastery, and not on any metaphysical weakness of the self. In this, then, by challenging the master's mastery (and thus the grand narratives of the master), the slave breaks the momentum that established existing relationships of mastery and slavery. Most critically, this different momentum reverses dynamics (or the order of things). Suddenly now, the slave no longer sees himself as the powerless slave, nor sees the master as metaphysically superior to the self. But further, realizing the existence of a dialectical relationship, the slave feels empowered since he realizes the very position of the master as the master had always depended on its acceptance by him, the slave. It is with such logic that Hegel argues that the awakened self-consciousness of the slave (his sense of self) leads to the slave's realization of a master–slave dialectic. And when this happens, the slave becomes the 'master' and the master becomes the 'slave.' Even if this transition is metaphorical and the slave remains physically shackled, this transition shatters the mirage that the master had absolute control over the slave and was superior in the absolute sense.

In Hegel's master–slave dialectic, this transition in the slave's perception of himself is passive and takes the form of a quiet 'self-recognition' on the part of the slave, the realization wherein the slave "becomes *for itself* being-for-self [as opposed to being-for-other]."[34] While I discuss the significance of the notions of 'being-for-other' and 'being-for-self' in Chapter 3 in this book, a brief explanatory note is in order here. Being-for-other implies the servitude of the self to the other, wherein the self lives only to serve the other. Being-for-self implies its opposite, wherein the self lives for itself, in complete independence (either physical or metaphysical) from the other. In contrast to Hegel's theoretic self-recognition, I argue that radical Islamist rhetoric promotes self-recognition through violence, an assertion that I illustrate with reference to radical Islamist rhetoric in the next two chapters.

Let us take a closer look at the logic implicit in Hegel's master–slave dialectic. As noted above, the most basic metaphorical sense of Hegel's master–slave dialectic can be summarized as a mutually reinforcing relationship where *there can be no master without a slave, and no slave without a master.* In other words, the existence of a master depends on, and leads to, the existence of a slave; and the existence of a slave depends on, and leads to, the existence of a master. Consider this cyclical causality in the simplistic Figure 1.2.

It is important to stress again that *the* most important component of Hegel's master–slave dialectic is that it assumes the existence of a *relationship*. What this means is that the master is not a master in the absolute sense, any more than the slave is a slave in the absolute sense. To put it in other words, it is not that the master is the master because he has god-like powers or is otherwise invincible; nor is the slave the slave because he is the weakest entity that exists on this earth. It is instead that the master is the master because he has *reasoned* himself as such, by pitting the myth of his superiority against the myth of the other's inferiority. One might understand Edward Said's central argument in his infamous *Orientalism* in such philosophical terms, wherein the 'othering of the other'—or the 'orientalizing' of the other—is motivated by the desire to present the self as 'civilized' and 'superior' and the other as the 'barbaric' and 'uncivilized.'[35] Here—as in Hegel's master–slave dialectic—it is the presentation of a *contrast* (between the self and the other) that is most critical in creating the image of the self as superior.

That the existence of a 'master' depends on the *relationship with the other* who is the 'slave,' and the existence of a slave depends on the relationship with the other who is the master, can further be appreciated in light of R.M. Hare's analysis of the notion of the 'slave.'[36] Hare argues that there are two critical aspects to the definition of the term 'slave'; the first relates to the *status* of the person/s in society and the second relates to the "*relation to the master.*"[37] In other words, the slave is a slave because he lacks rights and privileges *compared* to the others, but even more critically "he is a slave *of another* person or body."[38] Indeed, Hare stresses the point that lacking rights and privileges alone does *not* necessarily make one a slave if there is no other that this person is subordinate to, or negated by. After all, notes Hare, "the lowest castes in some societies are as lacking in legal rights as slaves in some others, or more so, but are not called slaves because they are not the slaves *of anybody.*"[39] Or, to put it in Kojeve's words, "the truth of the master ... [is] the slave."[40] This is where there master–slave relationship takes a turn, or where the momentum of the relationship changes direction. This is because, as notes John O'Neill, the slave eventually comes to "recognize his own subjectivity by a negative rebound."[41] In other words, the slave comes to realize his own worth through a realization of the subjective nature of his status as a slave. That is, the slave comes to realize his own *distinct* self-consciousness, his identity *independent* of the master. With this realization, the slave attains a *self-recognition*, a sense of self-worth that is independent of the master. Most critically, the slave realizes that the master's mastery is *dependent* on the slave's acceptance of such mastery and reflective only of established patterns of relationship that were, until now, left unchallenged. Self-recognition then results in the dismantling of the myth of the metaphysical superiority of the master and thus in challenging the master's mastery.

Terry Pinkard notes that the slave's awakened self-consciousness (his self-recognition) leads to his realization of the contingent and tenuous nature of the master's mastery, thereby changing the dynamic of the dialectic. Subsequently, through his awakened self-consciousness, the slave comes to challenge the master's *reason* upon which the master's mastery is based and justified and concludes that the master's reason too has no divine superiority, as Pinkard explains in the following:

> if the slave comes to an awareness that this is the case—that he takes the master's point of view as his own only because of *contingencies* in the past relationship between the two—then that awareness itself will transform the slave's own self-consciousness, since it shows him that *what he takes as authoritative* for himself is *only contingently authoritative.*[42]

In other words, the slave's realization of the contingent nature of the master's mastery leads the slave to a self-recognition as he comes to see the master as a façade ironically *dependent* on the slave for its perpetuation. And, subsequently, since the master never acknowledged the slave, the slave comes to acknowledge himself. At this point, the slave ceases to view himself as the slave, the metaphysically inferior self subordinate to the master, and comes to view himself instead as a equal to the master, a 'master' in his own right if you may. Reason in radical Islamist rhetoric, I argue, argues for such self-recognition in its promotion of violence and self-destruction. Violence and self-destruction then become not only demarcations of self-recognition, but instead are the very tools that challenge the master's mastery, as we shall see in Chapters 2 and 3 in this book.

A critical point about self-recognition needs to be emphasized here. Self-recognition is a *self*-acknowledgment, not an acknowledgment from the masters (the other) since the masters are typically (both in theory and practice) unwilling to offer such recognition to the slave. Self-recognition is promoted in radical Islamist rhetoric, I argue, through dialectical reason that emphasizes the tenuous nature of the master's mastery. The emphasis on the tenuous nature of the master's mastery seems reminiscent of Jean-Jacques Rousseau's (1712–1778) following assertion:

> Man is born free, and everywhere he is in chains.
> *Many a one believes himself the master of others,* and yet *he is a greater slave than they.*[43]

One can understand Rousseau's claim in terms of the Hegelian ethics of recognition, namely that if the master *depends* on the slave for the recognition of his mastery, then the master is not the independent entity (in absolute terms) that it is thought to be. Jean Hyppolite summarizes this logic thus:

> The dialectic of domination and servitude has often been expounded. [...] It consists essentially in showing that *the truth of the master reveals that he is the slave of the slave,* and that *the slave is revealed to be the master of the master.*[44]

To put it simply, William Shearson refers to this as the 'inner logic' of Hegel's master–slave dialectic, namely:

> [T]o be a slave means to have a master;
> [T]o be a master means to have a slave.[45]

Based on the realization of the existence of the master–slave dialectic, the slave realizes that if he simply does not accept his status as a slave, and the contrasting status of the other as master, then he challenges the entire existence of the master–slave relationship.

Such realization encourages a self-recognition that empowers the slave in two critical ways. First, the slave *no longer depends* on the master for recognition— for the master is unlikely to give the slave the recognition the slave desires as his mastery is based on the negation of the other, the slave. Second, and even more importantly, through his awakened self-consciousness, the slave no longer feels he *depends* on the master for recognition of his self-consciousness as he now attains a self-recognition. It is such empowering reasoning that is commonly found in radical Islamist rhetoric. To be more specific, I argue that self-recognition is promoted in radical Islamist rhetoric through a three-pronged logic. First, it recasts the self as *equally significant* to the masters in terms of identity and independence. Second (and as a result of the first), it at once challenges *and* rejects the servitude of the self and thus the subjugation of the self to the masters. Third, perhaps even more critically, such reason in rhetoric creates a sense of the *possibility* for its audiences (the potential recruits) that things *can* change to their advantage.

Self-consciousness as the 'ummah': the Islamic notion of a collective transnational identity

In their study of Islamist 'suicide terrorism,' Pape and Feldman seek to explain the "causal logic" behind the motivation of individuals "living in countries far removed from the occupied countries" to take part in transnational terrorism.[46] Pape and Feldman explain this causal link in terms of the existence of "multiple national loyalties to different stable communities of people associated with a territory, distinctive culture, and common language, one loyalty for their kindred community and another for their current country of residence."[47] But while multiple loyalties are indeed a reality, Pape and Feldman fail to pinpoint the very notion that explains the motivations of individuals for transnational terrorism in the Islamic context.[48] This notion is none other than the Islamic notion of the *ummah;* this notion is *not* itself a radical notion, but a notion instead that imagines the existence of a Muslim transnational community, a sort of sense of being that is collective, not individualistic. While much of the discussion of this notion appears in the varied discourses of the Islamic theologians and in debates of Islamic jurisprudence, it is also a notion that radical Islamists utilize to maximize their recruitment.

The best way to understand the notion of the ummah is to understand it as the notion that presents the self (the individual) as intricately tied to the collective (the group that the self belongs to, in terms of a religious kinship). In this way, self-consciousness is understood not merely as the *self*-consciousness of the individual (a sense of the individual's identity) but as the consciousness of the collective that the self belongs to, a sense of identity of the individual that is inseparable from the sense of identity of the collective that the individual belongs to. And so, references to the 'self' have both an individualistic and a collectivist meaning in radical Islamist rhetoric. Furthermore, based on a critical analysis of reason in radical Islamist rhetoric, I argue that the references to 'Islam' in such discourse are not

merely references to a religion but are also—if not more important
to the collective body of individuals that belong to the religion (of]
popularly noted as saying that "Islam is … [not] mere religion i
sense [of the word]," by which he meant that it is not merely a frai
individual's observation of religion but a vehicle for revolutiona
latter, of course, implies a collective agency.[49] Thus, references in r
rhetoric to the 'victory of Islam,' 'glory of Islam,' 'defense of Islai
popularly misunderstood as the intrinsically imperialistic nature ol
gion—are instead, I argue, implicit references to the agency of the
collective body. And so, victory for Islam, glory of Islam and defense of Islam are
best understood as calls for the revival of the collective identity of the Muslims
(the *ummah*), a revival in the sense of demanding a recognition in the Hegelian
sense: an acknowledgement of the distinctness and the autonomy of 'self'-con-
sciousness and thus a rejection of the negation of the 'self.' Thus, I argue, references to Islam in radical Islamist rhetoric are not intended to give agency to a
religious scripture but are intended instead to give agency to a collective people,
the Muslims, the ummah.

Let us take a closer look at the notion of the ummah. The *ummah*—derived
from the Arabic word *umm,* meaning literally mother—is a reference to the collective Muslim community.[50] Gordon Newby notes that today, "Muslims, regardless of differences, regard themselves as one *ummah.*"[51] John Esposito notes that
as a central concept in Islam, the *ummah* expresses the "*unity* and theoretical
equality of Muslims *from diverse cultural and geographical settings.*"[52] The
ummah is, if you may, a bond in the religious imagination of Muslims.[53] Esposito
makes the analogy of the *ummah* with the family which "pull together when
faced by a common external threat but then fall back" when the perceived threat
disappears.[54] The concept of the *ummah* can also be understood in terms of a
'nation' in the sense of a people with a shared religious identity. Indeed, such an
understanding can be seen in the speeches of numerous Islamist extremist
groups.[55] This is not surprisingly since in the Muslim context, broadly speaking,
identity *is* most frequently linked to Islam. In fact, in analyzing Pakistani civil
society, A.H. Nayyar and Ahmed Salim argue that "the process of equating
Muslim [Islamic] and Pakistani identities starts at early stages of school educa-
tion" based on a "need to nurture in children a sense of an *Islamic identity* and
pride in being Pakistanis."[56] Hence references to the *ummah*—an Islamic community—are essentially references to an Islamic identity. This means that
notions of 'self-consciousness' (a sense of distinct identity) also become understood in collective terms; so the 'self' in self-consciousness refers to the collective that the individual belongs to. To put it simply, identity becomes understood
in collective terms. Nonetheless, it should be noted that *ummah* remains an abstract concept and, for many contemporary modern Muslims, a notion in the
realm of idealism. A substantive analysis of the notion of *ummah* that situates it
within the context of Islam and Islamic discourse is beyond the scope of this
book. What is important here is to appreciate the strategic utilization of the
notion of the *ummah* in radical Islamist rhetoric.

The critical significance of the notion of the *ummah* is that it converts the notion of the 'self' as the individual into the 'self' as the collective. The 'self' thus becomes inseparable, and indivisible, from the collective that the self (the individual) belongs to. This mean that any reference to the 'self' is also a reference to the collective, and any reference to the collective—as in broad references to 'Islam,' 'victory for Islam' and the like—are references also to the individual. The larger significance of this is that victory (or defeat) of the collective is also victory for the individual, and victory for the individual is also victory for the collective. This logic becomes particularly functional, I argue, when it is applied [to] martyrdom (self-destruction) in radical Islamist rhetoric, and [the] rhetoric of martyrdom being a 'victory for the self.' As I [discuss in this] book, this victory, and indeed the promotion of self-[destruction] becomes defined in self-transcendent terms; here, the [self] refers to the individual who loses his/her life in a self-

[handwritten marginal note: How Ext, Apply Umnah principles to their actions]

[...implic]ation of the notion of the *ummah,* as it is utilized in [radical Islamist rhetoric] is that the imperative of demarcating one's *self*-[iden]tity as at once distinct and equally significant to the [collective rec]ognition indirectly puts the burden of this pursuit (of [the] self (the individual) and the 'self' (the collective *ummah*). In projecting a dual meaning of the 'self' (as individual and collective), radical Islamist rhetoric puts the onus of action on *each individual* for the benefits of his/her community. Indeed, one of the characteristics of radical Islamist discourse is that the 'duty' of jihad is defined as an individual duty, not a collective duty. This is most apparent in the now-infamous pamphlet *Al-Faridah al-Gha'ibah* (or *The Neglected Duty*) written by Muhammad Abd al-Salam Faraj, which became the creed of the assassins of the Egyptian President Sadat and, in more contemporary times, the creed of varied Islamist extremist groups.[57] This leaves little room for a free-rider mentality since now the 'self' (the individual) is also the collective (the ummah) and thus the responsibility for the plight of the community rests with the self, the individual. Thus, I argue, the desire for recognition in the Islamist context has the same meaning as the desire for recognition in the Hegelian sense, except the 'self' in the Islamist context is not understood merely as the individual but as instead the collective.)

David Cook tags the rise of the popularity of this collective notion of the 'self' to the decade when the Soviet Union invaded, and occupied, Afghanistan (1979–1989).[58] Cook argues that it was the sensational mobilizing rhetoric of the Palestinian Abdallah Azzam (who moved to Pakistan in 1979 in response to the Soviet invasion of Afghanistan for geographical proximity) that gave rise to a new trend of seeing the self as the collective in radical Islamist literature. Amongst the many sensational and highly mobilizing calls to the Muslim ummah for a unified action against the Soviets, Azzam also tried to mobilize the populace by turning a critical light on the Muslims themselves:

I believe that the Muslim *umma* [*ummah*] is responsible for the honor of every Muslim woman that is being violated in Afghanistan and is responsible for every drop of Muslim blood that is being shed unjustly—therefore they are an accessory to these crimes.[59]

Notions of a collective supranational Muslim self-consciousness are now evoked by contextually varied Islamist extremist groups even when the scope of their struggle may be strictly nationally defined—the scope and goals of a Lebanese struggle as being distinct from the Palestinian struggle, Palestinian struggle as being distinct from the Pakistani struggle, Kashmiri struggle as being distinct from the Egyptian struggle and so on. Thus, while the scope and goals of different Islamist extremist groups may vary according to their different contexts (as discussed in the previous chapter), their *essence* (essential nature, their reason) remains the same. Indeed, what is most notable in radical Islamist rhetoric from contextually varied groups is how violent struggles against servitude (actual or perceived) remain framed in the context of the interests of the larger *ummah*. That is, contextual contingencies aside, radical Islamist rhetoric at some point or other emphasizes the unity of the Muslims—the 'self'—as pitted against the non-Muslims—the 'other.' That such a framing offers considerable legitimacy to Islamist extremist groups is obvious and already documented in existing literature.[60] What is less obvious, I argue, is how such a framing converts regionally and geo-politically defined struggles and insurgences into broader struggles for the *recognition* of a distinct *Muslim self-consciousness*, and such recognition as an avenue to freedom and independence. Indeed, I argue that the references to the *ummah* both legitimize and *unify* the contextually varied Islamist extremist groups into essentially a collective struggle against the other. The net effect is the idealization of otherwise contextually varied Islamist extremisms into an essentially unified supranational 'moral' struggle against injustice.[61] Thus, I argue, that which appears to observers of Islamist extremism as disconnected, regionally defined struggles are essentially struggles that are *conceptually* the same.

This can be seen in the recruiting rhetoric of the Lebanese *Hizbullah*, the Palestinian *Hamas* and the Pakistani *Harkat-ul Mujahideen* to name a few. Amal Saad-Ghorayeb argues that *Hizbullah*, Lebanon's most nefarious Islamist extremist group of the 1980s, used Islamic rhetoric (references to Islam and to the larger *ummah)* to *redefine* Lebanese identity into a pan-Islamic identity.[62] Indeed, *Hizbullah* espoused a kind of 'Islamic universalism' if you may, in order to portray its particular struggle against the then Israeli occupation of southern Lebanon into a kind of a broader 'Muslim' struggle against the *ummah's* marginalization and servitude.[63] Hizbullah has also sought to portray the Palestinian struggle against he Israeli in such transnational terms. For example, Naim Qassem, the founding member of Hizbullah, noted the following:

No Arab or Muslim group has any excuse for negligence or for leaving the Palestinian people to suffer on their own.[64]

In a manner similar to that of *Hizbullah*, Saad-Ghorayeb notes that even the Palestinian *Hamas* has portrayed its cause as broadly 'Islamic.'[65] In fact, beyond Islamist extremist groups in the Middle East, the trend is similar in groups prevalent in South Asia. Pakistan's ultra-extremist group *Harkat-ul Mujahidin* also espouses a pan-Islamic ideology based on the romanticizing of the concept of the *ummah,* which it uses to frame its agenda of the secession of the predominately Muslim Kashmiris (in Jammu and Kashmir) from Indian administration.[66]

The framing of Islamist violence as essentially a part of a larger *unified* collective Muslim struggle against the *other* is most obvious in the assertions of the *Hamas* leader Khaled Mash'al in a speech he delivered to a congregation at a Damascus mosque in February 2006:

> We say to ... [the] West ... you will be defeated ... Israel will be defeated ... America will be defeated in Iraq. Wherever the (Islamic) nation [*ummah*] is targeted, its enemies will be defeated, Allah willing. The nation [*ummah*] of Muhammad is gaining victory in Palestine. The nation of Muhammad [*ummah*] is gaining victory in Iraq, and it will be victorious in *all Arab* and *Muslim* lands ... Today the Arab *and* Islamic nation [*ummah*] is rising and *awakening,* and it will reach its peak, Allah willing. It will be victorious ... Don't you see that they [the West and Israel] are spending their money in efforts to block the way of Allah, *to thwart Hamas,* to defeat it ... They do not understand the *Arab* or *Muslim mentality,* which rejects the foreigner [the oppressor] ... The *Arabs* will be victorious. The *Muslims* will be victorious. *Palestine* will be victorious.[67]

What is immediately notable in the above are the transitions from general references to the *ummah's* (defined in the above as Arab, Muslim *and* Islamic, that is, non-Arab) struggle against the west (America, Israel) to specific references to the Palestinian struggle (as seen in the reference to Hamas) and back again. It seems that Khaled Mash'al seeks to present the Palestinian struggle in terms of a broader *unified* Muslim struggle for the demarcation of its consciousness. More specifically, the references to the west and Israel being 'defeated' seem essentially references to them failing in their endeavors to oppress the Muslims, the *ummah.* This is interesting especially in the context of the references to the 'Arab *and* Islamic' *ummah* (nation) as 'awakening' and heading toward a 'victory.' Here, the awakening of the *ummah* can be understood in terms similar to that of the awakening of the self-consciousness of the Hegelian agent, a stage that precedes both the desire and the violent struggles for recognition. In this sense, 'victory' of the collective self (the *ummah*) can be understood as the freedom gained through the awakened self-consciousness and through the recognition of the 'self' sought violently (albeit in vain) from the 'other.' Most significantly, then, the 'defeat' of the 'other' (the west, American or Israel) in this context seems a reference to their failure in suppressing the self-consciousness of the Muslims (the *ummah*) and, by extension, their failure in quelling the *ummah's* life-and-death struggles for recognition.

Portrayals of a supranational Muslim consciousness can also be seen in the official statements of Pakistan's ultra-militant Islamist group *Harkat-ul Mujahideen*:

> Ours is truly *international network* of genuine *Jehadi Muslims*. We believe frontiers can never divide Muslims. They are *one nation. They remain a single entity.*[68]

Broad references in the above to 'Jihadi Muslims' and 'one nation' and a 'single entity' seem intended to portray a unified Muslim consciousness—the *ummah*— whose defense is incumbent on *all* Islamist extremist groups. The idealization of a *unity in essence* of otherwise regionally and contextually varied Islamist extremist groups is quite apparent here, an implication that substantiates the argument in this book that a conceptual explanation of Islamist extremism can be delineated while bracketing its geo-political contextual differences.

Assertions of Ayman al-Zawahiri, a former member of the Egyptian *Islamic Jihad* and a current member of *al-Qaeda* active in post-2003 US-occupied Iraq, are also noteworthy in its presentation of Islamist extremists as unified entities of the *ummah*:

> *Victory* for the *Islamic movements* against the *Crusader alliance* cannot be attainted unless these movements posses an *Islamic base* in the heart of the Arab region ... The *Jihad movement* must adopt its plan on the basis of controlling a piece of land in the heart of the Islamic world on which it could establish and protect the *state of Islam* ... if the successful operations against Islam's enemies and the *severe damage* inflicted upon them do not serve the ultimate goal of establishing the *Muslim nation* in the heart of the Islamic world, they will be nothing more than disturbing acts ... the dismissal of the *invaders* from the *land of Islam* ... must remain the basic objective of the Islamic jihad movement, regardless of the sacrifices and the time involved ... The jihad movement must realize that half the *road to victory* is attained through *unity* ... The movement must *seek this unity* as soon as possible if it is serious in its quest for *victory*.[69]

What is notable in the above are broad references to 'Islamic movements' and its perceived enemies 'the crusader alliance' that seem rhetorical efforts to present a unified Muslim consciousness against the agents of its marginalization, the 'crusader alliance'—or the 'other' in Hegelian analysis. References to an 'Islamic base' seem to substantiate my argument that stripped to its bare minimum—its essential features—all radical Islamist (jihadi) groups are conceptually the same and rhetorically present themselves as agents against the marginalization and the servitude of the *ummah* that subsequently seek recognition even if through violence. Broad rhetorical references to the 'state of Islam' and the 'Muslim nation' can be understood in this context, references that otherwise would be too broad to hold any significance. Indeed, calls for the establishment of a 'Muslim nation in the heart of the Islamic world' in the context of the 'dismissal of the invaders form the land of Islam' 'regardless of the sacrifices and the time involved' seem implicitly, if not fairly explicitly, calls to awaken the self-consciousness (identity) of Muslims as an avenue to demanding recognition from the masters (the invaders) even if through life-and-death struggles. Perhaps most noteworthy are al-Zawahiri's assertions that 'the road to victory' of Islamist extremism (jihadi movements) can only be attained through their 'unity,' an assertion that once again substantiates my argument that the essence of Islamist extremism can be delineated while bracketing its geo-political contexts since even references to the *ummah* in radical Islamist speeches seem intended to *minimize* the *contextual differences* and *maximize* the *conceptual similarities*.

In the weekly Pakistani Jihadi publication of the *Jaish-e-Mohammad, Zarb-e-Momin* (blow of the pious), the issue of the Al-Aqsa Mosque was addressed with the following heading: "Who will *free me* from the clutches of the Jews?"[70] Here, the Pakistani concern is presented as being the same as the Palestinian Muslim concern which is facilitated by an understanding of the fellow Muslims as part of the ummah. Similarly, the following official statement from an open letter put forth by Hezbollah also reinforces the notion of the Muslim 'self' that is indivisible from the Muslim collective (the ummah):

> what befalls the Muslims in Afghanistan, Iraq, the Philippines, or elsewhere befalls the *body of our Islamic nation* of which we are *an indivisible part* and we move to confront it out of a religious duty primarily and in the light of a general political visualization decided by the leader jurisprudent.[71]

Similarly, on being questioned about their relationship with al-Qaeda's supranational network, a representative of Pakistan's *Harkat-ul Mujahideen* replied:

> Osama bin Laden [leader of al-Qaeda] has his own *mission* [specific goal and scope] and we have our own. We are only fighting for the liberation of Kashmir ... As far as his [bin Laden's] *struggle* is concerned, that is the struggle of the *entire* Muslim nation.[72]

References to a sense of collective urgency can also be seen in Omar Shaikh's response to the question of why he abandoned his privileged existence in London in exchange for joining the Jihad in Bosnia in the 1990s and later in Kashmir:

> Watching the scenes of children being massacred in Bosnia, Palestine, Kashmir and other places, women being raped, mosques being destroyed ... I could not live a normal life.[73]

Indeed, according to Azmat Abbas, "belonging to a [Islamist] militant organization gives otherwise powerless men a strong sense of *identity* in an increasingly fragmented social structure."[74] According to Abbas, in the post-2001 era, the soaring ranks of Islamist extremists in Pakistan are attributed to a craving for a sense of belonging, a collective identity to stand for.[75] Abbas notes: "belonging to an [Islamist] militant organization … [gave] otherwise powerless men a strong sense of *identity* in an increasingly fragmented social structure."[76] So the notion of the ummah works not only to cater to the problem of the free-rider in struggles for recognition, but it also reinforces a sense of collective identity that is empowering. In the existential sense, notions of the collective can be understood as empowering as they do away with the angst associated with notions of the self as the lone individual.

In other words, the manner in which the notion of the *ummah* is evoked by the radical Islamists seems intended to portray a *unity* of the self with other such selves. In other words, radical Islamist portrayals of the 'self' (as the collective) as the endangered *ummah are* similar to the notion of the endangered self in Hegelian analysis. Leaders of Islamist extremist groups, through their recruiting rhetoric, in turn present themselves as the vanguards of the *ummah's* struggle for the recognition of its distinct Muslim self-consciousness. Just as the fear of servitude (fear of negation and marginalization) propels the Hegelian agents to engage in life-and-death struggles for recognition, so too, I argue, radical Islamist rhetoric justifies violence against the masters as an antidote to a lack of recognition (negation, marginalization and humiliation) of the ummah (the 'self' in Hegelian analysis). But since the incumbent masters are not willing to grant the slaves recognition, the slaves seek a 'self-recognition.' Thus, despite the difference in the meaning of the 'self,' the Hegelian and radical Islamist notions of self-consciousness are conceptually similar in that both are defined and understood in terms of a *distinct identity* which desires *recognition,* both in terms of an acknowledgment of one's distinct identity as well as in terms of the desired respect for one's distinct identity. The notions are also similar in that both the Hegelian notion of self-consciousness and the Islamist counterpart notion of the *ummah* play a pivotal role in the existential explanations of violence and in the moral consequentialist justifications of violence.[77]

Honneth and Nietzsche on struggles for recognition and moral consequentialism

I argue in this book that struggles for recognition necessarily lead to moral consequentialist justifications for any and all actions presented as a means to that end (the ends of recognition). Before elaborating this contention, it is first important to address the question of 'what' is morality. Generally speaking, notions that are presented as a 'morality' are understood in terms of their virtue and their 'right' versus 'wrong' character. But while stipulations of right and wrong are universal to notions of morality, the actual determinants and composition of the 'right' and 'wrong' vary according to different perspectives.[78] Indeed, the central debate in ethics revolves around the notion that morality is—or should be—'deontological' in nature versus the notion that morality is—or should be—'consequentialist' in nature. What is understood as the 'right' or the 'wrong' thus depends on whether morality is defined in deontological terms or consequentialist terms.

In its classic sense, a deontologist is a Kantian, "someone who believes that a moral person should act out of a sense of duty" and not desire, much less self-interest.[79] Kant presented the pursuit of duty (as opposed to a pursuit of socially contingent desires) as a *categorical* imperative. That is, not just what 'ought' to be done (an imperative) but what 'must' *necessarily* be done (a 'categorical' *imperative*). Actions that qualify the categorical imperative requirement much therefore be actions that are motivated *not* by desires, nor by some expectation of desired consequences, but motivated instead by a notion of 'virtue' (or the 'right' versus the 'wrong').[80] Proponents of consequentialist morality, however, criticize this Kantian assumption on grounds that it is static. In other words, what is understood as 'virtue,' or the 'right' and the 'wrong,' is argued by consequentialists to be temporally and circumstantially variable. The consequentialist critique of the deontological school of thought is thus that it critically ignores the fact that notions of morality are subjective. In contrast to a deontological view, then, "consequentialism in its purest and simplest form is a moral doctrine which says that the right act in any given situation is the one that will produce the best overall outcome."[81] If this is so, then morality cannot be understood in terms of some static or universal notions of 'virtue' and 'right' versus 'wrong' since these notions are vacuous, contingent as they are on who is defining them. And even if one may defend the Kantian deontological view—as does Henry Allison in his rebuttal to Hegel's criticism of Kantian notions of universal morals—by arguing that what is assumed to be universal is the universality of reason upon which notions of morality are based, and given notions of morality as universal, a Nietzschean consequentialist critique would argue that *reason itself is subjective* and thus temporally variable.[82] So the notion of the universality of reason does not tell us anything about the actual nature of reason that his employed at any given time as a justification for actions. In such a consequentialist critique then, deontological defense of the universality of reason is deemed as vacuous and useless as the notion of the universality of notions of morality. In other words, even though reason determines notions of morality, and even when this is universally so, this tells us nothing about *how* morality will be defined (and understood) at any given point since the nature of reason is variable. It is on such grounds that Nietzsche criticizes Kantian deontological notions of morality, as can be seen in his following assertions on morality in *Beyond Good and Evil*:

> What philosophers called 'the *rational* ground of morality' and sought to furnish was, viewed in the proper light, only a scholarly form of faith in the prevailing morality, a new way of expressing it, and thus itself a fact *within* a certain morality [emphases added].[83]

In other words, arguments of the rational grounds of morality (that notions of morality are determined by reason) do not negate the consequentialism of notions of morality since even these 'rational grounds' are subjective and variable. To defend the prevailing notions of morality as based on reason is thus, according to Nietzsche, just a banal acceptance of the prevailing notions of morality that are always justified and reinforced through consequentialist reason.[84]

That the desire and struggle for self-assertion—in the Hegelian sense of desire and struggle for recognition—produces, and indeed encourages, consequentialist notions of morality is an issue that Axel Honneth examines in detail in his work on the 'moral grammar' of struggles for recognition.[85] The critical implication here is that struggles for recognition (struggles for self-assertion) necessarily give rise to consequential notions of morality, *universally speaking*. When struggles for recognition are disguised through references to religious tenets, consequentialist notions of morality appear in terms of a 'religious imperative' (as in the case of radical Islamist rhetoric). Nietzsche's critique of what he referred to as 'Christian morality' was premised on his assertion that religious rhetoric becomes a mask to hide the vested interests of self-assertion of those who resort to references to religion to justify their actions; this argument is both implicit and explicit in his *On The Genealogy of Morals* (also known as the *Genealogy of Morality*) and his *The Will-to-power*. Nietzsche argued that actions for the ends of self-assertion (self-promotion) become presented as 'Divine' and thus 'moral.'[86] If violence now becomes contextualized within religious tenets—as it does in radical Islamist rhetoric—then violence becomes presented as a 'morality.'[87] Of course, when struggles for recognition are *not* disguised through references to religious tenets, consequentialist notions of morality appear in terms of the imperative of 'justice,' 'respect,' 'self-defense,' 'national security,' and even 'humanitarian action.' In the analysis of the latter, Honneth's work is widely respected.

Honneth on the 'moral language' of struggles for recognition: perceptions of reality and consequentialist morality

Axel Honneth's argument of the moral language of struggles for recognition follows along the lines of Marx who, broadly speaking, explained a people's aspirations for social movements in terms of their desire for equal *respect* and *dignity*; or Sorel who focused on issues of *honor* in explaining the critical motivations for a group's mobilization into a social movement; or Sartre who saw in Frantz Fanon's analysis of the violent anti-French Algerian rebellion a Hegelian struggle for recognition justified in terms of recourse to justice and justified thus as a morality.[88] In Honneth's paradigm of social conflicts, the sense of what one deserves is central to the understanding of the motivation for conflict and rebellion. The language of 'deserving' something is significant here as it implicitly frames desires for recognition in moral terms, as the 'right' (respect, recognition) contrasted with the 'wrong' (disrespect, marginalization). Given this equation then, disrespect and marginalization of the self become the 'immorality' that must be rejected. This implies that one's disrespect in society eventually becomes the intolerable status quo and it becomes framed in terms of the immorality (the wrong) that must be corrected. Critically still, notions of 'morality'—defined in terms of

the respect and recognition for the self—become designed so as to reject the intolerable status quo of the self and to emphasize instead what one deserves (that is,
respect and recognition). A sense of dessert then becomes linked to a sense of
justice and together they shape notions of morality. It is such that Honneth explains
the effective mobilization for social conflicts in terms of the moral grammar of
social conflicts. And it is this "internal connection," argues Honneth, "that often
holds between the emergence of social movements and the *moral* experience of
disrespect" that "has, to a large extent, been theoretically severed at the start" in
much of the sociological explanations of social conflicts.[89] In this way Honneth
develops an alternative paradigm that asserts a "connection between moral disrespect and social struggle"; or, if you may, in terms of the moral consequentialism
of struggles for recognition.[90]

Honneth's analysis of the 'moral motives' for social conflicts seem similar to
R.H. Hare's notion of the 'altruistic revolutionary.'[91] Hare argues that the rebel
or the revolutionary engages in violence for "some altruistic political reason" in
contrast to the criminal (the thief, the bank robber, the rapist and the like) who
engages in violence for selfish reasons of personal gain only and with no motivations to correct perceived injustices in society.[92] More specifically, the 'altruist
reasons' for conflict and violence to Hare—as the 'moral motives' to Honneth—
are those reasons that are based on (1) the oppression of a people that is "bad
enough" (this can be seen as similar to the intolerable status quo in Honneth's
model) and (2) when it is perceived that "the *evils* [of oppression] that will be
removed by the rebellion are greater than those which will be caused by it [such
as violence]," (this can be seen as the re-definition of morality and immorality so
that the former means recognition for the self and the latter means the negation
of the self through oppression).[93] The point to be emphasized here is not Hare's
consequentialist explanation of violence but instead the central role Hare gives
to notions of altruism in explaining revolutionary movements. Hare's analysis
thus seems complementary to Honneth notion of the imperative of moral language for the success of social movements for the recognition of the self (defined
in collective terms of 'self' as one's group). Indeed, Axel Honneth argues that
the redefinition of morality—from static notions to consequentialist notions—in
the context of struggles for recognition is inevitable because the group that perceives itself as disadvantaged comes to define the *rejection* (whether violence or
non-violent) of their negation and oppression as 'just' and thus as a 'morality.'[94]
Honneth's assertion of the inevitability of the moral language of struggles for
recognition is illuminating in understanding the resilience of radical Islamist
rhetoric which, I argue, also justifies violence in moral consequentialist terms.

Understanding the successful mass mobilizations on the part of the leaders of
social movements in terms of their re-definition of morality as 'recognition for
the self' sheds light on a few critical implications:

- If recognition (for the self) gets framed in terms of 'morality,' then recognition becomes understood by the masses as a timeless and universal good (as
  'morality,' however defined, is often presented as a universal standard).

- Recognition defined as 'morality' means that a lack of recognition then becomes understood as the 'immortality,' the injustice that must be rejected and challenged.
- A lack of recognition understood in terms of an 'immorality' also comes to have a timeless and a universal appeal (as characteristic of all notions of 'morality' and 'immorality'). This becomes critical in engendering a sense of a 'collective struggle' as "the emergence of social movements hinges on the existence of a shared semantics," such as that provided by the categorization of a lack of recognition in universal terms of an 'immorality.'[95]
- Collective struggle, understood in this way, then becomes the 'moral' struggle as it seeks to reject the 'immorality' and that, through reason of 'morality' (the necessary 'right' over all the 'wrongs'), then becomes presented as incumbent on all (all belonging to the disadvantaged group).
- Pursuits of recognition, through whatever means (non-violent or violent), then becomes understood and accepted as the 'morality' (the right thing to do) so much so that the legitimacy of its means (particularly when violent) becomes a matter beyond question.
- Ultimately, 'morality' becomes defined in terms of struggles for recognition, whether non-violent or violent. In the case of the latter, violence becomes defined as 'morality.' And such reason, I argue, can be seen in the radical Islamist moral consequentialist justifications of violence for the ends of struggles for self-recognition.

These implications, I argue, are relevant whether one is concerned with the examination of a disadvantaged group in society as in Honneth's analysis, or the hypothetical self-consciousness fighting to assert their mastery over the other as in Hegel's analysis, or the revolutionary as in Hare's analysis, or the radical Islamists as in my analysis.

In Figure 1.3 I have laid out key elements in Honneth's paradigm of social conflicts and their compatibility with what I see are the critical consequentialist justifications of violence in radical Islamist rhetoric. The bold letters in this diagram indicate Honneth's argument while the italicized letters indicate my analysis of radical Islamist rhetoric. As we can see, the rejection of the negation of the self becomes framed as the morality in both Honneth's analysis and in radical Islamist rhetoric. In Figure 1.3, we can see this from the box labeled 'intolerable status quo' to the far left of the diagram that then leads to the search for the 'right,' the morality, which in turn becomes defined as the rejection of servitude in radical Islamist rhetoric. The existence of intolerable status quo along with the notions of 'morality' then fuels the justifications for violence and destruction. This is similar to what Honneth refers to as the 'moral motives' of struggles for recognition, which are based on a sense of what one deserves. This sense of what one deserves appears in the context of self-recognition in radical Islamist rhetoric. Ultimately, as we can see in Figure 1.3, this line of reasoning creates the moral language for violent struggles for recognition and, in radical Islamist context, the moral consequentialist justifications for violence.

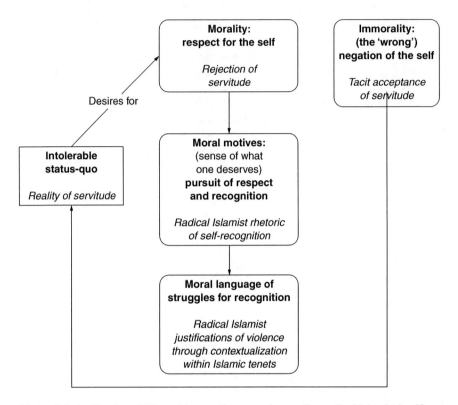

Figure 1.3 Application of Honneth's paradigm to understanding radical Islamist justifications of violence.

Note
Although Honneth talks about social conflicts in the general broad sense and nowhere does he touch upon the dynamics of Islamist extremist groups as a social conflict movement, I have summarized in this Figure Honneth's model (in bold font) and superimposed the findings of my critical analysis of radical Islamist rhetoric (in non-bold italic font) to illustrate what I see as the consistencies of his model with my assertion of the essence of Islamist extremism.

Nietzsche's critique of morality defined: the instrumentality of religion and moral consequentialism

Nietzsche's critique of morality (or of notions of morality) and his critique of what he called 'Christian morality' are perhaps the most widely misunderstood arguments.[96] Equally misunderstood are his following related claims: his denial of morality; his denial of the 'truths' that morality is based on; his description of himself as an 'immoralist'; his assertion (or hope) that "morality will gradually perish."[97] Some have understood these claims as Nietzsche's rejection of traditions, religion and rational thinking that is intended to "subvert the entire philosophical enterprise and replace it with a kind of thinking more akin to the literary exploration of human possibilities in the service of life—a kind of artistic play liberated from concern with truth and knowledge."[98] Others have understood these claims in terms of Nietzsche's desire to "find a way of *overcoming* the nihilism he believed to result from traditional ways of thinking."[99] I argue, however, that Nietzsche's critique of morality, and in particular his critique of Christian morality, were not so much intended to be normative or prescriptive assertions but were instead simply critical observations of *what there really is*; that is, they were critical observations of the nature and aims of morality, all morality, everywhere.

Quite simply, Nietzsche's critique of morality can be understood in terms of his assertion that morality is *not* static but temporally variable.[100] This means that morality is subjective and this subjectivity is contingent on the specific circumstances and necessities of any given point in time and space. The critical point here is that Nietzsche viewed morality as *consequentialist* in nature since he saw it as contingent on circumstances and exigencies (emergencies, necessities) of a particular time and in a particular space. Nietzsche thus saw morality as contingent on the needs and aspirations of those that are in the position to present certain notions in terms of a morality (such as political leaders or groups leaders). This means that even morality that is framed in religious terms—that is, morality that is contextualized within religious tenets—is consequentialist in nature, despite its deontological disguise. This can be seen in Nietzsche's following assertions:

> 'Christianity' has become something fundamentally different from what its founder did and desired. It is the great antipagan movement of antiquity, formulated through the employment of the life, teaching and 'words' of the founder of Christianity but interpreted in an absolutely arbitrary way ... [101]

> I regard Christianity as the most fatal seductive lie that has yet existed, as the great unholy life ... [...] [It is] Petty people's morality ... this is the most disgusting degeneration culture has yet exhibited. *And this kind of ideal still hanging over mankind as 'God'!!*[102]

> However modest one may be in one's demand for intellectual cleanliness, one cannot help feeling, when coming into contact with the New Testament, a kind of inexpressible discomfiture: for the *unchecked impudence* with which the *least qualified* want to raise their voice on the greatest problems, and even *claim to be judges of such things,* surpasses all measure. The shameless levity with which the most intractable problems (life, world, God, purpose of life) are spoken of, as if they were not problems at all but simply things that these little bigots *knew!*[103]

Particularly instructive in the above assertions is Nietzsche's critique of *Christianity as morality*, that is, the presentation of all that is framed within the context of Christian tenets as categorically and deontologically moral. This can be seen in his assertion that 'this kind of ideal' (in the sense of how Christianity as morality is presented by its advocates) hangs over 'mankind as God'; in other words, what is clearly not deontological in essence—at least not as far as Nietzsche saw it—is presented as such. His reference in the above to those that claim to know Christian morality as 'bigots' is also critically instructive as it sheds light on Nietzsche's view of such 'righteous' persons, as 'bigots,' presumably implying those individuals that wish to present the world in dichotomous terms in order to serve their self-interests.

Perhaps the most insightful of all of Nietzsche's assertions is the following as it most directly uncovers his critique of religious morality—whether it be Christian morality or any other religious morality—as but an effective tool for self-promotion and thus as distinctly consequentialist in nature:

> How can one wage war [...] of cunning, sorcery, lies ... First recipe: *one claims virtue* in general *for one's ideal*; one *negates the older ideal* to the point of *presenting it as the antithesis* of all ideals. [...] Second recipe: one *sets up one's own type* as the *measure of value* in general; one *projects it* into things ... *as God.* Third recipe: *one sets up the opponent of one's ideal as the opponent of God;* one *fabricates* for oneself *the right ... to power.*[104]

Nietzsche's critique of Christian morality in terms of its instrumentality is quite apparent in the above, especially with reference to how one presents oneself in terms of all that is moral (*"one claims virtue* in general *for one's ideal"*) in order to negate the other, and then even presents the self in Divine terms as 'God' (*"one sets up one's own type* as the *measure of value* ... *as God"*). However, the most insightful look into the nature of Nietzsche's critique of morality, particularly Christian morality, can be seen in the last sentence: *"one sets up the opponent of one's ideal as the opponent of God;* one *fabricates* for oneself *the right ... to power"*; here, Nietzsche very directly criticizes morality framed in religious as but a guise to legitimize the self in power, thereby unveiling for us his view of religion as instrumental. And by asserting that '*one sets up the opponent of one's ideal as the opponent of God,*' Nietzsche seems to highlight the ultimate instrumentality of religion, namely, the presenting of one's political opponents (or 'opponents of one's ideal' as Nietzsche refers to them) as blasphemous. This has very interesting implications in terms of how I argue radical Islamist groups use Islam as an instrument to create their legitimacy and to simultaneously delegitimize their opponents, as we shall see in Chapter 4 of this book. Nietzsche's above assertion also has very interesting implications in terms of all that is presented as 'just' and thus as 'moral,' even if in so doing it justifies violence and brutality, as in the case of the justifications of wars as 'just' and 'moral' in the internationally accepted Just War doctrine, as we shall also see in Chapter 4 of this book.

It should come as little surprise then that Nietzsche, who saw morality as reflective of ulterior motivations, should draw a distinction between the 'origins' and 'goals' (aims) of morality.[105] So even if the 'origins' may be presented in deontological terms (as pure, unselfish, divine, 'just') through references to religious tenets, the 'goals' are always self-serving. In other words, notions of morality, whether framed in secular or religious terms, are always consequentialist in nature; that is, notions of morality are always created with certain 'goals' (aims or consequences) in mind and are such a legitimizing means to selfish ends. As Keith Ansell-Pearson notes, Nietzsche's "major point is that the 'purpose' and 'utility' of a social custom [such as notions of morality] ... reveal nothing about their origin."[106] As such, Nietzsche argues that he is not interested in the origins of morality; he is interested only in the goals of morality, that is, the function, ulterior motivation and the instrumentality of morality.[107]

The view that morality has a consequentialist aim even if it is presented in deontological terms seems consistent with R.M. Hare's view of the two levels of morality. In *Moral Thinking* Hare argues that notions of morality have two levels: the critical level and the intuitive level.[108] Hare argues that notions of morality are created at the 'critical level' by critical thinkers who have self-interest in mind. And even though these critical thinkers are individuals with unique abilities to judge and evaluate what should be understood as a matter of morality, the notions of morality at this level are fundamentally instrumental for those that are in the position of presenting (or creating) certain notions as moral, indisputable and universal. But while the motivation of these critical thinkers is self-serving, these notions of morality get accepted as intuitive knowledge (as knowledge that is a given and hence accepted at the 'intuitive level') by the masses, the banal individuals in society, or the 'lower men' and the 'herd' to use Nietzsche's terminology.[109] This seems quite consistent with Nietzsche's claim that all morality is 'herd morality.' In other words, while the essence of morality is consequentialist (or utilitarian, as Hare puts it), morality gets accepted *as if* it were deontological in essence. This façade not only reinforces the power of the critical thinkers in society—their power to manipulate and dominate—but it does so under the guise of deontology. Hare's critical thinkers can be seen as analogous to Nietzsche's 'higher men,' both in terms of their critical ability and in terms of their selfish motivations.

But what of the 'goals' or 'aims' of morality that Nietzsche seems interested in at the cost of the 'origins' of morality? What kind of goals or aims is Nietzsche referring to? Answers to these questions can perhaps be found in the analysis of Nietzsche's unpublished work The *Will to Power,* which was translated and published in its most uncorrupted and un-manipulated form by the late Walter Kaufmann.[110] Nietzsche's notion of the will-to-power has excited much debate amongst scholars, ranging from those that challenge its importance in Nietzsche's overall arguments, to those who criticize it for its lack of clarity and its ambiguous nature, to those who argue for the critical centrality of this notion in understanding Nietzsche's philosophy.[111] Quite simply, Nietzsche's notion of the will-to-power can be understood as the human tendency and desire for self-assertion and domination.[112] Indeed, Nietzsche argues that "life itself is a will-to-power"; and since "this world is the will-to-power— and nothing besides," then morality too, is a will-to-power.[113] And if life is a will-to-power, as notes Nietzsche, then this implies that the struggle for self-assertion (the will-to-power) is existential in nature.[114]

Although my assertion that Nietzsche's will-to-power can be understood in terms of self-assertion is contested by some, the analysis of the following excerpts from Nietzsche's works indicates grounds for its validity. Consider for example Alphonso Lingis' interpretation of Nietzsche's will-to-power: "The will to power is not just power or force, but Will to power: always will for more power. It is ... transgression of all ends ... interpretations, valuations."[115] This seems to imply that the will-to-power is the desire to dominate, a desire for self-assertion. That will-to-power is critical thinking that challenges the sameness, a self-assertion that offers a counter reason to that which justifies the status quo can also be seen as implied in Lingis' following interpretation of Nietzsche's will-to-power:

> To affirm that the ground is Will to power means, it is said, that Nietzsche conceives of Being as force, as dynamism; to exist is to make one's presence felt. And it is to affirm that the ground is not only the support of constancy, but is also productivity, parturition, creativity. [...] But more radically, to affirm that the ground is will to power means that the ground is not identity, the One, but original difference.[116]

In the above, Lingis seems to be emphasizing—particularly in the last sentence—that Nietzsche believed in the transformative nature of human society. This belief has necessarily to be premised on the related belief that there is no 'One' standard that is categorically indisputable (which, of course, is also the way Nietzsche views notions of morality as we have already seen in earlier discussion). This point is perhaps emphasized in Lingis' following assessment of the meaning in Nietzsche's assertions:

> God is dead—specifically the God of *monotheism* ... The gods have died, Nietzsche writes, but they have died of laughter upon hearing the Jewish god claim to be the sole god.[117]

To claim monotheism is to claim absolute knowledge, the very thing that Nietzsche rejects both in its philosophical and epistemological sense.[118] For Nietzsche, there are no absolutes, in either notions presented by theists or notions presented by ethicists. All is ever changing in society, changing through the challenge posed by individuals in society with a will-to-power. This can be seen in Lingis' following clarification of Nietzsche's point:

> The will, in Will to power, is the differential element of force. Difference is enacted not in a reiteration of the same, but in the self-affirmation of a force exercised against another force. A will commands; it affirms itself.[119]

This means that Nietzsche's notion of will-to-power can be understood in terms of the Hegelian notion of the struggle for recognition in that in both the *self* is central, and central in terms of wanting to demarcate its independence (form the other) and its superiority (over the other). Both the Nietzschean will-to-power and the Hegelian struggles for recognition can then be understood in terms of desires for self-assertion and domination. That Nietzsche's notion of will-to-power can be understood in terms of the Hegelian notion of the desire and struggle for recognition (self-assertion), the desire to demarcate one's difference in the form of distinction can be seen in Lingis' following analysis:

> For a will to affirm itself is rather for it to affirm its difference. For Nietzsche, the feeling of distinction—the pathos of distance—is the fundamental affect of power. Power affirms its difference; difference occurs as power, as the *force* of Being [hence the existential nature of the will-to-power].[120]

But perhaps the best exposition of Nietzsche's will-to-power, particularly in the manner in which I argue it is compatible with the Hegelian notions of desires for self-assertion and self-recognition, can be seen in the following excerpt from Nietzsche's *Genecology of Morality:*

> Whatever exists … is again and again reinterpreted to new ends, taken over, transformed, and redirected by some power superior to it; all events in the organic world are a subduing, *a becoming master*, and all subduing and becoming master involves a fresh interpretation, an adaptation through which any previous "meaning" and "purpose" are necessarily obscured or even obliterated.[121]

Keeping in mind that Nietzsche's above assertions occur in the context of his examination of the genealogy of morality, it becomes fairly clear that he is implying that notions of morality are not static but also that notions of morality are a product of a will-to-power. If will-to-power is the desire to dominate, then the redefinition of morality for these ends of becomes necessarily for the transformation in society. This can be seen in the above when Nietzsche argues that the "becoming master … involves a fresh interpretation" (of societal norms) through which any "previous meanings … are obliterated."

The will-to-power is the very characteristic of life to Nietzsche or, as Arthur Danto puts it, "an elemental concept in Nietzsche's thinking."[122] If will-to-power is understood in terms of the desire for self-assertion and domination, then will-to-power can be understood as somewhat of a Darwinian concept, to the extent that it is assumed to be at once existential and necessary for the advancement of society.[123] Nietzsche thus considers morality as will-to-power; that is, the transformations in the notions of morality as powered by the desire for self-assertion on the part of the critical individuals in society. Any moratorium on such a critical and creative reassessment would only encourage a banal society, the domination of 'higher men' (critical thinkers) by the 'lower men' (the uncritical, banal individuals).

It is important to underscore, however, that while Nietzsche's will-to-power can be seen as Darwinian in essence in the sense that it is assume to be existential in nature, it is not Darwinian in the sense that it is a struggle for self-preservation; will-to-power is instead a struggle for self-assertion and self-domination. This can be seen in Danto's following analysis:

> Whether or not one preserves oneself has nothing to do with the blind exertion of Will-to-Power which characterizes each thing at each instant. Something survives and prevails only insofar as it is victorious in the struggle of wills, but it does not struggle in order to survive—if anything, it would be the other way round [the it survives in order to struggle].[124]

Danto's above interpretation of the meaning and significance of Nietzsche's will-to-power reinforces my assertion that it is compatible with Hegelian notions of the existential struggles for recognition (self-assertion and self-domination). And when morality is understood in terms of a will-to-power, then it becomes fairly clear that Nietzsche is pointing not only to the consequentialist nature of morality but, most critically, to the consequentialist nature of morality *in struggles for recognition*. This interpretation is perhaps best reinforced in Danto's following analysis of Neitzsche's will-to-power:

> The Will to Power is the desire for freedom in those who are enslaved, it is a will to dominate and overcome other in those who are stronger and more free.[125]

If the will-to-power is the desire to dominate and the desire for self-assertion, and if morality is a will-to-power, then this means that notions of morality are instrumental for the individual (or individuals) with a will-to-power; or, to put it in other words, the desire to dominate and the desire for self-assertion determine notions of morality. This seems a similar argument to that of Axel Honneth, namely that struggles for recognition are universally framed in moral terms, and hence that notions of morality are consequentialist in the sense that they have a desire for recognition as their aim, and instrumental in that they facilitate the struggle for recognition.

If morality is framed in religious terms, then not only does such morality become consequentialist and instrumental, but *rightfully* so! In other words, the self then presents itself as the *rightful* entity, the one that is guided by 'deontological' concerns (the divine concerns). It is in this way, then, that Nietzsche's critique of morality can be understood as linked to his critique of religious morality (or Christian morality as he called it) in terms of both having an instrumental (consequentialist) character. To be sure, in his critique of Christian morality, Nietzsche does not single out Christianity. Indeed, Clark notes that "the point here is *not* that his fight against morality is directed *only* against Christian morality," the point here is that Nietzsche was critical of all that is framed in terms of a religious 'morality.'[126] Ultimately, one can understand

Nietzsche's critique of morality as a desire to "question what has been considered unquestionable."[127]

Summary

This chapter illustrates the importance of understanding Hegel's notion of struggles for recognition for understanding the critical nature of reason in radical Islamist rhetoric. In particular, I argue that Hegel's notion of the master–slave dialectic is particularly instructive in understanding the nature of reason in the radical Islamist explanations of violence. In Hegel's master–slave dialectic, the slaves eventually undergo an awakening of their self-consciousness—they come to recognize their self-worth and their distinct identity upon which this self-worth is based—and come to therefore realize that there exists a dialectic in the perpetuation of the master–slave relationship. That is, the slaves come to realize that the master's mastery is contingent both on the existence of a slave and the slave's acceptance of such mastery. Upon such realization, the slaves no longer view themselves as the slaves and, indeed, no longer come to view the master as the master (at least not in the metaphysical sense of a superior entity). When this happens, the slaves achieve a self-recognition. While in Hegelian analysis this self-recognition is passive, I argue that self-recognition on the part of the radical Islamists is decidedly violent. Indeed, as I show in the next chapter, violence is itself explained in terms of the imperative of challenging the master's mastery in radical Islamist rhetoric.

This chapter also illustrates why and how struggles for recognition culminate into moral consequentialist justifications for any and all actions taken for the ends of the pursuits of recognition from the other, or for the ends of a self-recognition. In theoretical terms, such a relationship is argued in the works of Friedrich Nietzsche and Axel Honneth. In actual terms, I argue that such a relationship can be seen in the nature of the radical Islamist justifications of violence. Indeed, as I show in Chapter 4 in this book, radical Islamist justifications are decidedly consequentialist—the consequences intended being struggles for recognition and the demarcation of a self-recognition—even when they are contextualized within Islamic religious tenets. The tendency to disguise consequentialist reason within a deontological guise (such as that provided by references to religious tenets) is what Nietzsche criticized in both his critique of morality as well as in his notes on the will-to-power, as the analysis in this chapter shows. And this tendency, I argue, can be understood conceptually as the instrumentality of religion.

2 Recognition through violence

Critical analysis of radical Islamist rhetoric reveals that the radical Islamist explanations of violence fundamentally revolve around the fear of servitude and a categorical rejection of oppression. Indeed, I argue that violence is explained in radical Islamist rhetoric in terms of challenging the subjugation of the self through challenging the mater's mastery. Consistent themes in radical Islamist rhetoric that challenge the master's mastery are those that challenge the master's reason and those that emphasize the excessive brutality of the master. Challenging the master's reason not only challenges the master's mastery but also fundamentally challenges that reason upon which the servitude of the self is based. Similarly, in emphasizing the master's brutality, the radical Islamists challenge the master's self-proclaimed superiority since gross brutality, characteristic of excessive use of force, is portrayed as inconsistent with 'real' power.[1] Indeed, I argue that radical Islamist rhetoric portrays the self much as the Hegelian slave and, as such, challenges its oppression and servitude through highlighting the contingent nature of master's mastery; contingent as it is on the slave's acceptance of such mastery. Thus, much as in the awakened self-consciousness of the Hegelian slave, such reason challenges the status of the self as the slave.[2]

Such dialectical themes in radical Islamist rhetoric are strikingly reminiscent of the thought process that has been argued to crystallize for the Hegelian slave a self-recognition.[3] In self-recognition, as I had noted in Chapter 1 in this book, the slave does not seek the recognition from the master, as such recognition would be unlikely since it would result in the very undoing of the master's status as the master. In self-recognition, the slave instead realizes his self-worth and independence equal to the master. I argue, however, that the critical difference between the classic Hegelian struggles for recognition and what I call the radical Islamist struggles for self-recognition is the sequence of violence. While the Hegelian slave realizes a self-recognition passively, and only after violent life-and-death struggles have ensued and concluded with the creation of masters and slaves, radical Islamists demarcate self-recognition violently. The logic in radical Islamist calls for violence can thus be understood, I argue, through inverting the sequence of the classic Hegelian struggles for recognition, so that such struggles start from the point of the existence of masters and slaves and then culminate into violent life-and-death struggles for self-recognition (or self-assertion). Figure 2.1 illustrates this contrast and

Hegelian struggles for recognition

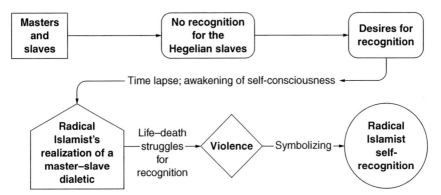

Figure 2.1 The inversion of Hegel's ethnics of recognition and the essence of Islamist extremism.

inversion. In this case, it is the radical Islamists that perceive themselves as the slaves and it is they who then explain the imperative of violence against the master in terms reflective of the anatomy of the classic Hegelian struggles for recognition and the Hegelian master–slave dialectic. The analysis in this chapter sheds light on three popular paradoxes: If extremism is linked to poverty, then how might we explain the motivations of individuals from privileged backgrounds? If Islamist extremism is *Islamic* in nature, then how might we explain the motivations of its secular recruits? If Islamist extremism is in essence a hatred for the Judeo-Christian world, then how might we explain radical Islamist sectarian violence?

Fears and desires that comprise the struggles for recognition

Violent struggles for recognition are essentially struggles against servitude, whether servitude is actual or perceived, present or feared. Both struggles for recognition and struggles for *self*-recognition have similar dynamics and features (what I refer to as the 'anatomy') in that both are centered around (1) the perception of the other as a threat to the self, and thus based on a fear of the other, and (2) a desire for honor and prestige. In this way, struggles for recognition are in essence the same as struggles for self-recognition, the only difference being the sequence of violence as I have noted above (see Figure 2.1). The other difference is in the expectations. The classic Hegelian violent struggles for recognition conclude with the desire and expectation of recognition from the other who the self has made into a slave. However, in violent radical Islamist struggles for *self-recognition*, while recognition is desired from the other, it is not expected from the other (the incumbent master/s) since this other is unlikely to grant recognition to the self. It is thus that such struggles, I argue, become struggles for self-recognition and not struggles for recognition. In the absence of an expectation of recognition from the master, violent struggles for self-recognition are intended to challenge the master's mastery and to thus demarcate the absolute independence of the self. So while the self may remain in chains (in actual or metaphorical sense), the self seeks to demonstrate that it is no longer a docile, banal slave that simply accepts, without resistance, its negation by the master. Such is the logic in the radical Islamist explanations of violence.

A note on who constitutes the 'other' in radical Islamist rhetoric is in order here. In the radical Islamist context, the other is presented not only as the non-Muslim other (the 'western' entities in the broad sense of the United States, Israel, India, Russia and so on) but also as the *sectarian* other (the Sunni versus the Shi'i). Indeed, Sunni Islamist extremist groups as well as Shi'i Islamist extremist groups do not consider the sectarian other as even Muslim and subsequently refer to such other in the same context as the non-Muslim other (the 'infidel' however specifically defined). The other is thus seen as *necessarily* a threat to the self, whether it be the non-Muslim agent or the sectarian Muslim other. Consequences of this perception have been as violent as the consequences of the perception of the threat of the non-Muslim other, as was seen in Pakistan during the 1980s and in the post-2003 US-occupied Iraq both prior to, and in the aftermath of, its US-sponsored national elections in January 2005.[4]

In Pakistan, prominent Sunni extremist groups such as *Sipah-e-Sahaba* (SSP), *Lashkar-e-Jhangvi* (LJ) and *Jaish-e-Mohammad* (JeM) emerged initially to counter what they perceived as the threat emanating from the Shi'ites in Pakistan in the 1980s (particularly in the aftermath of the successful Shi'i Islamic revolution in neighboring Iran and fears of a consequent revolutionary fervor among the Shi'ites in Pakistan) and later also metamorphosed into Jihadi groups. Muhammad Amir Rana notes that these groups saw the emerging strength of Shi'i organizations—based in part on the Shi'i awakened self-consciousness in reaction to General Zia ul-Haq's (1977–1988) Islamization policies that had a Sunni focus and in part on the ideological boost from the Iranian (Shi'i) Islamic revolution in 1979—as a threat to Sunni identity.[5] To counter what they saw as a Shi'i threat and to assert their Sunni identity, *Sipah-e-Sahaba* proposed the creation of an ultra-orthodox Sunni Taliban-type government in Pakistan.[6] Indeed, in public meetings during 1999, the leader of *Sipah-e-Sahaba*, Maulana Azam Tariq, demanded that the government of Pakistan declare Pakistan a Sunni state and terminate all social and commercial interactions with its Shi'i minority.[7] As well, *Lashkar-e-Jhangvi*, another ultra militant Sunni extremist group, took to the targeting of Shi'i leaders and government officials as a way to both intimidate the Shi'i power lords and assert their recognition violently.[8] *Jaish-e-Mohammad*, which initially operated solely as a Sunni sectarian extremist group, later expanded its missions to include a resistance against Indian suppression of Muslim Kashmiris in Indian administered Kashmir, and as such noted in its manifesto that its mission was "doing jehad against [all of] the enemies of the faith [a reference to Shi'ites as well as Hindu Indians]."[9] Prominent Shi'i extremist groups that emerged to counter what they perceived as the Sunni threat include *Tahrik-i-Jafaria* (TJP), *Sipah-e-Mohammed* (SM), and *Hizbul Momineen*. Tahrik-i-Jafaria was created in 1974, initially as a Shi'i political party, but during the decade of orthodox Sunni Islamization of Pakistan of General Zia ul-Haq (1977–1988) that marginalized Shi'i Islamic traditions, *Tahrik-i-Jafaria* turned to more militant activities in its quest for recognition and, as a result, was banned by General Musharraf's government in 2002.[10]

In the aftermath of the US military occupation of Iraq in 2003, one saw Islamist extremist violence targeting US elements (broadly defined) that was primarily of the *jihadi* variety. However, it was in the period leading up to January 2005 US-sponsored elections that one began to see the most aggressive efforts exerted by the extremist elements from both the Shia and the Sunni sectarian camps at mobilizing their constituencies against the other. The 2005 American-sponsored Iraqi national elections resulted in a drastic shift in the balance of power for the Sunnis, Shi'ites and Kurds in the country. While Iraq had historically been demographically dominated by the Shi'ites, the Sunnis (while a minority in numbers) had enjoyed being the group at the helm of power during the reign of now deposed and deceased Iraqi Present Saddam Hussein.[11] This population-power imbalance meant that the hitherto Sunnis' disproportionate hold on power could not translate into their dominance in the newly created Iraqi national assembly (national legislature) prior to the scheduled elections in January 2005. Not surprisingly, this change in the balance of power initiated a most violent reaction from radical Sunni groups that, as we shall see, presented their struggle in the most Hegelian manner as struggles for the *recognition of the self* in light of the *threat of the other*.

To be sure, however, Islamist violence in the post-2003 US-occupied Iraq has taken at least three distinct forms: (1) the radical Sunni anti-American violence targeting American military and civilian personal and their allies (the *jihadi* Islamist violence); (2) the Sunni–Shi'i sectarian violence (sectarian Islamist violence); (3) radical Sunni violence targeting moderate Sunni pro-US elements (a Sunni–Sunni violence) and radical Shia elements at war with contending Shia elements (intra-sectarian violence). In the remainder of this chapter and in my discussion the critical components of the radical Islamist self-recognition as based fundamentally on the perception of the 'other as a threat to the self' I shall focus only on two such forms of violence in post-2003 Iraq, the *jihadi* Islamist extremist violence and the *inter*-sectarian Islamist violence (based on the Shia–Sunni divide). This is because the *intra*-sectarian (Shia versus Shia, or Sunni versus Sunni) can not be conceptualized as based on the perception of the other as a threat to the self as the other here does not comprise entities with identities distinct from the self (since it is *not* the sectarian other or the non-Muslim 'infidel' other). In intra-sectarian violence then, the other is instead defined and understood as those non-compliant elements *within* one's sectarian group or, at times, the contending agents *within* one's sectarian group that are seen as a threat for reasons of competition for political power and status in society and *not* because they are perceived as obstacles in the way of the recognition of the self as a *distinct group*—Shia, Sunni as in the case of sectarian Islamist extremist group rhetoric or broadly the *ummah* as in the case of *jihadi* Islamist extremist group rhetoric.

The other as a threat to the self and the fear of the other

So central is recognition to human consciousness that, notes Hegel, its pursuits *necessarily* culminate in *life-and-death* struggles. Robert Williams explains this Hegelian logic in terms of the fact that the "master/slave is *preceded by* and is the *outcome of* a life-and-death struggle" where the one who lacks the courage to risk his physical life becomes the slave.[12] Pinkard restates this by noting that the "one who opts for life becomes the slave ... and the slave there-fore becomes a 'being-for-another' in that he accepts that his won subjectiv-ity—that what for him is an authoritative reason for belief or action—counts only in terms of how well it contributes to the master's desires and projects."[13] The dialectic takes shape when the slave comes to realize its opposite. That is, the slave comes to realize that he is but an extension of the master's plans. What is explicit and most critical in these assertions is that short of being willing to risk one's life in the struggles for recognition, one tacitly accepts servitude. Indeed, it is this very reason that, I argue, appears abundant in radical Islamist rhetoric wherein violence and even the destruction of the self becomes justified in terms of the pursuit of freedom. In other words, radical Islamist rhetoric presents logic reminiscent of the Hegelian ethics of recogni-tion wherein servitude of the self to the master is born *out of fear* of risking one's life in the struggles for recognition and not born out of any metaphysical superiority that the master possess over the slave.

The paradox of needing the other for the recognition of the self at the same time as the other also being a threat to the recognition of the self has already been outlined above. Indeed, as noted above, the inevitability of the culmination of any interaction between two competing self-consciousnesses into that of mastery and slavery is itself a testimony to this paradox. Hegel saw this inevita-bility as the inevitability of life-and-death struggles against servitude—the inevi-tability of violent struggles against servitude—which he argued was reflective of human history. Pinkard summarizes Hegel's argument to this effect as thus:

[t]he relation to the other is thus double-edged in that the other both *affirms* and *undermines* the subject's sense of himself, and it is this double-edged quality that leads to the dialectic of dependence and independence that structures the discussion of mastery and servitude.[14]

In other words, while one seeks to demarcate one's absolute independence from other/s one remains nonetheless dependent on other/s, in the sense of needing the other/s for the recognition of the self. And, perhaps even more importantly, it is this contradictory relationship with the other that makes the self at once a slave and a master and the other at once a master and a slave. Since the master–slave dialectic was discussed in detail earlier in this chapter, I shall not elaborate its dynamics here.

What is critical to appreciate at this point is that it is within the context of the Hegelian life-and-death struggles against servitude that Kojeve explains that if there is a multiplicity of desires for recognition then "each will want to subjugate the other, *all* the others, by a negating, *destroying action*."[15] Struggles for recognition and thus struggles against servitude are necessarily violent. Indeed, Kojeve sees violence for the ends of thwarting a life of servitude as the very *nature of history*, an absence of which could only signify an 'end of history,' that is, the 'end' of human interactions (or history) as we have thus far witnessed and therefore assumed.[16] This is apparent in his following assertion:

Man will risk his *biological life* to satisfy his *nonbiological* Desire … [because] the being that is incapable of putting his life in danger in order to attain ends that are not immediately vital—that is, the being that cannot risk its life in a Fight for *Recognition,* in a fight for pure *prestige*—is *not* a truly *human* being.[17]

If the nature of history is violent and contentious, as Kojeve argues, then the radical Islamists' violent pursuits of self-recognition should come as no surprise. Of course, whereas in Hegel's analysis the violent life-and-death struggles for recognition are fought to *thwart* a life of servitude, in the case of the radical Islamists violent life-and-death struggles for self-recognition are fought in order to *reject* the existing life in servitude (whether actual or perceived). Give that the radical Islamists are mobilized by negative *perceptions* of the other, and given that the other is the more dominating entity that is presented as subjugating the self (whether narrowly defined as a particular ethnic group or broadly defined as the Muslim world or the *ummah)*, radical Islamist demarcations of self-recognition take on a particularly violent fervor. After all, as Hegel argued, struggles against servitude—whether in pursuit of the recognition of self from the other or in pursuit of self-recognition—are inevitability violent. The understanding of the other as a threat to the self appears in the form of the imperative of revenge in radical Islamist discourse. For example, in a *Lashkar-e-Jhangvi* pamphlet entitled "Why are we waging Jihad?" commentaries argue for the "Muslim right to *revenge* in history."[18] As well, in one of the publications of the *Jamaat-ul-Dawa* (previously *Lashkar-e-Toiba)* it is postulated that:

ˈ Allah has created the human beings for only one mission—waging Jehad
(holy war) against infidels *who are out to destroy Islam.*[19]

Here, of course, 'Islam' is a broad reference to the 'self,' broadly defined as the
ummah and then even more broadly as 'Islam.' This notion of the self in the
Islamist and radical Islamist sense was discussed in Chapter 1. What is remarkable in the above is the assumption that the other is necessarily a threat to the self.
The perception of the other as a threat is quite explicit here in the reference to
'infidels who are out to destroy Islam.' References to the other as a threat that
must be violently overcome are also found frequently in bin Laden's rhetoric, as
in his following comments in the aftermath of September 11, 2001:

> Look at this war [against terrorism] that began some days ago against
> Afghanistan. Is it a single, unrelated event, or is it part of a long series of
> *Crusader wars against the Islamic world?* Since World War One…. the
> entire Islamic world has fallen under the Crusader banners, under the
> British, French, and Italian governments … This Muslim nation [Afghani-
> stan] has been attacked by the Russian *predator* … The Russians have exter-
> minated an entire people and forced them into the mountains, where they
> have been devoured by disease … Then there is the genocidal war in Bosnia
> that took place in front of the whole world's eyes … our brothers were mur-
> dered, our women raped, and our children slaughtered … For more than
> fifty years, our brothers in Kashmir have been tortured, slaughtered, killed
> and raped … Look at the Chechen war that is still going on today. An entire
> people is once again being subjected to war by this Russian *predator* … We
> should therefore see events *not as isolated incidents, but as part of a long
> chain of conspiracies, a war of annihilation in all senses of the word.*[20]

Aside from the obvious references to the *ummah* as one Muslim nation threatened by the other—as seen in explicit references to 'wars against the Islamic
world'—most striking in the above are the explicit portrayals of the other as a
threat to the realization of a 'Muslim' self-consciousness (defined in the broad
collective sense of independence and freedom). The references to the Russians
as the 'predator' scarcely need elaboration. Equally significant in the above are
references to multiple cases where the Muslim societies were attacked or otherwise threatened by the other, which seem intended to paint an authoritative
picture of the imminent threat to the *ummah* from what bin Laden broadly refers
to as 'crusader wars' which, given the context of the full text of his comments,
includes both the Christian crusaders as well as the Zionist crusaders. That bin
Laden refers to these events as *"part of a long chain of conspiracies"* further
points to his efforts at legitimizing violent jihad in the context of the 'reality' of
oppression.

In interpreting the defining element of Hegel's ethics of recognition, Alexandre Kojeve observed that "[m]an became a slave because he feared death."[21]
Interestingly, violence is explained in radical Islamist rhetoric in much the same

manner, as life-and-death struggles against servitude (whether actual or perceived). So, just as the fear of death created the Hegelian slave, it is the fear of death that radical Islamists portray as sustaining a life of servitude. Violence, therefore, becomes presented by extension as the only antidote to a life of servitude. Such Hegelian logic can be seen prevalently in radical Islamist rhetoric. *Jaish-e-Mohammad's* Maulana Masood Azhar's assessment of the atrocities committed by Indian forces in Indian administered Jammu and Kashmir and the plight of Muslim Kashmiris therein emphasizes the negation of one's being (the servitude of the self) as a justification of violence/insurgency:

> You [a reference to Indian forces] had *conquered* and *subjugated* the Muslims of India [a reference primarily to the Indian administered Kashmir given the context of his speech] and you had thought that you had *suppressed* them completely. But there are embers in that dying fire. When they shall blaze again they shall teach you a lesson you shall never forget![22]

This statement is theoretically instructive in light of the Hegelian assumption that a life-and-death struggle is an *outcome* of the fears of servitude, which in this context is seen as taking shape with the Indian occupation of Kashmir and the servitude of the Muslim Kashmiris therein. So, here the Indians become the masters and the Muslim Kashmiris the Hegelian slaves. This makes sense in the context of the fact that the grievance of the pro-independence groups—whether Pakistan-based or indigenous Kashmiri—is that their identity is not granted full recognition (in the German sense of the word meaning both identification and acknowledgment/respect), which is needed to foster independence. Also instructive is the following statement by Syed Saleem Gardezi, the founder of *Harkat-ul Mujahidin*, elaborating the reasons for the Muslim Kashmiri insurgency in Indian administered Jammu and Kashmir as founded on injustices in the legislative assembly elections of the Indian administered Kashmir in 1987:

> [The Muslim *Mutahida Mahaz* (Muslim Kashmir political party)] was deliberately made to lose the elections for the Occupied Kashmir Assembly ... [so that] these young men were *forced* to think that an *armed struggle* was their *only choice*.[23]

The stated *inevitability* of the use of violence in Gardezi's statement coincides in an inverse manner with the Hegelian assumption that the *lack* of willingness to risk one's life in the life-and-death struggles for recognition is a tacit acceptance of servitude.[24] In other words, fearlessness in life-and-death struggles for recognition (or self-recognition as I've argued to be the case in the radical Islamist context) is the only effective antidote to a life of servitude. Within this context, the reference to 'armed struggle' as the 'only choice' seems intended to portray armed struggle as the only antidote to a life of servitude.

An even more glaring compatibility of reason in Hegel's theory of violence and radical Islamist rationale is the fact that the *Muttahida Jehad Council*—a coalition of 22 militant Kashmiri groups (including *Hezb-ul-Mujahidin*), also known as the United Jehad Council—bases its raison d'être on a violent struggle against Muslim *servitude* in the Indian administered Jammu and Kashmir.[25] Indeed, when on July 24, 2000 the *Hezb-ul-Mujahidin* declared a unilateral cease-fire in Jammu and Kashmir, the *Muttahida Jehad Council* criticized the decision by labeling it "wastage of sacrifices and [a] *passage to servitude*."[26] The *Hezb* was only reinstated into the *Muttahida Jehad Council* after it withdrew the ceasefire on August 8 of the same year.[27] Broad spheres of influence of radical Islamist groups such as *Hezb-ul-Mujahidin*, *Lashkar-e-Toiba*, and *Hizbul Momineen* operating in the Indian administered Jammu and Kashmir point at the extent to which the reason espoused by such groups—violence as a struggle against servitude—appeals to the *existential sensibilities* of the disenfranchised masses, thereby reinforcing the validity of reason in Hegel's theory of violence.

The agents of one's servitude have also at times been broadly defined in radical Islamist rhetoric as those Muslim governments that have themselves become agents of the masters—the western powers. This can be seen in bin Laden's following statements:

> The *subserviency* of [Muslim] rulers is no different from the subserviency of the amirs or governors of provinces to the king or the president. The rule of the *agent* is the rule of the one who made him his agent [namely, the 'crusader United States'].[28]

The reference to the 'agent' in bin Laden's remarks is a reference to the subservience of the Muslim rulers to the United States, making the former simply an agent of the neo-colonialism of the latter. The perception of an alliance with the United States as being a demarcation of the servitude of the leaders of Muslim states seems a prevalent theme in the rhetoric of Pakistani Islamist extremist groups. Indeed, in the aftermath of Pakistan's post-2001 alliance with the United States' 'war on terrorism,' *Jaish-e-Mohammad* not only presented President Musharraf as a traitor and an 'agent' of the United States but also cited the Pakistani government's 'servile' policies as the justification for the conspiracy to assassinate President Musharraf.[29] Portrayals of the US–Pakistani alliance as a guise for Musharraf's servitude to the United States can be seen in Professor Hafiz Mohammed's critical remarks that Pakistan's decision to grant access to the United States over its land and space jeopardized Pakistani *independence*.[30] Within the broader context of such a mentality one can situate *Hezb-u-Mujahideen's* categorical rejection of any peace negotiations with India over the issue of Kashmir, which was their overt criticism of the India–Pakistan peace overtures in 2003:

> Thousands of militants have sacrificed their lives pursuing their dream of *liberating* Kashmir [from Indian administration]. Islamabad's *bowing* to US pressures on Kashmir is a *betrayal*.[31]

The presentation of the imperative of violent struggles against the other to thwart the servitude of the self to the other—and thus an acceptance of the Hegelian life-and-death struggles for recognition—can be explicitly seen in Abu-Mus'ab al-Zarqawi's following assertion:[32]

> The *price of jihad* ... as high and as onerous as it may be, is *not in any way comparable to the price of humiliation* and disgrace [and the price of] the loss of religion and [freedom in] this world. It should be noted that the infidel regime does not settle for enslavement to it, but completely uproots the believers from their religion, and [thus] they lose [their freedom] in this world.[33]

In his above remarks al-Zarqawi is referring to the American military occupation of Iraq and thus the reference to 'infidel regime' is a reference to the American regime. What is most notable in the above, however, is his presentation of the 'price of jihad' (namely one's life) as 'not in any way comparable to the price of humiliation' (namely servitude); in other words, the cost of one's life in violent struggles against servitude (jihad) is not as high (philosophically speaking) as the cost of servitude (namely the humiliation of the self). If there was any promotion of violent jihad in terms of the Hegelian life-and-death struggles against servitude then this is one quintessential example.

Even more conceptually consistent to the Hegelian thesis of the other as a threat to the self in struggles for recognition (self-assertion and independence) are al-Zarqawi's following remarks:

> *Humiliation* is when you see the Jews doing as they wish amongst the Muslims, yet you are silent and *cannot act*, you are *bound and cannot free yourself*. Humiliation is when *the Crusaders and their aides can take control*, and can build themselves [military] bases and then set forth from them to *kill Muslims* ... Humiliation is seeing your sisters crying out from the oppression of the Crusader jailer.[34]

In the above, the other is presented as both the Israelis (Jews) and the Americans (Crusaders) that is responsible for the bondage and lack of freedom of the self (defined broadly as the Muslims). Thus the other is a threat to the recognition of the self—in the sense of a demarcation and realization of one's independence and freedom—as the other is presented as taking control of the self and even killing the self. The implicit message in the above seems to be the inevitability, if not the desirability, of life-and-death struggles against servitude. A similar but slightly more implicit message can be seen in al-Zarqawi's following remarks:

> We have demands that we will not retract until we fulfill our obligations to Allah by being killed as *shahids* [martyrs] or by being victorious and living happily under the rule of Allah. Our demands are: The expulsion of the *invaders* from our lands in Palestine and Iraq, and in the rest of the *lands of*

Islam; the establishment of *shar'ia* [Islamic law] throughout the world; the dissemination of the *justice of Islam*; and the *elimination of the oppression* by [other] religions.[35]

Setting aside for now the rather theological sounding message in the above as apparent from references to the 'rule of Allah' and 'our demands' defined in terms of the 'establishment of shar'ia [Islamic law] throughout the world' (I shall address these rhetorical statements in the broader context of Promethean dreams and rhetorical claims of the return of the Caliphate in Chapter 4), what becomes immediately apparent is the rather Hegelian perception of the other as a threat to the self as demonstrated in the presentation of the other (ostensibly the Israelis and Americans given the reference to lands of Palestine and Iraq, respectively) as 'invaders' and oppressors by extension. Even more noteworthy are references in the above to 'lands of Islam' and 'justice of Islam' in the context of the struggle against the invaders (the other) and the 'elimination of the oppression' by the other as it sheds light on efforts to present (Sunni) Muslims as transnational entity—a 'self' consciousness if you may in the sense of the *ummah* as discussed earlier—that is united in its struggle against the other. Indeed, I argue that by presenting Islam and Muslims (the 'self') in such unified and homogenous terms al-Zarqawi's remarks by extension presents the other as the leviathan. In other words, if the struggle against the other is a matter of 'justice for Islam' and even more broadly as a matter of the 'lands of Islam' then the other must be an over-arching unified entity that beckons such a transnational struggle; the presentation of the other as the leviathan threat can also be seen in a lack of distinction deemed necessary in terms of the national origin of the invaders.

Another rather implicit promotion of violence for the ends of recognition can be seen in al-Zarqawi's following assertions:

> submission to the infidel rule and its oppression will over time generate *submissive, disgraced, and humiliated people* to whom disgrace and humiliation will taste good, and they will become *accustomed to a life of repression and enslavement* to someone other than Allah, and *will no longer see any of these things as condemned,* and *will certainly not [attempt] to repel them,* since they will be people who are led and dragged.[36]

The promotion of a life-and-death struggle against servitude is implicit but certainly present in the above. Instead of overtly calling for violent rebellion against the oppressors, al-Zarqawi presents its alternative as a life of servitude (humiliation, submission and disgrace). Thus, not only is the other presented as a threat to the independence of the self (as apparent in references to submission leading to a 'life of repression and enslavement') but the absence of a violent rebellion against the other is presented in terms of the consequences of a fear of death in the life-and-death struggles for recognition of that Hegelian agent that later becomes the slave. This is very apparent in the repeated references in the above to submission, humiliation, disgrace, enslavement and to a kind of numbness born of inaction that leads the self to 'no longer see any of these things as condemned' and therefore given in to servitude.

Explanations of Islamist (jihadi) violence in the context of struggles against the other and in terms of struggles against the servitude of the self can also be seen in bin Laden's response to the oft repeated question in the west, 'Why are they (Islamist extremists) doing this (a reference to terrorism)?':

> You [the Americans specifically, but also the British and the Israelis] attacked us in Palestine ... which has foundered under *military occupation* for more than 80 years ... you supported the Russian *atrocities* against *us* in Chechnya, the Indian *oppression* against *us* in Kashmir, and the Jewish *aggression* against us in Lebanon. Under *your ... orders,* the governments of our countries ... [have given] *us* [militant Islamist groups] a taste of *humiliation,* and [placed] us in ... a great prison of *fear and subjugation* ... These governments have *surrendered* to the Jews ... Your forces *occupy our countries;* you spread your military bases throughout them ... These tragedies and calamities are only a few examples of your *oppression* and *aggression* against us.[37]

The message in these statements seems to be that Islamist extremism is but a reaction to occupations, atrocities, oppression, humiliation and aggression committed by the other against the Muslims and the *ummah*—the 'us' in the above. The similarity between bin Laden's assertions of the essence of al-Qaeda above and Hizbullah's following definition of its essence are most noteworthy:

> They [the Americans] have attacked our country, destroyed our villages, massacred our children, violated our sanctities, and installed over our heads criminal henchmen who have perpetrated terrible massacres against our nation. They are still supporting these butchers who are Israel's allies and preventing us from *determining our destiny* with our *free will.*[38]

The message in both bin Laden and Hizbullah's statements seems clearly that their sanction of violence is a response to being placed in servitude to the other. References in the above to "determining our destiny" and "free will" deliver this point of *recognition through violence.* This substantiates my argument that the essence of Islamist extremism can be delineated independent of the particular geo-political context within which Islamist extremism may flourish.

Justifications for the creation of the *World Islamic Front* in 1998—an anti-American and anti-Zionist organization created by Osama bin Laden, Ayman al-Zawahiri (the Egyptian associate of bin Laden), member of the Egyptian *al-Gamaa al-Islamiyya* Abu Yasir Rifa'i Ahmad Taha, and the secretary-general of *Jamiat e Ulema* of Pakistan Sheikh Mir Hamzah—further reinforces my contention that Islamist violence is often framed by its recruiters as a Hegelian life-and-death struggle against servitude:

for over seven years America has *occupied* the holiest parts of the Islamic lands, the Arabian peninsula, plundering its wealth, *dictating* to its leaders, *humiliating its people* ... Some might have disputed the *reality of this occupation* before, but all the people ... have now acknowledged it.[39]

References to occupation, dictation, and humiliation in the context of the justifications for the creation of *World Islamic Front* seem intended to portray the latter as a *reactionary* (if not a revolutionary) group engaged in struggles against servitude. Less obvious but equally significant is the insinuation in the above that struggles against servitude are essentially struggles for honor; this is implicit in the reference to occupation (servitude) leading to humiliation (dishonor) which, given the context of the remarks (the declaration for the creation of a new militant group), seems intended to convey the message that the *World Islamic Front* offers a recourse through wars of honor and prestige. What is interesting here is that Alexandre Kojeve—one of the most prominent scholars of Hegelian philosophy—necessarily understood Hegel's ethnics of recognition, in particular the life-and-death struggles for recognition, as essentially *wars of honor and prestige.* I shall come back to this shortly. For now, let us consider the perceptions of the sectarian other as justifying violent struggles against servitude of the self.

The fear of the sectarian other

Until his death at the hands of the Americans in 2006, Abu-Mus'ab Al-Zarqawi (considered by many as the al-Qaeda representative in Iraq) represented the head of the radical Sunni insurgency in Iraq. A constant theme in Al-Zarqawi's rhetoric was his presentation of the Shi'ites as an arm of the American masters, as apparent in the following excerpt:

the new Crusader war that is taking place in Iraq, out of [the US's] desire to strengthen the Jews and to extend its [own era of] being the only [super-power], by taking control of the richest land in the world. Because it [the US] knew that it *would never find better help* in this region *than that of the Shi'ites*, as a tool for *destroying Islam*, it has turned this help [from the Shi'ites] and its reliance on them into a constant accompaniment to the measures of its *criminal plan.*[40]

In Al-Zarqawi's above remarks the Americans are presented as the nefarious masters (as explicit in the reference to the America 'Crusader') with desires not only to subjugate the Iraqis (as implied in the reference to Americans 'taking control of the richest land') but to 'strengthen the Jews' (a reference to the Israelis, that are implicitly presented as the extension of the American masters). Most notable in the above, however, is the demonization of the Iraqi Shi'ites as *co-conspirators* of the *master's larger plans of subjugation.* This is fairly explicit in the references to the Shi'ites as a 'tool for destroying Islam'; most interesting again is how Al-Zarqawi implicitly defines 'Islam' here as by definition Sunni and not Shi'i, thereby crystallizing the Shi'ites as the other that the self (the Sunnis) should be threatened by in its struggles for recognition. In the discourse context of the above, then, 'criminal plan' seems to warn against the American–Israeli–Shi'ite plan to subjugate the distinct Sunni self-consciousness and thereby to compromise Sunni independence (in the sense of being in total control of Iraqi affairs).

The demonization of the Shi'ite as the other that is a threat to the 'self'—here defined broadly as the Sunnis—can also be seen in the following remarks where al-Zarqawi explicitly pits Shi'ite against the Sunnis:

> The Shi'ite army—into which Bush, the enemy of Allah, is breathing life so that it will defend his back from the *blows of the jihad fighters*—is incapable of defending itself from the swords of the *faithful of Allah*.[41]

In his above remarks, al-Zarqawi not only relegates the Americans as the threat (the other) but also the Shi'ite and, perhaps even more remarkably, distinguishes between the Shi'ite Muslims and the 'jihad (Sunni Muslim) fighters' to reinforce his message that the other comes in the form of the Shi'ite as well. Indeed, in the context of his above remarks, the 'faithful of Allah' are presented only as the Sunnis which makes all others as the 'enemy of Allah' and thus a threat one's self-consciousness understood in the Islamist sense as the (Sunni) *ummah*.

Wars of honor and prestige

Kojeve's analysis of Hegel's ethics of recognition concludes that the struggles for recognition of one's distinct self-consciousness are essentially wars of honor and prestige.[42] Kojeve's sense of wars for the ends of 'honor' and 'prestige' can be understood in terms of wars for the ends of the demarcation of one's absolute independence and autonomy from the other, a demarcation that in the Hegelian sense can only be gained through life-and-death struggles for recognition. Wars of honor and prestige then come to mean wars for the demarcation of one's distinct self-consciousness. Thus, prestige in the Kojeveian sense can be understood as a status opposite to that of a life of servitude. It is in this context that Kojeve maintains the following:

> human, historical, self-conscious existence [that is, existence aware of its distinct identity and its worth] is possible only where there are, or—at least—where there have been, bloody fights, *wars of prestige*.[43]

To Kojeve, then, the inevitability of violent life-and-death struggles for recognition is essentially the inevitability of wars of honor and prestige. In fact, wars of honor and prestige, to the extent that they are violent extensions of struggles for recognition (or self-recognition), comprise for Kojeve the very nature of the history as noted earlier.

Most notably, one finds the radical Islamist justifications of violence as framed also in terms of the necessary 'costs' (in the real and not financial sense) of honor and prestige in the Kojeveian sense. This can be seen in Al-Zarqawi's following assertion of the imperative of violent insurgency against the American military and civilian elements in Iraq in 2006:

> Beware *not to lay down your weapons*, for your lot will be sorrow, regret, *shame and humiliation* in this world ... You used to pray day and night for ... jihad ... in Afghanistan, Chechnya, and elsewhere. Then Allah made ready for you the jihad deal in your own land.[44]

In his above remarks, passivity (or laying down one's weapons) is associated with dishonor and servitude (or shame and humiliation respectively). The references to jihad in the above can then be interpreted as the Hegelian life-and-death struggles against servitude, a retreat from which ushers a life of humiliation (or servitude). Thus much in a manner similar to Kojeve's analysis where self-conscious existence (independence existence, existence without humiliation and shame) inevitability ushers bloody fights (or jihad in this case) for the ends of prestige, al-Zarqawi in the above promotes violent jihad in a similar manner by highlight the consequences of its absence (a life of humiliation and lack of prestige).

The Kojeveian thesis that struggles for recognition (struggles against servitude) are essentially wars of honor and prestige takes on an added significance in the findings of Nasra Hassan's interviews of failed Palestinian suicide bombers in Israeli prisons. In his interviews with the prisoners, Hassan was told that it was *not* revenge but questions of *honor* that played a large part in the motivation for suicide missions:

> If that [revenge] alone motivates the candidate, his martyrdom will not be accepted to Allah. It is a military response, *not* an individual's bitterness that drives an operation. *Honor* and dignity *are very important* in our culture. And when we are humiliated we respond with wrath.[45]

References to honor and prestige seem frequently to be presented either as the very meaning of jihad, or its violation as an incitement to violence, or as the goal of violence and martyrdom. For example, Mujahid Akbar Khan, a member of the extremist group *Jaish-e-Mohammad,* blatantly noted that "[t]here is honor, fame and fortune in Jehad."[46] In a public speech delivered in Karachi, Pakistan in 1994, Maulana Masood Azhar, the co-founder of the ultra-extremist group *Jaish-e-Mohammad,* stated the following regarding the Indian attack on the *Babri* mosque in Ayodhiya:

> My proud Muslims elders, brothers and friends! It was ... [in] 1992 ... [that the] Kuffar [the non-believer/infidel] put us to the test ... chanting ... slogans against Islam, *challenging the honor* of the Muslims had advanced

upon the Babri Masjid [Mosque] in Ayodhiya. The entire Muslim world stood transfixed ... Finally, the heavens witnessed the scene, the earth watched too as defying the one billion and two hundred twenty million Muslims, the Hindus [Indians] attacked and martyred the 550 year old Babri Masjid ... By demolishing the Masjid [Mosque] the Hindus were testing the Muslims, watching what they would do.[47]

Azhar's focus on the sacredness of *Muslim honor*, and its abandonment or insult as a incitement to violence seem consistent in his speeches elsewhere, as in a speech he made regarding Pakistan's peace talks with India over the Kashmir conflict in 2003:

It seems their [Pakistani leadership's] *ghairat* (honor) has slept and there is a need to awaken it ... [this awakening] could be done by a true Muslim. It *will* be done through *jihad.*[48]

As well, violent jihad as a means of defending the *honor* of 'Islam'—which, as I noted in Chapter 1, should be understood not as religion but as the people who belong to the religion, the *ummah*—appear explicit in the speech delivered by the former chief of Pakistan's *Lashkar-e-Toiba*, Hafiz Saeed, at the *Jamia al-Qudsia* mosque in Lahore, Pakistan:

Islam is in grave danger, and the Mujahideen are *fighting to keep its glory* [honor, prestige, agency]. They are fighting the forces of evil in Iraq in extremely difficult circumstances.[49]

In the aftermath of the US-led invasion of Iraq in 2003, the publications of Pakistan's ultra-extremist Jihadi group *Lashkar-e-Toiba* started focusing on the need for a Jihad in Iraq. In June 2004, its Urdu language publication, *Ghazwa,* called for taking revenge against the Americans because of 'their' complicity in the *Abu Ghraib* prison atrocities. Amir Mir translated one such excerpt from the publication as thus:

The Americans are *dishonoring* our mothers and sisters. Therefore, *jehad* against America *has now become mandatory.* We should send our Mujahideen to Iraq to fight with the Iraqi Mujahideen. Remember that the Mujahideen are the *last hope* for Islam. If Mujahideen are not supported today, Islam will be erased from the map tomorrow.[50]

What is fascinating in such a rhetoric are the exaggerations that deliver the point that Jihad—and indeed violence against the other (the 'non-believers') as well as actions that endanger one's own life—is needed to defend the honor of Islam.

Explicit justifications of violence and martyrdom based on the defense of *Muslim honor and prestige* can be found in one of *Hamas'* rhetorical anthems:

O wonderful! We listen in astonishment to wonders and declarations concerning the international conference [a reference to the United Nations]. Even if your conference is held, it won't *bring back our rights* that we lost many years ago.

My rights were lost—where will I find them?

The honor of Islam—where will I find it?

... Dictate a message to the heart of the Cross [a reference to Christian world] and the Star [a reference to the Jewish world] ... .

But all the Arabs send are thousands of letters to the United Nations, crammed with statements of protest. They say the problem is solved, and a solution has been achieved.

I say that the problem [a reference to the servitude of the Palestinians at the hands of the Israelis] is not over yet ...

The only solution to the problem is blood, knee-deep. [51]

The above justifies violence in the context of the passivity of the Arab leaders, defined as their diplomatic negotiations and their compliance with the United Nations. Emotional disagreements between the Israeli–Zionist and Palestinian extremists over the rightful claims over land aside, what is important here is how reality is seen by the Palestinians, as that comprising of servitude and *dishonor* of the Palestinians and of the larger *ummah* (as seen in the references to 'honor of Islam'). Indeed, within the context of the criticism of diplomacy to what is presented as the brutal Israeli occupation, the anthem further *glorifies* Islamist violence in the context of the defense of the *honor* of Islam in general and, by extension, of Palestinians in particular.[52] The anthem concludes with quite explicit references to what Kojeve would call *bloody wars of honor and prestige* as the *only* solution to servitude, as reflected in the statement "The only solution to the problem is blood, knee-deep."

It is not surprising, of course, that in his speeches Osama bin Laden made frequent implicit or explicit references to the 'defense of Muslim honor' as the justification of *transnational* jihad. In a speech delivered in January 2006, bin Laden purported the following in the context of the perpetuation of jihadi violence:

As for us—we have nothing to lose. He who swims in the sea does not fear the rain. You have occupied our land and *violated our honor*. You have shed our blood and plundered our property. You have destroyed our homes and banished us. You have harmed our security, and we will pay you back in kind.[53]

When read carefully, the *transnational* scope of al-Qaeda's *jihad* is glaring in the above excerpt. For example, the references to the occupation of land, the violation of honor and the shedding of 'our blood' are much broader than any one area of conflict and seem at once to be a reference to the US occupation of Iraq, the US–NATO occupation of Afghanistan, the Israeli settlements in the West

Bank, and the like. This is perhaps the most dramatic validation of the universality of the Hegelian–Kojeveian thesis of *wars of honor and prestige* as a culmination of struggles against (actual or perceived) servitude as bin Laden frames *all* jihads as necessarily a response to a violation of Muslim honor. Such a view is also reflected in a speech delivered by Dr. Israr Ahmed, leader of the Pakistan's extremist *Tanzeem-e-Islami*:

> The process of the revival of Islam in different part of the world is real. *A final showdown between the Muslim world and the non-Muslim world*, which has been captured by the Jews, would soon take place. The Gulf war was just a rehearsal for the coming conflict.[54]

In the same spirit as bin Laden, Ahmad portrays all forms of Muslim insurgency as necessarily a competition of prestige, a 'final showdown' in the struggles for recognition.

The pursuit of honor and prestige also takes the form of an explicit rejection of the oppression of the self. This can be seen in the following assertion made by *Hezbollah*:

> We declare frankly and clearly that we are a nation that fears only God and *does not accept tyranny, aggression, and humiliation*. America and its allies and the Zionist entity that has usurped the sacred *Islamic land of Palestine* have engaged and continue to engage in constant *aggression against us* and are working constantly *to humiliate us*. Therefore, we are in a state of constant and escalating preparedness to *repel the aggression* and to defend our religion, existence and dignity.[55]

References to 'us' in the context of the reference to America and the Zionist entity seem references to the 'us' who has been subjugated. It is very clear in the above that violence is explained both in terms of the rejection of oppression and the rejection of the negation of the self. A desire for honor and prestige are implied herein. Consider also the following excerpt from *Hezbollah's* open letter to the 'downtrodden in Lebanon' and the world over:

> we have seen that *aggression* can be repelled only with scarifies and dignity gained only with the *sacrifice of blood*, and that *freedom* is not given but *regained* with the *sacrifice of both heart and soul.*[56]

The above not only rejects the oppression of the self but also challenges the oppression of the self. Violence is thus explained in such terms of struggles for self-recognition. It may be well to remind ourselves that a most intriguing aspect in Hegel's ethics of recognition is his argument that what the self fears the most is the negation of its self-consciousness (the self's distinct identity) and the subsequent life of servitude to the other. It is this fear of servitude that, according to Hegel, creates the motivation for a *life-and-death* struggle for recognition against the other.

Wars of honor and prestige and the sectarian other

Prior to its ban in August 2000, the Shi'i extremist group *Tahrik-i-Jafaria* met with the Governor of the province of Punjab in Pakistan to demand Shi'i rights and recognition, a statement that attests to the relevance of the following Hegelian claim: "to have value in my own eyes I must achieve value in the eyes of others."[57] To this end, *Tahrik-i-Jafaria* demanded the following:

> Shi'i Ulema [equivalent of a Shi'i clergy] should be allowed to address the public on television … relevant Shi'i books be made available in libraries. Plots [of land] should be allotted for Shi'i mosques in new housing schemes … Shi'i families victims of sectarian violence should be awarded financial aid. Lashkare Jhangvi [also spelled Lashkar-e-Jhangvi, the contending Sunni extremist group] camps in Afghanistan should be closed.[58]

The quintessential illustration of the Shi'i quest for recognition through violence, however, is found in the group *Sipah Mohammed*, which was created in 1993 primarily to counter the Sunni extremist group, *Sipah-i-Sahaba*. Upon its creation, the leader of *Sipah Mohammed* blatantly declared the following:

> We are tired of picking up corpses. Now, God willing, we will clear all accounts. *We will erase the very name of Sipah Sahaba* [also spelled *Sipah-e-Sahaba*, the contending Sunni extremist group] *from the annals of history.*[59]

Indeed, Muhammad Amir Rana notes that from 1993 to 2001, *Sipah Mohammed* was responsible for some 250 incidences of terrorism within Pakistan. Rana notes that

> [in] December 1994 its members attacked the offices of 'The Pakistan Observer' in Islamabad and accused the paper of not giving the organization sufficient coverage, and the paper's owner of having close relations with the leadership of [contending Sunni] Sipah Sahaba [*Sipah-e-Sahaba*] and utilizing the printing press for printing anti Shi'i literature for the organization.[60]

In the post-2003 Iraq theatre, in addition to the al-Zarqawi-led radical Sunni 'othering' of the Shi'ites, one also finds in Al-Zarqawi's speeches an implicit and explicit promotion of violence against the moderate Sunni pro-US elements that, in his view, comprised the Iraqi Islamic Party which cooperated with the US-sponsored elections in Iraq in 2005. Al-Zarqawi's response to such cooperation can be seen in the following excerpt:

> The [Sunni] Iraqi Islamic Party, whose history with jihad and with the Sunnis is well known, is the one that wanted to be the *lifesaver for the U.S.*

in the first battle of Falluja—which would have destroyed the American presence in Iraq had it not been for the *hudna* [i.e. temporary ceasefire] that his party worked so hard to attain, and which saved the *American master* from the quagmire in which it had sunk, after the noose drew tighter around the neck of the *Crusader and the Shi'ite forces* around Falluja.[61]

The Sunni moderates are presented here as the 'lifesavers' of the 'American master,' and thus guilty by association. This means that if the nefarious Americans represent the other to be feared, then their moderate Sunni sympathizers (the collaborators) are but puppets of the other and thus, by extension, also a threat to the self. Perhaps even more remarkable in the above is the reference to the 'crusader and the Shi'ite forces' that not only groups the sectarian other (the Shi'ite Muslims) with the nefarious masters (the American crusaders) but also implicitly presents the moderate Sunnis as no better than (or different from) the two aforementioned camps of 'the other.' The emotional gravity of rhetorically attacking moderate Sunnis in the context of the other is obvious.

Challenging the master's mastery

Radical Islamist rhetoric challenges the master's intellectual, spiritual and physical superiority and presents it as a myth using logic that is dialectical in nature. In so doing, it challenges the master's mastery and presents it as ironically contingent upon the self (the Hegelian slave) accepting such mastery. The master's mastery, radical Islamist reason implies, is not absolute. And so, radical Islamist rhetoric challenges the master's mastery by (i) challenging the master's reason upon which the master's mastery is based, and (ii) through the promotion of sporadic violence intended to render the master impotent and thereby to challenge the master's mastery.

Challenging the master's reason

That radical Islamist discourse frequently emphasizes the master's brutality and inhumanity is perhaps a well-known fact. What is less appreciated is the implicit logic behind such an emphasis, which, I argue, is intended to highlight the contingent nature of the master's mastery by presenting such mastery as contingent on the intimidation, humiliation and de-humanization of the self (the ummah, the Hegelian slave). The emphasis on the master's brutality thus seems intended to highlight the façade of the master's mastery, based as it is on the use of excessive force and not on compelling reason (thus challenging any perception of the master as metaphysically superior to the self). In other words, by emphasizing the master's brutality, radical Islamist discourse seeks to highlight the *illlegitimacy* of the master's control, a control that it presents as dependent on physical force and not moral superiority. Clearly, of course, challenging the master's mastery through emphasizing the master's brutality is an extension of challenging the master's reason for the master's coercive means (brutality) are often (if not always) *reasoned* through presenting the other (the radical Islamists, the Hegelian slaves) in categorically negative terms as 'terrorists,' as 'threats to peace,' or as 'axes of evil.' Radical Islamist rhetoric deconstructs such grand narratives by redefining the liberator, the reactionary and the terrorist. Thus, radical Islamist reason presents the masters as the 'terrorists' and the self (the Hegelian slaves) as the 'victims,' the 'liberators' and 'reactionaries' to the masters' oppression. The masters then get presented as categorically brutal and the self as categorically the victim.

A Chechen independence song starts with the following assertion: "*Chechnya is not a subject of Russia, it is a subject of Allah.*"[62] Theoretically speaking, if the master's mastery was based on the slave's acceptance of the master's reason as absolutely authoritative, then the awakened self-consciousness of the slave challenges the master's reason as it now sees the master's reason as *not* reflective of any metaphysical superiority of the master over the slave but as simply a matter of contingency—that of the slave's fear of challenging the master's reason. Challenging the master's reason, I argue, has two distinct but related components: (a) challenging the master's notions/perceptions of itself as the master and (b) challenging the master's definitions of 'good' and 'evil' and indeed the master's definition of 'victim' and 'aggressor.' The reference by the Iranian President Mahmoud Ahmadinejad to the United States as an "imaginary superpower made of straw" is a challenge to the master's notions or perceptions of itself and thus a broader challenge to the master's mastery.[63] The promotion in radical Islamist rhetoric of a distinct *Islamist reason* is, I argue, a component of the latter challenge, that of the master's definitions. Indeed, as we shall see, it is in this context that violence becomes presented in 'moral' terms as freedom struggle or even as a matter of sovereignty and not as an incidence of terrorism.

In the case of the Pakistani anti-Indian Islamist extremist groups, Amir Mir notes that their popularity is based fundamentally on their claims of providing an 'alternative worldview,' or, if you may, an alternative *reason* which challenges the master's reason.[64] This can be seen in the following statements of Masood Azhar of *Jaish-e-Mohammad*:

> They [the Pakistani leadership] are guided by the rules [reason] of international policies [implicit reference to the UN or US] and diplomacy, *not* by the teachings of Islam and the precepts of the Holy Prophet (PBUH). The intoxication of power has blinded them. They cannot think like an *independent* person. The fate of *ummah* (Islamic nationhood) cannot be left on them. We [are] all—the Mujahideen of *Jaish* [*Jaish-e-Mohammad*] are busy on this front—fighting a jehad against the worst enemy of Islam—the Indian army.[65]

Here, *Jaish-e-Mohammad* portrays the consequences of accepting the master's reason as a lack of independence of the self just as the Hegelian slave became a slave because he came to accept the master's reason as supreme and authoritative, thereby accepting by extension the mastery's mastery and the slavery of the self. Challenging the master's mastery is also most apparent in bin Laden's following statements:

> After the collapse of the Soviet Union ... made the US more haughty and arrogant, *and it has started to see itself as a Master of this world* and established what *it calls* the new world order. It wanted to *delude* people [into thinking] that it can do whatever it wants, *but it can't do this.* The US today ... has set a double standard, calling whoever goes against its injustice a terrorist.[66]

Most interesting in bin Laden's above comments are the fairly explicit references to the *contingencies* in history that have propelled the United States in the position of the master. In other words, just as the Hegelian slave realizes that his slavery and the master's mastery are "because of contingencies in the past relationship between the two," so too radical Islamists such as bin Laden portray American hegemony as a consequence of historical coincidence.[67] That bin Laden explicitly asserts that the United States "started to see itself as a Master of this world" and that it established "*what it calls* a new world order" is a clear indication at his efforts of challenging the master's reason. Even clearer are his remarks that the US "can't do this"—assert what bin Laden wants to portray as a baseless mastery—and his challenging of the master's definition of 'terrorism.'

Challenging the master's reason also popularly takes the form of challenging the master's definitions of 'good' and 'evil.' It would be a mistake, I think, to see such a challenge as merely a wasteful 'war' of semantics. Indeed, challenging the master's definitions of 'good' and 'evil,' of the master's presentation of the self as 'liberators' and the other as the 'terrorists,' fundamentally challenges the very legitimacy of the master's dominance by re-defining the terminologies and reversing their order so that the master's means are no longer seen as 'legitimate' for 'legitimate ends' (that of justice and liberation) but instead seen as nefarious for the ends of maintaining dominance and control. To put it more simplistically, challenging the master's definition of good and evil seeks to represent the master in an unfavorable light and to therefore challenge the grounds upon which the master's mastery is based—aggression and brutality, and not moral or legitimate authority.

Challenging the master's mastery through challenging the master's definitions—a subcomponent of the master's reason, as I have argued—is perhaps most explicit in the following except from an interview conducted by an independent Egyptian weekly *Roz Al-Yusouf* of an Egyptian Muslim Brotherhood member of parliament, Ragab Hilal Hamida:

> I specifically wanted to explain that [the term] *'terrorism'* is *not a curse* when given its *true meaning.* [When interpreted accurately], it means *opposing occupation* as it exists in Palestine, Afghanistan and Iraq! [...] From my point of view, bin Laden, Al-Zawahiri and Al-Zarqawi are *not terrorists* in the sense accepted by some. I support their activities, since they are a thorn

in the side of the Americans and the Zionists [...] anything related to *countering occupation is not a crime or* [an act of] *violence,* but rather jihad or 'terrorism' *in the sense of deterring and scaring* [the enemy] [...] We need an *accurate definition* of [the term] 'terrorism' in the negative climate in which we live—a climate that makes no distinction between a criminal and one who is prepared to sacrifice his life or a terrorist. *In defining* [this term] *we must not be influenced by American pressures ... They should not tell us to fight terrorism and to fight it as they command us to.*[68]

Numerous forms of the master's reason are challenged in the above. First, Hamida challenges the negative connotation of the term 'terrorism.' In defining it as "opposing occupation," Hamida presents the phenomenon of terrorism as an existential one, and thus reflective of the desires, aspirations, and fears of human existence. By so doing, he offers immediate legitimacy to the act. It then becomes a logical extension of his argument that he should present bin Laden, Al-Zawahiri, and Al-Zarqawi as "not terrorists in the sense accepted by some"; in other words, not terrorists in the negative sense, thus challenging the master's relegation of these individuals as undesirable and as criminals. The latter logic is apparent in his assertion "anything related to countering occupation is *not* a crime or [an act of] violence." Hamida then further challenges the dominant narratives related to the notion of 'terrorist' and 'terrorism' by arguing that a counter-narrative is needed, one that makes a distinction between a mere criminal and one who is "prepared to sacrifice his life." Perhaps the most instructive part of his commentary is the last two sentences. Here, he explicitly rejects "American pressure"—read, American reason—as well as the American 'war on terrorism.' The challenging of the master's reason then is complete.

The comments of Iraqi cleric Sheik Ahmad al-Kubeisi are also notable here in the context of challenging the master's definitions of victim and aggressor:

the world considers a plundering *occupier* [the Israeli government] *to be a man of peace,* and the *owner* [the Palestinians] of the *occupied land* to be a *terrorist.* The world [the masters] demands today from anyone whose land has been occupied ... that they shut up. If any of them [Muslims] complains, or picks up a gun to kill those who killed his family, and destroyed his land with missiles, *he is considered a terrorist.* On the other hand, *those who plundered, colonized, occupied, killed, executed, and dropped nuclear bombs and depleted uranium* (shells) are *considered men of peace,* who spread democracy.[69]

Since the above assertions represent al-Kubeisi's response to the question 'How do you view the Jihad in Palestine?' it becomes apparent that the references to the 'occupier,' 'owner of the occupied land,' 'terrorist,' the one who 'complains' are references to the entities that I have placed in parenthesis above. In the above, grand narratives related to definition and meaning of terrorism and democracy are turned on their head; this is as apparent from the first sentence in the above excerpt and the last sentence. Here, al-Kubeisi challenges the relegation of the self as the terrorist and the master as the 'man of peace.' He also challenges the master's reason by implying that brutal treatment by the master cannot be presented as the means to the ends of 'democracy'; this can be seen as implied in the last sentence of the above excerpt. Challenging the master's reason by challenging the master's notion of democracy can also be seen explicitly in following excerpt from al-Zarqawi's speech in 2006 that sought to challenge the legitimacy of the American occupation of Iraq:

> For they [a reference to Americans and Israelis] are the same ones ... who seek to bring upon themselves the *tyranny of human beings*—[that is] *democracy* ... They have deviated from the *right path*.[70]

Since earlier in this speech al-Zarqawi refers to the "Jewish and Crusader invaders" in criticizing the post-2003 American military presence in Iraq, the reference to "they" in the above seems to be a reference to the Americans and the Israelis. In a classic postmodernist spirit, al-Zarqawi redefines democracy as the "tyranny of human beings," a definition that stands in sharp contrast to the grand narratives of democracy as freedom for all human beings. If this is classic postmodernist reason, it is also classic dialectical reason in that by challenging the master's reason he challenges the master's legitimacy and ultimately his superiority.

Another example of challenging the master's reason through challenging the master's narratives as presented in the form of definitions can be seen in the way news is reported in the Chechen independent international Islamic Internet news agency—the *Kavkaz* Center—where frequent references are made to the Russian government as an "imperial state" with its "criminal policies of slaughtering, butchering, ethnic cleansing";[71] or the Russians as the "aggressors and occupiers."[72] Indeed, the Chechen Kavkaz Center often presents the global or regional military powers—a reference either to Russia, or the United States or regional powers such as Israel—in unfavorable and unconventional terms, as apparent in the following news headlines:[73]

1 "6 Israeli *Terrorists* Killed in East Lebanon."[74]
2 "Kremlin loses its grip on a *dying empire*."[75]
3 "10 Russian *Invaders* Gunned Down in Chechnya."[76]
4 "*War on Terror: 3 US Terrorists* on Trial in Vietnam."[77]

Most interesting in the above is the reversal of roles that is suggested wherein it is the masters, and not the Hegelian slaves, that are presented as the bandits. This can be seen in the headline that I have numbered as (1) above, where it is the Israelis that are presented as the terrorists in contrast to the popular use of this terminology to describe the Palestinians. In addition, the reference to Kremlin's 'dying empire' in headline (2) above seems equally intended to de-legitimize Russia's supremacy; the reference to a 'dying empire' is thus a challenge to the master's mastery. In headline (3) above, the reference to Russians as 'invaders' very clearly portrays them in the wrong and by extension the Chechens as the victims, thus very explicitly challenging the master's (Russian) reason that categorically portrays the Chechens as the only culprits. Most interesting perhaps is headline (4) above for it *redefines* the 'war on terror'—a terminology coined by the American administration in the post-2001 era—as comprising of the war against the 'US terrorists.' This is ironic as the American 'war on terror' is popularly, if not universally, understood as the American war against Islamist extremism. Thus, by reversing the implication of the master's terminology, the radical Islamist directly challenges the master's reason and, by extension, the legitimacy or the fact of their supremacy.

A similar effort at reversing the order of the master's reason can be seen in *Lashkar-e-Toiba's* reference to the self as *not* a terrorist group. In challenging the targeting of the self, the radical Islamist groups reversed the order of accusations so as to directly challenge the master's reason.[78] This logic can be seen in the statements of *Lashkar-e-Toiba*'s member, Professor Hafiz Mohammed:

> We have *challenged* the US authorities time and again to *prove* terrorism charges against the *Lashkar-e-Toiba* in any international … [forum]. *We repeat this challenge now.* We can prove who is the *real terrorist*: India, Israel, US, Russia or the Mujahideen? The world fully knows who was responsible for the *brutal killings* of hundreds of thousands of innocent people by nuclear bombs. Has the world seen a greater act of terrorism than that?[79]

What is most interesting in the above is the classification of the 'masters' as at once the United States, Israel, India, and Russia for it shows a kind of solidarity with the *ummah* that is targeted by the different manifestations of the master in different contexts and, by extension, implies a 'self-recognition' that is also broadly defined as the Hegelian slaves (the ummah) against the Hegelian masters. A similar challenge to the master's reason can be seen in the statements of Hamas' leader Khaled Mash'al in the following:

> The German [Chancellor Angela] Merkel pops up and says: Democracy and success in the elections are not sufficient for Hamas to gain legitimacy. *To hell with you all.* How are we supposed to gain legitimacy? When we said we had the legitimacy of resistance, *you called it terrorism.* Now, we say we have the legitimacy of democracy, but *you deny it.* In that case, you yourself are not legitimate, because you emerged through democracy. *This is the logic of a frail and defeatist person.*[80]

Khaled Mash'al directly challenges the contending perspectives of the superpowers in contrast to that of *Hamas* when he brings to light that what 'they' (the masters) called 'terrorism' (the evil) and viewed as immoral in instead 'resistance' (the good) and thereby legitimate and by extension 'moral.' This defiance of the master's reason is explicit in the assertion *"To hell with you all."* In other words, if the master's mastery is based on the master defining the actions of the other as terroristic, thereby giving the self the *authority* of action against such terrorism, then Mash'al challenges the definition of terrorism and therefore challenges the conceptual bases of the master's authority and his subsequent mastery. This seems quite clear in his reference to the master's logic as 'the logic of a frail and defeatist person,' which, by definition of 'frail' and 'defeatist,' means the master is not really a master. Similarly, the statements of Ayman Al-Zawahiri, member and deputy of *al-Qaeda,* are noteworthy here:

> With the collaboration of Musharraf the traitor and his security agencies, the *servants* of the Crusaders and the Jews, American planes attacked the village of Damdula, in Bajuar, shortly after the Feast of the Sacrifice. The planes killed 18 Muslims ... in their [the American] fight against jihad, *which they call terrorism* ... the whole word witnessed ... the extent of their barbarism, in its war against Islam and the Muslims.[81]

Here again, the master's definition of terrorism is directly challenged. Indeed, the fact that Al-Zawahiri makes references to 'jihad,' 'Islam' and 'Muslims' in the context of challenging the master's definition of 'terrorism' seems intended to reconstruct the master's reason by the self's own interjections. The implied conclusion seems to be that the masters are not engaged in a war against terrorism, but engaged instead in a war against Muslims; clearly a powerful rallying point for any Islamist extremist group.

Challenging the master's means

Radical Islamist rhetoric very clearly presents its use of sporadic violence—terrorist tactics by definition—as frustrating the master's conventional military means of defense and thereby as challenging the master's mastery. Such logic is in fact quite explicit in radical Islamist rhetoric. In light of this I argue that the Islamist extremist modus operandi of sporadic violence is also intended at challenging the master's mastery by challenging the master's capabilities of self-defense; or, to put it simplistically, by presenting the master as a 'paper tiger' with no absolute invincibility. In order to understand how violence can challenge the master's mastery, let us return to William Shearson's analysis of the "interior logic" of Hegel's master–slave dialectic that was introduced earlier and take a look at the related component of that logic:

> *[T]o be a slave means to have a master.*[82]

This logic, I argue, sheds critical light on the radical Islamist reason promoting violence as such missions are presented in terms of a tactic that, through its violence and its destruction of the others in the master's domain, seeks to *eliminate the master*. This elimination of the master is of course not actual but conceptual in the sense that sporadic violence does not actually eliminate the master in its entirety—for the 'master' is not an individual but a people considered to be the oppressors. To the extent that violent missions *challenge* the very role sub-scripted to the Hegelian slaves by the masters—that of subservience, servitude and submission—such missions *defy* the master's control over the self and, thereby I argue, are reasoned to *challenge the master's mastery.*

Let us focus on the radical Islamist use of sporadic violence—that often but not always comprises of self-destructive missions—to illustrate the manner in which they are presented as challenging the master's mastery and thus as frustrating the masters. This dimension is based on an alarmingly simple logic derivative of the very nature of terrorism. It is the sporadic and surprise element of any terrorist action that is, by definition, frustrating for the targeted entity because most often, if not always, the targeted entity is familiar only with conventional means of war and defense. Radical Islamist rhetoric capitalizes on this age old knowledge by glorifying its violent and martyrdom missions as not only comprising of a surprise attack that frustrates the enemy but as one that therefore challenges the master's ability to ade-quately combat the unconventional nature of its warfare—thus challenging the master's mastery. This logic is quite apparent in the following except from Reuter's interview of a Palestinian man in Gaza, a self-declared "author-ity on Hamas":

> We don't have tanks or F-16 jets. But we have something better: our explod-ing Islamic bombs [a reference to martyrs or suicide bombers]. All they cost is our lives, but *nothing can beat them—not even nuclear weapons.*[83]

The above clearly presents the destruction of the self as challenging the very bases of the master's mastery, namely his possession of nuclear weapons, as such weapons are useless against the martyr's surprise operations, thus 'nothing can beat them.' Indeed, Khalid Mash'al, the leader of *Hamas,* explicitly chal-lenges the master's conventional means of mastery in his promotion of martyr-dom missions:

> The Arabs have said: We don't want [conventional] wars, thank you very much. Leave the war to the peoples. Today, *the Israeli weapons are of no use against the peoples. We have imposed a new equation in the war.* In this equation, *our tools are stronger.* That is why *we will defeat them,* Allah willing.[84]

Most interesting in the above are references to martyrdom as having introduced a 'new equation in the war' against the Israelis where their 'weapons' are of 'no use' to their people as this presents Islamist violence as challenging the Israeli conventional means of mastery.

A similar logic can be found in Osama bin Laden's glorification of the Sep-tember 11, 2001, suicide missions:

America is a great power possessed of *tremendous military might* and a wide-*ranging economy,* but all this is built upon an *unstable foundation* which *can be targeted,* with special attention to its obvious *weak spots. If America is hit* in one hundredth of these spots, God willing, *it will stumble,* wither away and relinquish world leadership and its oppression. A small group of young Islamic fighters managed ... to provide people with *proof of the fact* that it is *possible to wage war* upon and fight against a *so-called* "great power" ... because they used Jihad ... [to bring] *victory.*[85]

References to suicide missions are implicit in the above but apparent in references to 'Islamic fighters.' What is quite explicit, however, is the presentation of suicide missions as challenging America's mastery as seen in use of the terms 'American is a great power' with 'tremendous military might' juxtaposed with reference to America's 'weak spots' in the context of 'Islamic fighters' that illustrated that weakness through jihad (martyrdom operations). The message in the above seems to be that while America can not be challenged through conventional means as it is far too superior in that domain, it can be challenged through unconventional operations of Islamic fighters and, more specifically, through the means of violent jihad.

The portrayal of martyrdom by Fathi Shikaki, the founder of the Palestinian extremist group *Islamic Jihad,* is also noteworthy here:

We can achieve our aims by causing an explosion which gives the mujahid [the martyr] no chance to hesitate or to escape. This would enable him [the martyr] to carry out a *successful operation* in the name of jihad and the faith, *destroy the enemy's morale,* and *sow the seeds of fear in the enemy's people.*[86]

Here, 'success' is defined as frustrating the masters through destroying the 'enemy's morale' and challenging the master's dominance and superiority through instilling 'fear in the enemy's people.' Christoph Reuter argues that it is the impact of such a justification that encouraged the first Palestinian suicide bomber operation against Israeli citizens in 1993.

Conclusion

Radical Islamists explain violence in terms of a rejection of oppression with logic that is Hegelian in nature. That is, I argue that reason in radical Islamist rhetoric seeks a recognition (acknowledgment) of the self's autonomy from the other (the master); but since it does not achieve this recognition from the other, it demarcates its autonomy and independence through use of sporadic violence against the master (the other) that is intended to at once challenge the master's mastery and the status of the self as the slave. In this violent 'self-recognition,' radical Islamist rhetoric uses reason that is dialectical in logic as it challenges the servitude of the self through challenging the master's reason upon which his mastery is based and through the use of sporadic violence to which the master's conventional means of recourse are impotent.

It is important to note that in the classic Hegelian model, struggles for recognition are violent but *self-recognition*—which is attained through the realization of the existence of the master–slave dialectic—is passive and non-violent. In the radical Islamist context, however, I argue that the explanations of violence are argued in terms of a self-recognition that is a product of the realization of the master–slave dialectic but this self-recognition is demarcated violently. Self-recognition then, in the radical Islamist context, has a decidedly violent manifestation as opposed to its Hegelian theoretic counterpart. Thus, I argue in this chapter that the nature of reason in radical Islamist explanations of violence can best be understood through inverting the sequence of Hegel's ethnics of recognition, so that the life-and-death struggles for recognition start from the re-awakening of the self-consciousness of the slave (the realization of a self-recognition by the slave) and thus start from already existing masters and slaves and then culminate into the classic Hegelian violent struggles for recognition. So while in the classic Hegelian model masters and slaves are the outcome of violent struggles for recognition, where the slaves over time achieve a very passive self-recognition, in the radical Islamist case, I argue that the existence of masters and slaves *itself* gives rise to violent struggles for self-recognition. In this way, struggles for self-recognition are fundamentally struggles that violently reject the oppression of the self using dialectical reason that challenges the master's mastery as an impetus. Violence then gets explained in radical Islamist rhetoric as an imperative that demonstrates the tenuous nature of the master's mastery—the very mastery that the self once categorically accepted—since it renders the master impotent given the sporadic nature of such violence to which the master's conventional capabilities are rendered impotent. This dialectical logic can be simply understood as thus: if the master is not really the invincible entity that the master portrays himself to be, then the slave is not really the weak and besieged entity that the slave understood himself to be. And it is this logic, I argue, that can be seen through a critical analysis of the nature of reason in radical Islamist rhetoric.

By illustrating that the nature of reason in the radical Islamist explanations of violence is reflective of the existential Hegelian struggles for recognition, the analysis in this chapter readdresses the following paradoxes: (1) those created by the fact of voluntary recruits of Islamist extremist groups that come from privileged socioeconomic backgrounds which invalidate the poverty–terrorism nexus arguments; (2) those created by the fact of radical Islamist sectarian violence (which targets the Shia or the Sunni other) which invalidates the clash-of-civilizations arguments that presume that radical Islamist violence is motivated by a theological and cultural hatred of the Judeo-Christian world. This is because the analysis in this chapter shows that it is the fear of being negated (oppressed) by the other—whether the other is the non-Muslim entity or the Muslim sectarian other—that is used in radical Islamist rhetoric as explanations of violence and not the fact of economic destitution, much less the hatred for the Judeo-Christian world simply for what it is.

3 Self-transcendent recognition

Radical Islamist 'suicide bombers' are often explained in popular western media as being motivated by the promise of 'virgins in heaven,' or by the desire to escape a life of drudgery through an act of suicide, or motivated simply by fanaticism unique to the Islamic context. The explanation of the 'virgins in heaven' as a motivation for self-destruction is contradicted by Daniel Brown's observation that there exists a tendency in the writings of the popular Shia and Sunni Islamic revivalists "to emphasize the ideological value ... of martyrdom [self-destruction] *rather than* the pleasures of the hereafter."[1] The explanation that self-destruction is motivated by a desire to escape a life drudgery is challenged by two facts: (1) that the socio-economic backgrounds of those that take part in self-destruction are not always reflective of economic impoverishment, contrary to the theoretical expectations of the poverty–terrorism nexus; and (2) such an assumption offers no explanation for why the other is also targeted in the act of self-destruction. In other words, such an explanation does not address the paradox of 'why kill the other if the motivation is to extricate the self from a life of drudgery?'[2] Finally, the explanation that self-destruction reflects a uniquely Islamic fanaticism is contradicted by Daniel Brown's observation that the notion of martyrdom "could quite easily thrive in a *secular context*, where the individual has little hope for the afterlife."[3] Then there are those that explain the radical Islamist act of self-destruction in terms of a Muslim culture that is reflective of a 'culture of death.'[4]

In this chapter, however, I argue that the radical Islamist explanations of self-destruction are neither uniquely *Islamic* (conceptually speaking) nor reflective of a uniquely apocalyptic culture. The radical Islamist explanations of self-destruction are instead, I argue, at once Hegelian (in the dialectical sense relevant to the slave), Gilgameshian (in the sense of what radical Islamist discourse understands about the master), and de-constructive in reason (in the sense of how it defines 'life' and 'death'). Along with the analysis of such reason, this chapter readdresses the following paradoxes: *Why kill the other, along with the self, if the motivation is to extricate the self from a life of drudgery? Why kill the self, along with the other, if the motivation is to exact revenge from the other?*[5] As we shall see, the logic in the radical Islamist explanations of self-destruction, as apparent from the nature of reason in rhetoric, is (1) to negate the masters, and thus to negate the master's control over the self, and (2) to achieve a self-transcendent recognition. The notion of 'recognition' in the Hegelian sense, as we saw in Chapter 1, relates to either the acknowledgment by the others, or to the demarcation by the self, of the absolute autonomy and absolute freedom of the self (and thus as the opposite of being negated or put in chains). The notion of a 'self-transcendent' recognition, particularly in the context of the radical Islamist explanations of self-destruction, has a two-pronged logic: one that relates to the 'self' as the individual, and one that relates to the 'self' as the collective (the *ummah*). In both these senses, a self-transcendent recognition is a symbolic demarcation of the absolute freedom and autonomy of the self (in both the individualistic and collectivist sense).

The dialectical, gilgameshian and paradoxical logic of self-destruction

While Hegel's dialectic is the story of the reawakening of the self-consciousness of the slave through which the slave takes a critical look at his fear of death which made him into a slave and thereby challenges the bases of the master's

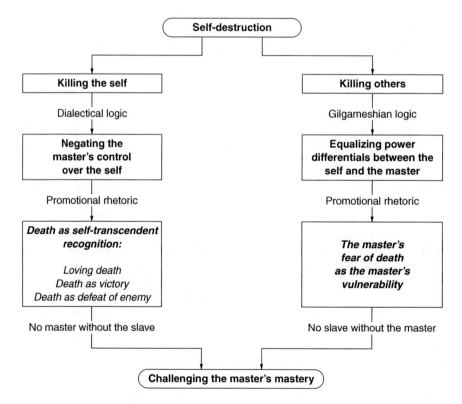

Figure 3.1 Dialectical and Gilgameshian logic in radical Islamist promotion of self-destruction.

mastery, the story of Gilgamesh is the "story of the master … dreading death."[6] In addressing the paradox of 'why kill the self if the motivation is to exact revenge from the other?', I argue that the nature of reason in radical Islamist rhetoric is dialectical in the Hegelian sense.[7] In addressing the paradox of 'why kill the other if the motivation is to extricate the self from a life of drudgery?', I argue that the nature of reason in radical Islamist rhetoric is Gilgameshian in the sense of the awareness of the vulnerabilities of the master. And in promoting self-destruction that is fundamentally based on a willingness to sacrifice the self, I argue that the nature of reason in radical Islamist rhetoric is deconstructive in the sense that it re-defines the meaning of 'life' and 'death.' The Hegelian and Gilgameshian logic can be broadly understood in terms of *challenging the master's mastery* through an act of self-destruction in which the master neither has any control nor any immunity. The de-constructive logic that redefines the meaning of life and death can be broadly understood in terms of promoting a self-transcendent recognition that comes to signify a *self-transcendent victory*. Figure 3.1 summarizes these points. Let us take a look at these categories in more detail.

Self-destruction as negating the masters

The logic of negating the masters through an act of self-destruction has two components: *killing the self* (the Hegelian slave); and *killing the other* (the Gilgameshian master).

Killing the self: challenging the master's control over the self

The nature of reason in radical Islamist rhetoric that promotes self-destruction can be understood, I argue, in terms of the Hegelian master–slave dialectic: there can be no master without a slave; there can be no slave without a master. This means that both the slave's servitude as well as the master's mastery is contingent on the physical existence of both the slave and the master. In this way, the slave's decision to choose death—as in acts of self-destruction—destroys the slave's life in servitude as well as the master's control over the slave which was contingent in the first place on the slave's fear of death. In other words, as in Hegelian analysis, the slave becomes a slave because of his fear of death, and his resultant decision to choose a life of servitude over his death (his physical demise) in struggles for recognition. If now the slave relinquishes his fear of death, and in fact embraces death himself, then he challenges the fundamental bases of the master's control over himself since this was premised on the slave's desperation to hold on to his life. The decision to choose self-destruction, then, neutralizes this desperation—which led to the slave's servitude in the first place—and replaces it with a sense of empowerment. This can perhaps best be seen in the remarks of a madrassa teacher in Karachi, Pakistan, whom Sharmeen Obaid-Chinoy asked the question 'Who do you think will win this war?' (referring to the US–NATO military operations in Afghanistan and Pakistan since 2001). The madrassa teacher replied:

A person who is not afraid of death, then who can kill him.[8]

The context of the teacher's remark was a discussion regarding the question of the recruitment of individuals for self-destructive (suicide) missions. What is interesting, of course, is that a person's fearlessness of death has nothing to do with another person's ability to kill him, at least not in the physical sense of death. Clearly, then, the above remark seems intended to portray a *metaphysical invincibility* of the person who chooses to engage in self-destructive missions, since in so doing, the person not only relinquishes his fear of death and stands eye-to-eye with the master (metaphorically speaking), but in choosing death himself, he takes away from the master the control the master has over the self, both in terms of the master's intimidations and in terms of the master's decision to kill the slave. Logic that challenges the master's mastery by relinquishing one's own fear of death can also be seen in promotion of self-destruction in the following statement by the founding member of Hezbollah, Sheikh Naim Qaseem:

> The enemy's [master's] only weapon is to *threaten* [the slave's] *life*, and it *only works against those who seek life*. In consequence, *it is futile to fight those who believe in martyrdom*.[9]

Similarly, Sebastian Smith's translation of a banner hung in Sheikh Mansur square in Grozny that draws upon a nineteenth century Chechen 'Song of the Death of Khamzad' that rhetorically negates the master's control over the self by welcoming the physical death of the self is instructive here:

> As a wolf tired and hungry longs to reach the forest, as a horse unfed and mettlesome the fresh clean meadow—so do my companions *thirst for the fight unto death. Nor do I fear thee*, oh Kagherman. *I laugh at all thy force*.[10]

The above emphasizes fearlessness, even that of death, and uses that to challenge the master's mastery and the master's control over the self with reference to 'I laugh at all thy force.' Similarly, Smith reports a verse from a 1995 Chechen war song that reads: "*Freedom or death*, the cry was heard again in the mountains."[11] Here, of course, the freedom of the self is more directly linked to the *physical death of the self* in a kind of *a reciprocal causality* where freedom is demarcated through death, and where death demarcates freedom. In such dialectical reasoning, freedom seems to be implied in its absolute sense, that is, freedom from *all* desires, even that of life. Only then can both freedom and death symbolize each other.

In his analysis of death and dominion, Bamyeh argues that for the master, death is *not* the opposite of life; death is the opposite of power.[12] But while this may be true for the Gilgameshian master, it is not true for the Hegelian slave— the radical Islamists—for whom death is the very *symbolization* of power, in the sense that death of the slave takes away from the master the object he needs to demarcate and demonstrate his mastery. If death of the slave negates the master's mastery, then the death of the slave empowers the slave. Indeed, it was the Hegelian slave's very *fear of death* that awarded him a *life of servitude* to the master, as I noted above.[13] For the Hegelian slave, then, death is the opposite of servitude and, as such, at once a symbolization of his absolute autonomy and his power (in terms of his ability to challenge his life circumstances and to challenge the master's control over himself). Thus, in contrast to the Gilgameshian master who in death loses his power, the Hegelian slave is empowered through his death.

Robert Williams sheds critical light on this Hegelian dialectical logic by examining the role played by the slave's *fear of death* in maintaining the master–slave relationship. In his analysis of the phenomenology of mastery and slavery, Williams notes that the fundamental assumption of such a relationship is that the slave *fears death* more than he fears a life of servitude to the other.[14] This assumption translates into the acceptance by the slave of *being-for-other*, in contrast to the master whose existence is characterized by *being-for-self*.[15] When life (in servitude to the other and as thus a 'commodity' of the other, as being-for-other) becomes valued more than self-autonomy, a slave is created. Indeed, argues Williams, the master's control over the slave is contingent on the master's *assumption* that the slave *fears* death and would thus prefer a life of servitude to physical death.[16] Thus, "the master relates immediately to the slave through the *threat … of death*."[17] In other words, the master is able to control the slave through threatening him with an axe over his head, and to the extent that this intimidates the slave, the master gains absolute control over the slave. But if the slave were to relinquish his fear of death, the master would become immediately powerless over the slave; the master would become immediately impotent. The simple reason for this is that oppression relies on compliance. And it is this compliance that makes the master the master, and the slave the slave. But if the slave is no longer compliant, and indeed not only relinquishes his fear of death (that made him into the slave in the first place) but becomes willing to take part in actions that challenge the master's mastery at the cost of his own life, then the master loses his mastery since the master is unable to control the slave.

The Hegelian notion of the being-for-self can also be understood in another way: the very act of self-destruction takes away the master's control over the self, the slave, since the very act of self-destruction is, by definition, completely autonomous of the master. Such logic is explicit in the assertions of Hezbullah's founding member, Sheikh Naim Qassem:

> Understanding the notion of martyrdom and its acceptance are not subject to international conventions, the politics of the intimidators or the appraisal of the enemy. It is only normal for these to launch an organized and intensive assault destined to condemn martyrdom, describing it in various notorious ways. For the notion [of martyrdom] is a weapon that is *primarily beyond their control* and, secondarily, *one that cannot be defeated*.[18]

In the above, Qassem asserts that the notion and practice of martyrdom is beyond the understanding of the international community and, in arguing such, criticizes the manner in which radical Islamist martyrdom is popularly portrayed in the west. He seems to argue in the above that western (international) criticism toward martyrdom is a consequence of the west (the masters) being intimidated by the act. He offers two reasons for this. First, because martyrdom, as an act, is "beyond their control"; that is, it is an act that is completely independent of the masters and thus—it seems implied—negates the masters' mastery since this is contingent on controlling the slave. Second, he seems to argue that the west is intimidated by the act of martyrdom because it is an act "that cannot be defeated"; if martyrdom is an act that cannot be defeated then it implies that the masters are defeated by the act since—again—mastery is contingent on control and subjugation of the other (the slave). If the slave takes part in actions that are completely autonomous of the masters, then the slave negates the masters' mastery.[19]

In analyzing what he refers to as "Iran's Suicide Brigades," Ali Alfoneh notes that in a speech delivered at Martyr's Section of *Behesht-e-Zahra* (Tehran's Iran-Iraq war cemetery), Mohammad Ali Samadi—"member of the editorial board of *Shalamache* and *Bahar* magazines, affiliated with the hard-line *Ansar-e-Hezbollah* [emphasis added] (followers of the Party of God) vigilante group"[20]—noted the following:

> The *[martyrdom] operation* against the [US] Marines [in 1983] was a hard blow in the mouth of the Americans and *demonstrated* that despite their *hollow prestige* and *imagined strength* ... they (have) many vulnerable points and weaknesses. We consider this operation [namely, martyrdom] a good model.[21]

Samadi's above assertions can be seen as challenging the master's mastery (as seen in the reference to 'hollow prestige' and 'imagined strength') through the promotion of an act (or 'operation') of self-destruction that is absolutely independent of the master's control. Self-destruction (martyrdom) is thus presented as at once negating the master's control over the self and thus negating the master.

Since recognition in the Hegelian sense is the acknowledgment of one's autonomy and independence, the recognition of one's distinct self-consciousness (one's identity), a self-transcendent recognition is thus a symbolization of the *absolute* autonomy of the self through the decision to take one's own life. In this way, self-destruction symbolizes a self-recognition that negates the master's mastery. This is because by choosing to take his own life, the slave demonstrates his absolute autonomy and freedom over the master. This is consistent with the central logic in Hegel's ethnics of recognition:

> I am released from slavery or imprisonment, or, conceivably, *I attain freedom by my own DEATH.*[22]

And:

> *He who dies in battle dies a free man.*[23]

The above can be understood in the context of Hegel's assumption in the *Phenomenology of Spirit* that the slave becomes a slave because he values "physical life more than freedom."[24] Indeed, as Pinkard notes, since the slave's slavery is "not based on any metaphysical difference between him [the slave] and the master but only on the fact that, *out of fear* [of death] he accepted the status of slave in relation to the other, who became the master," then by discarding his fear of death, the slave challenges his status as a slave.[25] The connection between death and freedom can also be seen in Hegel's assertion that the action of suicide *is* the quintessential—not necessarily ideal—manifestation of the *absolute freedom of the will* (absolute freedom to reason) to the extent that such an action demonstrates *self-assertion* as well as negates the master's control over the self.[26] Indeed, for Hegel *absolute* freedom can only be attained if one is able to abstract oneself from "every determinacy, *including life itself.*"[27] Williams underscores this fact by noting the following:

> [In the Hegelian sense] ... *freedom ... can transcend mere natural existence;* this possibility of *self-transcendence* is concretely demonstrated by a *willingness to risk one's life.*[28]

Here again, one sees a link between *death and freedom* in Hegelian thought, which is conceptually similar, I argue, to the logic displayed in radical Islamist rhetoric linking death (self-destruction) with freedom (which is 'recognition' in the Hegelian sense). Thus, the transition in radical Islamist reason, from the desire for recognition *in this life* (see the analysis in the previous chapter) to the pursuit of a self-transcendent recognition, is less a contradiction than a dialectical reason reminiscent of a Hegelian logic, as depicted in Figure 3.2.

The implicit assertion that self-destruction challenges the master's control over the self and symbolizes a self-transcendent freedom can be seen in the following confession of a Palestinian man contemplating self-destruction:

> At the moment of executing my [self-destructive] mission, it will *not* be purely to kill Israelis. The killing is *not* my *ultimate goal* ... My act will *carry a message* beyond to those responsible and the world at large that the ugliest thing for a human being is *to be forced to live without freedom.*[29]

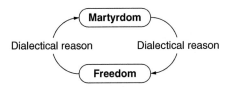

Figure 3.2 The radical Islamist martyrdom and absolute freedom dialectic.

The logic in the above seems reminiscent of the Hegelian logic "man demon-strates his capacity for freedom only by risking his own life and that of others."[30] And so, the references in the above to 'killing' as 'not my ultimate goal,' in con-junction with references to killing as carrying 'a message beyond,' that the 'ugliest thing for a human being is to be forced to live without freedom' point to the symbolism implied in an act of self-destruction: namely, a demarcation of absolute freedom. The above assertion thus presents self-destruction as challeng-ing the master's oppressive grip and thus the master's control over the self. This can also be seen as implied in the following leaflet distributed by the Palestinian Hamas in 1988:

> Every day the earth absorbs the blood of the righteous, (and) kneels in front of the graves and bows before the martyrs of grace. *This is part of the price of pride and honor, liberation and salvation.*[31]

In the above, physical death of the self is linked to the freedom of the self in the self-transcendent sense. Since in a martyrdom operation, the martyr loses his or her life, the reference in the above to the 'price of pride and honor, liberation and salvation' refers to the price paid by the martyr (through giving up his life) for the ends of autonomy from the masters. Or, as I have noted earlier, the price is the cost of life for the martyr and the reward is the symbolization of the absolute freedom of the collective that the martyr once belonged to.

Quite simply, then, radical Islamist rhetoric presents self-destruction in terms of a self-transcendent recognition. In so doing, self-destruction gets presented as negating the master's control over the self and as thus a *victory for the self* and the *defeat of the masters* (the enemy). Let us examine this formulation further. To the extent that self-destruction is an entirely autonomous decision, it chal-lenges the masters' oppressive grip over the self. And to the extent that it chal-lenges the masters' oppressive grip, it challenges the masters' mastery. And to the extent that it challenges the masters' mastery, it negates the masters' control over the self since if the master has no absolute control over the self, then the master is not the master in the absolute sense.[32] As such, self-destruction becomes presented in radical Islamist rhetoric as at once a victory for the self and as the defeat of the enemy (the masters).

And so, despite its *justifications* with reference to Islamic religious tenets, I argue that radical Islamist rhetoric explains martyrdom (self-destruction) as empowering because it challenges the master's mastery.[33] Such a promotion has a two-pronged logic, one that is reflective of a Hegelian dialectical logic and the other that is reflective of an understanding of the vulnerability of the Gil-gameshian master. In the first incidence, death of the self is presented as victory over the masters (and thus defeat of the masters) since death is associated with a self-transcendent recognition. And since the master's mastery depends on his successful intimidation of the slave, and depends further on the slave's *tranqui-lized existence*, which assumes his fear of death, the slave's decision to take his own life challenges the bases of the master's mastery on all accounts, as I have noted above. In the second incidence, the death of others in the master's domain is promoted through emphasizing the master's fear of death in contrast to the self's love of death. To the extent that it is now the master that feels intimidated, and the fact that in death the master looses all mastery, self-destruction is rhetorically promoted as equalizing the power differentials between the self (the slave who was *once* intimidated) and the other (the master who is *now* intimidated).

Killing the other: exploiting the master's vulnerability, equalizing power differentials

If radical Islamist promotion of self-destruction is framed in terms of negating the master's control over the self and thus as at once negating the master and challenging the master's mastery, it is equally promoted in terms of exploiting the master's vulnerability in such a way so as to equalize the power differentials between the self and the master. The master's vulnerability—necessarily a singular not a plural terms since the master is otherwise (militarily and economically) almighty—can best be understood with reference to *The Epic of Gilgamesh*. In analyzing the epic of Gilgamesh, Mohammed Bamyeh argues that for Gilgamesh—the semi-god, the master—death symbolized the opposite of *power*, not life, for Gilgamesh could only demonstrate his mastery so long as he was physically alive.[34] Death (physical demise) for the master then neutralizes all the power the master can exert in life. Gilgamesh's desire to escape mortality was thus his desire to remain the semi-god that he was, a master of all masters; thus the fact that he remained a mere mortal challenged the absolute nature of his power and his mastery since these were contingent on his physical existence.[35] For Gilgamesh then, the inevitability of his (physical) death meant a complete loss of his power and, even more importantly, symbolized his one weakness which, if exploited, could equalize the power differentials between himself and his subjects.[36]

And we see in Leo Tolstoy's *Master and Slave* that the slave welcomes his (physical) death, as "in death he [the slave] will attain his freedom."[37] In contrast, Tolstoy paints a picture of the master who desperately tries to hold on to his life in the chill of the winter, since death means his complete negation. The slave, on the other hand, feels content in allowing "the chill of nature to do its ordinary work and freeze into death its unfree being."[38] Death, of the slave and the master, thus negates not only the slave's status as the slave, but also negates the master's status as the master. As such, death (of the self, the slave, and the other, the master) becomes an equalizer of power differentials.

Critically, then, the meaning of physical death for the master is very different from the meaning of the physical death for the slave. Death for the slave, as I have noted above, means empowerment as it breaks the chains of servitude that are contingent on the physical existence of the slave. So death for the slave is empowerment as in death the slave is finally free. Death for the master, however, means a complete loss of his power for without his physical existence he cannot exert his mastery. It is in light of these contrasting perceptions of physical death that, I argue, radical Islamist rhetoric makes frequent references to the master's 'fear of death' in contrast to the self's 'love of death.' To put it simply, in promoting self-destruction in crowded places, radical Islamist rhetoric highlights the vulnerability of the Gilgameshian master for whom power is contingent on his physical existence, his life. And so, *killing the other* along with the self is promoted in radical Islamist rhetoric as *neutralizing* the *power differentials* between the self and the master.[39] To this end, Christoph Reuter makes a significant observation regarding the Palestinian Islamist extremist groups of Hamas, Islamic Jihad and the Al-Aqsa Brigades in the following:[40]

> The attackers, their supporters … understand that their enemy is stronger in a conventional military sense. *Yet they also believe that their opponent is weaker in a deeper, existential, or spiritual sense.* 'They have grown soft, the attacker believes; they want to live, and live well, and *they are afraid of death*'. Despite their own obvious military inferiority, the suicide bombers … draw consolation and strength from the assurance of this 'cowardice' of the other side.[41]

To understand the enemy (in this particular case, the Israeli masters) as weaker in the *existential* sense is to understand the enemy—the master—as weaker because of his fear (of death) and his desire (for life). Fears and desires are central in the philosophical debates of all that is existential (that is, characteristic of human existence). But even more importantly, to understand the enemy in any kind of an existential sense is to understand that the power differentials between the self (the slave) and the enemy (the master) are *not* absolute but contingent since the master, too, is a mere human being like the self.[42] In other words, it is to understand that the power differentials are not categorical since there is a point where the differentials equalize, and that point is where the master's *fear of death* meets the slave's *love of death*. Faced with death, the master is suddenly fearful but the slave is fearless. And so, to believe that the enemy is "afraid of death" is to exploit the one glaring vulnerability that the enemy does possess: the fear of death. After all, much like Gilgamesh, the master's exertions of power and his domination are only tapered by the master's realization of his own inherent vulnerability. Fundamentally, this vulnerability is the realization that the self, the master, is *not* invincible. Gilgamesh was, therefore, only god-like and not the god he wished to be. See Figure 3.1 which illustrates this point.

The strategy of playing upon the master's *fear of death* is probably most explicitly stated in the following excerpt from Nawwaf al-Takruri's book *al-'Amaliyyat al-istishhadiyya fi al mizan al-fiqhi* (*Martyrdom Operations in the Legal Balance*) where al-Takruri discusses the virtues of martyrdom (self-destruction):

> They [martyrdom operations] are a deterrent by means of causing terror among the enemy.

[...] They *equalize* what would otherwise be unequal conflicts (such as that against Israel).[43]

The above implies that martyrdom operations, by 'causing terror among the enemy,' turn the tables around so that it is not the self but the master that is now terrified. Causing 'terror among the enemy' is thus to exploit the master's weakness and thereby to expose his vulnerability. In so doing, power differentials between the self and the master come into question. Although the above makes reference to equalizing 'unequal conflicts,' the mere reference to 'equalize' points to the radical Islamist logic of killing the other, namely as a way to challenge the very bases of the master's mastery by attacking his façade of invincibility.

In the Palestinian context, it was Yahya Ayyash who was the "first to propose that human bombs be adopted in Hamas's military operations."[44] The logic implicit in Ayyash's strategy was to instill *fear* amongst the enemy and to damage its morale. In elaborating this strategy, the Hamas members whom the international relief worker Nasra Hassan interviewed explained that "spreading fear among the Israelis was as important as killing them."[45] Indeed, according to Fathi Shiqaqi, the founder of the Palestinian Islamic Jihad, the central logic of martyrdom operations is to "destroy the morale of the enemy and plant terror into the people."[46] If the physical death of the master equalizes power differentials between the self (the slave) and the master, then instilling the *fear of death*, and thereby damaging the *morale* of the master, also equalizes power differentials as it showcases the master's vulnerability.

Similar logic can be seen in Ayman al-Zawahiri's assertion of 'the importance of martyrdom operations' in his publication *Knights under the Prophet's Banner* (December 2, 2001):

> (we must) be sure to inflict maximum causalities on the enemy, *kill the greatest number of people, for this is the language understood by the West,* no matter how much time and effort such operations take.[47]

In his above assertion, al-Zawahiri seems to imply the master's fear of death by emphasizing that "killing the greatest number of people" is the only "language understood by the West." What is implied here is that only by killing as many as possible in the master's domain will the master, *because of his fear of death,* come to be humbled. And, in this way, the façade of his invincibility will be revealed.

References in radical Islamist rhetoric to the 'love of death' are thus intended, I argue, to showcase the existential (and spiritual) strength of the self compared to the master's existential (and spiritual) weakness. The intention in such rhetoric is therefore to equalize power differentials by recasting the self as the strong one and the master as the weak one, much in a Hegelian master–slave dialectical sense. Consider, for example, the following two excerpts, the first from the Palestinian context and the second from the Iranian context:

From the barrels of guns, we will take back our rights and forge our glory ... *Passionately we love death* ....[48]

The martyrdom-seeking Iranian women and girls ... are ready to walk in the footsteps of the holy female Palestinian warriors, *realizing the most terrifying nightmares of Zionists* [namely, the latter's fear of death].[49]

The first excerpt is from a Palestinian graffiti, and is cited by Oliver and Steinberg.[50] The second excerpt is taken from *Baztab*, the news website of the Islamic Revolutionary Guard Corps (1981–1997), and cited by Ali Alfoneh.[51] One's fearlessness of death in the first is contrasted with the master's fearfulness of death in the second. It is interesting to reconsider the Hegelian assertion here, that the "fear of death" is "the first condition of the slave mind," as this sheds light on why the assertions of 'loving death' that are found in radical Islamist rhetoric are intended to challenge the existence of the self as the slave.[52] And, if we were to analyze the second excerpt through Mohammed Bamyeh's philosophical prism, that death for (and of) the master is the opposite of power not life, then it becomes apparent that the radical Islamist assertions of the master's 'fear of death' are intended to challenge the master's mastery since such fear challenges the very status of the master as master.[53]

It is in the context of defying the fear of death and presenting the self as loving death that one finds references in radical Islamist discourse to death (of the self) as desire. Consider, for example, the following Palestinian slogan praising martyrdom:

O mother, my religion has called me to jihad and self-sacrifice.
O mother, I am marching toward immortality; I will never retreat
O mother, don't cry over me if I am shot down, laid out on the ground. For death is my path; martyrdom, *my desire*.[54]

The words in the above challenge the fear of death through presenting death instead as a desire. And if the slave's fear of death is what the master relies on in order to exert his control over the slave, then converting this fear into desire takes away from the master the very assumption that allowed him to intimidate and control the slave.

Self-destruction as a self-transcendent victory through the deconstruction of the meaning of 'life' and 'death'

Radical Islamist reason deconstructs the meaning of 'life' (existence) and 'death' so that life in servitude is considered the 'death' of the self (the death of self-consciousness, the death of autonomy). In this way, 'death' does not necessarily refer to physical death; it may refer to the death of one's autonomy. And in this way too, physical death is considered better than a life of servitude, or better than the 'death' of the self, the 'death' of one's self-consciousness. This logic can be understood in the following way: while physical death is the death of one's being, a life in servitude is the 'death' of the *very essence of being* (that of autonomy and independence). And so, actions that challenge a life in servitude—such as self-destruction that destroys the physical existence (life) in chains of the self—are presented as demarcating a 'victory' for the 'self.' Here, two things are immediately important: the meaning of 'victory' and the meaning of the 'self.' Victory, in radical Islamist rhetoric, almost always implies a self-transcendent victory; a victory at the cost of the physical existence of the self (as the individual) but one that symbolizes a victory for the 'self' as the collective that the individual once belonged to and the collective that one leaves behind. The 'self' is thus understood both as the individual that dies in the act of self-destruction and the collective that the self belonged to, the *ummah* that the self as an individual is inseparable from and that lives on.[55] Either way, self-destruction becomes a 'self' transcendent victory both because the victory transcends the physical existence of the self as the individual and because the victory symbolizes the absolute freedom of the collective that transcends the individual and that lives on beyond the self as the individual.

In sum, life is understood as having meaning only if it is *free of chains*. A life in servitude is thus not considered a 'life' worthy of living since it marks the 'death' of the self (the death of self-consciousness). In this way, 'death' of one's self-consciousness is considered worse than physical death. To the extent that physical death, in ending one's life in servitude to the masters, challenges the masters' control over the self, physical death is presented in radical Islamist rhetoric as negating the masters and thus as a victory over the master's control over the self. Physical death then gets valued (glorified) over a 'life' in chains.[56] In this way, one finds frequent references to self-destruction (physical death) as 'victory' for the self and as defeat for the masters (the enemies).[57] This logic can also be understood in the sense of the Hegelian master–slave dialectic in terms of the Hegelian slave's awakened self-consciousness that comes to realize that *there can be no master without a slave.*[58] In this way also, physical death of the self is a victory over the master's control over the self. And it is also in this way that self-destruction is presented as self-transcendent victory, a self-transcendent recognition of the absolute autonomy of the self.

Let us take a closer look at the notion of the *essence of being* which I described above as meaning the autonomy of the self and which, I noted above, 'dies' in a life of servitude. The notion of the essence of being presents itself in the Hegelian analysis as the *being-for-self* (the autonomous self that is not a slave to any other), as opposed to the *being-for-other* (the negated self who is a slave to the other). Indeed, Quentin Lauer points out that 'death' that is feared in Hegel's 'life-and-death' struggles for recognition is not to be understood in the conventional sense of physical death, but it is instead the 'death' of one's autonomy, the *negation* of one's being, the *marginalization* of one's *identity,* leading ultimately to enslavement and servitude.[59] It is thus that I argue that the promotion of self-destruction in radical Islamist rhetoric is Hegelian in essence since it promotes the physical death of the self (the individual) in order to challenge the 'death' of the self (as the individual and the collective). Certainly, such reason has a kind of an existential tone that Kojeve saw in Hegel's notion of life-and-death struggles, whereby struggles for recognition are motivated by the rejection of a "*slavish* recognition of another's superiority."[60] Critically then, if negation of the self is the 'death' of the self (the death of self-consciousness), then 'existence'—in the sense of life worth living—must challenge the negation of the self (the servitude of the self). In this way, physical death of the self can symbolize the 'existence' of the 'self' as the collective since physical death challenges a life in servitude and thus symbolizes the autonomous 'existence' of the collective (the 'self' in quotation marks, the *ummah*). It is in this way that I contend that in both Hegelian reason as well as radical Islamist reason, existence can be a self-transcendent demarcation of one's autonomy. Indeed, in Hegel's life-and-death struggles for recognition, the weaker entity engaged in struggles for recognition may opt for his death in order to avoid a life in servitude to the other. In such a circumstance, death symbolizes a self-transcendent recognition; one might be reminded here that recognition, in the Hegelian sense, is the acknowledgment (by the other) of the absolute autonomy of the self, the acknowledgment of self as distinct (autonomous) and equally significant to the other (thus not a slave to the other).[61] Consequently, the recognition of one's autonomy (one's distinct self-consciousness) can then be self-transcendent. And thus, I argue, self-destruction is promoted in radical Islamist rhetoric in terms of a *self-transcendent recognition*. Here, while the recognition (in the Hegelian sense of acknowledgment of one's autonomy and independence) that is attained through self-destruction transcends the self as the individual, it symbolizes the recognition of the 'self' as the collective, the *ummah*.

Let us take a closer look at the manner in which 'life' (physical existence) and 'death' are portrayed in radical Islamist rhetoric. In arguing that suicide operations are a legitimate defense, Sheikh Muhammad Sayyed Tantawi notes that "*honorable* people prefer to die than to live in humiliation."[62] Here 'honorable' refers to a belief that life in chains is not worth living. One can make sense of this in the context of the Hegelian slave to whom death is *not* the opposite of life (since life in servitude is not considered a worthy existence anyway), nor it is the opposite of power (as Bamyeh argues is the case for the master). For the Hegelian slave, death is the very symbolization of self-empowerment. Indeed, Fawaz Gerges notes that doctrinaire jihadis present self-destruction as "martyrdom on the battlefield [that] *will not* signify our end but a new beginning."[63]

The unique meaning of 'existence' can be understood further with reference to the following last testament of Abdullah Azzam, a Palestinian suicide bomber:

> What *value* has life *if* we live like a small child *under the feet of the unbelievers?*
> What value has life if we accept to sit with those who remain behind?[64]

In the above, life in servitude is relegated little value, thus living 'under the feet of the unbelievers,' or leaving in servitude to the masters is not 'living' in the sense of what a self-consciousness desires, namely a recognition from the other of one's distinct and yet equally significant identity to the other (the masters). Oliver and Steinberg argue that the second sentence, in particular the reference to 'those who remain behind,' is an indirect call to pious young Palestinians to become suicide bombers. I would argue further that the choice of the words 'those who remain behind' is intended to imply slavish cowardice of those who choose *not* to take part in self-destructive missions.

A critical component of the redefinition of 'life' and 'death' is the emphasis on the *abandonment* of the *fear* of (physical) death. Since life in servitude is the 'real' death of the self, physical death becomes portrayed as desirable to the death of self-consciousness in a life of servitude to the other. Thus, numerous rhetorical references can be found urging the abandonment of the fear of physical death. Sebastian Smith cites a poem composed by a Chechen named Mussa "in honor of the *fearless wolf,* who even when trapped and wounded by a *shepherd* tries to kill his tormentor—a truly Chechen wolf."[65] The Chechen poem reads:

> Hatred boils in the *wolf,*
> Agony grips his strong body,
> Then the *shepherd* sees the *wolf's eyes in the darkness*
> And for the first time feels mercy,
> Mercy for his grey-skinned thief *who died so well.*[66]

The references in the above to the 'fearless' wolf who 'died so well' are significant since they point to the abandonment of the fear, even that of death, on the part of the Chechens (the 'wolf') in challenging the oppression of the 'shepherd' (the Russians, the masters). But not only is the Chechen wolf portrayed as fearless in the above, the reference to the wolf's 'eyes in the darkness' imply a silent reawakening of the self-consciousness of the wolf, the oppressed Chechen, the Hegelian slave. The 'shepherd' is of course a reference to the one who leads, the Russian, the master who thinks of himself as metaphysically superior. But, as noted in the poem above, the shepherd will no longer have the wolf to lead, as the wolf will no long follow. In death, the wolf defies both the shepherd's *control over the self* and the shepherd's direction, thereby negating the very essence of the shepherd (the one who portrayed himself as the master).

A paradoxical understanding of 'life' (physical existence) and 'death' is most explicitly depicted in the following poem *Li-i-shuhada* (For the Martyrs) by Ghazi al-Qusaybi, published in 2002 in *al-Hayat* pan-Arab newspaper:

> God bears witness that you are martyrs; [...]
> [...] Have you committed suicide?? (No) we [the living] are the ones who have committed suicide in life, *but our dead are alive,*
> O people, we [the living] have died, so prepare to listen to how they eulogize us.
> We were impotent until even impotence complained of us, we wept until weeping had scorn for us.

We prostrated until prostration was disgusted by us, we hoped until hope
asked for assistance.
We licked the shoe of (Israeli Prime Minister Ariel) Sharon until the shoe
cried: Watch out, you are tearing me!
We repaired to the illegitimate rulers of the White House, whose heart is
filled with darkness.
O people! *We have died* but dust is ashamed to cover us.[67]

David Cook analyzes the above poem in the following manner: "For al-Qusaybi
those who are *still alive* are the *ones who are really dead*. They are dead from
shame, from humiliation and from self-abasement."[68] But there is a larger significance to the above poem than just that.[69] The more significant aspects of the
poem, I argue, are its implicit assertions that life in servitude is the 'death' of the
self, while physical death (through self-destruction) is the symbolization of
'existence' since in challenging the servitude of the self, self-destruction stays
true to the essence of existence: autonomy and independence. These assertions
are evident in the following ways: (1) the poem portrays the living (as in references to 'we' in the poem) as living in servitude (as in reference to impotence,
prostration, licking the shoe of Sharon); (2) through asserting that the living are
the ones who are truly 'dead' (as in references to 'we are the ones who have
committed suicide in life' and 'we have died') the poem connects physical existence (the living) in servitude to the 'death' of the self (the death of self-
consciousness, the death of autonomy and independence); (3) and then in
glorifying the martyred (the physically dead) in terms of "our dead are alive,"
the poem portrays 'existence' as a life that challenges servitude even if such
'existence' means the physical demise of the martyr. Thus 'life' is worthy only
if it is not in chains, *real* 'death' is the death of self-consciousness (a life in servitude), and meaningful 'existence' (where the living are not the 'dead') is
demarcated through the physical death of the self (to the extent that the latter
challenges one's subservience and complacency to a life in servitude).

Such unique understanding of 'life' (physical existence) and 'death' in radical
Islamist rhetoric forges a link between self-destruction and a self-transcendent
recognition. That is, such paradoxical definitions of existence and death translate
into understanding physical death as the demarcation of the absolute autonomy
of the self and the collective that the self belonged to. Here, it seems appropriate
to begin with the Sayyid Qutb's promotion of martyrdom given that Qutb is
often credited as the ideological forefather of much of contemporary radical
Islamist groups and movements.[70] In his analysis of the *Muslim's Nationality
and his Belief*, Sayyid Qutb asserted the following:

the *victory* of the Muslim, which he celebrates and for which he is thankful
to God, is *not a military victory*.[71]

Here, Qutb seems to be implying that 'victory' through martyrdom is not glory
in the sense of the material benefits during life on this earth. Victory through

martyrdom is instead a self-transcendent victory, one that not only transcends the self but transcends one's earthy existence. Victory through martyrdom is thus portrayed an everlasting glory. This notion, I argue, can be understood in Hegelian terms as a self-transcendent recognition.

The presentation of self-destruction as a self-transcendent victory, in much the Hegelian sense of a self-transcendent recognition, can be more explicitly seen in the following excerpt from *The Martyr,* written by Mortaza Motahhery (a prominent Shia religious figure):

> What does a martyr do? His function is *not* confined to resisting the enemy and, in the process, either giving him a blow or receiving a blow from him. Had that been the case, we could say that when his blood is shed it goes waste. *But at no time is a martyr's blood wasted ... Every drop of it* is turned into hundreds and thousands of drops, nay, into tons of blood and *is transfused into the body of his society ...* Martyrdom means transfusion of blood into a particular human society, *especially a society suffering from anemia, so to speak, of true faith.*[72]

The italicized portions of the above excerpt point to the inner logic of martyrdom. As such, the emphasis here is that martyrdom is not merely physical death, much less an action taken out of weakness and in desperation. Martyrdom in the above is portrayed as symbolically rejuvenating the society that the self belonged to, as implied in reference to 'blood' that is 'transfused' into the 'body' of the society. But what kind of rejuvenation is this? The answer to this, I argue, can be found in the assertion "Martyrdom means transfusion of blood into a particular human society, *especially a society suffering from anemia, so to speak, of true faith.*" Here, 'true faith' appears to be a reference to absolute freedom. Indeed, Islamist literature commonly depicts Islam as a faith that encourages one to disconnect from the material world—with its implied desires and servitude to desires—in exchange for 'true freedom,' that is, freedom from all desires. And in radical Islamist rhetoric, freedom from all desires means even that of life.

The link between faith (Islam) and freedom (freedom in the absolute sense) can be seen quite explicitly in the following except from Sayyid Qutb's *Milestones:*

> this religion [Islam] is really a universal declaration of the *freedom* of man from *servitude* to other men and from *servitude to his own desires,* which is also *a form of human servitude.*[73]

Interestingly, Qutb also defined violent jihad as "*freedom from the shackles of this earthly life.*"[74] This link between faith and freedom can also be seen in the following excerpt from the *Majjalatul Dawa,* a monthly newsletter of the ultra-militant Pakistani Islamist organization *Jamaat-ul-Dawa* (formerly *Lashkar-e-Toiba*):

> O boys, *forget about this material world,* join the Mujahideen [freedom fighters] and fight the devil forces of India who are killing and raping your mothers, daughters and sisters.[75]

Here, violent jihad against the Indian forces is framed implicitly in the context of an abandonment of all worldly desires, which is implied in the reference to the 'material world.' Here, what is underscored is not unlike the Hegelian assertion that "the ability to abstract from one's desires ... [as] an essential ingredient of higher types of freedom."[76] These assertions seem conceptually similar to what Alan Patten explains as the fundamental premise of Hegel's notion of absolute freedom:

> *Risking my life* in combat is this kind of demonstration [of absolute freedom]: it shows that I am indifferent to, and *not dependent* on, my *natural existence.*[77]

Thus, Hegel's notion of absolute freedom is premised, fundamentally, on the abandonment of *all* desires, even that of life, especially if 'life' has become a life in servitude to the other. Patten explains further the centrality of the abandonment of desire in Hegel's notion of absolute freedom as:

> To come to the point where one is reflectively *independent* of one's given *desires* and inclinations requires a certain set of attitudes, goals and capacities. It demands, for instance, a capacity and willingness to *distance oneself* from one's *immediate desires* and inclinations and to subject them to critical examination ... [and] it *requires the self-disciple* to tear oneself away from one's desires and inclinations.[78]

It is this very 'self-disciple' and 'critical examination' of the self that is implicit in both the assertion made in the *Majjalatul Dawa* and by Qutb.

From connections between faith and freedom to an explicit connection between self-destruction (justified in the context of faith) and a self-transcendent recognition (self-transcendent freedom) can also be seen in Ayman al-Zawahiri's following remarks (2005):

> *Jihad* for the sake of Allah *is greater than any individual* ... It is the struggle between truth and falsehood ... [and] the struggle between truth and falsehood *transcends time.*[79]

The references in the above to jihad as being 'greater than any individual' in the context of a 'struggle between truth and falsehood' (or between victors and losers) alludes to jihad as quite possibly comprising of self-destruction, and of self-destruction symbolizing a self-transcendent victory. The reference to 'jihad' as a struggle that 'transcends time' also appears to marginalize the individual in the interest of the collective. This again seems intended to emphasize the self-transcendent nature of such struggles and their victories. A similar connection between self-destruction and a self-transcendent victory, with references to 'blood' as a medium of liberation and freedom, can be seen in following remarks by Osama Hamdan, *Hamas'* representative in Lebanon:

> As for us, if we are required to *sacrifice our lives* and our *blood* in order to *liberate* our land and *restore our rights*, then we will do so. We do not love war or fighting, *but we are prepared to sacrifice for the sake of our future.*[80]

Notions of a self-transcendent freedom can also be seen as implied in the video-taped last testament of Abu-Surur, a Palestinian suicide bomber:

> we will, insha'Allah [God willing], present our spirits and *make our blood cheap* for the sake of Allah [God] and out of love for this homeland and *for the sake of freedom* and *honor of this people* in order that the Palestine remain Islamic, and Hamas remain a torch lighting the road of all the perplexed and all the tormented and *the oppressed,* and *Palestine be liberated.*[81]

In the above excerpt, Abu-Surur justifies the destruction of self—implicit in references to 'make our blood cheap'—by referring to it as 'for the sake of freedom' and, no less emotional, for the sake of honor.[82] Indeed, in addition to linking 'blood' (death) with 'freedom,' Abu-Surur presents his self-destruction not only in terms of challenging the servitude of the self—and thus the master's control over the self—but in terms of a self-transcendent freedom. Death of the self is thus presented as symbolizing the freedom of the Palestinian people.

Such self-transcendent recognition can also be seen as implied in the following martyrology (to use Cook's expression) in *Martyrs: The Building Blocks of Nations*, authored by Abdallah 'Azzam (a Palestinian who travelled to Afghanistan during the 1970s to fight a jihad against the Soviets):

> The life of the Muslim Ummah is solely dependent upon ... the blood of its martyrs. [...] History does not write its lines except with blood. Glory does not build its lofty edifices except with skulls. Honor and respect cannot be established except on a foundation of ... corpses.[83]

Here, the reference to the ummah is clearly a reference to the collective for whom the blood of the martyrs is shed. Or, to be more specific, the martyr's death symbolizes the glory, honor, respect and, one might add independence, of the collective (the ummah) that the martyr belonged to.

If self-destruction symbolizes a self-transcendent recognition that negates the master's control over the self, then self-destruction comes to symbolize a victory over servitude and thus a victory over the masters. In explaining this logic of martyrdom, Hezbollah's Sheikh Qasim has noted:

> The act of jihad bears two fruits: martyrdom *and* victory. The martyr earns martyrdom, while the community and its freedom fighters gain victory.[84]

The association of death with victory can also be seen in following translated text of *The Islamic Ruling on the Permissibility of Martyrdom Operations*:[85]

> The name "suicide operations" used by some is inaccurate … How great is the *difference* between one who commits *suicide*—because of his unhappiness, lack of patience, and *weakness* or absence of iman (faith)—and the self-sacrificer who embarks on the operation *out of strength* of faith and conviction, and *to bring victory* to Islam *by sacrificing his life* for the uplifting of Allah's word.[86]

Most interesting in the above is the pitting of "weakness" of the one who commits mere suicide with the "strength" of the one who takes part in martyrdom. This, in conjunction with a reference to the martyr as bringing "victory" to "Islam" by "sacrificing his life," the text alludes to challenging the master's mastery through the willingness to face one's own death (in an act of martyrdom). Thus, the combined references seem to allude to a self-transcendent recognition, defined at once as 'strength' of the self as opposed to the weakness of a slave, and thus 'victory' over servitude for the collective. If, as in the Hegelian sense, the first condition of a slave mind is the fear of death, then the relinquishing of this fear—as described in the above—is a victory over servitude.

The association of self-destruction with victory can also be seen in the following excerpt from a popular Palestinian slogan inciting the *intifada* (the uprising against the Israelis):

> I swear by the One [a reference to God] who made fast your mountains and set your clouds in motion, O Palestine, that I will erase *shame* in every house and *from my blood and bones* I will weave banners of *victory* for Islam.[87]

The reference in the above to "my blood and bones" is a reference to the death of the self. Since the above slogan ends with reference to Islam, it would be popularly misunderstood in popular western media as proof that Islamist extremism is *Islamic* in essence, thereby reinforcing the popular vilification of Islam (as an entire religious and cultural context). However, the reference to 'victory for Islam' in the above reflects instead a moral consequentialist justification for violence and self-destruction that is framed in deontological terms. References to Islam offer a sense of morality in the deontological sense for something that is otherwise a life-and-death struggle for recognition (as implied in the reference to erasing 'shame' through 'blood and bones'). Since I have relegated the discussion of the radical Islamist moral consequentialist justifications to the next chapter, I shall not elaborate the significance of the deontological hinting in the above Palestinian slogan.

Equally significant in the above Palestinian slogan is the connection forged between self-destruction and erasing shame as this alludes to self-destruction as victory for the self. To elaborate this logic further, death is argued to translate into a victory as it extricates the self from servitude to the master. As such, death is victory for the self as it negates the master's control over the self and, thus, negates the master's mastery. Similar logic can also be seen in the following last testament of a Palestinian suicide bomber:

> Thanks be to God who brings about the *mujahedeens' victory* and the *dictators' defeat*.[88]

In the above testimonial, the reference to 'mujahedeen' is a reference to the martyr, the person who challenges the master's mastery through violence or self-destruction. The reference to the 'dictator's defeat' is a reference to the *controlling* master to whom the self is linked dialectically, so that the master's mastery depends on its passive acceptance by the slave, and indeed on the very existence of the slave. But if the slave then becomes a mujahedeen, then the master loses his absolute control over the slave. The master is thus defeated and the slave emerges victorious.

Further references to self-destruction as victory over servitude can also be seen the following song of the Palestinian *intifada* (1987):

> By the points of daggers and knives, the road of victory with be ours

> With the tears of bereaved mothers and orphans, we will draw the map of the homeland

> From the barrels of guns, we will take back our rights and forge our glory [...].[89]

The reference to the "tears of bereaved mothers" appears to be a reference to the martyr who takes his/her own life, through a self-destructive mission, since in such an act, the mothers lose their offspring. The reference in the above to "points of daggers and knives," "the road to victory," "from the barrels of guns," and "take back our rights" are clearly references to the life-and-death struggle that the self is engaged in since it is clearly a promotion of violence for the ends of rights and justice.

The following Palestinian song is directed by a member of the *Hamas*:

> Kill me, rend me
> Drown me in my blood
> *You will never live in my land*
> *You will never fly in my sky*
> O swords of Allah, rise up from sleepiness to light
> Teach the usurpers a lesson and send them to their destruction.[90]

The assertion that 'you will never live in my land, you will never fly in my sky' are meant as emotionally arousing rhetoric that imply that the Israeli masters will not succeed in putting (or keeping) the self (the Palestinians) in servitude, even if such a victory for the self takes a self-transcendent form. One can also contextualize such radical Islamist logic in terms of the Hegelian assertion: *He who dies in battle dies a free man.*[91] Indeed, in analyzing Qutb's attitudes towards martyrdom, as outlined in his *Ma'alim fi al-tariq* (Signposts along the Way), David Cook notes that Qutb equated "real victory" to the act of martyrdom (self-destruction) since the martyr abandons all worldly desires (even that of life, signifying absolute freedom) in exchange for "human dignity."[92]

If self-destruction is presented dialectically as the victory for the (collective) self, then it should come as little surprise that self-destruction is also dialectically presented as symbolizing the defeat of the enemy in radical Islamist rhetoric. If the master cannot succeed in maintaining control of the other—the very feature that is required for him to maintain his title as the 'master'—then the master stands defeated. Such logic is implicit in radical Islamist rhetoric which presents the destruction of the self (an act that is entirely independent of the master) as not only negating the master's control over the self, but as also therefore signifying the defeat of the master. The radical Islamist notion of 'defeat' is not conventional in the sense that it implies the military defeat of the master. The radical Islamist notion of 'defeat' refers instead to *metaphysical* defeat of the master, the defeat of the very essence of the master, that of control and domination. The association between self-destruction and the defeat of the enemy can be seen in Abdelaziz al-Rantisi's (second in-command of *Hamas* prior to his assassination by the Israeli Defense Force) following remarks:

> He who wants to kill himself because he's sick of being alive—that's suicide. But if someone wants to sacrifice his soul in order *to defeat* the enemy and for God's sake—well, then he's a martyr.[93]

Martyrdom in the above excerpts is portrayed not as hopeless suicide but as a calculated action based on reason to 'defeat' the enemy and thus to challenge the master's mastery in absolute terms. In this way, self-destruction is portrayed not only as the 'defeat' of the enemy (the master) but also as thus a 'victory' for the self.

Conclusion

I argue in this chapter that the radical Islamist promotion of self-destruction is fundamentally premised on a logic that is Hegelian dialectical, Gilgameshian, and paradoxical. Ultimately, self-destruction is promoted in terms of a measure that negates the master's mastery. This is done in two ways: (1) through the use of dialectical logic which presents self-destruction as a measure that takes away the control the master had over the self; (2) through the presentation of the master as the Gilgameshian master whose very mastery depends on his physical existence. And in this way also, self-destruction is presented in radical Islamist rhetoric as empowering—*not* as the weapon of the weak (as presented in some scholarship because it is reasoned to challenge the master's mastery through an act that negates the master's control over the self and that highlights the master's vulnerability (that of his desire for life).

But beyond such dialectical and Gilgameshian logic, radical Islamist rhetoric also presents the act of self-destruction as an act that symbolizes the victory over the masters. This paradoxical reason—at least in the context of conventional warfare when the death of the self is understood as the defeat of the self—is facilitated through the radical Islamist deconstructive reason which redefines the meaning of 'life' and 'death.' 'Life' becomes defined in radical Islamist rhetoric as worthy only if it is a life free of servitude to the other (as free of chains, meta-phorically speaking), so that a life of servitude is considered the 'death' of self-consciousness, the death of one's identity, the death of the very essence of being, namely that of autonomy and independence. In this way, radical Islamist rhetoric argues that physical death is better than the 'death' of the essence of being, since in the former scenario an individual challenges the master's subjugation of the self and thereby attains a self-transcendent recognition, in the latter the indi-vidual looses all sense of his worth and becomes merely an object for the master to use and abuse to his advantage.

The analysis in this chapter readdresses the paradox of 'why kill the other if the motivation is to extricate the self from a life of drudgery?' since in killing the other—the Gilgameshian master—the self takes away from the master the very life the master needs to exert his mastery. In this way, killing the other (the master) negates the other (the master). In death, the master is no different from the slave as he too becomes powerless. Thus killing the other is reasoned in terms of equalizing the power differentials between the self (the slave) and the other (the master). The analysis in this chapter also readdresses the paradox of 'why kill the self if the motivation is to exact revenge from the other?' since killing the self takes away from the master any and all control the master once exerted over the self (the slave). In this way, killing the self challenges the mas-ter's mastery since the decision to kill the self—in self-destructive missions—is entirely independent of the master's control, wishes or expectations. Killing the self is also explained as an imperative in radical Islamist rhetoric since in so doing the self symbolizes a victory for the 'self' (in both the individualistic and collectivist sense), a victory that at once challenges the master's control over the self and the status of the self in servitude to the other (the master). In this way, killing the self is argued in existential terms as giving rise to a self-transcendent recognition (in the Hegelian sense).

4 Violence as morality

Radical Islamists define violence as a morality. This can be seen in their contextualization of violence within religious tenets that are understood as divinely sanctioned. The radical Islamist reference to jihad, which they define as a divinely sanctioned *violent* struggle, is a classic illustration of this.[1] Such radical Islamist rhetoric has been popularly understood in the west as an illustration that "Islam is violent, no matter what terms you use, and Muslims are *prone* to wage war, or jihad, against their enemies, no matter what context you conjure."[2] Western neo-conservative pundits—the proponents of the clash-of-civilizations argument—present such logic as reflection of a uniquely *Islamic* 'culture of death.' But the equation of violence with morality—whether through references to religious tenets or through references to the necessity of self-preservation (self-defense)—is nothing new, much less unique to the radical Islamic context. Such logic, of course, is fundamentally consequentialist in essence. Consequentialist reason, as we saw in Chapter 1 in this book, defines as 'moral' all those actions that are expected to achieve the desired goals (or consequences). Such 'moral consequentialist' reason can also be understood in simple terms of the popular logic *the ends justify the means*. Consequentialist morality, far from being an anomaly specific to any one religious or cultural milieu, is in fact a universal narrative. So universal is this tendency that Hans-Georg Moeller argues that it is *not* remarkable that war, genocide and ethnic cleansing have taken place in the name of 'morality'; it is remarkable instead that such tendency is ubiquitous.[3]

Even more significantly, I argue that while consequentialist morality (morality defined in terms of the desired consequences) may appear distinct in nature from religious morality (morality defined through references to religious tenets), the two are fundamentally the same in that both are consequentialist in essence. The only difference between the two is appearance: while notions of morality that point to consequences as a justification for actions are, if you may, unpretentious in terms of their consequentialist nature; notions of morality that point to the divine sanctions of religious tenets as justifications for actions are inconspicuous in terms of their consequentialist nature. In other words, I argue that notions of morality legitimized through references to religious tenets are as consequentialist as the straightforward consequentialist morality that makes no pretences to divine sanctions. In this way, religious morality is nothing more than consequentialist morality that is disguised in deontological terms (with references to religious tenets) for an added sense of urgency and legitimacy. This view, of course, is compatible with Nietzsche's view of morality, as we saw in Chapter 1. Indeed, Nietzsche's very critique of 'morality' is premised on his assertion that all morality—whether presented in terms of religious principles or secular principles—is consequentialist in nature.[4] This can be seen in his assertion that everything in life, including morality, is a will-to-power. To the extent that Nietzsche's notion of the will-to-power can be understood in terms of the desire for self-assertion that is similar to the Hegelian notion of the struggle for recognition—as I argued in Chapter 1 in this book—the claim that morality is a will-to-power implies that notions of morality are created in order to achieve the aims (goals or ends) of self-assertion. In this way, then, morality is necessarily consequentialist and, most importantly, linked to the struggles and desires for self-assertion. Axel Honneth goes as far as to argue that there necessarily exists a moral grammar for all struggles for recognition.[5] Given Nietzsche's critique of morality and my assertion that reason used to justify actions is fundamentally consequentialist whether it is framed in secular or religious terms, and my assertion (in Chapters 2 and 3) that radical Islamist reason is reflective of Hegelian struggles for recognition (self-assertion), the justifications of violence as a morality must then be understood in terms of the negative manifestations of the *human condition* and not as something unique only to the radical Islamist context.[6]

Let us return to my assertion that all morality is consequentialist in nature, even morality that is contextualized within religious tenets. References to divine sanctions then only gives a deontological façade to otherwise consequentialist reason. Indeed, Nietzsche's critique of what he referred to as 'Christian morality' was fundamentally his critique of *religion as morality*; that is, the utilization of references to religion to create notions of morality. And so, Nietzsche's critique was not limited only to 'Christian morality' but was a critique of all morality framed in religious terms.[7] Nietzsche's skepticism of religion as morality was essentially based on his view that religion becomes used as an *instrument* that legitimizes self-promotion (self-assertion, self-recognition). Hence his claim that 'morality is a will-to-power' seems to point to his critique of the instrumentality of religion; that is, the practice of using religion as an instrument to promote the self and to justify all actions towards the promotion of the self. In this way, actions escape the criticism of ulterior motivations and get viewed instead in terms of divine authenticity by the 'herd' (to use Nietzsche's expression) or the masses.[8] The instrumentality of religion, as a phenomenon, can also be understood in the words of Iranian sociologist, Ali Sharyati:

> Religion is an amazing phenomenon that *plays contradictory roles* in people's lives. It can destroy or revitalize, put to sleep or awaken, enslave or emancipate, teach docility or teach revolt.[9]

The instrumentality of religion that disguises consequentialist justifications of violence in terms of 'divine sanctions' for added legitimacy can be explicitly seen in the rhetoric of the Christian Crusades that justified violence and brutality.[10] For example, Mark Gregory Pegg observes the following:

> the Albigensian Crusade ushered genocide into the West by linking *divine salvation* to *mass murder*, by making slaughter as loving an act as His sacrifice on the cross.[11]

Indeed, argues Pegg, the Christian Crusades were justified in terms of a "redemptive homicide."[12] Certainly, such presentation of violence as morality was not—and is not—limited to the context of the medieval Christian Crusades. Robert L. Holmes notes that "it is clear ... from the Old Testament that wars commanded by God are considered righteous."[13] Of course, this leaves open to subjectivity what wars god commands and what wars god forbids. This very subjectivity, in either the interpretation of religious tenets or in the selective emphasis on certain religious tenets in order to legitimize the actions that the self engages in, is the reason why I argue that even religious morality—along with its more obvious secular consequentialist morality—is consequentialist in essence. Consider, as another example, Alan Kramer's observations of the nature of the German justifications for war and violence during World War I. Kramer notes that in Germany, the 'League of Free Church Preachers' declared the following:

> The members of the Evangelical Free Churches serve the Kaiser and the Reich as do all other patriots. They are second to no one in love of their dear fatherland. Their knowledge, *gained from the bible* and history, teaches them that *bloody wars* between peoples are a *natural necessity* until the end of time.[14]

If the above seems somewhat Darwinian in reason (with its reference to 'natural necessity'), it is no less consequentialist in essence since the 'necessity' it refers to is clearly (given the wartime context of this assertion) that of victory for the self. Yet, the above assertion is presented in terms of a religious morality, as apparent in its reference to the bible as teaching the self that 'bloody wars' are 'natural necessity.' That reason presented as religious morality is essentially consequentialist in essence is further illustrated by Kramer's following observations:

> pastors spoke of *Germany's 'holy war'*, and that it was a 'crusade'; another wrote that this war was a *war of defense,* a '*moral duty* and thus a work pleasing to God.[15]

Here clearly references to 'holy war' and 'moral duty' are intended to offer a deontological disguise for an otherwise purely consequentialist justifications for war and violence, the latter is apparent in the explicit reference in the above to the 'holy war' being a 'war of defense.' This is all too explicit in the following statement made by the German theology professor Dr. Titius:

> He who is ready *as a Christian* not only to give his life to the fatherland but also, if it must be, *to kill* or to throw the flaming torch, in short, to do what is alien and loathsome to his innermost desire, *does not stand far from the warm love of the Apostle* ... not far from the sense of the great sufferer who was ready to bear the sins of his people and all the world and to atone for them.[16]

The above quotations illustrate that it is not only radical Islamist rhetoric that makes references to Islamic religious tenets in order to justify violence in terms of divine sanctions and as thus a 'religious morality'; one finds similar justifications of violence in the Christian Crusades and the German war efforts.

Even more notably, I argue that radical Islamist justifications of violence are not only similar to the historical justifications of violence in the context of Christianity but that they are also *conceptually* similar to the secular justifications of violence found in the contemporary version of the internationally accepted Just War doctrine. This assertion has two implications, both of which underscore what I have noted earlier: (1) that violence has always been justified as a morality by those engaging in violence, whether such justification is framed as a religious morality or a secular morality; (2) that morality that is framed in religious terms (with references to religious tenets) in order to justify an action (particularly a violent action) remains fundamentally a consequentialist morality despite its deontological guise since such reason typically makes references to the *need* for self-defense and other *exigencies* of the time that are argued to make resort to violence 'necessary' (as we saw above and as we can see in radical Islamist rhetoric). However, such consequentialist-deontological fusion in reason often goes unnoticed or overlooked. For example, in reference to the charter of the Palestinian Hamas, Roxanne Euben and Muhammad Qasim Zaman contend that the "Qur'anic verses that punctuate the text ... have little substantive connection to what is actually being said."[17] Contrary to this assertion, I argue that the 'Qur'anic verses that punctuate the text' are intended to offer a deontological urgency to a consequentialist reason and, as such, have a significant substantive connection to what is being said. In other words, such religious punctuations are intended to 'divine' actions that are otherwise reasoned in consequentialist terms. In other words still, such punctuations offer a deontological guise to consequentialist reason, thereby fusing deontological reason with consequentialist reason so that the two become essentially consequentialist in essence.

In the context of radical Islamist rhetoric, the utility of a consequentialist-deontological fusion in reason is that it offers compelling arguments to audiences receptive either to a deontological (religious) reason or to those receptive to a secular (non-religious) reason. Thus, such consequentialist-deontological fusion in reason has two advantages: (i) it appeals to those non-secular, religiously inclined individuals for whom mere references to religious tenets offer unquestionable sanctions for any action (including violent action and even the action of self-destruction), and (ii) it also appeals to those secular minded individuals for whom references to religious tenets hold little meaning but for whom the framing of an action in terms of its desired consequences (such as challenging oppression) holds greater appeal. Such fusion in reason presents violence as both a *categorical imperative* (in the conceptual Kantian sense of an imperative duty) as well as a necessity (in the consequentialist sense for the *ends* of justice and self-recognition). Kant had defined the categorical imperative not only as that action that *must necessarily* be done, but an action whose maxims (principles) are *known to all* and that need *never be questioned*.[18] Thus, by contextualizing violence within Islamic religious tenets, radical Islamist rhetoric frames violence within religious principles *known to all* and thus that *never need to be questioned*, this gives reason framed in religious terms a kind of an unquestionable legitimacy, a kind of a 'categorical imperative.' The intention in such rhetoric, I argue, is to create a sense of 'right intentions' for violence so as to disguise the underlying consequentialist nature of such reason. And this, I argue further, is both *conceptually* and *functionally* similar to the notion of 'right intentions' as stipulated in the internationally accepted Just War doctrine; this points to the universality of moral consequentialist justifications of violence and brutality.

'Just Wars' and the universal narratives of the justifications of violence

The brutality and violence of the medieval Christian Crusades that were justified through references to religious sanctions stands as a classic example of the equation of violence with morality; and, further, as a classic example of disguising consequentialist reason (the desire for the Christian conquest of Jerusalem) in deontological terms (the references to religious sanctions). Mark Gregory Pegg notes that "the crusade, far from being a Christian aberration, epitomized the sanguine beauty and bloody savagery of thirteenth-century Latin Christendom."[19]

That such violence was presented as religiously sanctioned and as thus a 'just' war can be traced, in part, to the writings of St. Augustine of Hippo (354–430) during the Christian antiquity era and the writings of Thomas Aquinas (1225–c.1274) during the Christian medieval era.[20] Both St. Augustine and Aquinas had intended to create guidelines for the just conduct during wars. Alex Bellamy notes that although St. Augustine "did not put forward a single or coherent theory" of war, he had nonetheless intended to create a legal framework for wars.[21] This framework was intended to offer principles for going to war that would act to legitimize the act of war and violence. This principle has come to be known as *jus ad bellum*. As far as *jus ad bellum* was concerned, it is argued that St. Augustine's main contribution was to declare that wars must be "inspired by the *right intentions* and declared by a *proper authority*."[22] The 'right intentions' were understood as all those intentions that were divinely guided—which was likely premised on his belief that "God praised the profession of soldiering"—and 'proper authority' (or 'legitimate authority' as it is now known) which he understood as the divine right of the Kings.[23]

Thomas Aquinas extended the stipulations of St. Augustine's Just War doctrine and, most importantly, secularized the Just War doctrine.[24] Aquinas reiterated the need for 'proper authority,' which he saw as situated only in a prince, and the requirement of 'right intention,' which he defined broadly and vaguely as one that intends to "promote good or avoid evil."[25] To these, however, Aquinas added the stipulation of a 'just cause,' which he defined as meaning that the "enemy must have violated the rights of one's community."[26] The popular, contemporary understanding of this is the right of self-defense. Not surprisingly therefore, contemporary Just War doctrine defines a war as just if it is fought for the ends of self-defense. But 'self-defense' has come to mean a wide variety of things in the contemporary international arena, particularly as it has come to be re-defined by the powerful hegemonic states. Thus, the re-definition of 'self-defense' has come to include even forceful 'democracy promotion,' such as in the case of the justification of the American military occupation of Iraq in 2003.[27]

Quite apart from its glaring consequentialist reason, the view that military occupations—an otherwise aggressive act of war that stands in contradiction to what can easily be understood as 'just' or 'moral,' at least in the deontological sense[28]—can be justified under the banner of 'democracy promotion' and as part of the larger component of 'self-defense' is premised on the historical Kantian notion of perpetual peace.[29] Kant had argued that beyond strictly defensive wars (where one responds to an attack on one's sovereign integrity), aggressive wars can also be just if they are 'prevent' hostilities and thus 'preemptive' hostilities.[30] Kant's view was premised on his belief that lasting world peace could only be attained through the democratization of all the states in the world, even if this was forced and through aggressive military action. However, Kant's notion of forced democratization for the ends of long-term perpetual peace critically overlooks two important realities. First, as brought to light by Thomas Aquinas, is of the possibility of 'double-effect' whereby a war may give rise to unintended outcomes in addition—and perhaps even contrary—to what was intended or even expected.[31] Second, the perception of occupation, by those that are being occupied, is often starkly different from the theoretical (and, I might add, hegemonic) portrayal of occupations and their benefits.[32]

'Just' versus 'Unjust' wars

The contemporary Just War doctrine does not justify violence with reference to any religious tenets. It does, nonetheless, present violence as 'just' (and thus as both moral and legal) in 'select circumstances' which, not surprisingly, are always defined to benefit the self, both in terms of giving the self—the state in question—the license to engage in wars and violence and to absolve the self from the human catastrophes that have resulted from the engagement in wars. Indeed, a closer look at the many stipulations of the contemporary Just War doctrine reveals their problematic nature in terms of their hypocrisy and their subjectivity, both of which I argue are products of the consequentialist nature of the doctrine. The hypocrisy and subjectivity of the Just War doctrine is most apparent in its categorization of some wars as 'just' and others as 'unjust.'[33] This translates into subjective and hypocritical assessments where the actions of violence and brutality that the self engages in are presented as 'just' while the actions of violence and brutality that the other engages in are presented as 'unjust.' But beyond its hypocrisy and subjectivity, the very notion of a 'Just War' is problematic because it assumes some universality in the perceptions of what is considered as 'just' and 'moral.' Not only does such universality not exist, but assumptions of some universal (and universally uncontested) notion of 'just' war is as vacuous as the Kantian notion of 'universal morals' in that both are disconnected—perhaps intentionally so—from the varying perceptions that create an understanding of what is 'just' or 'unjust,' perceptions that I argue are based on the consequentialist assessments of the utility of wars and violence. Robert L. Holmes affirms this point when he notes that the interrelations between notions of 'just' and 'unjust' war are "complex in light of the fact that both are subject to different interpretations."[34]

Critically then, in its insistence on 'just' and 'unjust' wars, the Just War doctrine functions less as a moral standard for the conduct in wars and more as a *justification* for the *conduct of the self* in wars. This then leads to proclamations that the brutality that the other engages in are reflective of a uniquely barbaric culture, while the brutality that the self engages in is reflective of a civilized culture in pursuit of a 'Just War.' The larger implications here are that regardless of the perceptions of the other, the self that is engaged in violence and wars will always present it as 'moral' and thus 'just'; the self as a reluctant participant in war and violence, the other as the evil entity prone to violence and destruction; the self as engaging in war and violence for the sake of justice, the other as engaging in war and violence for the sake of oppression and domination. And in these formulations, the radical Islamist promotions of violence are no different from the promotion of wars by a state entity.

Not surprisingly then, gross destructive actions committed by the self are always presented as measures of 'last resort' while similar gross atrocities committed by the other are presented as ends in themselves. The lack of acknowledgement of the subjectivity of the Just War doctrinal stipulations makes the problematic of these stipulations dire for two reasons. First, not acknowledging that different perspectives and perceptions influence the meaning of 'Just War'—and particularly its stipulations of 'just cause,' 'right intention,' 'legitimate authority,' and 'supreme emergencies'—takes us farther from understanding the *dynamics* of violence, justified as they always are rhetorically in terms of a morality. A lack of understanding of this takes us farther away from an understanding of the motivations of individuals that voluntarily take part in violence and destruction, be that under the auspices of a formal military institution or informal paramilitary units (such as insurgent or extremist groups, organizations and movements).[35]

Second, not acknowledging, or completely ignoring, the subjectivity of the stipulations of the Just War doctrine, and presenting them instead in terms of a universal consensus, fuels the resentments of the non-hegemonic actors (whether state or non-state) that interpret such dogmatic assertions as paternalistic and thus negating. This is particularly true when stipulations such as 'extreme emergencies' are used to excuse the sporadic and disproportionate killing of civilians by the self as 'just'—as, for example, in the case of the United States CIA sponsored predator drone bombings of areas populated by civilians in Afghanistan and in Pakistan's federally administered tribal areas (FATA) often in pursuit of one individual—while labeling similar disproportionate killings by the other as 'unjust' and 'immoral.'

To his credit, Thomas Aquinas noted that "war could never be *just,* because the very act of killing always contained some element of injustice."[36] However, noted Aquinas, in certain circumstances, when the reasons for going to war are 'just,' war could be *"justifiable."*[37] Aside from the very obvious consequentialism implied in the notion of something being 'justifiable,' let us take a closer look at the stipulations that are thought to make a war 'just' in the contemporary understanding of the Just War doctrine. One can categorize the Just War stipulations into two broad categories: *jus ad bellum* (the moral or right reasons for going to war) and *jus in bello* (the moral or right conduct during war). The stipulations of *jus ad bellum* can be summarized as thus: legitimate authority (a legitimate governing authority must declare war); right intentions (intentions must be 'right' or 'moral)'; just cause (the reason for going to war must be 'just' and 'moral'); last resort (violence must be chosen only after non-violent means have been exhausted); probable success (the probability of success must be greater than the probability of failure); proportionality (benefits of the war must outweigh the costs of the war). The stipulations of *jus in bello* can be summarized as thus: discrimination (combatants must be clearly distinguished from non-combatants and the latter must always be spared); proportionality (only that amount of violence that is absolutely necessary to achieve a goal must be used; this precludes massive bombing campaigns, torture, and rape). It does not take much imagination to realize that all of the above stated stipulations are subject to a wide range of interpretations and, even more importantly, a wide range of justifications for the violations of these stipulations thereby rendering such stipulations meaningless.

Even more significantly, as we shall see in the analysis in the rest of this chapter, all above stipulations that are used to present violence and brutality in terms of a 'just' and 'moral' war are also used by entities (such as radical Islamists) that otherwise do not recognize the legitimacy of the Just War doctrine. Specifically, as we shall see, radical Islamist rhetoric justifies its promotion of violence and brutality in the following ways: as sanctioned by legitimate authority; as reflective of right intentions; as a matter of self-defense; and as reflective of a supreme emergency. Thus, regardless of the radical Islamist contextualization of violence within Islamic religious tenets, the following analysis shows that the nature of reason in the radical Islamist justifications of violence is as morally consequentialist as is the nature of reason in the Just War doctrine. Both doctrines of justifications present their violence in moral terms. In illustrating this point, I analyze some of the popular Just War doctrinal justifications of violence and brutality and juxtapose them with the radical Islamist justifications of violence and brutality. In highlighting the moral consequentialist nature of the justifications of violence in both doctrines, I analyze the nature of the hypocrisies that are inherent in the Just War doctrinal justifications of violence in order to show why such a doctrine would fail to understand the similar moral consequentialist justifications of violence offered in the radical Islamist doctrines. The larger consequences of the misunderstanding of the nature of radical Islamist justification of violence—understanding them instead as reflective of a uniquely barbaric culture of death—are, I argue, misguided policies that are intended to combat the threat of Islamist extremism but that only exacerbate its threat in the long term.[38]

Legitimate authority: kings, heads of state, Caliphates and Mahdis

In medieval Christian times, a legitimate authority was considered to be the king whose authority was believed to be divinely sanctioned.[39] The immediate irony of such a right and authority of the kings is pointed out by Uwe Steinhoff in the following:

> For medieval thinkers 'civilized living' consisted perhaps not least in a situation in which authorities supposedly appointed by God told the subject, at whose expense they were living, what to do and what not to do. That such thinkers should set the highest value on the principle of legitimate authority is perhaps *due more to their own self-interest* than to their care for the public.[40]

The self-interest that Steinhoff points to is relevant even today and, I argue, translates into a myopic definition of what is, or is not, a legitimate authority. This leads observers farther away from an understanding of the dynamics of violence, of which moral consequentialist justifications are central. Consider for example the contemporary the stipulation that "war must be declared by those with responsibility for public order, not by private groups or individuals."[41] The latter stipulation is popularly understood, at least in the west, as referring to the head of state. In order to understand the implicit self-interest (consequentialist reason) in the latter assumption, let us take as an example the war that the American and NATO forces are engaged in Afghanistan.[42] In this, it is indeed a matter of self-interest that the American and NATO forces present their engagement in terms of a 'Just War' based, in part, on the fact that it has been declared by a 'legitimate authority.' Conversely, the immediate implication of this is that the Afghani Taliban—with whom the western forces are at war and who do not represent the head of state of Afghanistan—represent an illlegitimate authority who are thus engaged in an 'unjust' war. The self-interested net result is that in the eyes of public opinion—both domestic (in the respective countries of the American–NATO alliance) and international—all the actions and excesses of war on the part of the American–NATO alliance are excused (even those that give rise to civilian deaths) since their engagement is presented in terms of a Just War.

Advocating the notion of 'legitimate authority' strictly according to one's own criterion ignores the fact that the meaning of 'legitimate authority' in one context is different from its meaning in another context. Yet, as I have argued before, this does not alter the fact that war is always presented as 'just' by *all* contending sides engaged in a war. For example, the Afghan Taliban considers the *Shura* councils (comprised of group tribal elders) as legitimate authority and not President Karzi who is the formal head of state. All violent actions taken by the Taliban, if explicitly or tacitly sanctioned by the *Shura* council, are thus viewed by the members of the Taliban as 'just.' Thus, the fact that such actions are labeled as terrorism or insurgency (implying its illegality) by the American–NATO contingencies is entirely irrelevant to either the momentum of Taliban violence or to the manner in which such violence is presented by the Taliban to its recruits. The critical point here is that the momentum of war and violence is not affected by exogenous labeling of an authority as 'legitimate' or 'illegitimate,' and thereby the ensuing war as 'just' or 'unjust.' The momentum of war and violence is based instead on *self-determined* moral consequentialist reason that decides which entity is going to be accepted as 'legitimate authority.' Combating violence, from whatever entity the violence may be emanating, necessitates such an understanding.

However, scholars of the Just War doctrine most often overlook such a nuanced understanding of the universality of moral consequentialist justifications of violence. For example, consider A.J. Coates' assertion:

> The criterion of legitimate authority has become the most neglected of all the criteria that have been traditionally employed in the *moral assessment of war*. Nowhere is this more evident than in the popular assessment of contemporary terrorism.[43]

Coates completely ignores here that terrorists do indeed follow the commands of a *legitimate authority*, but it just so happens that the notion of legitimate authority is understood differently in the radical Islamist context than it is in the western-oriented Just War doctrine. As far as they are concerned, they are engaged in a 'moral' (not an immoral) war. In order to understand the dynamics of radical Islamist violence, it is important to understand that the problem is not the absence of a legitimate authority; the problem is instead that of a different understanding of a legitimate authority.[44] Uwe Steinhoff criticizes Coates rather myopic understanding of the problem of legitimate authority in a similar manner. Steinhoff notes:

if, for example, the community that stands behind the members of the Israeli army is a legitimate authority and can therefore make the Israeli soldiers agents and executives of public force, why should the community that stands behind the members of, say, Hamas not be such a legitimate authority, making the Hamas fighters the agents of publicly legitimized force?[45]

Steinhoff offers another, rather different, criticism of Coates assessment in the following:

If Hamas—or better yet—if an unorganized single fighter in the Gaza strip blows up an Israeli tank (which, according to international law and the laws of war, is a legitimate action against soldiers of an occupying power, or at least no war crime), it is terrorism; if Sharon, elected democratically, has helicopters fire into groups of Palestinian civilians (according to international law and the laws of war unequivocally a war crime), it is at once something completely different [because Sharon was recognized by international law as a legitimate authority].

Steinhoff points out the absurdity in Coates assertion, particularly if the ultimate humanitarian (and indeed human) concern in any situation of violence is that of the tragic killings of innocent civilians.

The carte blanche that is offered for the actions of a 'legitimate authority' understood in the western sense of an elected democratic state is quite shocking. The hypocrisy implicit in such double-standards is quite apparent in Janna Thompson's following assertion:

A state which unjustly invades the territory of another isn't necessarily committing acts of terror by attacking and killing those who oppose it. Its aims may be limited ... Nor should a state be accused of terrorism just because it sometimes violates just in bello restrictions. Those who fight an *unJust War* [presumably because such a war is not commanded by an authority recognized as 'legitimate' in the western sense] ... deserve condemnation. But the term "terrorist" should be reserved for those whose actions or ideological commitments show that they are truly outside of the law ... and have no intention of obeying *reasonable* restrictions [quotation marks found in the original text].[46]

The fact that atrocities are allowed, and indeed considered legal, if they are committed by recognized states but considered terroristic if they are committed by non-state actors is a contradiction that has dire consequences for humanity. Furthermore, Thompson's above claim stretches the notion of 'Just War' to an absurd point where anything committed by a sovereign state passes the test of a Just War. Steinhoff criticizes Thompson's above assertion on rather different grounds. He notes that if Thompson's assumption is that "legitimate authorities have the violence of their members under their control," then this "is hardly less true of Hamas than of the Israeli army or the Israeli state."[47]

But the problems with western-centric notions of 'legitimate authority' are not only their subjectivity and their myopic understanding of the dynamics of violence. Even when the notion of a 'legitimate authority' is applied to a western context as a criterion of a 'Just War,' they are problematic. For example, Robert L. Holmes notes that "even Hitler arguably had the legitimate authority to declare war in World War II."[48] Does that therefore make Hitler's wars 'just' and 'moral'? Certainly not. But proponents of the German Nazi machinery would have argued as much. For example, Otto Adolf Eichmann, at his trial held in Jerusalem in 1961, defended his brutality against his Jewish victims in terms of the 'morality' of following orders that had been given to him by Hitler's regime—a 'legitimate authority' in German eyes—and to which he was loyal and committed. Indeed, as Hannah Arendt points out in her report *Eichmann in Jerusalem,* Eichmann went as far as to defend his actions in terms of Kantian categorical imperative, a deontological (not consequentialist) notion of morality that he clearly reinterpreted (or misunderstood) as meaning simply the unquestioned commitment to duty commanded by an authority that the self recognizes as legitimate.[49] Of course, as far as his perceptions of morality were concerned, Arendt points out that "Eichmann was ... 'no exception within the Nazi regime.'"[50] Being 'no exception' meant, to Arendt, that he was but one of the many 'banal' individuals that were so critical to the Nazi machinery because they were uncritical beings.[51] To Arendt, a banal (uncritical) individual was either one that was unable to think critically for him or herself or one who had no courage to do so, and it is this that made such individuals easy 'foot soldiers' in the implementation of the brutal and inhuman policies of the Nazi state.[52]

Legitimate authority in radical Islamist rhetoric

What is presented as comprising legitimate authority in the Islamic context is very different from what is presented as comprising legitimate authority in the western Just War doctrine. Historically speaking, legitimate authority for an Islamic community was that which was relegated the title of the caliphate (*khali-fah*) in the Sunni tradition, and that which was relegated the title of the *imam* in the Shia tradition. Thus, broadly speaking, the Sunnis have sought a caliphate while the Shias have sought an 'imamate' (which is interchangeably referred to as the *Mahdi*).[53] In order to understand the radical Islamist justification of violence in the context of a legitimate authority, one has to understand the implicit meaning and significance of the notions of caliphate and the Mahdi.

In the internationally accepted Just War doctrine, war is considered 'just' if it is declared by a legitimate authority, which in contemporary times means an incumbent *elected* head of state. In radical Islamist discourse, war and violence are considered 'just' if they are fought *for the ends* of a legitimate authority. While the notion of a legitimate authority declaring war and wars fought for the ends of establishing a legitimate authority are different, war justified for the ends of a legitimate authority nonetheless earn the same *perception* of being 'just' as those that are declared by a legitimate authority. It is within this context, I argue, that one can understand the utility of the frequent references in Sunni radical Islamist rhetoric to the calls for the return of the caliphate as justifications of violence. A caliphate means literally the "the successor to the Prophet Muhammad as the political-military ruler of Muslim community."[54] John Esposito notes that "the first four successors to that office were chosen by consensus of the Muslim community's elders and were known as the leaders of the believers." As such, the notion of the caliphate has come to be associated with the notion of a legitimate authority. Esposito notes that the "Ottoman sultans were ... widely recognized as caliphs until abolition of the caliphate in 1924."[55] Rhetorical reference to the return of the caliphate in contemporary radical Islamist discourse is thus intended to offer legitimacy to the actions of radical Islamist groups, a sort of 'ends justify the means' logic. Since historically the functions of the caliphate were "the enforcement of law, defense and expansion of the realm of Islam, distribution of funds (booty and alms), and general supervision of government," the notion of the caliphate can be understood in terms of the western notion of 'legitimate authority.'

But calls for the return of the caliphate are not only calls for a legitimate authority, but they are calls for self-governance and self-representation. Thus, quite contrary to how this notion is misunderstood by western audiences (as merely calls for world domination or imperialism in the classic sense), calls for the establishment of the caliphate or the return of the caliphate are emotionally arousing because they are existentially appealing (since self-governance is universally favored over oppression as a human tendency). And in their existential appeal, they are presented in terms of a morality (the right versus the wrong). The notion of the caliphate is thus, in essence, the same as the western notion of legitimate authority in the sense that both imply an authority that is representative of the self and thus reflective of self-representation and self-governance. This can be seen in the following excerpts from Abd al-Salam Faraj's *The Neglected Duty* wherein he justifies violence for the ends of the establishment of a caliphate as not only just but as incumbent on all Muslims:

> it is obligatory for every Muslim to seriously strive for the return of the Caliphate ... [...] One of the characteristics of such a state [and Islamic state ruled by a Caliphate] is that it is ruled by the laws of Islam. [...] if it is ruled by other laws than those of Islam ... [then one can expect] the *disappearance of safety* for the Muslim inhabitants ... to such an extent that this is a source of *danger to the Muslims* and a cause for the disappearance of their safety.[56]

It is clear in the above that the imperative of the return of the caliphate is argued to be the safety of the Muslim inhabitants of the country in question. As such, the notion of the caliphate is justified in the above in decidedly consequentialist terms, as being in the larger safety interests of Muslims. And thus, the notion of the caliphate implies the notion of legitimate authority, as that authority which is representative of the self. Faraj goes on to note the following:

The State (of Egypt in which we live today) is ruled by the Laws of Unbelief [that is, secular, un-Islamic laws] although the majority of its inhabitants are Muslims. [...] The laws by which the Muslims are ruled today are the laws of Unbelief, they are actually codes of law that were made by infidels who then *subjected the Muslims* to these (coded).[57]

In the above, laws other than those of the caliphate are presented as leading to the subjugation of the Muslims; again, the consequentialist justification of Islamic laws is implicit in the above. Thus violence is presented as 'just' as it is argued for the ends of self-representation and the rejection of subjugation.

Ayman al-Zawahiri's publication *Knights under the Prophet's Banner*, published on December 2, 2001 in reference to what he refers to as the oppressive 'western' forces (a broad term which implies Israel and Russia along with the United States and its traditional western allies) is also instructive here:

> *Liberating* the Muslim community, attacking the *enemies of Islam*, and waging a jihad against them require a *Muslim authority, established on Muslim territory*, that raises the banner of jihad and rallies Muslims around it. If we do not achieve this goal, our actions will be nothing more than small-scale harassment and will not bear fruit—[which is described as] the *restoration of the caliphate* and the *departure of the invaders* from the land of Islam.[58]

A number of things are notable in al-Zawahiri's above assertions. First, the reference to "liberating the Muslims" in the same context as the "restoration of the caliphate" indicates that the latter notion is indeed a notion attached to self-determination in the modern sense. This can also be seen in al-Zawahiri's assertions of the imperative of a "Muslim authority, established on Muslim territory," ostensibly by the consensus of Muslims themselves. Finally, it should be noted that the reference to "enemies of Islam" is not a reference to religion but a reference instead to the Muslim ummah (the collective transnational Muslim community). In this way, 'attacking the enemies of Islam' is to be understood as attacking the enemies of the Muslim ummah. This can be seen in his references to "our Muslim world" (193), "in the various lands of Islam" (193), "wounds of the tortured people throughout the land of Islam, from Eastern Turkistan to Andalusia" (194), "young Muslim fighters" (194), "the Islamic movement in general" (195), "mobilizing the community to participate in the struggle" (196), and so on.[59] In the context of the rest of *Knights under the Prophet's Banner*, al-Zawahiri appears to justify violent rebellion for the ends of a legitimate authority.

In Shia radical Islamist rhetoric, it is the references to the imam and, more specially, to the *Mahdi*—or the 'Mahdi Army,' as in the case of the anti-occupation and anti-American Shia extremist group that sprouted during the years of the American occupation of Iraq—that are intended to offer moral justifications for any and all means authorized by the imam or the Mahdi.[60] While I discussed the role of the Mahdi Army in sectarian violence and in the context of struggles for self-recognition in Chapter 2, what I wish to emphasize here is the legitimacy inherent in the notion of the 'Mahdi' or the 'Mahdi Army.' The notion of the Mahdi refers to a 'right guidance,' as that offered by a guardian, a vanguard. It is significant to note that the notion of "divine guidance" in the Quran is often understood as the notion of the Mahdi.[61] Indeed, Esposito defines the notion of the Mahdi as the "divinely guided one."[62] More specifically, Esposito notes that the Mahdi is "an eschatological figure who Muslims [particularly Shia] believe will usher in an era of *justice* and true belief just prior to the end of time."[63] Connections of divine guidance and justice with the notion of the Mahdi bolster the legitimacy of an individual presented as the Mahdi or a group presented as the Mahdi Army. In other words, the notion of the Mahdi offers at once a sense of legitimate authority and of morality. It is within this context that one can understand the immediate legitimacy Muqtada al-Sadr earned when he created the al-Mahdi movement (also referred to as the Mahdi Army) in Iraq in 2003.[64] Sadr's Mahdi army was created as a reaction, and indeed a rejection, of the American occupation of Iraq. But its legitimacy was not limited to its anti-occupation stand; its legitimacy was also bolstered by its presentation of itself as the vanguard of not only the Shia but also of the Sunni in Iraq. Indeed, the Shia Mahdi Army was critical in the part it played in aiding Sunni anti-American violence in Falluja, Iraq.[65] The Mahdi army in Iraq thus presented a sort of a united front against the American occupiers. Thus, al-Sadr earned the reputation of a legitimate authority through his creation of an army based on notions of divine guidance and justice.

Beyond the notions of the Caliphate and the Mahdi, radical Islamists also justify violence in terms of themselves being the legitimate authority to authorize violence. This can be seen in the frequent reference in radical Islamist discourse to the teachings of the Qur'an and the Prophet as providing the guidelines for violent action. This, I argue, is less an accurate interpretation of Islam, much less the essence of Islamist extremism, as it is an effort to forge a sense of the self as legitimate authority so as to mobilize the populace.[66] For example, Article 8 of the Charter of the Islamic Resistance Movement (HAMAS) of Palestine notes the following:

> Allah is its Goal.
> *The Messenger [Prophet Muhammad] is its Leader.*
> *The Qur'an is its Constitution.*
> Jihad is its methodology, and
> Death for the sake of Allah is its most coveted desire.[67]

By presenting the Prophet Muhammad himself as its leader, and the Qur'an as its very constitution, Hamas presents its authority—and the authority of any of its contemporary and changing leaders—as legitimate authority. Based on such contextualization, all actions authorized by Hamas—including calls to violence and war—are now portrayed as that which are authorized by a legitimate authority and thus imperative in the deontological sense.

One other way in which radical Islamist leaders and recruiters portray their authority as legitimate, and therefore their cause as just, is through carefully selected references in the names of the groups they head. Understanding the meaning and symbolisms in the names of the Islamist extremist groups is critical to understanding the dynamics of Islamist extremism, by which I mean the possible nature of the motivations of those that voluntarily join Islamist extremist groups and the equation of violence with morality.[68] Consider the symbolisms in the following names of some of the most popular Islamist extremist groups; the following list is presented in terms of the name of the group, its acronym and sectarian affiliation, and the translation of its title in English. Consider, for example, those groups operating in Pakistan and Pakistan administered Kashmir: Lashkar-e-Jhangvi (LJ; Sunni)—Army of War (Jhangvi means 'of war'); Sipah-i-Sahaba (SSP; Sunni)—Soldiers of the Prophet's Companions, an ultra-radical splinter group of Lashkar-e-Jhangvi; Lashkar-e-Toiba (LoT; Sunni)—Army of the Pure (the good); Sipah-e-Muhammad (Sunni)—Soldiers of Muhammad; Hezb-ul-Mujahideen (Hezb; Sunni)—Party of the Freedom Fighters; Jayash-e-Muhammad (JeM; Sunni)—Army of the Prophet Muhammad; Harkat-ul-Mujahidin (HuM; Sunni)—Movement or Actions of the Freedom Fighters; Tehreek-e-Taliban Pakistan—(TeT; Sunni)—the Path of the Taliban in Pakistan or the Taliban Movement of Pakistan. Consider also those groups operating in Palestinian territories: Harakat al-Muqaqama al-Islamiyya (Hamas; Sunni)—Islamic Resistance Movement; Islamic jihad (Sunni)—Islamic Struggle.[69]

Right intentions: from divine reason to moral duty

In the medieval Christian Crusades (the century following the Albigensian Crusade), Mark Gregory Pegg notes that "the *moral imperative* demanding the extermination of heretics through mass murder became the *ethical basis* for eliminating Muslims and Jews from Christendom [emphases added]."[70] That murder and violence were framed in deontological terms as the 'moral imperative' points not only to the deontological guise for consequentialist reason, but points also to the Crusaders' efforts to present violence in terms of 'right intentions.' In the contemporary secular version of the Just War doctrine, 'right intentions' are defined not in terms of a religious duty, much less in terms of a divine reason, but defined instead in terms of 'national interests' and 'duty' to safeguard those interests (particularly in sense of following your duty as a member of the armed forces of your country).[71] That such a sense of duty would give rise to human rights atrocities under the guise of 'right intentions' is perhaps best illustrated in the atrocities committed by US soldiers in the infamous *Abu Ghraib* prison in Iraq. American soldiers accused of torturing Iraqi prisoners typically defended their actions in the following terms: as following duty "when others failed";[72] as their actions having little significance, as they were "allowed";[73] as doing something that was "accceptable."[74]

Indeed, in popular interpretations of the contemporary Just War doctrine, it is not 'unjust' to kill innocent civilians during a war as long as such killing is *not* intentional. Quite apart from the intangible nature of intentionality, such a stipulation means that unbridled actions taken out of a lack of concern for the other (namely, the innocent civilians on the enemy's domain) but without the 'intention' of targeting innocent civilians passes the criterion of a 'Just War.'[75] For example, consider the case of the unmanned predator drones that are used by the CIA to target and kill actual or suspected Taliban extremists in Afghanistan and the tribal areas of Pakistan. It is not unreasonable to think that a bomb with such destructive power, thrown in the middle of populated areas, would cause the deaths of innocent civilians along with the particular individual that is targeted. Yet, the deaths of innocent civilians in this case are largely unreported and underemphasized and, further, do not factor into the considerations of what is or is not a 'just' war.

Alex Bellamy argues that one of the important criterions distinguishing a terrorist act from a non-terrorist act is that the former *intends* to kill innocent civilians (or non-combatants) while the latter does not (where the killing of non-combatants is consequential not intentional).[76] Even if it could be established, without a doubt, that soldiers of a formal military institution under the command of a recognized sovereign state had *not* intended to kill innocent civilians during war, is it not absurd to think that the deaths of innocent civilians in such an action should still be presented as 'just' and 'moral' since they were not intended? The fact is that intentions mean very little to the families and relatives of those innocent individuals who are killed pointlessly in such unbridled actions. Such violence, to the ones left behind, is anything but 'just' in either the moral or the legal sense. But such justifications are certainly moral consequentialist for those evoking them.

And if right intentions are the main focus, does this mean that good deeds committed with bad intentions (or selfish intentions) should therefore be relegated as unjust? Steinhoff points to such a contradiction in the following:

> If, for instance, genocide is committed in a country and stopping it is a just cause for military intervention, even considering the moral costs of the war, such an intervention would nevertheless be illegitimate if it were not carried out in order to prevent the genocide but rather in order to expand one's own sphere of influence. [...] Correspondingly ... it is unclear why an intervention which saves a people from extermination should be foregone only because it will not be carried out *in order* to save the people from extermination.[77]

Steinhoff seems to be saying in the above that surely it is actual actions and their outcomes that should *also* be considered in the relegations of war as just and moral. The problem with the notion of 'right intentions' is, I argue, that it is rhetorical and decidedly subjective and consequentialist. This holds true whether a hegemonic state entity presents its *intentions* in terms of 'democracy promotion' or the 'liberation' of a people as justifications for a military intervention of another state, or when individuals such as Eichmann present their brutality in terms of the *intention* to follow orders and thus as a 'categorical imperative.' In addition, the rhetorical nature of the claim to right intentions offers a carte blanche to powerful states that can then escape accountability based on the proclamation of a good intention. But, not surprisingly, powerful sovereign states do not have the monopoly over the claims of 'right intentions.'

The notion of right intentions in radical Islamist rhetoric

In his infamous pamphlet *Al-Faridah al Gha'ibah*—literally the duty that has been ignored or has disappeared, but popularly understood as *The Neglected Duty*—Mohammed Abd al-Salam Faraj (1952–1982) argued that it was the *duty* of each Muslim individual to challenge injustices, particularly those for which one's own government was responsible. This can be seen in section 84 of the pamphlet, entitled 'Fighting is now a duty upon all Muslims'; Faraj asserts that jihad "becomes an individual duty" either when one is ruled by unrepresentative government or when "infidels descend upon a country."[78] The claim of jihad as an individual duty stands apart from the classical Islamic thought which prescribed jihad as a *collective* duty, and *only* when the enemy was "an external one."[79] The deviation from classical discourse can be seen as pragmatic, intended to attract as many recruits as possible and to bypass the problem of free riders which would be created with the abstract notion of 'collective duty.' It can also be argued that the emphasis from the notion of a collective duty to an individual duty is intended to give violent jihad a kind of spontaneity. This is because the onus for violent rejection is placed on each individual such that no time need be wasted in attaining sanctions from higher authorities or from a collective for violent actions. This can be seen in Faraj's following assertion:

> Know that when jihad is an *individual duty*, there is no (need to) ask permission of (your) parents to leave to wage jihad, as the jurists have said.[80]

In other words, the radical Islamist assertion that violent jihad is a duty (thus deontological in essence and based on 'right intentions') incumbent on each individual has the effect of catalyzing violent resistance. This is because it takes the 'duty' of violent resistance away from the abstract realm of the 'collective' and places it in the concrete realm of the individual. In this way, the problem of free riders is eliminated and any delays in action are eliminated as now the individual can act as the 'judge and the jury' in judging when a violent action is necessary. Faraj paints the picture of violence jihad as incumbent on each individual (as in individual's duty) in a variety of different ways in his pamphlet. For example, he selectively emphasizes the verses in the Quran that sanction violent offensive actions while ignoring those that sanction violence only as a defensive measure. Indeed, Faraj questions the very legitimacy of defensive and nonviolent jihad, arguing that such "argument shows either complete ignorance or excessive cowardice."[81]

The references to violent resistance as a duty in Faraj's pamphlet implied that it was the right thing to do, even if in so doing one were to resort to actions that were violent. Indeed, the notion of '*al-faridah*' also implies right intentions, not simply duty. It is perhaps not too surprising that such a deontologically disguised document would became the creed of President Sadat's assassins in 1978 and, later, the creed of numerous other Islamist extremist groups in Egypt and beyond.[82] In presenting violence as a religious duty, Abd al-Salam Faraj sought to present violence as a categorical imperative and as thus based on 'right intentions.' So that even if the notion of *religious* duty did not much appeal, the notion of *duty* retained its appeal.

Interestingly, I argue that the radical Islamist justifications of violence and destruction in terms of the 'right' (struggles for self-recognition and struggles against servitude) against the 'wrong' (negation of the self and tacit acceptance of such negation and oppression) are Honnethian in formulation, in that they are moral consequentialist in essence.[83] In other words, violent struggles for recognition become justified in radical Islamist rhetoric in terms of a morality, the 'right' (seeking justice) against the 'wrong' (injustice in the form of negation and subjugation of the self by the other). The equation of violence with morality by the radical Islamists—the Hegelian slaves—is thus pragmatic as it is consequentialist, despite its more obvious religious dressing. The radical Islamists' selective emphasis on those Islamic tenets that sanction unbridled violence—as for example in Abd al-Salam Faraj's *Neglected Duty*—then point to the instrumentality of religion. Since these justifications (references to religious tenets) are connected to the explanations of violence (references to grievances), they are framed in terms of a 'Just War.'

In strict Islamic religious terms, right intentions, or "righteous intentions" as Muhammad Abdel Haleem refers to them, are a central requirement for the engagement in war.[84] This can be seen, argues Abdel Haleem, in the emphasis on 'righteous intentions' for going to war in the Qur'an and the hadith.[85] Broadly speaking, righteous intentions are described as belonging to "the one who fights in the way of God" so that "the word of God is uppermost."[86] Abdel Haleem notes, however, that this broad reference is often misunderstood as 'spreading of Islam' in the world.[87] Nothing could be farther from the word of the Holy book, argues Abdel Haleem, since "nowhere in the Qur'an is changing people's religion given as a cause for waging war."[88] Yet, references to fighting as reflective of God's will or fighting as reflective of a divine duty are frequently cited in radical Islamist rhetoric, which has the impact of framing violence as a morality. For example, consider Qutb's following commentary on the Qur'anic *sura 9, al-Tawba* dealing with war:

> Fighting is targeted only against real forces which *prevent people's liberation from subjugation* by other creatures, so that they submit to God alone.[89]

The consequentialist justifications for war and violence can be found in Qutb's assertion that war and violence are sanctioned if they *liberate people from subjugation*, which in the context of Qutb's writings is a reference to General Nasser's Egyptian government. However, the reference in the above that people should be liberated from subjugation so that "they submit to God alone" offers, I argue, a deontological framing for an otherwise consequentialist reason. The result is the framing of violence as a product of right intentions and as thus a morality. Qutb's tendency to frame consequentialist reason within a deontological framework is perhaps more obvious in the following assertion taken from his influential work *Milestones*:

> This religion [Islam] is really a universal declaration of the *freedom of man from servitude* to other men ...
> [...]
> This *universal declaration of the freedom of man* on the earth from every authority except that of God, and the declaration that sovereignty is God's alone and that He is the Lord of the universe, is not merely a theoretical, philosophical and passive proclamation. It is a *positive, practical and dynamic message with a view to ... actually freeing people from their servitude to other men.*[90]

In the above, Qutb justifies violent revolt against an oppressive government (General Nasser's regime) with references to consequences (freedom of man from servitude) and right intentions (as implied in his reference to God as being the legitimate sovereign). In other words, Qutb justifies violence through fusing consequentialist and deontological reason. Qutb pursues this line of logic throughout his arguments in *Milestones*. For example, consider also Qutb's following assertion, which perhaps even more explicitly weds consequentialist reason with a deontological justification:

> The jihad of Islam is to secure complete freedom for every man throughout the world by releasing him from servitude to other human beings so that he may serve his God.[91]

The framing of violent jihad in the context of references to God or Islam, and as thus in terms of 'right intentions,' can also be seen in the manner in which the Palestinian Islamist extremist group Hamas presents itself. Roxanne Euben and Muhammad Qasim Zaman observe that Hamas weds "Islamism to *wataniyya* (patriotism, derived from *watan*—or homeland)" and indeed welds "nationalist aspirations to an Islamist framework."[92] This, I argue, is intended to present nationalistic violence (decidedly secular in nature) in terms of divine sanctions (with references to Islam), and thus in terms of right intentions. Indeed, Article 6 of the Charter of the Islamic Resistance Movement (HAMAS) of Palestine notes that "it gives its loyalty to Allah."[93] Similar presentation of violent action in terms of right intentions can be seen in Article 12 of the Hamas Charter:

Nationalism, from the point of view of the Islamic Resistance Movement, is part and parcel of *religious ideology*.

[...]

If other nationalism have material, humanistic, and geographic ties, then the Islamic Resistance Movement's nationalism has all of that and, more important, *divine reasons* providing it with life and spirit ... raising in the heavens the divine banner to connect earth and heavens with a strong bond.[94]

The reference in the above to Hamas' aims being "part and parcel of religious ideology" and, more significantly, as reflective of "divine reasons" is a quintessential illustration of what I refer to as a consequentialist–deontological fusion in reason that is intended to offer a sense of 'right intentions' for violent actions. Packaged in such a manner, calls to violent action are less likely to face resistance from the people (to whom the call for action is directed) who now reinterpret violence as a morality. This is not unlike the presentation of the brutal Christian Crusades of the medieval times as 'divine' and as thus based on 'right intentions,' as I discussed earlier in this chapter.

Let us now consider the references in radical Islamist rhetoric that present violence and fighting as reflective of a *divine duty*. In fact, I argue, radical Islamist rhetoric often presents violent jihad as a *categorical imperative* in a way that is *conceptually* similar to a Kantian categorical imperative (that is, in the sense of the obligatory nature of duty), but different of course in its content. For example, Sayyid Qutb, in his publication *Milestones,* argues that 'God's law' is a 'universal law.' As such, Qutb argues for the inviolability of "universal laws" which to him reflect the contents of the Shariah (Islamic law).[95] A strict adherence to these 'universal laws,' argues Qutb, is *categorically imperative* on each individual. In addition to presenting anything (including violent action) as based on 'right intentions' if it is framed within notions of 'universal laws,' the claims of 'universal laws' in the context of morality have a larger, more damaging consequence. There is an implied *inviolability* of assumptions and declarations that are passed off components of 'universal laws.' Thus, all actions justified in the context of universal laws become presented as reflective of divine reason, divine duty and thus right intentions.

Deontological disguise for consequentialist reason, which presents violence as 'duty' and thus as based on 'right intentions,' is also apparent in the assertions of *Hizbullah*'s founder member, Sheikh Naim Qassem:

When a Muslim dies in defensive Jihad, he fulfils ... his religious *duty* by waging a holy war as well as gratifying God by making the ultimate sacrifice.[96]

Violent jihad is clearly portrayed in terms of divine sanctions, as can be seen in references to 'holy war' and 'gratifying God.' The implications are clear, violent jihad is thus based on 'right intentions' for what could be more 'right' then following divine sanctions. But beyond proclamations of divine sanctions, there is an additional deontological logic in the above, one that is based on presenting violent jihad as a "duty." So the imperatives of defense or 'defensive jihad' (a distinctly consequentialist reason) become presented in terms of a deontological urgency (with reference to violence as divine duty and then as individual's duty).

It is interesting to pause here and reconsider Kant's deontological argument.[97] Wood notes that Kant "clearly does not conceive of actions done from duty as done with repugnance" and, in this way, Kant "thinks of acts done from duty as done *willingly,* with a *desire* to do them."[98] In other words, Wood argues that to Kant *duty is always desired.* In this way, the notion of desire exists in Kant's formulation of absolute freedom, but this desire is defined in terms of a *desire for duty* and not a socially contingent desire (as that for material goods and other such things that enhance personal pleasure and satisfaction). Thus, 'desire' in the Kantian notion of absolute freedom and in his notion of deontological morality is defined as self-determined desire, to the extent that the *desire for duty* can be seen as a self-determined since what it desires (duty) is itself self-determined and not socially contingent.[99] Such logic can be seen as implied in the following popular Palestinian children's anthem that seems intended to reinforce radical Islamist sentiments:

> O mother, my religion has called me to jihad and self-sacrifice.
> O mother, I am marching toward immortality; I will never retreat
> O mother, don't cry over me if I am shot down, laid out on the ground. For death is my path; martyrdom, *my desire.*[100]

Martyrdom is defined as a duty in the above song, as implied in the sentence "my religion has *called me* to jihad and self-sacrifice." Even more critically, jihad and martyrdom are presented in the above as an individual *desire*, as explicit in the assertion "my desire." The implication seems to be that not only is violent jihad reflective of 'right intentions,' but is reflective of a 'desire' for the 'right intentions.'

Self-defense: the classic justification of unbridled violence

The Just War doctrinal notion of 'double-effect' allows for the framing of unbridled violence as 'just' and 'moral.' This is because the doctrine of double-effect suggests that an action of self-defense can have two effects, one that is intended (to safeguard the self) and one that is not intentional but is consequential (namely, the killing of the aggressor or even the innocent civilians in the aggressor's domain). So, for example, as long as the death of innocent civilians in an act of war was not *intended* but a product of the 'double-effect' of self-defense, it is excused, and actions that are responsible for such deaths remain qualified in terms of a 'Just War.' Given such a claim, particularly if made by a powerful state entity, even the most grotesque actions get qualified in the realm of a 'just'

war. This, of course, is one of the many classic cases of the resort to consequentialist morality that the Just War doctrine helps to facilitate.

The doctrine of *double-effect* was initially introduced by Thomas Aquinas,
ostensibly to warn against the unforeseen outcomes of war. Since it is assumed
that in self-defense the *intention* is merely to defend the self and not to kill the
other, the killing of the other cannot therefore be considered "unlawful" or
immoral.[101] Bellamy points out that Francisco de Vitoria (*c.*1492–1546) understood Aquinas' notion of double-effect in the following manner:

> It is occasionally *lawful to kill the innocent* not by mistake, but with full
> knowledge of what one is doing, if this is an *accidental effect* [double-
> effect] ... this is proven since it would otherwise be impossible to wage war
> against the guilty, thereby preventing the *just side* from fighting ... care
> must be taken to ensure that the *evil effects* of war do not outweigh the pos-
> sible benefits sought by waging it.[102]

But, as Holmes points out, one of the problems with the notion of self-defense is
that "whenever hostilities break out, each side accuses the other of aggression
and proclaims that it, on the other hand, acts only in self-defense."[103] Should this
therefore mean that all sides can apologize for the excesses of their military
actions in terms of a double-effect? And if that be the case, does that not bring
into question the carte blanche that is afforded an entity (state or non-state) in
the name of 'self-defense'? And does that therefore mean that the Just War doctrine allows for unaccountability in the deaths of innocent civilians so long as
the aggressor frames it as 'unintentional' and 'regrettable' in its rhetorical
apology?

Steinhoff notes that one of the starkest "abuses of the doctrine of double
effect" was "Truman's attempt to justify dropping the atom bomb on Hiroshima
and Nagasaki."[104] In a speech delivered to the American people in August 1945,
President Truman noted the following:

> We have used [the bomb] against those who attacked us without warning in
> Pearl Harbor ... against those who have abandoned all pretense of obeying
> international law of warfare. We have used it in order to *shorten the agony
> of war.*[105]

The above is ironic for two reasons. First, it justifies the dropping of the bomb
(with all the civilian causalities that it entailed) by noting that the *other* had
"abandoned ... international law of warfare." That the dropping of the bomb
entailed excessive and disproportionate use of force—a clear violation of the
proportionality principle and an abuse of the 'double-effect' principle—is completely ignored. Second, it justifies dropping the bomb in clearly consequentialist
terms as shortening "the agony of war." As even Walzer notes: "I can find ... no
way of defending such a procedure. How did the people of Hiroshima forfeit
their rights?"[106]

However, Steinhoff notes that the problem with the principle of double-effect is that this "doctrine interprets, it would seem, the prohibition against killing in such a way as to maintain it while simultaneously allowing to kill."[107] As such, the double-effect clause actually functions to broaden the definition of self-defense so that *any* action, even that which is taken for self-interest and demonstrations of power, may be justified in terms of a self-defense. And since "aggression is commonly regarded as a criterion of the illegality of war as well as the immorality of war" as Holmes notes, I argue that this further motivates the broadening of the definition of self-defense.[108] This is particularly true for those entities that engage in actions which straddle the line between defensive and aggressive. The Flotilla controversy is a case in point.

Other more contemporary justifications of the use of legal force that implicitly invoke the double-effect clause can also be found. Amnesty International reports that in March 2010 Harold Koh, the Legal Advisor to United States Department of State, justified the use of predator drones in the war in Afghanistan as legal and thus 'just' under international law. Koh asserted:

> as a matter of international law, the United States is in an armed conflict with al-Qa'ida, as well as the Taliban and associated forces, in response to the horrific 9/11 attacks ... [and thus, the United States] ... may use force consistent with its inherent right to self-defense under international law ... [he argued that this included] ... authority under international law ... to use force, including lethal force, to defend itself, including by targeting persons such as high-level al-Qa'ida leaders who are planning attacks.[109]

Koh's above justifications stand in contrast with perceptions of those upon whom the bombs are being dropped, as is apparent in the following warnings and reports found in Pakistan's popular newspaper *Dawn:*

> Last week, a UN human rights expert warned that the "prolific" use of US drone attacks amounted to "a license to kill without accountability" and was setting a damaging example that other countries would follow.[110]

> In a report to the UN Human Rights Council, Philip Alston sharply criticized the legal arguments used to justify them, their civilian toll and the involvement of the Central Intelligence Agency (CIA).[111]

In addition, Amnesty International notes that Koh's justifications does not provide any information as to the bases of the American decision to target the individuals that it targets with the use of predator drones. Such information includes:

> who the targets were, what justification there was for using lethal force against them, whether non-lethal alternatives were tried or even considered, what safeguards were put in place to ensure that civilians are not

endangered, who was killed or injured, what investigations took place in cases where violations of international legal rules are suspected and more.[112]

Such ambiguity points to the use, and indeed misuse, of the doctrine of 'double-effect' so that any action taken by the self in terms of a 'self-defense' is presented as 'just' regardless of the scale of atrocities caused by such an action.

The subjectivity in the resort to claims of self-defense is quite glaring. The question of whether both sides in a war can feel they have a 'just cause' has concerned Just War theorists for years. Following Francisco de Vitoria's (*c.*1492–1546) assessment on the matter in the sixteenth century, the contemporary consensus appears to be that while a war can be viewed as 'just' by both sides engaged in a war—and indeed, it always is, as I have argued earlier—only one side can have an 'objective' just cause while the other must necessarily have a 'subjective' just cause.[113] But, of course, the very labeling of a cause as 'just' and thus 'objective' is itself a subjective judgment. This is because no entity engaging in war presents its engagement in terms of an 'unjust' war. If this is so, then no entity perceives its cause as only 'subjectively just'—and at the very least, will not *present* its cause as only subjectivity just—since this would imply that the motivation of the self is consequentialist and not altruistic. This is because presenting oneself in terms of altruism affords more legitimacy to the violence and brutality that one engages in than presenting oneself in self or consequentialist terms.

While morality—or the 'right' thing to do—is often presented in deontological terms (such as commitment to duty and other such selfless proclamations), admitting that the self is motivated by consequentialist aims (and thus by a cause that is only subjectively just) takes away the carte blanche that only claims to a deontological morality offer.[114] This means, quite simply, that one opens oneself up for criticism from the other, from all others, for its engagement in violence and brutality. This would not only negate claims to a 'Just War' but also substantially weaken the rhetoric that is used to recruit voluntary individuals to take part in violence (whether the recruitment is to an official military institution of a state or to a sub-state and non-state militant group). As a result, no entity engaged in a war will present its cause as only subjectively just. The distinctions between an objective and a subjective just cause are thus naïve. Thus, contrary to Vitoria's qualification of an 'objective' just cause and a 'subjective' just cause, I argue instead that all proclaimed 'just causes' are subjective, and all such subjective causes are rhetorically framed as objective. Axel Honneth's argument of the moral grammar of struggles for recognition is particularly illustrative of my latter point.[115]

But, for the sake of an argument, let us entertain Vitoria's stipulations of an 'objective' just cause and a 'subjective' just cause. The deeper implication of this distinction is that one side is more enlightened and operates on absolute facts only (itself a debatable notion) thereby giving it a objective just cause, while the other side is ignorant and operates on perceptions (which some epistemologists would argue is not divorced from experience, or 'facts') thereby giving it an subjective just cause.[116] Even if this may be so, such an assessment beckons a critical question: Who might be the authority that judges the objectivity or the subjectivity of a cause? And, further, who might offer this authority the legitimacy to make such a judgment? It is a well-known fact that in judgments of crises and conflict, even the most well-regarded international government organizations lack objectivity so that they may label a cause as objective when it is subjective, and subjective when it is objective. That the national interests of member states are at stake in such judgments is the obvious culprit in the pendulous assessments of international government organizations.[117] For example, despite the proliferation in the deaths of innocent civilians as a result of the American CIA-operated predator drone strikes in Afghanistan and the tribal areas of Pakistan's northwest frontier, which claim to target militants but kill anyone in the vicinity, the Obama Administration continues to present its involvement as objectively just by framing it in terms of 'self-defense.'[118] To the thousands of innocent civilians in these areas that are killed or displaced, the American use of predator drones would hardly be excused as 'just,' much less as objectively just. The theoretical distinctions between 'objective' and 'subjective' just causes are thus meaningless as they are necessarily subjective themselves.

Furthermore, if the essence of violence is a struggle for recognition (a struggle against the negation of the self), as I have argued in this book, then biased stipulations of an 'objective' just cause and a 'subjective' just cause would only breed more resentment on the part of the Hegelian slaves (the entities that have been made to feel inferior to the master). As a result, the Hegelian slaves would come to view such subjectivity in assessment as but another way for the master to keep the self oppressed. This would breed resentments which would only fuel violence as they will reinforce the justifications of the non-hegemonic entities (the Hegelian slaves) of being *in fact* engaged in an 'objective' Just War, a war against the injustice of dehumanization and the negation of the self. My latter assessment takes on a rather insightful implication in light of the fact that "following Augustine, he [Vitoria] argued that the only just cause for war was to right a prior wrong."[119] As we shall see later in this chapter, radical Islamist rhetoric justifies its violence in these very terms, as addressing the wrong that has been done to the self.

One might bring to light here Emmerich de Vattel's (1714–1767) analysis on the question of an 'objective' just cause and a 'subjective' just cause.[120] Vattel addressed this question with reference to his distinction between a 'legally Just War' and a 'morally Just War.' In his view, if all sides follow the protocols of war as stipulated in the Just War doctrine and as thus consistent with international law, then all sides can be said to be engaged in a 'legally' Just War.[121] However, for a war to be 'morally' just, the causes for war must be 'objectively' just. In this way, according to Vattel, while both sides can be legally just in a war, only one side can be morally just. It is interesting to note that Vattel does not address the *subjectivity* in the very assertions of the 'objectivity' of 'just causes,' as I noted above, but introduces instead the criteria of the 'legality' of war in the hopes of introducing a measure of 'objectivity' in the judgment of whether a war is just or unjust. Vattel's criteria of Just War in the context of the legality of war makes 'unjust' the two major wars of the decade of 2000–2010 since the conduct of the American forces in Iraq and the conduct of the American–NATO forces in Afghanistan have, on many occasions, violated the stipulations of both *jus ad bello* as well as *jus in bello*.[122]

Another point to keep in mind, and one that weakens the utility of Vattel's distinctions between the 'morality' and the 'legality' of war, is that the distinctions such as these are blurry at best in both rhetoric and reality. In his critical look at the Just War doctrine, Andrew Fiala makes a similar point when he notes that theoretical standards are a far cry from actions in reality.[123] Furthermore, it is critical to understand that all actors that engage in war and violence (whether hegemonic states, non-hegemonic states or non-state entities) do indeed present their engagement in a manner that fits a legal framework that they recognize. Thus, a legal framework may either be viewed as provided by the western-oriented Just War doctrine or, for that matter, by the Islamic tradition of jihad. This is not to say that the Islamic tradition of jihad is categorically interpreted by all Muslims as violent, much less that the indiscriminate killing of civilians is categorically understood as acceptable. As Reuven Firestone notes, "like Judaism and Christianity, Islam is multifaceted, offering a variety of responses to the questions and perplexities of the human condition."[124] In fact, notes Fazlur Rahman, "armed jihad is only one form" of jihad.[125] Indeed, the Arabic root of the term jihad can mean any of the following: "to strive, to exert, to fight."[126] Or, as Aziz al-Azmeh notes, "there are many 'Islams'."[127] The critical point here is not of the different interpretations of jihad. The critical point here is that legal frameworks vary according to the context. This means that while notions such as legitimate authority and self-defense are ubiquitously utilized in the western and non-western contexts as justifications for war and violence, how they are defined (as reflected in the actions that are justified under their banner) and carried out varies tremendously.

But this variation is not necessarily between contexts; it may even exist within a particular context. For example, as we shall see later in this chapter, the US–NATO contingencies in Afghanistan that ostensibly justify their actions in the context of the Just War doctrine nonetheless include a broad spectrum of violent actions under the banner of 'self-defense,' actions that have otherwise been criticized for their inhumanity by international human rights organizations such as Amnesty International. If variations in the interpretations of the stipulations of the Just War doctrine can exist *within* the context of the Just War doctrine—thus leading to variations in what is understood as a 'Just War' in the legal sense—then might not one expect variations in the interpretations of the legality of war at the global level? In other words, Vattel's assertion that more than one entity may be engaged in a legally Just War is not as critical as realizing that the legal frameworks that outline stipulations of Just War—along with their customary understanding of symbols and taboos—are characterized by variations in the observations of the stipulations, both within a particular framework as well as between different frameworks.

This is a point that is completely overlooked by Elaine Scarry when she argues that there are some actions that are "categorically prohibited by international law [such as those outlined in the Just War doctrine]."[128] It is not that her argument is false; it is instead that she overlooks the fact that international law is not recognized by those warring entities whose frameworks of legality and morality are provided by radical interpretations of their religious traditions. Any extremist group that justifies violence in the context of its religious scriptures is a case in point, and here Islamist extremist groups are no exception. In other words, Scarry fails to realize that the actions that are understood as legal and moral vary tremendously, not only amongst those that proclaim to adhere to stipulations of international law, but most certainly amongst those that do not recognize *international* law. And thus she presents the following incident as an unconscionable violation of international law:

> A memorable example of such treachery occurred during the spring 2003 invasion of Iraq by the United States, when an Iraqi taxi driver allegedly displayed a while flag at a checkpoint and then, having gained the trust of the guards, exploded a car bomb, killing four American soldiers.[129]

A final loophole in Vattel's distinctions between a legality of war versus the morality of war in determining whether a war is 'just' deserves attention. Often, what is presented as a 'legally' Just War is also presented as a 'morally' Just War by entities justifying their engagement in war. I can think of no exceptions. For example, in his speech to the United States Military Academy at West Point, New York on December 1, 2009, United States President Obama justified the American military troops' surge in Afghanistan in the following terms:

> And as Commander-in-Chief, I have determined that it is in our vital national interest to send an additional 30,000 U.S. troops to Afghanistan. [...] I do not make this decision lightly. [...] Of course, this burden is not ours alone to bear. This is not just America's war. Since 9/11, al Qaeda's safe havens have been the source of attacks against London and Amman and Bali. The people and governments of both Afghanistan and Pakistan are endangered. [...] Our overarching goal remains the same: to disrupt, dismantle, and defeat al Qaeda in Afghanistan and Pakistan, and to prevent its capacity to threaten America and our allies in the future. [...] ... we are ... heirs to a *noble struggle* for freedom. And now we must summon all of our might and *moral suasion* to meet the challenges of a new age.[130]

In the above remarks, President Obama presents war in Afghanistan as both legally and morally just. The reference to the "burden is not ours alone to bear" with earlier reference in the speech to support from NATO allies seems intended to bolster the legality of the war. The references to "noble struggle" and "moral suasion" in the context of justifying the troops surge in Afghanistan seem intended to present the war in moral terms.

Self-defense in the radical Islamist rhetoric

As in the internationally accepted Just War doctrine, the notion of 'self-defense' is also defined quite broadly in radical Islamist justifications of violence. First, the notion of 'self' defense is understood both in terms of the defense of a particular ethnic or linguistic entity (such as, for example, the Afghan Taliban) as well as in terms of the defense of the larger *ummah*. Second, broadening the definition of self-defense also broadens the definition of the enemy, so that the enemy is not perceived exclusively as the entity at war with the self (in terms of a particular ethnic and linguistic group) but also as the entity at war with the larger *ummah*. In this way, the enemy is often understood to mean at once the entity far away (a foreign entity or as an occupying force) as well as the entity at home (one's own repressive government). And hence, an enemy maybe the 'far enemy' or the 'near enemy,' two notions that have been most recently been popularized by Fawaz Gerges' analysis of the notions.[131] However, Gerges points out that the notion of a 'near enemy' and a 'far enemy' was originally coined by Mohammed Abd al-Salam Faraj in his pamphlet *Al-Faridah al Gha'ibah* (or the neglected duty).[132]

Hasan al-Banna (1906–1949), the founder of the first Islamic revivalist political party *al-ikhwan al-Muslimun* (Muslim brotherhood) in Egypt in 1928, popularly defined violent jihad as "the road to salvation from Western *colonialism.*"[133] To the extent that history records western colonialism of the non-western as entailing subjugation, dehumanization and oppression, al-Banna's assertion can be understood in terms of a justification of violence in terms of a *self-defense*. Indeed, in his justifications of violent jihad, al-Banna challenged the notion that the 'greater jihad' was in fact a struggle of the heart and the spirit and instead redefined 'greater jihad' to mean violent, defensive wars.[134] This is not surprising, for Brown notes that the very difference between Islamist radical thought and Islamist revivalist thought is that the radicals emphasize the "superiority of the physical jihad … [lesser jihad] over other spiritual … understandings of the idea [of the greater jihad]."[135] Indeed, for al-Banna the ultimate jihad could only be realized through martyrdom missions.[136] The "*right* cause"—or just cause—was thus portrayed by al-Banna in terms of self-sacrifice in the absolute sense.[137] And for this, al-Banna proclaimed that violent jihad and martyrdom was "the most *noble* of goals."[138]

Sayyid Qutb (1906–1966) vehemently argued that "*jihad* was never defense, in the narrow sense that the term 'defensive war' generally denotes today.*"[139] What Qutb meant by this is that jihad was not defensive in the sense of *only* protecting the self (in the individual or collective sense) from immediate and imminent harm. Jihad, to Qutb, strove to defend *humankind at large* from servitude and humiliation. As such, jihad to Qutb had a much larger legitimacy than merely a 'reaction' (defense of self) to an 'action' (threat to the self directed by the other). This seems apparent in the following:

> *jihad*, for God's cause represents a positive movement that aims to liberate man throughout the world, employing appropriate means to face every situation at every stage.[140]

But just because Qutb rejects the notion of 'self-defense' in its limited sense this does not detract from the fact that he presents jihad—and any violent action therein—as a 'just cause'; the latter is clearly implied in Qutb's assertion that jihad aims to "liberate man," for what could be more 'just' (moral) than freeing humankind from humiliating subjugation. This is clearly noted in Qutb's following remarks:

> If we must describe Islamic *jihad* as defensive, then we need to amend the meaning of the term 'defense' so that it means the defending of mankind against all factors that hinder their liberation and restrict their freedom.[141]

What is also noteworthy in Qutb's above assertions is that along with presenting jihad in terms of a just cause—and as self-defense in the larger sense of the word—he also presents violent action (as in references to jihad and "God's cause") in deontological terms. Thus again, I argue, one sees a fusion of consequentialist-deontological reason in radical Islamist rhetoric. In Qutb's above assertions, it is consequentialist because it seeks the freedom of humankind, 'freedom' being the consequences sought; and it is deontological because it also frames such action in non-selfish and non-self-serving terms as "God's cause." One other way of understanding Qutb's criticisms of the notion that violent jihad is merely for self-defense is the following. While violent jihad is seen as done *out of necessity of defense* in the revivalist sense, Qutb seems to define violent jihad as done *out of necessity for a revolutionary change*. Qutb's views seem reflected in Mawdudi's depiction of jihad. Mawdudi presented violent jihad as a grand revolutionary struggle and not simply as a defensive measure, implying its timelessness and the permanency of the struggle to forge a radical Islamist *sittlichkeit*.[142] This is apparent in Mawdudi's following assertions:

> the objective of the Islamic *Jihad* is to eliminate the rule of an un-Islamic system, and establish in its place an Islamic system of state rule. Islam does not intend to confine this rule to a single state or to a handful of countries. The aim of Islam is to ring about a *universal revolution*.[143]

Notwithstanding Qutb's objection to the narrow meaning of 'self-defense,' contemporary radical Islamist groups and movements explicitly justify their violence in terms of self-defense, and thus in terms of a Just War. For example, Article 7 of the Charter of the Islamic Resistance Movement (HAMAS) of Palestine notes the following:

> The Islamic Resistance Movement is a link in (a long) chain of the jihad against the Zionist occupation, which is connected and tied with the initiation (of the jihad) of the martyr 'Izz al-Din al-Qassam and his mujahid brothers in 1936.[144]

The portrayal of Hamas' cause as being based on self-defense and as thus 'just' is apparent in the reference to jihad (violence) "against the Zionist occupation." This is also explicit in the following excerpt from Article 15 of the Hamas Charter:

> When an enemy *occupies* some of the Muslim lands, *jihad* becomes *obligatory for every Muslim*. In the *struggle against* the Jewish *occupation* of Palestine, the banner of jihad must be raised ... in the Arab (world) and in the Islamic (world), and that the spirit of jihad—fighting and joining the ranks—must be broadcast among the umma (Muslim community).[145]

What is particularly interesting in the above excerpt is that in addition to presenting its violent actions in terms of a self-defense (as implied in references to struggle against the occupation), Hamas presents any violent jihad for self-defense in terms of transnational obligation of all Muslims. Thus, the above presents violent jihad as 'just' not only in the Palestinian context, but also in any other context where Muslims feel threatened and where therefore self-defense is called for. This, of course, is similar to assertions made by Shaykh Muhammad Husayn Fadallah (who Euben and Zaman note is considered in the west as the spiritual leader of the Lebanese Hizbullah):

> Concerning violence, jihad in Islam is a defensive movement and a deterrent.[146]

Similarly, the commander of *Hezb-ul-Mujahidin*, Syed Salahuddin, describes the *raison d'être* of his group in the following manner:

> Ours is an armed *resistance movement* of all the people of Jammu and Kashmir.[147]

Violence jihad can be seen as framed in terms of a 'just cause' and as self-defense in the following commentary by Egyptian Grand Mufti Sheikh Muhammad Said Tantawi:

> It is the right of all Muslims, Palestinians, and Arabs to blow themselves up in the heart of Israel. *A noble death* is better than a *life of humiliation*. There is *no other way* than the battle, the jihad, and whosoever tries to evade it, is not a believer.[148]

The reference to violence and self-destruction as a 'noble death' frames these acts as a morality and as thus a Just War. The reference to the "right" to engage in such violence seems intended to emphasize justice over a "life of humiliation." That is, violence (in the form of self-destruction) is presented as the 'right' (as moral) over the 'wrong' (tyranny and oppression).

That morality may be defined in consequentialist terms as fighting for one's rights or fighting against tyranny is implicit in the following proclamation of Shaykh Muhammad al-Ghazali. Here, al-Ghazali offers justifications for violence on grounds that subjugation (the 'wrong,' the 'immorality') must be rejected violently, presenting such a violent rejection as the 'right,' the 'good,' the 'morality':

> peace is to be welcomed *when rights are protected* and beliefs respected; but *if peace means abject surrender and subjugation, it cannot be defended on moral or realistic grounds.*[149]

The urgency of self-defense in the calls for violent jihad can also be seen in the following statement of Mohammed Masood Azhar, the leader of Lashkar-e-Toiba:

> Fellow Muslims! We cannot appeal to the unbelievers to assist us, we have to understand that *the annihilation of Muslims is their main purpose and mission*; they are overjoyed upon seeing the free flow of Muslim blood.[150]

The presentation of jihad as self-defense and as thus a 'just cause' is not, of course, limited to the Muslim Arab and South Asian contexts. Such discourse is ubiquitously characteristic of all radical Islamist groups and movements. For example, Sebastian Smith reports a song written by a Chechen fighter in Bamut in April 1995 in which, I argue, the justifications of violence are presented not only in terms of self-defense but as thus based on a 'just cause.' The Chechen fighter asserts:

> We swear to you we'll give our lives
> So the Caucasus may be *free* [from Russian control].
> You [the Chechen fighters] could have stayed at home.
> And looked on *evil* [the Russians] from the sidelines,
> But you come to this land,
> For the *freedom* of this little country.
> You come to this land, you come to *save*
> Chechnya from its *enemies*,
> And today, *you've died for freedom.*[151]

The references in the above to "freedom" and being "free" seem intended to present the self as endangered, especially since it is presented in contrast to the other (the enemy) who is presented as "evil." What is further implied is that the actions of the self are matters of *self-defense* and are thus 'just' and moral.

Supreme emergencies: self-defense and beyond

Michael Walzer argues that the principles of proportionality and discrimination maybe overridden in cases of 'supreme emergencies.' The clauses of 'necessity' and 'supreme emergency' in the Just War doctrine are intended as legal exceptions, if you may, for violating the principles of proportionality and discrimination. These clauses suggest that in cases of 'necessity' (however defined) and 'supreme emergency' (however defined), sovereign state actors may overlook the requirement of using only that amount of force that is absolutely necessary (the 'proportionality' clause) as well as the requirement of sparing innocent civilians and non-combatants (the 'discrimination' clause). In every sense, then, the exceptions of 'necessity' and 'supreme emergency' make legal—and indeed sanction and make 'just'—unbridled brutality. In this way, the Just War doctrine is stretched to the point where any action, including one that employs excessive force and violence and that completely disregards the humanity of the other, can be qualified as 'just' and 'moral' as long as it is argued to be a product of 'necessity' and 'supreme emergency.'

It may be useful to begin the analysis on the most subjective criteria of *jus in bello* (the just conduct during war) with the following fact: "Whereas Aquinas grounded his defense of a relationship between *just ad bellum* and *jus in bello* in right intentions, Grotius insisted that ... the *conduct of war* became the *more powerful normative test*" of whether a war could be judged as just or unjust.[152] Grotius's qualification can be understood in terms of how one of the central tenets of Aquinas' assertions is understood, namely that "going to war to readdress an injury must not be likely to do *more harm* than leaving the injury unaddressed."[153] This principle has come to be understood as the principle of 'proportionality' in the contemporary Just War doctrine and it claims that the use of force during war should be proportional to the nature of the threat and that it should not exceed what is absolutely *the minimum* necessary to achieve one's aims. In other words, disproportionate (or excessive) use of force that has the potential and the likelihood of indiscriminately killing innocent civilians in your enemy's domain are not allowed. The latter stipulation is also understood as the principle of 'discrimination' of the Just War doctrine. Fiala explains the principle of discrimination that of noncombatant immunity based on a "good-faith effort" to avoid "harming noncombatants."[154]

The notion of extreme emergency is interesting in terms of the exceptions to rules that it offers. This notion was originally coined by Churchill in describing the threats facing Britain in 1939.[155] Walzer resurrected this notion in order to justify his assertion that violations of the proportionality and discrimination principle may be allowed in contemporary Just War doctrine in extreme cases.[156] Supreme emergencies, Walzer argues, makes legal and moral both preemptive and preventative wars and broadly allows for the overriding of the rules of war in cases of military necessity. Walzer defines the criteria for the invoking of a supreme emergency as thus:

> Though its use is often ideological, the meaning of the phrase is a matter of common sense. It is defined by two criteria, which correspond to the two levels on which the concept of necessity works: the first has to do with the imminence of the danger and the second with its nature.[157]

With this criteria in mind, Walzer judges the "adoption of a policy of terror bombing [of Nazi Germany] by the leaders of Britain, [where] some 300,000 Germans, most of them civilians, were killed and another 780,000 seriously injured" as an example of a Just War since, according to him, the Nazi regime threatened "human values."[158] However, Walzer criticizes the American President Truman's decision to drop two atomic bombs on the Japanese cities of Hiroshima and Nagasaki because, according to him, this did not qualify as a supreme emergency. Walzer cites as a reason the contradictory assertion offered by President Truman in his justifications for the dropping of the bombs, namely that the Japanese were "fighting an aggressive war." Wars, of course, are always aggressive. This hardly qualifies for a supreme emergency. Walzer criticizes Truman's decision on a second account, that of the claim that the Japanese were "fighting [the war] ... unjustly."[159] To this, Walzer notes the following:

> It is worth noting ... that the [Japanese] raid on [American] Pearl Harbor was directed entirely against naval and army installations ['just' targets according to the Just War doctrine]: only a few stray bombs fell on the city of Honolulu.[160]

Despite Walzer's careful qualifications that relegate what he himself refers to as the 'terror bombing' of Germany as 'just' given the threat of Nazi Germany to "human values," and the 'terror bombing' of Japan as 'unjust' given the nonsensical justifications offered for such an extreme action, there remains one glaring problematic that Walzer fails to consider.[161] If 'we' can declare a supreme emergency to justify our violation of the rules of war, 'they' can also do the same. Holmes brings this criticism to light when he asks "would one be willing to acknowledge the right of Nazi Germany to make such a claim?"[162] Holmes notes that Hitler presented "the German nation (meaning the German people, not the state) as confronting the very kind of threat to its survival and values that Walzer takes to justify supreme emergencies and that Just War theorists almost universally take to constitute a just cause."[163] Holmes' question underscores my point that Walzer's judgments of what does or does not qualify for a Just War tends to be myopic and self-centered.

Holmes' point also underscores my assertion earlier that wars and violence are always presented as just by those engaging in them. This means that the disparity between a just and unjust war is merely theoretical since no entity engaged in war and violence would ever present its actions as 'unjust.' Walzer's stipulation of supreme emergency can thus be understood in realist terms, notes Holmes, where its definition is contingent on national interest.[164] Such logic seems reminiscent of clauses offered to justify violence and destruction in the U.S. Army and Marine Corps *Counterinsurgency Field Manual.* According to Marshall Sahlins, one Lt. Colonel in the counterinsurgency manual asserts the following:

> There will be no peace ... The de facto role of the US armed forces will be to keep the world safe for our economy and open to our cultural assault. *To these ends, we will do a fair amount of killing.* We are building an information-based military to do that killing.[165]

Since 2001, the Americans have described their 'war on terror' in terms of such supreme emergencies, granting themselves somewhat of a carte blanche in any and all actions taken under its banner. The use of the remote controlled predator drones in Afghanistan and the tribal areas of Pakistan is a case in point. Predator drones are justified not only in terms of 'self-defense' (as we saw earlier) but also in terms of extreme emergencies created by the threat and imminence of terrorism. However, a US military officer—who shall remain unnamed here—once noted to me that the use of predator drones to bomb remote tribal areas in Pakistan that target militants but that also kill scores of innocent individuals indeed amounted to "instilling terror" in these areas; but, he boasted, "we'll fight terror with terror."[166] But what then of a similar justification offered by radical Islamist groups of their terrorism? It is naïve to think that exceptions to rules of war may only be invoked by the self and not the other. It is also naïve to think that unbridled actions that are justified by the self as a necessity may not also be justified by the other as such, regardless of whether such justifications are within the parameters of a stated doctrine or not. Ignoring this fact—which I argue applies equally to state and non-state actors—takes us farther away from the understanding of the justifications of violence and brutality, which takes us farther from an understanding of the dynamics of violence. A lack of understanding on both grounds leads only to misguided, and indeed flawed policies intended to combat the threat of violence.[167]

It seems appropriate to conclude this section with Steinhoff's following assertion: "whether an act is one of terrorism or not is a question to be *decided by the act itself*, and *not* with reference to the perpetrator."[168] Steinhoff notes, however, that Bruce Hoffman completely overlooks this critical point. Hoffman asserts instead:

> [such a proposition plays] into the hands of terrorists and their apologists who would argue that there is no difference between the 'low tech' terrorist pipe-bomb placed in the rubbish bin at a crowded market ... and the 'high tech' precision-guided ordnance dropped by air force fighter-bombers from a height of 20,000 feet or more that achieves the same wanton and indiscriminate effect on the crowded market-place far below.[169]

If international law prohibits indiscriminate killing of civilians, then surely this stipulation applies to *state* as well as non-state actors. Steinhoff offers a similar rebuttal to Hoffman in the following:

> But in fact, whoever does *not* apply a double standard [as those implied in considering actions of a non-state actor as terrorism but actions resulting in similar indiscriminate killing of civilians by a state actor as not terrorism] plays only into the hands of objectivity and universalism, whereas Hoffman himself plays into the hands of partisanship and state terrorism.[170]

In addition, one might also counter Hoffman's assertion by arguing that "high tech' precision-guided ordnance dropped by air force fighter-bombers from a height of 20,000 feet" has the potential of even a *greater* scale of destruction. In other words, a "precision-guided" bomb dropped from a "height of 20,000 feet" has the physics of momentum on its side, causing a far more destructive outcome than that which results from a "pipe-bomb placed in the rubbish bin."[171] Hoffman's assertions bring to light another peculiarity which reflects a popular mentality of American audiences regarding the morality of violence. This peculiarity is most poignantly brought to light by Vicki Divoll (former CIA lawyer and lecturer at the U.S. Naval Academy in Annapolis) in her following observation: "People are a lot more comfortable with a Predator strike that kills many people than with a throat-slitting that kills one." But she added, "mechanized killing is still killing."[172]

Supreme emergencies in the radical Islamist rhetoric

Much as in the internationally accepted Just War doctrine, 'necessity' of self-defense is often presented in radical Islamist rhetoric as negating all other moral principles; here, as elsewhere, consequentialist reason takes over deontological reason. Thus, 'necessity' of action that violates the safety of non-combatants is explained in terms of the outcomes of a 'supreme emergency' wherein actions that would otherwise be considered immoral are now considered moral. This can be seen in article 121 in Faraj's pamphlet entitled "The permissibility of attacking the infidels at night and firing at them even if it leads to killing their dependents."[173] Such a qualification, which ultimately invalidates the courtesy of 'discrimination,' is not unlike the qualifications offered by scholars of the internationally accepted Just War doctrine for the violations of the principle of discrimination.[174] Indeed, in his pamphlet *The Neglected Duty*, Faraj in fact allows for the targeting of noncombatants in the following situations:

> when they [those targeting the noncombatants] *do not do it on purpose* [thus implying a 'double-effect' of self-defense] without *need for it* [thus implying a 'necessity' or a 'supreme emergency'].[175]

The notion of necessity, as such therefore, narrows the parameters of what are considered 'innocent civilians' or 'noncombatants' and broadens the definition of 'aggressor.' To take the example of Faraj's pamphlet *The Neglected Duty* again, Faraj defines an 'infidel' as not only that non-Muslim foreign aggressor, but also the unrepresentative Muslim leader (head of government) that has become an 'infidel' because he has become unrepresentative of the Muslim people.

On the matter of necessity, let us first consider Hezbollah's reason. Hizbullah has long justified Jihadi violence in terms of the *necessity* of defense.[176] In discussing the issue of targeting Israeli civilians, the founding member of Hizbu'llah, Naim Qassem noted the following:

> How should the Palestinians react in self-defense? There is no alternative to resistance activity that targets first and foremost the Israeli military. But where these members of the military alienate themselves from the battle domain and

seek refuge in village and towns behind a shield of civilians, and when Israeli settlers continue to murder and aggress, thus turning the Israeli civilian population into a form of military, then *the target becomes this society of militants.*[177]

The above is remarkable for a number of reasons. First, in citing 'self-defense' it implies a 'necessity.' Second, in portraying the threat as emanating from both the Israeli military as well as the Israeli settlers, it portrays the threat as much larger than one that is concentrated to a uniformed entity (namely the Israeli military). This can be seen in the reference to the Israelis as comprising a "society of militants." Such references not only create a sense of emergency, but they inevitability override the courtesy of discrimination since the scope of threat is presented as much larger and nebulous in nature. The implication here is that the protection of Israeli civilians—as would be expected in the notion of discrimination—is de facto the protection of the Israeli military, the very entity that threatens the self.

What is most interesting here is that Qassem's assertions, that essentially override the principle of discrimination, are not unlike the justifications offered by American military command in its use of the unmanned predator drones that are known to kill militants along with scores of innocent civilians. The oft-repeated justification of such atrocities is that the 'militants hide amongst the civilians.' Notwithstanding the fact that such justifications are not theoretically acceptable as violations either of the proportionality principle or the discrimination principle in the Just War doctrine, it is important to note that such justifications are nonetheless commonly dispensed. And, even more notable, they are common not only in radical Islamist rhetoric but also in the rhetorical apologies of civilian causalities on the part of the American–NATO contingencies in Afghanistan, and on the part of the broader western and non-western state entities.

Osama bin Laden's justifications of violent jihad as last resort or a necessity is also notable here:

> [Violent] Jihad is part of our religion. *Is there another way to drive away infidels?* Those who sympathize with the infidels, such as the PLO in Palestine, or the so-called Palestinian Authority, have been trying for tens of years to get back some of their rights, and they laid down their arms and abandoned what is called 'violence' these days and ran after peaceful bargaining but what did the Jews give them? They did not give them even one per cent of their rights.[178]

The reference in the above to "jihad is part of our religion" in the context of the justifications for violence seems intended to give the message that unleashing violence and destruction upon the "infidels" (the enemy that threatens the self) is the *duty* of all Muslims and therefore an obligation, a 'morality,' and indeed a necessity. The necessity seems implied in his assertion "is there another way to drive away infidels?" The connection here seems to be between 'necessity' creating an obligation in much the same way as morality implies obligation. Thus if necessity leads to violence then violence must be a 'morality,' a 'Just War.'

Essence, motivations, and flawed policies

...nalysis thus far has challenged the orientalist assertion that Islamist extrem-...an be explained in terms of an inevitable clash between the Judeo-Christian ...and the Islamic world, an assertion that is popularly understood as the ...-of-civilizations.' The proclaimed inevitability of conflict between these ...orlds is premised on a number of related assertions, such as the claim that ...lamic world is uniquely barbaric and, further, prone to violence due to ...s born of jealousies of the western world. However, critical analysis of ...l Islamist rhetoric in this book has revealed that violence is instead ...ned by the radical Islamists in terms of a rejection of the negation of the ...d justified in terms of consequentialist reason that makes moral all actions ...for the ends of the rejection of the negation of the self. Such findings point ...existential nature of reason in radical Islamist rhetoric (both in its rejection ...ation and in its moral consequentialism) which stands in sharp contrast to ...ientalist narrative that such reason is grounded in an inherently violent dis-...on and a hatred for the other simply because of who the other is (the other ...the Judeo-Christian world or the 'western' world). For example, Michael ...n, a leading neoconservative and a former consultant to the United States ...al Security Council, asserts that "[t]he tyrants [Islamist extremists] hate ...ited States for *what it is*, not for *what it does*."[1]

...nay be that the radical Islamists hate the United States for "what it is," but ...so most certainly that they hate the United States for what it is *perceived* ...ng. It is this perception that is all too often ignored by neo-conservative ...al pundits and popular western media in their analysis of Islamist extrem-...his leads to simplistic and dichotomous answers to the question of 'why ...y do this?' as simply 'because they hate us for who we are.' But under-...ng 'why do they do this?' requires a critical analysis of reason presented ...ical Islamists in their explanations and justifications of violence. Such ..., I have argued, portrays the self as engaged in a Hegelian life-and-death ...e for recognition, which then creates a perception of the other (the west) ...oppressive master intent on keeping the self (the Muslim world and ...ns) in subjugation, much as a Hegelian slave. Thus, most critically, servi-...umiliation, and subjugation become presented in radical Islamist rhetoric ...rely as the consequences of western policies but *as the intention* of such

Osama bin Laden's very questioning of the immorality implied in the term 'violence'—as apparent in his statement "what is called 'violence' these days"—is thus most striking in this context as it seems intended to redefine 'morality' and 'immorality' in light of a necessity of self-defense. That the failures of the Palestinian Authority (and the PLO before that) are simplistically explained in the context of their abandonment of violence—ignoring other important variables of failure such as the complex internal Palestinian political dynamics and complex historical Palestinian–Israeli equations—seem further intended to highlight violence as a prerequisite of self-defense and as a necessity. Thus, not only is violence justified as a *necessity* but its very immorality is brought into question, thereby reversing the equation of violence as an immorality.

The notion of necessity also redefines the meaning of 'defensive measures' and the meaning of 'aggressors,' both of which become very broadly defined which further serves to justifies violence in terms of a 'morality.' In radical Islamist rhetoric, defense of the self does not just mean an immediate self-defense but also defense of a people (the ummah if you may) against the negation of the 'self' (defined collectively) and against the continued servitude of the self even when the latter does not entail an immediate threat to the life of the self. In this way, not only does violent self-defense become a 'morality' but violent life-and-death struggles for recognition, broadly speaking, become an imperative (a duty) and a virtue (a morality). So violent and self-destructive jihad ('martyrdom') becomes presented as challenging the servitude of the 'self' (collectively defined) and in this way self-destruction becomes presented as the 'morality' (the pursuit of the recognition of the self) over the 'immorality' (the negation of the self). Much as in Honneth's analysis, the 'good' (morality) becomes defined as challenging the servitude of the self and the 'bad' (immorality) becomes defined as the servitude of the self very subjectively and broadly speaking.

Along these lines, the justifications of violence in radical Islamist rhetoric portray the 'aggressors' as not only those that directly oppress Muslims, but also those that are indirectly complicit through their associations with the aggressors. For example, radical Islamists in Pakistan came to view President Musharraf as a traitor, an aggressor and even an infidel based on his alliance with the United States (considered by most radical Islamists as the oppressor). As well, in his justification of the destruction of civilians (non-aggressors by conventional standards) in suicide missions, Yusuf al-Qaradawi (Al-Jazeera's TV cleric) argues that *all* Israelis are 'aggressors' since "Israel is in its very essence is a military society" and all men, women and children that ultimately serve in the military become tools of the oppressive Israeli military machinery and are thus guilty by association and thereby legitimate targets.[179] Broad definition of 'aggressors' can also be seen in bin Laden's statements in 1999:

> The Saudi government sent several delegations to negotiate with me in Sudan to convince me to keep silent on the *unjust* American *occupation* of Saudi Arabia. We [the erstwhile Taliban and al-Qaeda] rejected these attempts ... I would ... like to add that our primary targets are the world's

infidels, and then *by necessity* those regimes in Islamic countries which have become *tools* of the infidels.[180]

Here again, not only is American military presence presented as an aggressive and unjust 'occupation,' the Saudi government is painted as the collaborator for the American aggression and thus, 'by necessity,' the necessary target of the al-Qaeda and the *International Islamic Front*—a jihadi anti-American and anti-Israeli jihadi movement inspired by bin Laden. An even broader reference to complicit Muslim governments can be seen in bin Laden's following allegation:

> The Muslim countries today are colonized. Colonialism is either direct or veiled … masking colonialism … is exactly what happened in Afghanistan when the United States occupied that country and installed an Afghan agent, Hamid Karzai … There is no difference between the Karzai of Yemen, the Karzai of Pakistan, the Karzai of Jordan, the Karzai of Qatar, the Karzai of Kuwait, the Karzai of Egypt, and the long list of Karzai traitors ruling the Muslim countries.[181]

It is interesting to note that the radical Islamist notion of necessity is not defined as an imperative in its own right, but it is seen instead as a recourse to oppression and subjugation. That martyrdom as embodied in suicide missions indiscriminately kills innocent women, children and the elderly—an immorality in the deontological sense—is thus often glossed over or justified in utilitarian/ consequentialist terms as necessity for the ends of struggles against servitude.

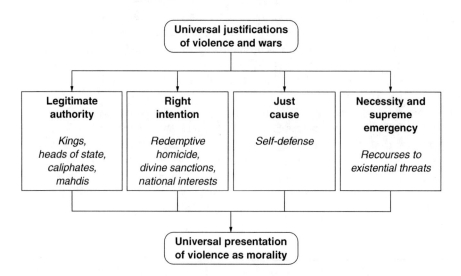

Figure 4.1 The universality of consequentialist justifications of violence.

Such selective reasoning can be seen in the following justification of Palestinian suicide bombers offered by the Islamic cleric Yusuf al-Qaradawi:

> These operations ... [suicide bombers] are the *highest form of jihad* and most certainly permitted by the Shari'a [Islamic law] ... a person who becomes a martyr sacrifices himself for the faith and the nation ... if a child or an old person is killed ... then its not intentional but an oversight; a mistake for reasons of military necessity. *Necessity justifies what is forbidden.*[182]

Most striking in the above is the reference to violent jihad as the "highest form" of jihad, which seems to reverse the order of what is meant by 'greater' jihad versus the 'lesser' jihad, an interpretation that is quite contrary to the reformist understanding of 'greater' and 'lesser' jihad.

Conclusion

Radical Islamists justify violence by presenting it as a morality. But, I argue, the presentation of violence as a morality is not a reflection of a *uniquely* barbaric Islamic religious and cultural milieu but a reflection instead of the universality of the instrumentality of religion and of the consequentialism in struggles for recognition. I refer here to Axel Honneth's contention that all struggles for recognition are framed in moral consequentialist terms, and Friedrich Nietzsche's assertion that notions of morality (including morality framed in religious terms) are contingent on struggles for self-assertion (the 'will-to-power') and are there-fore consequentialist in nature. The radical Islamist contextualization of violence within Islamic religious tenets is thus, I argue, a tactic to disguise consequential-ist reason (struggles for recognition) in deontological (religious) terms. Indeed, I show that not only are radical Islamist justifications of violence consequentialist in nature, but that such consequentialist justifications of violence are *conceptu-ally* similar to the justifications of violence found in the internationally accepted Just War doctrine. This substantiates my assertion that justifications for violent actions are always consequentialist in nature even when they are presented in deontological terms (that is, contextualized within religious tenets as in the case of radical Islamist rhetoric) and therefore the radical Islamist contextualization of violence is not a reflection of a uniquely barbaric religious context. The glaring implication of this is that it readdresses the paradox of the secular volun-tary recruits of Islamist extremist groups since I argue that the fundamental *nature of reason* in radical Islamist rhetoric is *not Islamic* but moral consequen-tialist. Thus, it is *not* calls to religious duty but the framing of violent actions in terms of a consequentialist morality that resonates with its voluntary recruits. And such moral consequentialism is theoretically expected in all struggles for recognition since such struggles are driven by the expected consequences of actions, namely the desire for recognition of the self as distinct and equally significant to the other (and as thus not inferior to the other).

5 Essence, motivations, and flawed policies

My analysis thus far has challenged the orientalist assertion that Islamist extremism can be explained in terms of an inevitable clash between the Judeo-Christian world and the Islamic world, an assertion that is popularly understood as the 'clash-of-civilizations.' The proclaimed inevitability of conflict between these two worlds is premised on a number of related assertions, such as the claim that the Islamic world is uniquely barbaric and, further, prone to violence due to hatreds born of jealousies of the western world. However, critical analysis of radical Islamist rhetoric in this book has revealed that violence is instead explained by the radical Islamists in terms of a rejection of the negation of the self and justified in terms of consequentialist reason that makes moral all actions taken for the ends of the rejection of the negation of the self. Such findings point to the existential nature of reason in radical Islamist rhetoric (both in its rejection of negation and in its moral consequentialism) which stands in sharp contrast to the orientalist narrative that such reason is grounded in an inherently violent disposition and a hatred for the other simply because of who the other is (the other being the Judeo-Christian world or the 'western' world). For example, Michael Ledeen, a leading neoconservative and a former consultant to the United States National Security Council, asserts that "[t]he tyrants [Islamist extremists] hate the United States for *what it is*, not for *what it does*."[1]

It may be that the radical Islamists hate the United States for "what it is," but it is also most certainly that they hate the United States for what it is *perceived as doing*. It is this perception that is all too often ignored by neo-conservative political pundits and popular western media in their analysis of Islamist extremism. This leads to simplistic and dichotomous answers to the question of 'why do they do this?' as simply 'because they hate us for who we are.' But understanding 'why do they do this?' requires a critical analysis of reason presented by radical Islamists in their explanations and justifications of violence. Such reason, I have argued, portrays the self as engaged in a Hegelian life-and-death struggle for recognition, which then creates a perception of the other (the west) as the oppressive master intent on keeping the self (the Muslim world and Muslims) in subjugation, much as a Hegelian slave. Thus, most critically, servitude, humiliation, and subjugation become presented in radical Islamist rhetoric not merely as the consequences of western policies but *as the intention* of such policies.[2] This perception is then used to present violence as a necessity using consequentialist reason that defines an individual's responsibility in terms of challenging the oppression of the self by all means possible.[3] In this way, if the west is *perceived* as subjugating the self for the ends of its own domination, then "what it does" (military occupations, however justified) becomes equated to "what it is" (a ruthless master who acts with impunity).

In contrast to the popular 'clash-of-civilizations' narrative stands a counter-narrative; consider, for example, Graham E. Fuller's assertion that a 'world without Islam' would *not* be any less violent than it is today since it is not Islam (as specific to a cultural context) that forms the bases of violent conflicts but territorial disputes and the rejection of occupations.[4] In this book, I have argued further that the essence of Islamist extremism is not *only* a rejection of foreign occupations, but a rejection of *all forms* of oppression that result in the negation of the self; such negation of the self may be at the hands of a foreign entity or at the hands of one's own government or at the hands of the sectarian other (Shia or Sunni). However, such a counter-narrative is unlikely to easily penetrate the dogma of the western meta-narratives. Beyond misunderstanding the essence of Islamist extremism (as reasoned in radical Islamist rhetoric itself), meta-narratives of a clash-of-civilizations lead to a misunderstanding of the nature of the motivations of individuals that voluntarily join Islamist extremist groups. This misunderstanding leads further to a misunderstanding of the nature of the resilience of Islamist extremism. And a misunderstanding on both these accounts leads only to misguided and ill-suited policies that are intended to combat the threat of Islamist extremism but that only exacerbate its threat.

Examples of misunderstanding the essence of Islamist extremism are ample. For example, in analyzing the jihadi and sectarian violence in Iraq in the aftermath of the American occupation of Iraq in 2003, David Frum criticizes former President G.W. Bush for his supposed optimism that democracy could be introduced in Iraq. Such a statement, of course, critically overlooks the elephant in the room. To put it in other word, that democracy should be introduced using military force and military occupation is an acute contradiction in terms. The concept of democracy is, after all, liberal and as such opposed to any use of force and oppression; indeed, democracy as a concept is by definition the opposite of oppression.[5] Leaving this irony aside, Frum goes on to quote Huntington as having once warned that "in the Arab world ... Western democracy strengthens anti-Western political forces."[6] This implies that no matter what good the west does for the Muslim world, it will get only ingratitude, hatred, and violence in return because of the inevitable clash of fundamental values and hatred for the west for what it is. Indeed, Frum concludes that "Islam really is inherently hostile to democracy and the West."[7] Such assessments are critically misguided since they fail to understand the nature of the problem at hand. Samuel Huntington might have been correct in his assertion that the new post Cold War threat to western security would emanate from the Muslim world, but he was critically wrong in his assumptions of the *reasons why* such a threat would come from the

Muslim world. Huntington wrongly assumed that the nature of this threat is a 'clash-of-civilizations' when in essence, as I've illustrated in this book, the nature of this threat is instead an existential rejection of the oppression of the self (whether actual or perceived, at the hands of one's own government or at the hands of a foreign entity).[8]

Critical analysis of radical Islamist rhetoric points to a conclusion contrary to that which is forwarded by David Frum. Indeed, it shows that it is *not* that the 'anti-western political forces' (to use Frum's words) in the Muslim world reflect a 'Muslim' aversion to all that is western, culminating in a rejection of democracy and freedom for the sake of the rejection of democracy and freedom. It is instead that violence in radical Islamist rhetoric is explained in terms of an aversion to the *manner* in which democracy is introduced: through military means and unapologetic occupations. Since 2001, US foreign policy has embraced the objective of 'democracy promotion,' especially in the Middle East, "as antidote to international terrorism."[9] But this promotion of democracy has tended to be through military means and physical occupation of the host states. As a result, 'democracy promotion' has come to be understood in radical Islamist rhetoric as meaning *the freedom of the West to do as it wishes*, unbridled and unchallenged. The radical Islamist explanations of violence then become presented in terms of the rejection of Western 'democracy' on grounds of its oppressive nature. Not surprisingly, the anti-American Iraqi extremist group *Islamic State of Iraq* (ISI) presents the American military presence in Iraq as reflective of a classic American hegemonic oppression that is only masquerading as 'freedom' and 'democracy' for Iraq. Scandals of torture and humiliation of *suspected* Iraqi anti-American insurgents by the American soldiers at the Abu-Gharib prison in 2003, and similar abuses of *suspected* Afghani Taliban at the hands of the American soldiers at Bagram US Air Force detention camp in Afghanistan, have only served as fodder for radical Islamist rhetoric.[10] Such incidences then get presented as evidence of the nefarious intentions of the western masters (in this case, the American–NATO contingencies in Afghanistan) to subjugate and domesticate the self (the Muslims).

Bruce Hoffman has argued that "defeating al Qaeda" in Iraq would require new strategies "anchored firmly to sound, empirical judgment and not blinded by conjecture, mirror-imaging, politically partisan prisms and wishful thinking."[11] While this assessment offers some hope as it points to the importance of understanding the *nature of the motivations* of those that join al-Qaeda, it stops short of a critical understanding of the *essence* of Islamist extremism. For example, Hoffman goes on to argue that the success of these new strategies would depend on "systematically destroying and weakening enemy capabilities alongside the equally critical ... imperatives of countering the continued *resonance* of the radical's message ... that has sustained and replenished al Qaeda."[12] Ironically, however, understanding the anti-American insurgency in Iraq (whether fueled by al-Qaeda's rhetoric or the rhetoric of the Shia *al-Mahdi* army or the many Sunni anti-occupation militias) in terms of the "enemy" takes us farther away from an accurate understanding of the 'resonance of the radical's message' (to use

Hoffman's words) in Iraq or elsewhere. This is because 'enemy' implies a threat to the self (in this case, the Americans) and thus a subsequent need for the unbridled 'defense' of the self.[13] In such an understanding, the self is the hero and the 'other' is the entity of aggression, categorically speaking (in this case, the Islamist extremists). But such an understanding completely ignores the critical reason for the resonance of radical Islamist rhetoric, based as it is on the presentation of the Americans or western entities (the 'self') as the aggressors and the occupiers. The resonance of the rhetoric is the existential reason with which occupation and oppression is rejected.[14] In other words, if 'we' (the self) see ourselves as being on the defensive, the other (the anti-American groups and movements) also sees itself as being on the defense. In this way, unbridled violence is presented in radical Islamist rhetoric as the heroism needed to fight aggression, much in the same way that unbridled American military operations in Iraq or Afghanistan are presented as heroic, defensive measures, despite the fact that they are over 10 years removed from the initial defensive reaction that was universally considered as legitimate.

The problem in understanding the resilience of radical Islamist rhetoric can then be situated in the impasse of perceptions; or, if you may, in the parallel lines of logic by which the self and the other understands 'reality.' In other words, a dichotomous understanding of the self as always the 'victim' and the 'hero' and the other as categorically the 'aggressor' and the 'terrorist' obscures an understanding of the *perceptions* of the other. Perceptions of what 'reality' is play a critical role in the motivations for action. Dichotomous understanding of the self versus the other leads not only to a misunderstanding of the essence of violence—which I have argued is Hegelian in its explanations and consequentialist in its justifications—but, worse, to a misunderstanding of the essence of Islamist extremism and to thus misguided policies intended to combat its threat. An accurate understanding of the essence of violence might benefit from a dialectical understanding of violence, that is, where violence has a reciprocal causality.[15] Such an understanding necessities a discarding of the reductionist explanations of violence, such as those encapsulated in the notion of a clash-of-civilizations, and an understanding of violence as instead an action–reaction dynamic.

With this in mind, it becomes clear that Bernard Lewis wrongly concludes that Islamist extremism is motivated by a desire for supremacy, if by that is meant a desire unique to the radical Islamist context. If the desire for supremacy can be said to motivate the radical Islamists, the same can be said to motivate the western entities in their many military engagements in the Middle East. I have argued in this book that Islamist extremism is a Hegelian rejection of oppression (whether actual or perceived). And to the extent that such a rejection is the rejection of the self as the slave, it can be argued that such a rejection is also inherently a desire for supremacy, a desire to see the self as the master. After all, in Hegel's analysis of the primordial life-and-death struggles for recognition, competing self-consciousnesses (the competing beings) are motivated by the fear of servitude and a desire for recognition through domination. This, Hegel argues, is existential and thus universal to the human existence. Such desires can hardly be seen as distinctly *Islamic* in nature, as Lewis argues.

This chapter examines two major implications of a misunderstanding of the essence of Islamist extremism: (1) a misunderstanding of the motivations of individuals that voluntarily take part in violence and self-destruction; and (2) a support for flawed policies designed to combat the threat of Islamist extremism but that only exacerbate its threat. I argue in this chapter that the nature of reason in radical Islamist rhetoric (which I have argued reflects a Hegelian struggle for recognition that is justified in moral consequentialist terms) shapes the nature of the motivations of individuals that voluntarily join Islamist extremist groups. In this assertion, I draw upon epistemological assumptions that relate reason (in radical Islamist rhetoric) to knowledge of 'reality' (or circumstances), and logical deductions that connect knowledge of 'reality' to perceptions of 'reality' and thus motivations for action. This means that if the nature of reason in radical Islamist rhetoric is Hegelian and consequentialist, one can expect that the nature of the motivations of individuals that are attracted to violent action based on such reason in rhetoric will be equally Hegelian and consequentialist. This has critical implications for the nature of the American policies of 'war on terrorism' since such policies are primarily premised on either a direct military occupation of countries in question (such as Iraq, Afghanistan) or on the use of aggressive firepower (such as through the use of predator drones in the northern areas of Pakistan), both of which are vehemently criticized in radical Islamist rhetoric as both giving rise to the deaths of innocent civilians and as violating the sovereignty of Pakistani air and land space. And if the essence of Islamist extremism is a rejection of oppression (whether actual or perceived, direct or indirect), then such policies only reinforce the recruiting rhetoric of Islamist extremist groups, both in their explanations of violence and in their justifications of violence. I elaborate this contention in the last section of this chapter.

From radical Islamist rhetoric to an individual's motivations

Fanaticism, argues R.M. Hare, does *not* reflect an absence of reason; it reflects instead an *unbridled devotion* to reason. And this, Hare argues, also applies to a 'fanatical terrorist,' as he explains in the following:

> The fanatical terrorist is a person who attaches so much importance to some ideal that he is prepared to prescribe that he himself should be murdered, kidnapped, tortured, etc., if it were necessary in order to advance the cause which he has embraced. He is *not* seeking self-centered ends—indeed the true fanatic is the most unselfish and self-sacrificing of people.[16]

Hare's above assertion can be used to understand the motivations of individuals that voluntarily join Islamist extremist groups and that take part in violence and self-destruction. These individuals are, then, not 'fanatics' in the sense of irrational persons devout of reason (as popularly understood, particularly by western neoconservatives); these individuals are instead 'fanatics' in the sense of their *unquestioned devotion to reason*, reason being that which is presented in terms of the explanations and justifications of violence in radical Islamist rhetoric. The connection between reason in radical Islamist rhetoric and individuals' motivations for violence and self-destruction can be understood in light of epistemological assumptions and logical deductions.[17] In this section, I draw upon Kantian epistemological assumptions as encapsulated in his notion of transcendental idealism, as well as logical deductions as those related to the philosophy of logic.[18]

In its most fundamental sense, Kant's transcendental idealism is a notion that reason, as opposed to experience alone, *can* add something new to our knowledge of a thing. This, Kant argues, is because reason (cognitive variable) systemizes and categorizes experience (sensory variable), thereby presenting (or understanding) experience in a certain light. Knowledge of that experience is thus shaped by one's reason that frames experience in a certain way. So while reason alone can be argued to be insufficient for knowledge, experience alone is also insufficient in forming knowledge of a thing. I argue here that reason in radical Islamist rhetoric presents that reason that categorizes and systemizes experience. In other words, reason in radical Islamist rhetoric can be seen as providing for its audiences a framework of interpretation, that is, a particular framework to understand experience. In this way, knowledge of 'reality' on the part of the individuals that comprise the audiences of Islamist extremist groups is based on the reason in radical Islamist rhetoric.[19] Knowledge in turn creates perceptions of reality, which then determines the motivations to engage in violence for individuals that voluntarily join Islamist extremist groups.

A brief explanatory note on the meaning of 'experience' is in order here since the notion of 'experience' concerns all epistemologists, whether those empiricists that argue that experience is central to knowledge or those rationalists that argue that it is not. Anil Gupta argues that 'experience,' in its philosophical and epistemological sense, can mean a variety of things; from events that you observe, to things or actions that directly impact you, to even historical narratives that you are exposed to. Fundamentally, Gupta argues that anything presented as an 'experience' has a "what it is like" quality to it.[20] Even more significantly, Gupta argues that any experience is perceived by the one experiencing it as being objective when actually all experience is subjective. For example, Gupta gives the example of the experience of visiting temples in Nepal; the temples are indeed an objective existence but what this experience means to the observer (how the temples are viewed by, perceived by, or impact on the observer) is decidedly subjective. It appears from this that what Gupta is saying is that a large part of experience is based on what we think (or perceive or believe) we saw. Experience is thus interpreted subjectively. What is most interesting in Gupta's assertion that 'experience' may take the form of historical narratives is that such 'experience'—experience of others that preceded you, as recorded in history books—is actually 'experience' based on reason (namely, history as recorded). This means that knowledge based on 'experience' need not be firsthand. Knowledge based on 'experience' may be knowledge based on someone else's firsthand experience, that someone whose experiences you consider to be valid and legitimate enough to inform your knowledge of a thing. Such epistemological logic thus sheds light on the paradox of the motivations of those individuals that voluntarily join Islamist extremist groups but that have not *themselves* experienced events that could explain their motivation for violence (such as economically privileged individuals or individuals spatially removed from the 'realities on the ground'—such as occupations—to which to they are willing to react). Such epistemological logic therefore sheds light on the importance of understanding the nature of reason in radical Islamist rhetoric since such reason presents an experience to which it then argues an action must be taken. Reason in radical Islamist rhetoric, then, at once shapes the knowledge of 'reality' for its audiences, as well as their perceptions and motivations for violent actions. Understanding the nature of reason in radical Islamist rhetoric is thus critical to understanding the nature of the motivations of individuals that take part in radical Islamist action.

From reason to knowledge, from knowledge to motivations

In attempting to delineate motivations of individuals based on reason in radical Islamist rhetoric, I draw upon the rationalist epistemological perspective (not to be confused with the 'rational choice' paradigm of comparative politics). This epistemological school of thought, which competes with the empiricist school of thought, argues that knowledge of a thing can be based on reason alone. Epistemological rationalists, then, place a significant importance on our cognitive functions which are the bases of reason. Knowledge, then, does not *require* actual experience (sensory input) of the thing whose knowledge is in question. So, for example, the 'knowledge' of God according to rationalists is not based on any actual sensory or visual (actual) experience of God but based instead on the *reason* (extrapolative logic if you may) that God *must* exist for X or Y to have happened. In sharp contrast, the empiricists believe that knowledge of a thing can *only* be attained through the actual experience of a thing and that in fact there can be no 'real' knowledge without sensory or visual (actual) experience of it. In this case, the empiricists might give us an example of the necessity of actual experience (sensory data) of having a limb blown off in military combat in order to gain the *knowledge* of the *exact* nature of the sensory (physical) pain as a result.

There are, of course, many variations in the specific formulations of rationalism (focusing on reason) and empiricism (focusing on experience) that form the two major schools of thought in epistemology. Despite these variations and nuances, both are known for their characteristic assumptions. For example, all empiricists (in sharp contrast to rationalists) deny the possibility of *synthetic a priori* knowledge, that is, "knowledge that is both informative about the world and also knowable *independent* of experience due to the mode of function of the human mind."[21] Or, to put it in other words, knowledge that is based on the use of reason (thus *a priori*) but that also adds something new to the understanding of a thing (thus synthetic) but that which is independent of experience. Empiricists believe *only* in the possibility of *synthetic a posteriori* knowledge, or knowledge gained from experience (thus a posteriori) and that thus adds something new to the knowledge of a thing (thus synthetic).[22] Or to put it most simplistically, empiricists believe only in the possibility of *a posteriori* knowledge, that is, judgment or knowledge that has to be "known from experience."[23] In contrast, all rationalists agree that knowledge *can* be attained through *reason alone* and that therefore the experience of a thing is not necessary. As such, rationalists argue that we can have knowledge of a 'non-empirical reality,' a reality we may be able to see but whose knowledge is based on reason and not sensory (tangible) input or experience. Such knowledge, rationalists argue, yields knowledge that subsequently does *not* need to be *empirically proved* or demonstrated given that its validity is based on reason that has made its knowledge possible. In other words, knowledge of a thing that is based on reason need not require sensory or visual experience to substantiate it, nor require empirical evidence (demonstrations through experience) to prove it. The outcome of course is *a priori* knowledge, that is, knowledge based on reason.

As might be expected, a priori knowledge yields 'analytical truths,' that is, 'truths' or judgments whose "predicate is contained in the concept of the subject" and that is delineated through reason.[24] Another way of understanding this is how Kant understood it, namely, a "conceptual connection ... [where] one concept is contained in another."[25] To put it simply, an analytical truth is that 'truth' or knowledge that is logically *implied* within a statement, or something that is implied within the definition of something. For example, the foreign 'occupation' of one's land implies by definition oppression, injustice, and the use of force; the latter three are therefore analytical truths of a military occupation. Let us take another example, "when we say that a moon is a satellite of a planet, we are not reporting the results of an astronomical discovery, but explaining the meaning of a term [namely, the meaning of moon]."[26] In other words, the "truth or falsity" of this statement can be judged or "established by purely deductive reasoning."[27] Such sentences are thus not only "analytic but *a prior*," that is, sentences that are rich with implications and that are based on reason and that add to our knowledge of a thing.[28]

In addressing epistemological questions (questions related to the knowledge of a thing), Kant disagreed, in part, with both the empiricists and the rationalists. Kant's criticism of empiricism was based on its central *unwavering* tenet that all knowledge must *absolutely* "come from experience."[29] His criticism of this view was based on his own assertion that *reason* can indeed *add* something new to empirical knowledge (knowledge based on experience) and so not all knowledge need absolutely be based on experience alone since reason too plays a part in shaping (categorizing and systemizing) experience. Kant thus saw the pure empiricism of Locke and Hume as leading only to *skepticism* as it denied the possibility of "everyday 'commonsense' knowledge," knowledge that is *necessarily* based on reason.[30] Kant found arguments of the possibility *only* of a posteriori knowledge (knowledge based on experience) as limiting because he believed in the *possibility* of *synthetic a priori* knowledge, that is, knowledge based on intuitions, reason, and 'common sense' that add something new to the knowledge of a thing (beyond the experience of that thing). To put it simply, Kant acknowledged that while knowledge often is *initially* based on experience (sensory data, observations[31]) he disagreed with the empiricists in their negation of the impact of reason in the knowledge of a thing.

To be sure, Kant also objected to pure rationalism and categorically rejected the rationalist claim that knowledge can be based entirely or solely on reason *alone* and it is this that he set out to debunk in his *Critique of Pure Reason*, namely that "traditional metaphysics is impossible."[32] To Kant, knowledge based on reason *alone*—such as 'knowledge' of God—was *not* knowledge in the true sense of the word (as it was not substantiated or supplemented to *some degree* with actual experience) but was knowledge based on mere beliefs (sentiments). Indeed, it is important to underscore the point that Kant's disagreement with the empiricists was based on the *extent* to which experience determines knowledge and not on the (empiricist) assumption that experience is necessary. We might understand from this that while some experience is indeed necessary, *reason plays an equally important part in shaping the knowledge of the thing that we have experienced.* In other words, one uses reason to systemize and categorize one's experience in a certain manner to then understand that experience as knowledge of a thing. In the case of our current analysis, we can understand 'reason' as that rhetoric in radical Islamist discourse that presents the experience of occupations or the oppression of the self in a certain light. This then creates the knowledge for its audiences which, in turn, can then be said to be both empirical and rational; empirical since occupations are not imaginary, and rational since how occupations are portrayed (for example, the intentions behind such harsh military tactics) are matters of reason and interpretation. This assertion may be seen as similar to Kant's theory of knowledge, which can be seen as comprising components of both empiricism and rationalism.

It is within such an understanding of Kant's epistemological views that we can understand his notion of *transcendental idealism.*[33] A critical point is in order here. The notion of the 'transcendental' must not be confused with 'transcendent,' as notes Mohanty.[34] While 'transcendent' means 'to go beyond' something, 'transcendental' refers instead to the cognitive functions (that is, refers to reason) that makes knowledge possible.[35] Thus, notes Mohanty, the notion of *transcendental* in the Kantian (or Husserlian) senses does *not* imply transcending (going beyond or excluding) the empirical (experience) in the knowledge of a thing. Indeed, that knowledge can be based on reason alone is a belief that Kant criticized in his *Critique of Pure Reason* as noted earlier. Transcendental (in Kant's transcendental idealism) refers instead to "that which constitutes and thereby renders the empirical possible."[36] In other words, "while it is usual to contrast the transcendental [a priori] with the empirical [physical experience], *that* is *not* the fundamental contrast" since 'transcendental' for Kant is but an "*a priori condition* of the possibility of empirical cognition ... the transcendental ... [thus] explains how any cognition ... is possible."[37] Or to put it in other words still, Kantian *transcendental idealism* examines how reason systemizes and categorizes experience (sensory data, observation), thereby yielding a particular 'knowledge' of 'reality' reflective of a synthesis of experience *and* reason.[38] This means, as Dicker puts it, "we cannot know things *apart* from *the way they appear to us* in sensibility" (in experience) nor know things apart from how they are "conceptualized by our understanding."[39] Indeed, in explaining and reinforcing the Kantian notion of transcendental idealism, Dicker argues the following:

> Suppose ... we stand the traditional assumption [about knowledge] on its head. Instead of assuming that it is the object known that dictates the content of knowledge to the knowing subject, suppose that the knowing subject *contributes* to the object *as known* certain of its structural features. This will *not mean* that the knower *creates* or even alters *things as they are in themselves*. Nor will it mean that knowers need be aware of the fact that they are contributing to the content of knowledge. But *it will mean* that in knowing, humans *unconsciously* and *inevitably*, because of their own, built-in nature, *impose* on the object as known *certain of its basic structural features*.[40]

It now becomes apparent that the *idealism* in Kant's notion of *transcendental idealism* is the belief that the human mind, through the use of reason, can actually *supplement* empirical knowledge of a thing to give rise to a knowledge that is based on a *synthesis of experience and reason*. This synthesis is based on the cognitive systemization and categorization of experience. This means, of course, one's perceptions of how things are cannot be divorced from an *understanding* (through systemization and categorizing of experience) of actual experience. Perceptions then are a product of a categorization and systemization of experience, or a product of a particular knowledge of a thing, and therefore perceptions are based on knowledge. And if this knowledge is presented in radical Islamist rhetoric in terms of reason that portrays a certain reality, then individuals' perceptions of reality are based on reason in rhetoric. This highlights the *power of reason* in shaping knowledge and in both determining the *composition* of knowledge as well as the *nature* of perceptions. Of course, this does not mean that reason creates a certain imaginary 'reality' but only that reason is necessary to make sense of 'reality' and further, that such reason (or reasoning) is inevitable in both knowledge and perceptions of reality. Transcendental idealism thus assumes the unavoidable marriage of experience (the empirical) with reason (transcendental logic).

A most critical implication comes to light if we take the Kantian notion of transcendental idealism as valid, and that is that knowledge of 'reality' need not *necessarily* reflect concreteness or absoluteness (or *the thing in itself*, reality as it really is); knowledge of reality may reflect instead a particular understanding of reality (through the systemization and categorization of experience). This, of course, is consistent with how Dicker explains transcendental idealism, that "instead of assuming that it is the object known [say, for example 'reality' in itself] that dictates the content of knowledge [of reality] to the knowing subject, suppose that the knowing subject [the individual or individuals] *contributes* to the object as known [through reason that categorizes and systemizes experience]."[41] Perceptions of reality are thus necessarily *subjective* since they are based on subjective reason that creates the knowledge of a thing. In this way, transcendental idealism assumes, I argue, the inevitability of the subjectivity of the knowledge of reality and thus the subjectivity of the perceptions of reality. Synthesis of experience and reason can then be seen as leading to the knowledge of reality which in turn shapes the perceptions of reality. I have illustrated this in Figure 5.1.

The resonance of radical Islamist rhetoric can then be understood in terms of the Kantian transcendental idealism. In other words, what is presented by the recruiters (leaders) of Islamist extremist groups as the 'reality' of things is in fact a product of their particular reason (their systemization and categorization of experience that appears in their discourse) and which in turn shapes knowledge (through reason in rhetoric) of their audiences and shapes their perceptions. Perceptions of reality then ultimately determine the motivations of individuals to engage in violent and self-destructive missions. If such reason in rhetoric presents reality in terms of a Hegelian struggle for recognition—as I have argued in Chapters 2 and 3 in this book—then it gives rise to the perceptions of the self as the Hegelian slave which in turn creates the motivations of the individuals to challenge the negation of the self. In other words, if we hold the reason–knowledge–perceptions–motivations rubric to be valid (see Figure 5.1), then it follows that the *nature of motivations* of the individuals that voluntary join Islamist extremist groups can be deduced from the analysis of the *nature of reason* in radical Islamist rhetoric. In other words, if the rationalists' argument of the possibility of *synthetic a priori* knowledge holds any validity—namely, that reason shapes and contributes to knowledge of reality—and if Kant's transcendental idealism can also be assumed to be valid—that is, the contention that reason can contribute to the knowledge of a thing—then the importance of reason in radical Islamist rhetoric in shaping its audiences' perceptions and motivations becomes apparent. Quite simply, this means that if reason in radical Islamist rhetoric is existential and consequentialist, as I have argued in this book, then the motivations of individuals based on such reason can also be expected to be existential and consequentialist given the reason–knowledge–perceptions–motivations rubric. Thus, I argue, it is the *nature of reason* in radical Islamist rhetoric that sheds light on the *nature of motivations* of the individuals that voluntarily join Islamist extremist groups. This means that if we are to accurately understand the motivations of individuals that voluntarily join Islamist extremist groups, we must accurately understand the nature of reason in radical Islamist rhetoric. It is thus this nature of reason that forms the *essence* of Islamist extremism (the 'what is' of the Islamist extremism).

There is one other important implication that arises out of Kant's notion of transcendental idealism (the notion that reason contributes to knowledge of experience) that is critical to understanding the diverse profiles of the individuals that voluntarily join Islamist extremist groups. This implication can be understood in light of Nietzsche's contention that "language is not simply a means of describing what there is [for example, the thing in itself]; rather, it imposes a *framework of interpretation* on our thoughts."[42] In other words, language plays a manipulative role in society. If we understand language as reason—as in the 'language' of the radical Islamists that translates into reason in radical Islamist rhetoric—then it implies that language as well as reason are manipulative. In this, the 'framework of interpretation' can be seen as the product of a particular categorization and systemization of experience through reason (such as reason in radical Islamist rhetoric). Such reason then offers a framework as to how something 'should' be understood or perceived; that is, it offers 'a framework of interpretation' for its audiences. This framework of interpretation then shapes the knowledge of its audiences and thus their perceptions and their motivations; see Figure 5.1.

This, again, highlights the importance of understanding the *nature of reason* in radical Islamist rhetoric in order to understand the nature of the *motivations* of individuals based on such reason in rhetoric. This further explains why voluntary recruits to Islamist extremist groups do not always fit the stereotypical category, either that of the underprivileged and disgruntled individual with nothing to live for or an individual that directly experiences atrocities.[43] In other words, if reason in radical Islamist rhetoric presents a particular 'framework of interpretation' (as I noted above), then personal experience of atrocities becomes an unnecessary variable in creating the motivations for violent action for individuals that voluntarily join Islamist extremist groups. And if personal experi-

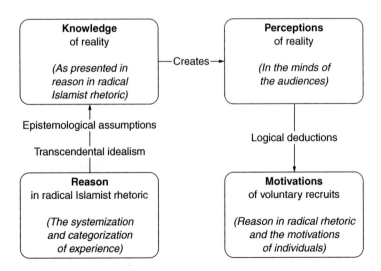

Figure 5.1 The reason–knowledge–perceptions–motivations rubric.

ence becomes unimportant in understanding 'reality' and in the knowledge and perceptions one has of reality, then radical Islamist rhetoric broadens its reach into audiences that are either privileged or not directly affected by atrocities (such as foreign occupations) that are thought to lead to voluntary recruitment into violent reactionary groups. And it is thus that we can explain, for example, the British-born Pakistani millionaire Omar Sheik who joined the jihad in Bosnia in the early 1990s. Consider also the example of the individuals who took part in the self-destructive missions on September 11, 2001, none of whom had direct experience with oppression or atrocities.

From misunderstanding essence to flawed policies

A misunderstanding of the essence of Islamist extremism leads to a misunderstanding of the nature of the motivations of individuals that voluntarily join Islamist extremist groups; and a misunderstanding on both accounts leads to flawed and misguided policies intended to combat the threat of Islamist extremism. Such misguided policies, I argue, only consolidate the long-term threat of Islamist extremism even if they translate into short-term successes. In other words, such misguided policies lead to strategic failures even if they comprise tactical successes.[44] In this book, I have argued that the essence of Islamist extremism is an *existential* rejection of oppression (whether actual or perceived) and as a struggle for self-recognition.[45] That this essence is *existential* in nature is based on my analysis of Hegel's assertion of the inevitable awakening of self-consciousness in the development of human consciousness and its implications for conflict in human relations. Based on this, one can understand existential 'fears' as broadly the fears of the negation of the self, and existential 'desires' as broadly the desires for self-assertion and self-recognition.[46] And if such is the nature of reason in radical Islamist rhetoric then, given epistemological assumptions and logical deductions, we can expect that the motivations of its voluntary recruits will also likely be existential in nature. That motivations are existential in nature is to say that motivations are not economic in essence but are instead reflective of, and catalyzed by, fears and desires that are common to *human existence* (such as the fear of oppression and the desire for autonomy and independence). Given that the U.S. 'counterinsurgency' policy in both Iraq and Afghanistan has been based on the *occupation* of these countries, it is easy to see how such policy is fundamentally flawed as it reinforces those very existential fears on the part of the local populations. And it is this very fact, I argue, that explains the resilience and indeed the resonance of radical Islamist rhetoric. The outcome of such flawed policies is likely to be the consolidation—not the fracturing—of radical Islamist groups and movements in the long term.

Counterinsurgency as foreign policy

Traditional counterinsurgencies are domestic in scope. A counterinsurgency comprises of a government's strategy and tactics of defeating an insurgency that has developed within the boundaries of its sovereign state; hence 'counter-insurgency.'[47] In its simplest sense, then, counter-insurgency is a counter-offensive, where the insurgents are the anti-government elements that are the offensive elements, and the counter-insurgents are the government elements that are the counter-offensive elements. Indeed, one can argue that a counterinsurgency can only hope to be successful if it is *domestic* in scope since a most critical component of a successful counterinsurgency is the *legitimacy* of the counter-insurgent entity (which is the incumbent government in a traditional counterinsurgency), and this legitimacy is hard to attain if the 'counter-insurgent' is a foreign entity. Yet the 2006 United States Army and Marine Corps manual endorse the strategy and tactics of *traditional* counterinsurgency as a new strategy in its *international* 'war on terrorism.'[48] Traditional counter-insurgency has now been paralleled with what has come to be known as modern counterinsurgency; the former represents a domestic policy, the latter represents a foreign policy. In order to understand why the appropriation of the strategy and tactics of counterinsurgency as a foreign policy is fundamentally flawed, one needs first to understand the basic components of a successful counterinsurgency.

One of the classic historical examples of a successful counterinsurgency is the one conducted by the Indonesian government against the Darul Islam insurgency in Indonesia during 1947–1962.[49] There are two main components of a traditional counterinsurgency, the so-called 'enemy-centric' component and the so-called 'population-centric' component. The enemy-centric component is more informally known as the 'search-and-kill' strategy of a counterinsurgency, where the counterinsurgent searches for and kills all known insurgents as a way to destroy the insurgency movement. The population-centric component is more informally known as the 'hearts-and-minds' strategy of counterinsurgency, where the counterinsurgent tries to destroy the resonance of the ideology of the insurgents amongst the population at large in order to (1) destroy the insurgent networks and thus to destroy its movement and (2) gain the liking and trust of the population. The intention in any successful counterinsurgency is to kill as many insurgents as possible while at the same time winning as many hearts-and-minds of the population as possible.

A closer look at the strategy and tactics of counterinsurgency sheds light on what is thought to be components of its success. The enemy-centric (search-and-kill) component of counterinsurgency has the following features:[50]

- the use of over-whelming force to crush the enemy (the insurgent);
- the use of tactics to 'break'—dehumanize or eliminate—the enemy.

These features are based on the following assumptions:

- Killing insurgent leaders will terminate the insurgency.
- Insurgency is about insurgents, so if there are no insurgents, there is no insurgency.

On the other hand, the population-centric (hearts-and-minds) component of counterinsurgency has the following features:

- an effort to understand the nature of the insurgency—that is, the narrative used by the insurgents that has mobilized some of the population to engage in violence—and to then offer a *counter*-narrative in order to undercut the legitimacy of the insurgents;[51]
- to offer economic or social incentives to the populace in order to make insurgents appear an unattractive option.

The above features are based on the assumptions that the popular support for insurgency is based on either a lack of knowledge on the part of the populace of a better alternative or the unavailability of a better alternative (in terms of either political or economic options).

The success of a counterinsurgency is typically measured in terms of its (1) tactical success and (2) strategic success. Tactical success can be understood in terms of a purely military success, that is, the success in physically eliminating the enemy—the insurgents—through use of firepower in search-and-kill tactics. Tactical successes are often short-terms successes and cannot, on their own, secure a long-term success for the counterinsurgency operation in the absence of strategic success. Strategic success can be understood in terms of successfully winning the hearts-and-minds of the population—to use counterinsurgency lingo—through methods *other than* military. Strategic success, if achieved, tends to be long-term successes and is thus considered critical in *winning the war* (through winning hearts and minds) and not just *winning the battles* (through search and kill tactics). Providing the population with access to economic sources of sorts is an example of the latter in cases of traditional counterinsurgency (that is, counterinsurgency that is decidedly domestic in scope). Providing funding for the creation of schools, roads, bridges or the technical assistance for the better functioning of democratic institutions are examples of efforts towards strategic success in the case of a non-traditional counterinsurgency, as in the case of the American 'counterinsurgency' in Iraq (2004–2008) and in the case of the US–NATO 'counterinsurgency' in Afghanistan (2001–2011).[52] However, I argue that the presentation of a foreign policy based on military aggression (however justified and warranted) as a 'counter-insurgency' has two critical and inherent flaws: (1) it creates an impasse in the perceptions of the self and the perceptions of the other leading to the ultimate long term failure of such a policy; (2) it requires a protracted occupation of the host state which is a tactic that also leads to long term failure. Ultimately, the appropriation of such tactics fundamentally misunderstands the essence of Islamist extremism.

Occupation as counter-insurgency

That the US military operations in Iraq qualify as the US *occupation* of Iraq is a fact that is not much contested, despite the many different justifications that were offered by the Bush administration for the military operations that started in 2003.[53] Indeed, M. Cherif Bassiouni notes that "on October 31, 1998, US Congress passed the Iraq Liberation Act in support of a democratic government to replace Saddam Hussein's regime, laying the foundation for forceful regime change in that country."[54] Indeed, the US administration officials argued that "the US was authorized under ... legal sources to preemptively attack Iraq and to *occupy* it."[55] This authorization was based on the following resolutions and stipulations: the post-2001 Joint Resolution of the Congress that authorized the use of force against those entities that "planned, authorized, committed or aided" the 2001 attacks on the United States; "Joint Resolution of the Congress, Authorization for Use of Military Force Against Iraq Resolution of 2002"; Article 51 of the UN Charter that allows the right of self-defense in response to an attack.[56] In response to the charge of occupation, Thomas Donnelly notes that "Americans in Iraq have never been simple 'occupiers' ";[57] it appears that 'not being simple occupiers' is a reference to the counter-insurgency tactics that the US military employed not long after its occupation of Iraq in order to dampen the growing anti-Americanism in Iraq that was based on the US occupation of Iraq and that subsequently led to the growth of the anti-American insurgency in Iraq.[58]

Qualifications aside, there remain two critical problems in the presentation of a military occupation (an offensive action by definition) as 'counter-insurgency' (a counter-offensive action by definition):

- Such a presentation is a contradiction in terms since an offensive action (such as a military occupation) cannot also double-up as a counter-offensive action (as a 'counter-insurgency').
- In such a presentation, while the self (the American military in this case) presents itself as the counter-offensive element (the counter-insurgent), the other (the Iraqi anti-American contingents) also presents itself as the counter-offensive element since it views the occupation by a foreign entity (in this case the US) as *the* offensive action.

Since the first point above does not need any further elaboration, let us focus on the second point. It is important here to highlight the obvious, that the act of a military occupation itself fuels the mobilization of local anti-occupation forces, so that while the self (the US forces in this case) seeks to present itself as the 'counter-insurgent,' the other (in this case the anti-American groups and movements in Iraq) also presents itself as the 'counter-insurgent' (counter-offensive) element since it presents the occupation (by the US in this case) as the offensive action to which it is a counter measure. For example, in an interview aired on *al-Jazeera* on March 29, 2008, Muqtada al-Sadr (leader of the Iraqi Mahdi Army) described the US military operations in Iraq thus:

> this was occupation, not liberation. I call it occupation. I have said in recent years: Gone is the 'little Satan', [a reference to Saddam Hussein], and in came the 'Great Satan.'[59]

Indeed, radical Islamist discourse explains its violence in terms of a *counter-offensive* and in terms of the rejection of the offensive directed at them, in this case, the occupation of their country by a foreign entity. Such radical Islamist narrative, by challenging the status of the self as the 'slave'—the negated and violated—then explains violence as a *defensive* measure, a counter-offensive and not an offensive. This means, for example, that while the US–NATO contingencies in Afghanistan may present the Afghani Taliban as the 'insurgents'—and thus, by definition, the aggressors and the offensive entities—the Taliban themselves present themselves as the *counter*-insurgents, the defensive entity at war with the aggressive entity comprising the foreign occupation. Such a narrative can be seen in bin Laden's following remarks:

> The [Muslim] governments of the region said: 'The Americans came for only a few months', and they lied from start to finish. [...] a few months passed; a year passed, and then another: nine years have passed, and the Americans are lying to everyone, saying: 'We have interests in the region, and we will not move as long as we have not secured them'. An enemy breaks into your home to steal your money. You ask him: 'Are you robbing me?' He replies: 'No ... I am defending my interests'. They are tricking us, and the governments of this region fell into the trap. [60]

The matter of the conflicting perceptions—or the parallel lines of logic as I referred to it earlier in this chapter—is made quite apparent in the above assertion. That bin Laden's statements are rhetorical and sensational is beside the point; the point here is of how reason in radical Islamist rhetoric (as in the above) shapes the perceptions of its audiences. In the above, the Americans are categorically presented as the aggressors, the offensive entity, the 'insurgents' if you may.

This also highlights the point I had noted earlier, that dichotomous classifications of the self as the defensive and heroic entity that is engaged in a 'counter-insurgency,' and the other as the aggressive and immoral entity that represents the 'insurgents' only takes us farther away from understanding perceptions that motivate violence. Consider, as another example, the following assertion made by Akhmed Zubarayev, a Chechen fighter in Grozny who, in August 1996, categorized the Soviet military as the offensive, aggressive entity in Chechnya, while presenting the self as on the *counter-offensive* (quite contrary to how the Soviet military rhetoric presented the Chechen fighters as offensive and insurgent):

> A year and a half ago we were forced to retreat. Now it's the *counter-offensive*. We're *liberating our city from Russian occupation.*[61]

Of course, the American military labels its actions (whether in Iraq or Afghanistan) as a 'counter-insurgency.' In the case of Iraq, such a classification preceded the rise of Sunni and Shia violent resistance groups opposed to the American occupation. But despite this, the American military labeled its actions as a 'counter-insurgency,' relegating the actions of the radical Sunni and Shia opposition to occupation as 'insurgent' elements. But such reason is paradoxical since it is akin to creating the problems yourself and then presenting yourself as an antidote. Such paradoxical logic also creates an impasse in the perceptions that the self has of itself (in this case the US military) and the other has of itself (in this case the anti-American contingents in Iraq). The result is a misunderstanding of the nature of the motivations of the enemy, which in this case came in the form of either the radical Shia Islamist *Mahdi Army* or the many radical Sunni anti-occupation militia groups such as *al-Mujahideen Army, al-Fatiheen Army, Islamic Front for the Iraqi Resistance, Iraqi Hamas.*[62] Michael Schwartz's analysis of the anti-American resistance in Fallujah is notable here.[63] Schwartz points to the fact that while the US military labeled this resistance as the 'insurgency' in Fallujah, the so-called 'Fallujah insurgents' labeled themselves instead as the 'mujahidin' (freedom fighters, or the counter-offensive elements if you may).[64] Indeed, according to one independent reporter that Schwartz spoke to, the Fallujah mujahidin were not "isolated 'extremists' repudiated by the majority of the Fallujah's population" but were instead "of the community and fully supported by it."[65] Far from the US 'counter-insurgency' succeeding in Fallujah, "US troops withdrew to a base outside Fallujah [in April 2003] and rarely ventured into the city" and "Fallujah became a national symbol of successful resistance to the occupation."[66]

Beyond the example of Fallujah, the larger point here is that the label of 'Islamist insurgents' that the American military command attaches to Islamist extremists (whether in Iraq or in Afghanistan) is diametrically opposed to how the Islamist extremists perceive themselves and present themselves: as engaged in a *defensive war* and as thus the counter-insurgents, not the insurgents. And, conversely, how the American forces present themselves is diametrically opposed to how the American forces are viewed: as the aggressors and the insurgents, not the counter-insurgents. If perceptions are everything, as Merleau-Ponty would have argued, then there is a debilitating stalemate here since all actors involved view and present themselves as engaged in a defensive war. If all sides are defensive, then all sides are right.[67] And if all sides are engaged in self-defense and are thus in the right, then aggressive actions from the 'other' (whether the aggressive actions of the US military or Islamist violence) will only reinforce the resolve of the 'self' (whether the US and its allies or the radical Islamists) to 'counter' such aggression. And if this is the dynamic we are looking at, then we can expect two outcomes: (1) an endless, protracted war for the Americans and their allies in the countries that they are perceived as an occupying force; (2) the consolidation of the threat of Islamist extremism.

Michael Walzer has been known to argue that an occupation of a country by a foreign entity may, at times, be 'just' if it leads to a "decent postwar political order."[68] Walzer's assertion not only ignores the negative perceptions attached to an occupation but is also far removed from an understanding that a rejection of occupation is existential in nature. To the extent that occupations are perceived as negative—even when they may be presented as 'benevolent' occupations, overlooking for the moment the contradiction in terms that is implied herein—occupations will always be rejected, and violently so. To argue that an occupation of a country may at times be 'just' is to overlook the human sensibilities of the other, and to thus critically misunderstand the essence of violence. This means that even an establishment of some "decent postwar political order" as a consequence of an occupation will likely be rejected, or replaced in the long term, since it will be perceived as having been negotiated by an occupying entity. Hegel's analysis sheds light on the inevitability of the slave's rejection of the master's reason in what Hegel calls the master–slave dialectic. Contemporary assertions of the master's will—that is, actions that are *perceived* as denoting the master's will and that are perceived as the master asserting his mastery—will also be inevitability rejected. Walzer's support of the protracted American occupation of Iraq in terms of being "responsible for the well-being of the Iraqi people" thus ignores the elephant in the room: the *occupation* that will always be rejected, and violently so.[69]

Counterinsurgency through occupation

Prior to the drafting of the 2006 US Army and Marines Corps manual, David Kilcullen (former Senior counterinsurgency advisor to General Petraeus in Iraq) argued that the US military contingents in Iraq and Afghanistan should employ the strategy and tactics of a traditional counterinsurgency since, according to him, the threat emanating from al-Qaeda can best be understood in terms of what he calls "global Islamist insurgency."[70] In referring to Islamist extremism as 'global Islamist insurgency,' Kilcullen stretches the meaning of insurgency, which typically refers to a *domestic* offensive against one's *own* government. Kilcullen's rationale seems to be that since the 2001 attacks on the United States constituted an offensive, those conducting the attacks must be the offensive (or insurgent) entities (in this case elements of al-Qaeda) and the US reaction to such attacks must therefore be the counter-offensive (or counter-insurgent).[71] In other words, Kilcullen sees the US military engagement in Afghanistan—which is now spanning over a decade since 2001—as a defensive war.[72] To this end, he endorses a military campaign in Afghanistan that is counter-offensive or 'defensive' as Kilcullen calls it. And in light of the unconventional nature of the anti-American 'insurgency' (in both Iraq and Afghanistan), Kilcullen argues for an equally unconventional counter-insurgency, namely a counter-insurgency that is international in scope but that utilizes all of the same tactics and strategies of traditional counterinsurgency. But since such an unconventional counterinsurgency must follow the formula of a successful traditional counterinsurgency (as that of the Indonesian government noted earlier), Kilcullen notes that such a policy "demands a residential approach."[73] In simple terms, then, Kilcullen endorses a protracted occupation of Afghanistan (and Iraq before that) for the ends of an 'international counterinsurgency.'[74] To this end, in September 2010, the American Defense Secretary Robert M. Gates and Admiral Mike Mullen (the chairman of the Joint Chiefs of Staff) "defended the contentious, administration-wide debate … that produced a new strategy for Afghanistan approved by President Obama ... [This strategy] called for a *substantial buildup of forces*" stationed in Afghanistan.[75]

The immediate problem with employing the strategy and tactics of traditional counterinsurgency for the ends of a modern counterinsurgency (that is, counter-insurgency through the occupation) is that it ignores the circumstances that have historically lead to successful counterinsurgencies, namely that counterinsurgen-cies have been a domestic operation with no foreign intervention. Kilcullen himself notes the example of Indonesia as classic example of a successful coun-terinsurgency. Yet the 2006 US Army and Marines Corps counterinsurgency manual ignores this very important circumstance and creates a manual that necessitates the occupation of host states as part of its counterinsurgency policy.

I argue that the strategy of counterinsurgency through occupation is doomed to fail in the long term for the following reasons:

- Counterinsurgency through occupation critically misunderstands the *essence* of Islamist extremism which is fundamentally a *rejection of oppression* (foreign occupations being one quintessential manifestation of oppression).
- Counterinsurgency through occupation thus *retards* the 'population-centric' hearts-and-minds component of a counterinsurgency strategy (which is crit-ical for the long-term success of a counterinsurgency) so that what becomes emphasized in the eyes of the populace are the harsh 'enemy-centric' search-and-kill tactics.[76]

In elaboration of the points above, the policy of counterinsurgency through occu-pation ignores the fact that occupations are ubiquitously rejected since occupa-tions are universally viewed as oppressive, and that this rejection is existential in nature. Thus, such a policy at best makes impotent the campaigns to win hearts-and-minds and, at worst, backfires through the expansion of the support base for the local anti-oppression elements (such as, for example, the Taliban in Afghani-stan). Thus, I argue, any strategy based on occupation critically misunderstands the essence of Islamist extremism.

The two most significant net outcomes of the US–NATO counterinsurgency through the occupation of Afghanistan are therefore likely to be: (1) that it only *rein-forces* (not weakens) the resonance of radical Islamist rhetoric and (2) that therefore it *consolidates* (not fractures) Islamist extremist networks at both the domestic and transnational levels. In other words, given what I have argued is the fundamental essence of Islamist extremism, employing the strategy of counterinsurgency through occupation may lead to short-term tactical successes but will lead to long-term stra-tegic failures. If the aim of the U.S. 'war on terrorism' is the long-term reduction in the threat of Islamist extremism, then the strategy of occupation towards that end is as much of an oxymoron as a 'preventive war' for the ends of 'perpetual peace.'[77]

While it is true that a substantial military deployment is necessary for a tradi-tional counterinsurgency (judging by the success of the Indonesian government's counterinsurgency during 1947–1962), the operative word here is 'traditional,' which means a counterinsurgency where *all players are domestic*. But if now 'counterinsurgency' involves an occupation by foreign entities then the tactics and strategy of counterinsurgency become akin to throwing fuel on fire.[78] What is then completely ignored in such a non-traditional counterinsurgency is the elephant in the room: the *occupation* that it is based on. And it is this occupation, and the oppression that accompanies it, that is fundamentally rejected in radical Islamist rhetoric of temporally and contextually varied Islamist extremist groups, of which the Taliban (both the Afghani and the Pakistani) and al-Qaeda are no exceptions.

However, such an understanding of the essence of Islamist extremism seems entirely missing in the actions that General Petraeus took immediately after taking command of US–NATO forces in Afghanistan on June 24, 2010.[79] Instead of understanding how harsh enemy-centric (search-and-kill) tactics may be *perceived* by the local population, particularly when they are accompanied by an occupation, General Petraeus called for the reversal of the "curb on U.S. strikes and artillery in Afghanistan."[80] Indeed, a few months after assuming command, General Petraeus had "been pulling out all the stops—aggressively using the American troops buildup, greatly expanding Special Operations raids (as many as a dozen commando raids a night) and pressing the Central Intelligence Agency to ramp up Predator and Reaper drone operations in Pakistan."[81]

Under the former command of General Stanley McChrystal, the US–NATO contingents in Afghanistan employed the following enemy-centric and population-centric strategies:[82]

- Enemy-centric—the 'search-and-kill' campaign:

  - Separating 'insurgents'—Taliban and their 'foreign fighters'—from civilians and killing them through offensive U.S. Marines 'Special Operations.' General Petraeus' former aid explained this strategy in the following words: "reconcile with those who are willing and kill the people you need to."[83]
  - Using CIA operated predator drones to fire missiles on targets *suspected* of being Taliban insurgents.[84]

- Population-centric—the 'hearts-and-minds' campaign:

  - Focusing on forging deals with the moderate Taliban members.[85]
  - Limiting the use of lethal force and air strikes (including the use of predator drones) based on an acknowledgement that such unbridled actions only alienate a population that is ideologically undecided in such a war.[86]
  - Offering economic incentives—such as jobs and security—to those Afghanis not yet sympathetic to, or members of, the Taliban.[87]

Interestingly, even though General McChrystal's counterinsurgency strategy in Afghanistan was shaped after General Petraeus' counterinsurgency strategy in Iraq, and was reflective of the strategy as outlined in the 2006 U.S. Army and Marine Corps *Counterinsurgency* manual—which was itself created "under the direction of Army general David Petraeus"[88]—General Petraeus, upon taking the command of U.S. forces in Afghanistan, immediately instituted a reversal of General McChrystal's policy of making it "more difficult to call in airstrikes to kill insurgents because [this] ... risked civilian causalities."[89] This effectively hardened the rather softer enemy-centric strategy that had been employed by the US–NATO contingents under the former command of General McChrystal.[90]

While aggressive search-and-kill tactics have to always be carefully balanced by a counter hearts-and-minds tactics in a traditional counter-insurgency, this is all the more imperative—and all the more difficult I argue—in a counter-insurgency conducted by a foreign occupation force (as in the case of the US–NATO forces in Afghanistan). David Kilcullen argues that this delicate balancing act can best be achieved through offering a counter-narrative to that which is offered by the insurgents (a strategy he calls 'exploiting a single narrative').[91] Kilcullen notes:

> Since counterinsurgency is a competition to mobilize popular support, it pays to know how people are mobilized. [...] Nationalist and ethnic historical myths, or sectarian creeds, provide such a narrative. The Iraqi insurgents have one, as do Al-Qa'eda and the Taliban. To undercut their influence, you must exploit an alternative narrative—or, better yet, tap into an existing narrative that excludes the insurgents.[92]

There are, however, two critical problems in Kilcullen's above prescription. First, in understanding the central narrative of al-Qaeda, the Iraqi and Taliban insurgents as based on 'nationalist and ethnic historical myths,' Kilcullen critically *misunderstands* the *essence* of such Islamist extremist groups. This essence, at its very core, is far more fundamental than nationalistic, ethnic or sectarian creeds. It is, as I have argued in this book, an existential rejection of oppression and a parallel struggle for self-recognition through violence if need be. This means that any effort on the part of a foreign occupying force to offer a counter-narrative is doomed to fail. In other words, if the fundamental narrative of the 'insurgents'—the Islamist extremists, or Taliban in particular, who incidentally see themselves as the counter-offensive elements—is a rejection of foreign occupation, a counter-narrative to that must be equally appealing in existential terms. And while economic incentives are certainly appealing, economic incentives offered by an occupying force—by definition, aggressive and oppressive—are not likely to counter the narrative of the insurgents, which is based on a more fundamental rejection of the negation of the self.

Second, the problem with Kilcullen's prescription of tapping into the existing narrative of the insurgents in such a way as to exclude the insurgents (or make them appear illegitimate) is that it is impossible to do so long as the US–NATO contingents remain the occupying force in Afghanistan. This is because the central narrative of the insurgents is an anti-occupation narrative; such narrative cannot be exploited without a change in the policy of the foreign contingents that is based on the occupation of Afghanistan. In other words, exploiting the narrative of the Taliban in Afghanistan can only be achieved through the end of the US–NATO occupation of Afghanistan. Short of this drastic change in policy, the US–NATO actions in Afghanistan are likely to experience short-term tactical victories (since the military means of the latter are far superior than any military means at the disposal of the Taliban and its affiliates) at the cost of a long-term strategic defeat. The danger in this, for the American and NATO forces, is that this war is likely to become a strategic defeat, Soviet-style.

One might be reminded that negative perceptions of the foreign occupying force as the embodiments of the Hegelian masters bend on the negation and oppression of the self (in this case the Afghanis) makes defunct any efforts at winning 'hearts-and-minds' on the part of the foreign counterinsurgency contingents which then only spotlights the more aggressive 'search-and-kill' counterpart of a counterinsurgency. Thus, the American strategy of 'counter-insurgency' in Afghanistan is doomed to fail in the long-term since it is pursued by a foreign entity (the US–NATO contingents) which is viewed as the *occupation* entity by the leading anti-American Taliban contingents and their Pakistani counterparts, the *Tehreek-e-Taliban Pakistan* (or the Taliban movement of Pakistan). Any strategy of winning hearts-and-minds in such set-up inevitability deteriorates into *losing* hearts-and-minds. And while Nadia Schadlow defends the US counterinsurgency tactics in Afghanistan by noting that "the current COIN [counterinsurgency] doctrine emerged as a corrective to the American tendency to take an engineering or technological approach to war, one that divorces war from its enduring human, psychological and political nature," Schadlow completely overlooks the fact that counterinsurgency through occupation has a worse psychological impact on the host population since it is seen as oppressive.[93] So if a military wishes to understand the enduring human nature of war, it must understand that occupations will always be categorically rejected. And if this can be understood, then the resonance and resilience of Islamist extremist groups can be understood.

Losing hearts and minds

Harsh enemy-centric counterinsurgency tactics of the US occupation force in Iraq, Afghanistan and the northern tribal areas of Pakistan are bound to translate into the long-term strategic failure for the United States military operations as, I argue, such actions translate into the losing of hearts-and-minds in the long term. Consider for example the following harsh tactics: the "FISH strategy (Fighting In Someone's House) which involved 'throwing a hand grenade into each room before checking it for unfriendlies'" in Iraq;[94] the torture of naked Iraqi prisoners in Abu Ghraib prison (all of whom subsequently proved to be innocent); daily intimidations such as stopping "civilians at gunpoint and dump[ing] their breakfasts out of their baskets while asking them questions and yelling obscenities";[95] the unbridled use of the CIA remote controlled predator drones to target known or *suspected* terrorists in Pakistan's semi-autonomous FATA (federally administered tribal areas) as well as in the *Khyber-Pakhtunkhwa* province that have exacted a huge tool in the deaths of innocent civilians.[96] In fact, in reaction to the deaths of innocent civilians in the tribal areas of Pakistan, there has started (since December 2010) a broad based social movement against the US and its use of predator drones.[97] That this is the clearest sign of losing hearts-and-minds does not need any elaboration. Furthermore, in Pakistan's *Khyber-Pakhtunkhwa* province, even those elements in the population that once did *not* object to the US use of predator drones (despite the guarantee in such attacks of civilian causalities) have now become vociferous in their objection to these bombs that are dropping from the sky.[98]

Perhaps the best illustration of the strategic failure of a 'counterinsurgency' that is based on an occupation of a host state (in which the population-centric hearts-and-minds strategy becomes inevitably eclipsed by the harsh enemy-centric tactics, as I noted earlier) is the support that was offered by the Shia *al-Mahdi Army* to the various anti-American radical *Sunni* Islamist fighters in 2004. This is notable since the *al-Mahdi Army* is a radical Islamist sectarian group and thus by definition an anti-Sunni group, which makes it an unlikely alliance for its Sunni counterparts with whom it had engaged in sectarian violence before. This paradox can be explained by the fact that *al-Mahdi Army* was created in opposition to the US occupation of Iraq in 2003 and, as such, found itself in *informal* alliances with its Sunni anti-US-occupation groups in what can classically be explained as 'my enemy's enemy is my friend.'[99] In fact, Michael Schwartz notes that in 2004:

> Residents of Fallujah and other Sunni cities expressed the same sentiments with banners and graffiti containing slogans that explicitly called for unity— such as "Sunni + Shia = Jihad against Occupation"—or that grouped together Sunni and Shia centers of insurgency, such as "The Martyrs of Fallujah, Najaf, Kufah, and Basra Are the Pole of the Flag that Says God is Great".[100]

Given such existential rejection of oppression and occupation, it is the radical Islamist rhetoric that in its explanations and justifications seems to win the 'hearts-and-minds' of the people. I base this statement on the recruiting success of anti-occupation Islamist groups and movements in Iraq and the recruiting success of both the Afghani and the Pakistani Taliban.

The critical problem in seeking to win hearts-and-minds through a policy of occupation that also uses heavy-handed enemy-centric actions is that the aim of winning hearts-and-minds becomes understood as a rhetorical guise for the negation of the self by the occupier. For example, a *New York Times* article clearly noted that:

> [US] Special Operations raids have caused an unspecified number of innocent deaths that *have outraged the local population.*[101]

Similarly, Pakistan's popular English-version newspaper, *Dawn,* reported:

> more than 900 people have been killed in nearly 100 drone strikes in Pakistan since August 2008 ... [killing militants as well as innocent civilians] ... the attacks *fuel anti-American sentiment in the country.*[102]

That aggressive enemy-centric tactics make impotent the population-centric strategy of winning hearts-and-minds can also be seen in the following excerpts from interviews conducted by William Dalrymple of local Afghanis:

> [On his visit to an Afghani village, accompanied by his Afghani host, Dalrymple was told] "the foreigners have come for their own interests, not for ours. They say, 'We are your friends, we want democracy, we want to help.' *But they are lying.*"[103]

> [One of the tribal members from Jegdalek told Dalrymple] "How many times can they apologize for killing our innocent women and children and *expect us to forgive them?* They come, they bomb, they kill us and then they say, 'Oh, sorry, we got the wrong people.' And they keep doing that."[104]

> [Dalrymple asked his Afghani hosts if the Taliban were likely to come back to power and they relied] "The Taliban? [...] They are here already! At least after dark."[105]

> [In his visit to Jalalabad, Dalrymple was taken to a jirga (assembly of tribal elders) where he had an insightful interaction with one of the tribal members]: "After the jirga was over, one of the tribal elders came and we chatted for a while over a glass of green tea. 'Last month,' he said, 'some American officers called us to a hotel in Jalalabad for a meeting. One of them asked me, *'Why do you hate us?'* I replied, 'Because you blow down our doors, enter our houses, pull our women by the hair and kick our children. We cannot accept this. We will fight back, and we will break your teeth, and when your teeth are broken you will leave, just as the British left before you. It is just a matter of time'."[106]

Negative perceptions, on the part of the Afghanis, that the American–NATO occupation of Afghanistan is but another episode of the Great Game can be seen in the following commentary:

> Since the British went, we've had the Russians ... We saw them off, too, but not before they bombed many of the houses in the village ... Afghanistan is like the crossroads for every nation that comes to power ... Next, it will be China. *This is the last days of the Americans.*[107]

Based on the above analysis, I argue that there are three inter-related critical lessons to be learnt from the outcomes thus far of the American occupation of Iraq and the US–NATO counterinsurgency policy in Afghanistan that is also based on an occupation of the country:

1   A focus on 'tactical victory' compromises—and, indeed retards—a 'strategic victory.'[108]

2   One cannot act as the aggressor, on the one hand, and hope to be accepted as the benevolent entity, on the other hand; such thinking completely overlooks the negative perceptions created from the very act of occupation.[109]

3   Seeking to win 'hearts-and-minds' through offering economic incentives to the not-yet-radicalized population critically *misunderstands* the essence of Islamist extremism (and that of the Afghani and the Pakistani Taliban in particular) which is fundamentally a rejection of the *negation of the self*. One may be reminded that the Hegelian life-and-death struggles for recognition are life-and-death struggles for self-assertion, which are essentially struggles motivated by the fear of being negated by the other and the dread of the possibility of a life of servitude to the other; all such fears, of course, are only catalyzed by the fact of a foreign occupation of one's land.

Yet, it is interesting to note that while American soldiers have typically complained about "losing the tactical-level fight in the chase for a strategic victory" and had before also complained about the limits imposed on them on the use of fire power by General McChrystal, the loosening of those restrictions under General Petraeus is likely to enhance short-term victories (tactical victories) at the cost of long-term victory (strategic victory, that is, winning hearts and minds).[110] To be sure, General McChrystal had warned against such a grim eventuality (of a strategic loss in Afghanistan) in the following terms: "The Russians killed 1 million Afghans, and that didn't work."[111] Yet, popular reports in the widely read *New York Times* often include misleadingly optimistic reports alluding to the strategic successes of the war by confusing tactical successes with strategic ones, or worse, by not distinguishing between the two. These reports often highlight facts such as the following: "about 130 important insurgent figures have been captured or killed in Afghanistan over the past 120 days";[112] "Special Operations forces are carrying out an average of five raids a day against a constantly updated list of high-value targets, mostly in southern Afghanistan";[113] and that the killing of actual or *suspected* Taliban members in the numerous Special Operations raids are intended to either force the Taliban to "lay down their arms" or to "neutralize the Taliban."[114] In all these reports and assessments, the element of the perceptions of those that are the targets of the harsh US–NATO enemy-centric 'counterinsurgency' tactics—particularly the innocent civilians in Afghanistan and Pakistan—is completely overlooked or, worse, not considered at all. Such tendency to ignore the human reactions on the part of the population wherein one is engaged in military combat is the quintessential illustration of negating the other. The US–NATO explanations of the deaths of innocent civilians in Afghanistan and Pakistan (and Iraq before that) in terms either of double-effect, the lack of intentionality or supreme emergency are thus irrelevant in the momentum of losing hearts-and-minds.[115]

Optimistic reports of the outcomes of the US–NATO counterinsurgency in Afghanistan or Pakistan thus completely misunderstand the essence of Islamist extremism, particularly when they assume that the Taliban (whether Afghani or Pakistani) can be intimated or coaxed into laying down their arms through the use of aggressive measures to which it is a reaction. Further, to 'neutralize' the Taliban is to neutralize their rhetoric, and this cannot be achieved through the continued US–NATO occupation of Afghanistan and the de facto occupation of northern part of Pakistan. No amount of killing the actual or suspected members of the Taliban or al-Qaeda and its many variants will reduce the resilience of the rhetoric since it is premised on the very *rejection of oppression and occupation.* Since the nature of reason in their rhetoric is existential, it is timelessly resilient. As Thomas Friedman rightly noted:

> You know you're in trouble when you're in a war in which the only party whose objectives are clear, whose rhetoric is consistent and whose will to fight never seems to diminish is your enemy: the Taliban.[116]

In light of the lack of understanding of what I have argued is the fundamental essence of Islamist extremism, and the consequent long-term failure of a war focused on tactical successes grounded in occupations of host states, long-term strategic success seems unlikely, if possible. This assessment is probably best summarized by Thomas Friedman in the following: "the only real choices are lose early, lose late, lose big or lose small."[117]

Conclusion

The essence of Islamist extremism is largely misunderstood amongst political pundits in the west and elsewhere. A critical component of this lack of understanding, I argue, is the popular inability to distinguish between the nature of reason in the radical Islamist *explanations* of violence and the radical Islamist *justifications* of violence. The result is a misunderstanding of the essence of Islamist extremism as *Islamic* in nature, and thus as a phenomenon that is unique not only to the Muslim religious and cultural milieu but to Islam itself. A misunderstanding of the critical essence of Islamist extremism—which I argue is reasoned in terms of an existential struggle for recognition and justified in terms of moral consequentialism—leads to a misunderstanding of the motivations of individuals that voluntarily join Islamist extremist groups. Indeed, I argue that the motivations of secular recruits are based in large part on the manner in which 'reality' is depicted in radical Islamist discourse (as that necessitating violent struggles for recognition). In other words, in following the rationalist epistemological tradition, I argue that knowledge of 'reality' is based in part on 'reason' and in part on 'experience,' and therefore that experience itself need not be necessary for an individual to be motivated for action. 'Reason'—by which I mean reason as presented in radical Islamist rhetoric—thus *adds* to the knowledge of 'reality' (in following the Kantian epistemological tradition of transcendental idealism). The critical implication here is that the voluntary recruits of Islamist extremist groups *need not* have *themselves* experienced atrocities—whether at the hands of their own government or at the hands of foreign governments and entities—in order to be motivated for violent action. This readdresses the paradox of the motivations for extremist action on the part of individuals far removed from atrocities (such as government repression, foreign occupations, wars and torture); this also explains the motivations of the many foreign fighters in Afghanistan (the so-called 'Arab-Afghans') and the larger transnational recruitment success of the Taliban (both the Afghani and the Pakistani) as well as al-Qaeda.

A misunderstanding of the essence of Islamist extremism, and thus of the motivations of individuals that voluntarily join Islamist extremist groups, leads ultimately to misguided policies. Misguided polices are those that are intended to reduce the threat of Islamist extremism but that in fact only exacerbate its threat in the long term. A quintessential example of a misguided policy is one where the central component is the *occupation* of a host state; this is because such a policy—given the essence of Islamist extremism—is guaranteed only to reinforce the narrative of Islamist extremist groups and thus strengthen (not weaken) its constituencies. In this chapter, I offer the example of the United States' new approach to its 'war on terrorism,' which employs the strategy and tactics of a counterinsurgency through *occupation* of host states (whether Iraq or Afghanistan). I argue that whether an occupation is presented as a 'counter-insurgency' (the hyphen emphasizes the irony in the latter) or is presented as necessary for a 'counterinsurgency,' in both cases the long-term consequences are likely to be the loosing of hearts-and-minds of the very populations that the US and US–NATO contingents operate amongst in their fight against trans-national Islamist extremism. And if the intention is to dismantle the radical Islamist threat, then alienating the host populations (through protracted occupa-tions and harsh military tactics that do not—and perhaps cannot—distinguish between innocent non-combatants and combatants) is not the avenue to success since it is likely (at best) to lead to the tacit acceptance of Islamist extremist groups or (at worse) the support of Islamist extremist groups given the latter's anti-oppression narrative.

Concluding remarks

Nothing Islamic about Islamist extremism

The analysis in this book offers a counter-narrative to the clash-of-civilizations explanation of Islamist extremism. It argues instead that there is nothing *distinctly* Islamic about Islamist extremism. This is not to offer an apology for Islamist extremism, much less to excuse its violence and brutality. This is to highlight instead that the *essence* of Islamist extremism cannot be explained in simplistic terms as a reflection of a uniquely barbaric Muslim religious and cultural milieu or as something unique to Islam. The essence of Islamist extremism, I argue, can only be accurately understood by drawing a conceptual distinction between the radical Islamist *explanations* of violence and the radical Islamist *justifications* of violence. In its explanations of violence, radical Islamist reason is reflective of existential Hegelian struggles for recognition. That is, radical Islamist rhetoric explains violence in terms of a rejection of the oppression of the self and a rejection of the negation of the self (the 'self' defined collectively). While in its justifications of violence, radical Islamist rhetoric is fundamentally consequentialist in reason. That is, while radical Islamist justifications of violence are undoubtedly contextualized within *Islamic* religious tenets, the references to religious tenets serves the purpose of presenting all actions—including violent actions—in terms of a 'morality,' a logic which may be understood in terms of the instrumentality of religion, a phenomenon which itself is universal. As such, the creation of such moral consequentialism, through the aid of references to religious tenets, is *not* unique to the Islamic religious context but in fact reflective of the classic justifications of violence found throughout history.

That Hegel based his magnum opus on the argument that violent life-and-death struggles for recognition reflect the *very nature* of *human existence,* and that Nietzsche based his critique of what he referred to as 'Christian morality' on his assertion of the instrumentality of religion attests to the universal tendency towards both the explanations of violence in terms of struggles for recognition and the justifications of violence in terms of moral consequentialism. Here, the classic example of the medieval Christian Crusades is particularly instructive. The medieval version of the internationally accepted Just War doctrine justified the brutality of the Christian Crusades in terms of Christian religious tenets, as salvation and redemptive homicide.[1] But the brutality of the Christian Crusades are rarely—if at all—seen as *uniquely Christian* or reflective of the broader

Christian religious and cultural milieu, while the brutality of the radical Islamists are popularly seen as *uniquely Islamic* and reflective of the broader Muslim religious and cultural milieu.

Narratives that point to Islam (as a religion) as *the* explanation of Islamist extremism and violence essentially create what has come to be popularly known as 'Islamophobia' (or, phobia of all that is Islamic or Muslim). This demonization of the other (in this case, the entire Muslim population worldwide) takes two forms: one that argues that Islam is itself compatible with terrorism; and one that argues that Muslims are both sympathetic and prone to terrorism. In terms of linking Islam to terrorism, consider for example the British National Party (BNP)—which, despite its exclusionary and prejudice rhetoric, insists that it is not racist[2]—that believes that "while not all Muslims ... [are] dangerous fanatics ... that itself ... [is] dangerous."[3] This perception has been consumed by the larger society—or at least by banal individuals in society[4]—and manifests itself in the fear that British society is turning into a so-called 'Londonistan.'[5] Narrative that links Islam to terrorism can also be seen in choice of the photographs placed on the jacket cover of books dealing with Islamist extremism, many of which depict ordinary Muslims (not extremists) engaged in their daily prayers. In terms of presenting Muslims (as a collectivity) as both sympathetic and prone to terrorism, consider for example the remarks of Narendra Modi (the Chief Minister in Gujarat, India, and a member of the ultra-nationalist Hindu party *Rashtriya Swayamsevak Sangh* (RSS)[6]): "All Muslims are not terrorists but all terrorists are Muslims."[7] Similar generalizations can also be seen in the post-2001 neoconservative narrative in the United States which calls upon Americans to beware of the Muslim terrorist 'sleeper cells.'[8] Kevin Passmore goes as far as to argue that "for some national-populists [in the west] the figure of the Muslim has taken over from that of the Jew as the embodiment of evil."[9] The demonization of the Jews as a collective people was perhaps best illustrated in the Russian anti-Semitic document *Protocols of the Elders of Zion* which, based on conspiracy theories and racist generalizations, argued that Jews (as a collective people) were planning to take-over the world. It may be surprising to some to know that such writing became popular in the inter-war period of the 1920s and 1930s not only in "central and western Europe" but also in "England and the United States."[10] The point I wish to emphasize here is that whether generalizations are based on conspiracy theories (as in the case of the *Protocols of the Elders of Zion*) or on a sense of threat (as in the Islamophobic narratives that link Islamist extremists with Muslims at large), they are always based on exaggerations that are facilitated by racist thinking. It is most troubling that such easy answers have historically tended to resonate in societies.

Ironically, the very pundits that explain the violence and brutality of Islamist extremists as *uniquely Islamic* also equate Islamist extremism with fascism, a phenomenon so characteristic of early twentieth century western Europe so as to always be defined with reference to it.[11] The irony in presenting Islamist extremism as *uniquely Islamic* yet linking it also to a phenomenon that has been *characteristically European* is striking here. Nonetheless, popular public figures such as former President Bush and Milton Friedman (to name just a few in the American context) vociferously explained Islamist extremist in term of 'Islamo-fascism.'[12] Of course, the intention seems clearly to present Islamist extremism as the kind of evil that had once been associated with the evils of Hitler and thereby to *elevate* the perception of its threat to the levels that had once ema-nated from fascist Germany. The intention seems also to create urgency for pro-tracted military action and, worse, a carte blanche for any and all actions taken to combat its threat, so that even the death of civilians in the process gets pre-sented as 'just.'[13] While deaths of innocent civilians are inevitable in any war, this probability is multiplied when wars comprise of military occupations of host states and the use of guided missile aerial bombings.

The 'Islamo-fascism' narrative, of course, is ill-suited to explain Islamist extremism. This is not only because of its irony (as noted above) but fundament-ally because the nature of reason in radical Islamist rhetoric focuses *not* on the projections of one's supposed supremacy through violence (as in fascism) but on a *rejection of the negation of the self* through violence.[14] Here, a popularly mis-understood notion of the *caliphate* deserves a mention. In explaining Islamist extremism in terms of Islamo-fascism, political pundits point to radical Islamist references to the 'return of the caliphate' as an indication that the motivation—and indeed the essence—of Islamist extremism is a desire to take over the world and to convert it to Islam.[15] Such an understanding is not only misguided—since it completely disconnects any notion of causality for Islamist violence and thereby absolves the self from any notion of responsibility for actions that might have fomented and exacerbated Islamist violence[16]—but it also misunderstands the critical reason in the notion of the *caliphate* which ultimately centers around the notion of *self-governance* and *representative governance*. It is true that the rhetoric of transnational Islamist extremist groups such as al-Qaeda has tended to glorify this notion with references to its global reach, but an accurate under-standing of this notion can perhaps be gained from the rhetoric of domestically confined Islamist extremist groups, such as those that were catalyzed by the writ-ings of Sayyid Qutb which emphasized the pursuits of a representative govern-ment for the ends of self-governance and a rejection of oppression (in this case, at the hands of one's own government).[17]

In sum, the analysis in this book concludes that the recruiting success of Islamist extremist groups and movements is *not* situated in the appeal of their religious (Islamic) rhetoric but situated instead in the appeal of their existential and consequentialist rhetoric.[18] This assertion re-addresses the paradoxes created by the fact of voluntary recruits to Islamist extremist groups that have either secular mindsets or come from privileged socioeconomic backgrounds since, I argue, recruitment success is neither about religion (in and of itself) nor about economic destitution (the 'nothing to live for' argument). This is not to say that these factors are irrelevant. Certainly, a religiously inclined (non-secular) indi-vidual who is easily convinced with any reason contextualized within religious tenets would be susceptible to the religious rhetoric of Islamist extremist groups. And certainly, an individual who is economically destitute would be more prone to the calls for justice and recourse that are explicit in radical Islamist rhetoric. This is to say instead that the recruiting success of Islamist extremists groups and movements can be most accurately understood in terms of the *critical reason* that radical Islamists themselves offer in terms of their explanations and justifications of violence. And this reason, I argue, is existential in its appeal and moral consequentialist in its zeal.

Appendix I

On essence

The notion of an 'essence' is necessarily abstract since an essence "cannot be seen in any ordinary sense of that term."[1] However, the 'essence' of a phenomenon refers to those characteristics that remain the same despite the existence of many other variations of the phenomenon. To the extent that I argue in this book that the *nature of reason* in radical Islamist rhetoric from temporally and contextually varied Islamist extremist groups displays common *themes* (see the *Introduction* of this book), such reason can be understood as the *essence* (the 'what is') of Islamist extremism, since such reason remains the same despite the many temporal and contextual variations of Islamist extremist groups. And so, in delineating the essence of Islamist extremism in this book, I have drawn upon the linguistic and sociological tradition of *critical discourse analysis.* The discourse that I examine presents itself in the forms of varied radical Islamist communiqués—their speeches, declarations (fatwas), charters—that form the rhetoric that is so characteristic of Islamist extremist groups. Interestingly, the method of critical discourse analysis also makes tangible what is otherwise intangible, namely the essence of a thing.

The delineating of the essence of a phenomenon requires a conceptual analysis of the phenomenon in question (the 'what is' of the phenomenon). In a conceptual analysis, a conceptual imagination is critical as only through such a categorization could one distinguish the essence from the other non-essential features (such as context-specific particularities). It should come as no surprise, then, that the notion of an *essence* is often seen as compatible with the notion of *essentialism.* Mohanty defines essentialism as the notion that all things have their core essences, their 'necessary truths' or, if you may, those features that *remain the same* despite all the variables of a phenomenon. Focusing on the essence thus necessarily yields a broadly generalized conceptual study and not a nuanced context-specific causal study. But if it is general, it does not lack merit. Indeed, the merit of a conceptual study is arguably that it generates findings that are more widely applicable than the findings of context-specific study, thereby offering a more comprehensive cross-contextual understanding of a phenomenon.[2]

It deserves to be mentioned that the notion of an essence (or essentialism) has come under attack from the empiricists, those that rely only on observable data and a posteriori judgments (judgments based on experience or tangible data or evidence). It has also come under attack from those philosophers who Mohanty notes are:

> so impressed by the open-endedness of the course of experience as well as of scientific research [provable, observable data] ... [and] so impressed by the historicity of all truths [based on nuanced analysis of contexts] ... and the *fallibility* of all cognition [responsible for making a priori statements about things such as essences] that they find in examinations of essences or in essentialism the opposite of everything they stand for.[3]

In other words, the notion of an essence—the view that anything can be reduced to a *core* essence—has been criticized on grounds that it is at once subjective, normative (thus unscientific) and static (since it does not account for temporal or contextual variations). To this, I might note that while my analysis in this book can be criticized as static (since it argues that Islamist extremism can be understood in terms of a singular essence) and normative (since it is based on my critical analysis of radical Islamist rhetoric), it is nonetheless not entirely divorced from a posteriori analysis since it is based on tangible data in the form of actual radical Islamist discourse.

Of course, the analysis in this book is also extrapolative, particularly in its judgments of the motivations of individuals that voluntarily join Islamist extremist groups. But since such extrapolation is based on epistemological assumptions and logical deductions based on the reason in radical Islamist rhetoric, it cannot be criticized as entirely hypothetical. In this way the analysis in this book cannot be criticized as *entirely* subjective or normative since my conclusions are based on critical analysis of reason that actually comprises radical Islamist rhetoric and not on any purely normative imaginations. Of course, to the extent that any *critical* analysis is subjective by definition, the critical analysis of radical Islamist discourse in this book can also be seen as subjective. But since this book cites actual excerpts from radical Islamist rhetoric (of temporally and contextually varied Islamist extremist groups), the subjectivity of my assertions are at least in part kept in check since the readers too have access to the excerpts that form the bases of my assertions. And, if the analysis in this book is logically convincing, then my assessments about the essence of Islamist extremism can be seen as illustrations of an *analytical truth*—a judgment, assessment, 'truth' or knowledge based on the apparent and logical relations between the concepts within a statement. So if normative and extrapolative it is, it is because such is the nature of a conceptual analysis which, by definition, requires the re-opening of the dialogue of the 'what is' of the phenomenon under question, a venture that unavoidably engages critical analysis which in turn is, by definition, normative and extrapolative.

Finally, the nature of this book, focusing as it does on the essence of Islamist extremism, is very different from the more traditional context-specific causal studies of Islamist extremism. A focus on the essence is a focus on "generalities rather than with particular cases."[4] Schmitt defines essence as the "necessary and *invariant* feature of a given kind of thing that the ... [thing] must possess in order to be an example of that kind of thing."[5] In other words, the essence of a thing is its most essential features, those features that are common to all things in the same category. So, for example, Schmitt argues that the fundamental essence of a human being is the possession of sensory organs. Thus, stripped of all their physical variations and interactive individualities, human beings can only be called a *human* if and only if they possess some basic sensory organs without which the being could not be definitively called a human. The conceptual analysis of Islamist extremism in this book has a similar aim of examining those features of Islamist extremism, as a phenomenon, that remain the same across the temporal and contextual divides of the many varied Islamist extremist groups. Only through such an analysis, which must necessarily be based on empirical generalizations, can one understand the essence of Islamist extremism.

Making essence tangible: the use of critical discourse analysis

This book relies on two variations of discourse analysis: *conversation analysis* (CA) and *critical discourse analysis* (CDA). As such, the method of analysis in this book is a hybrid of both the sociological approach (epitomized in CA) and the linguistics approach (epitomized in CDA) to *discourse analysis* (DA).[6] Critical discourse analysis and conversation analysis represent only two of the many different approaches to *discourse analysis* (DA); however, in the interest of brevity and relevance to this study, only CA and CDA will be discussed here and then only those components of its methods that are reflective of the method employed in this study.[7] Since, as Julia Gillen notes, "there are no blueprints as to how 'best' to proceed" with DA, liberties in its application seem almost inevitable.[8] Before discussing the nature of the liberties taken in this study regarding its DA—in particular, its particular combination of CA with CDA as a method of analysis—it may be instructive to first define the terms 'discourse' and 'discourse analysis.'

Gilbert Weiss and Ruth Wodak note that the term 'discourse' has held many different meanings; in the German and Central European contexts, "a distinction is made between 'text' and 'discourse'," while in the "English-speaking world, 'discourse' is often used for *both* written and oral texts."[9] Norman Fairclough defines 'discourse' as meaning language—broadly defined to include various manifestations of social communications including "visual images, etc."[10] Consistent with this, Julia Gillen and Alan Petersen define DA as a method that accepts "as data any language *as it occurs*, whatever the channel or mode."[11] The emphasis on language 'as it occurs' is to point to the fact that DA often analyzes "discourse produced as part of everyday and institutional life, *rather than* data obtained through, say, research interviews."[12] In this way, DA as a method is quite different from phenomenology *as a method* (to be distinguished from phenomenology as a framework of analysis, as used in this study) as the latter typically requires the researcher to immerse herself literally in the context of the phenomenon under examination and to conducted interviews herself while DA does not require such first-hand data collection.[13]

One of the distinguishing features of CA, is that CA "explicitly *rejects* the notion that you have to understand the *context* before you can approach texts."[14] In other words, the interpretation of discourse need not proceed from a detailed analysis of the context within which the discourse takes place, as it does not in this study as well. Although the discourse in this study is not strictly 'conversation' analysis—to the extent that the discourse analyzed does not comprise of a direct dialogue among Islamist extremists in the form of their conversations but instead comprises of what radical Islamists publish—the aforementioned distinctive feature of CA still gives legitimacy to the method of empirical generalizations. In other words, much of the radical Islamist discourse makes explicit who and what the object of grievance is; thus references are either made to particular governments and/or military occupations that the particular discourse is surrounding. Given this, a context-specific analysis is unnecessary for a conceptual analysis of Islamist extremism that is based on a critical analysis of reason in radical Islamist rhetoric.

A critical qualification

In generalizing the essence of Islamist extremism as a Hegelian struggle for recognition, I do not negate the importance of the context-specific geo-political causes that create and consolidate Islamist extremist groups. The method of critical discourse analysis that I utilize in this book intends instead to focus on that which remains the same across the temporal and contextual variations of Islamist extremist groups, that which I argue is the *essence*—the essential nature—of Islamist extremism. Indeed, as notes Schmitt, in a phenomenological examination "descriptions of ... *situations* do not serve as premises for an *inductive generalization* [about essences]."[15] Here, 'situations' can be understood as the equivalent of specific contexts (temporal and/or geo-political) within which Islamist extremist groups are formed. In other words, in moving away from the traditional context-specific analyses of Islamist extremism, the analysis in this book does *not* doubt or negate the importance of contexts in creating and fomenting Islamist extremist groups. In this way, a conceptual analysis of Islamist extremism based on critical analysis of radical Islamist discourse is intended to imaginatively 'lift' Islamist extremist groups from their specific contexts in order to focus instead on that reason that remains the same regardless of temporal and contextual variations—thus to focus on the 'what is' and not the 'why' of Islamist extremism.[16] Furthermore, to say, as does Schmitt, that 'descriptions of ... *situations* do not serve as premises for an inductive generalization' is to say that the descriptions of temporal and geo-political contexts of Islamist extremist groups do not serve as premises (thus are not necessary) for delineating the *essence* of Islamist extremism since the essence can be delineated—as in this book—through critical analysis of the nature of reason in radical Islamist rhetoric. Assessments of 'essence' that are based on critical analysis of radical Islamist discourse are thus essentially inductive generalizations. They are 'inductive' (as opposed to deductive) because such assessments are necessarily intangible even if they are based on observable data (such as radical Islamist discourse). They are 'general' because such assessments describe an *essence* common to temporally and contextually varied Islamist extremist groups and not the particular causes of specific Islamist extremist groups.

Equally, it must be noted that in delineating the essence through empirical generalizations of sorts (that are characteristic of a method of discourse analysis), the analysis in this book does *not* assume uniformity in the scope and goals of the temporally and contextually varied Islamist extremist groups, it assumes only a common essence. It is indisputable that the specific scope and goals of Islamist extremist groups do indeed dependent on the temporal and/or geo-political context of the groups. Thus, for example, while the specific *goals* of the Palestinian *Hamas* are the destruction of what it sees as the Zionist government of Israel, the specific *goals* of the Pakistani *Lashkar-e-Toiba* are the destabilization of what it sees as the US-puppet Pakistani government.[17] A great variation of *scope* can also be found in temporally and contextually varied Islamist extremist groups, so while *al-Qaeda* has a transnational scope, *Hamas* and *Lashkar-e-Toiba* have geographically limited if not a predominately intrastate scope. Indeed, the Lebanese *Hizbullah* prides itself in its distinction from *al-Qaeda* in terms of its scope and goals in the following manner:

> Al-Qa'ida has adopted a position against the Americans to go after them directly … *wherever the U.S. may be in the world* [its scope], whereas Hezbollah's choice has been *entirely different*. Hizballah perceives that the confrontation *must be restricted* to the Israelis where *they are occupiers of the land* [and not if they are no longer occupiers], and that does not involve going after all the Jews in the world.[18]

My intention in the conceptual analysis of Islamist extremism in this book is thus to illustrate that the *essence* of Islamist extremism remains the same even when the scope and goals of Islamist extremist groups vary according to their temporal and geo-political contexts and even when, given the same temporal or geo-political contexts, the goals of Islamist extremist groups vary based on whether they are *jihadi* groups (where the scope is often inter-state or 'transnational' and where the 'other' is defined as the non-Muslim 'other') or *sectarian* groups (where the scope is often intra-state and where the 'other' is defined as the Muslim sectarian 'other,' the Shi or the Sunni as the case may be).[19]

Appendix II

Virgins in heaven

The notion of the '72 virgins in heaven' that is oft cited by radical Islamists as a reward for martyrdom (self-destruction), and that is also popularly thought of as the very bases of an individual's motivation for self-destruction (martyrdom) in the western media is a fundamentally distorted notion. Indeed, the notion of the 'virgins in heaven' is a misrepresentation of the theological notion of the *houris*;[1] the notion refers to persons in heaven made "anew," *as if* "made virgin," and not literally virgin in the sexual sense.[2] Thus, contrary to its popular presentation and its popular understanding in literal terms, this notion, in its accurate theological sense, has instead a metaphorical meaning. Though this claim is oft-cited in radical Islamist rhetoric, and it also forms the popular western understanding of the motivation of radical Islamists based on what is proclaimed in radical Islamist rhetoric, Muhammad Abdel Haleem (a leading Islamic theologian) argues that this notion is a most perverted understanding of the Quranic verses dealing with *al janna* (heaven) and all the pleasures therein.[3] Haleem argues that 'pleasures' in heaven are *not* of the flesh, but refer instead to *spiritual* pleasures derived from the serenity to be expected in heaven. Haleem refers to numerous verses in the Quran as substantiation of his point. It appears therefore that the notion that martyrdom (self-destruction) will be awarded by the physical pleasures of 72 virgins is but a falsification conspired by the recruiters of Islamist extremist groups to sensationalize an act which is fundamentally reasoned in radical Islamist rhetoric in terms a self-*transcendent recognition* in much the Hegelian sense.[4]

Indeed, David Cook argues that the entire notion of special rewards awaiting martyrs in heaven—as depicted in radical Islamist rhetoric—is itself a misrepresentation of both the notion of rewards and the notion of martyrdom.[5] Cook points out that the notion of martyrdom has been stretched to a point of losing much of its original theological meaning. Indeed, he notes that "there are no verses in the Qur'an, other than ... [Qur'an 3: 169–170] that single out the martyr for special treatment in heaven."[6] However, notes Cook:

> In the transition from the Qur'an to the *hadith* (traditions) literature, the situation changes completely. Inside the *hadith* literature, the figure of the martyr is delineated and described in great detail as a unique person set

apart from all other Muslims. The first problem that arises is who precisely could be counted as a martyr (*shahid*) in Islam. [...] The early *hadith* reflect a process of widening the definition of martyrdom to the point where it began to lose all meaning and simply came to cover anyone who had died a worthy death and should be admitted to paradise.[7]

Even more significantly, Cook notes that "there is a striking difference between the popular *jihad* literature ... and the formal Islamic legal literature. Lurid descriptions of the rewards of the martyr are entirely *absent* from the legal literature, which consists of discussions of definitions of what constitutes a martyr and what describes the legal boundaries of a martyr's actions."[8] Cook's observation substantiates my argument in Chapter 3 of this book that radical Islamist promotion of martyrdom (self-destructive missions) should be understood less, if at all, as a testimony of faith (in the sense of a demarcation of a religious duty), and more as a challenge of the status of the self as the slave through reason that is dialectical in nature.

Some other comments deserve a mention here. It is important to keep in mind that the notion of martyrdom (self-destruction) is originally a uniquely Shia notion of the "theology of redemptive suffering."[9] That martyrdom was originally a Shia phenomenon may be explained, argues Cook, by the fact that Sunnis, who comprise approximately "85 percent of world Muslims ... have hardly ever been in the situation where they were oppressed (compared ... to Shi'ites)."[10] Here, my argument that martyrdom is reasoned in terms of a tactic that challenges the servitude of the self seems particularly relevant in light of the fact that this very notion has been traditionally a Shia notion, representing a group that has been traditionally oppressed. Daniel Brown notes that it is only in contemporary times that Sunni revivalists have "made an ideology of martyrdom central to their program."[11] This may make sense in light of the more recent Sunni perception of being oppressed by the other (whether one's own unrepresentative governments or foreign entities). The rise of 'suicide bombers' in the years of the American occupation of Iraq is a case in point, since many of these actions were committed by the anti-American *Sunni* insurgents and the al-Qaeda (also Sunni) contingents in Iraq.

Brown argues that one of the reasons for the Sunni adoption of the Shia tradition of martyrdom is the desire to promote a "*self-assertive* Islam."[12] This assessment is consistent with my argument in Chapter 3 of this book, namely that the radical Islamist (Sunni or Shia) promotion of self-destruction can be conceptually understood in terms of a rejection of the negation of the self through an action that takes away the control of the masters over the self. Hence, as I argue in Chapter 3, self-destruction becomes reasoned in terms of an action that demarcates the absolute autonomy of the self, which can otherwise be understood in terms of *self-assertion*. In other words, the Sunni adoption of the Shia tradition of martyrdom for the ends of what Brown calls "self-assertive Islam" can be understood conceptually in recognition-theoretic terms, as the desire for the *assertion of the self* as at once distinct and equally significant to the other. The reference to 'Islam' in the calls for a 'self-assertive Islam' may thus be understood, I argue, in terms of Islam as a symbolization of a collective identity, the *ummah,* as opposed to Islam strictly as a religious tradition.[13] So the promotion of a 'self-assertive Islam' may be conceptually understood in terms of the promotion of the *self-assertion of the ummah*, as in the rejection of the self (in the collective sense of the ummah) as the slave.[14] In this way, martyrdom becomes a symbolization of a self-transcendent recognition since in the symbolization of 'self' assertion, the individual is killed in the act; see my analysis in Chapter 3. Within this context, we can also conceptually understand the Shia notion of 'redemptive suffering' in that it redeems the collective 'self' (the *ummah*) in exchange for the suffering of an individual through death. Not surprisingly then, Brown points out that such Shia redemptive suffering was promoted during "the Iranian Revolution; in the Iran-Iraq war; in the bitterness of the Lebanese civil war";[15] all of these cases, I argue, are of conflicts characterized by the perception of the self as oppressed and as thus characterized by struggles for recognition in the Hegelian sense.[16]

Appendix III

Humanitarian interventions

I argue in Chapter 4 that stipulations of wars as being 'just' and 'unjust' are useless in understanding the nature of violence since violence and wars are always justified in terms of a 'morality'—and thus presented in terms of a 'just' war—by all those engaging in wars and violence. Thus, I argue, violence and wars are always justified in terms of a consequentialist morality. Critics of my argument might well ask 'what of humanitarian interventions,' since such interventions are popularly viewed as altruistic and thus not consequentialist in reason. Such criticism, of course, overlooks the politics of humanitarian interventions and views such interventions—or lack thereof—in terms of how they are *rhetorically presented*: as unquestionably altruistic and thus 'just.' But the consequentialism inherent in the decisions to engage in military interventions for the ends of 'humanitarianism' can be seen in: (1) their selective nature; (2) in the varying perceptions of the citizens of host states regarding such interventions; (3) in the varying perceptions of others regarding such interventions.

The hypocrisies in the designation of what qualifies for a humanitarian intervention, as well as the contradictions in actions taken for the ends of a 'humanitarian intervention,' renders its stipulation as a 'just war' subjective at best, and dangerous at worst.[1] Indeed, even Michael Walzer, who otherwise argues that there are clear demarcations between 'just wars' and 'unjust wars,' views humanitarian interventions with caution:

> clear examples of what is called 'humanitarian intervention' are very rare. Indeed, *I have not found any*, but only mixed cases where the *humanitarian motive* is *one among several. States don't send their soldiers into other states, it seems, only in order to save lives.*[2]

Yet, the proclaimed altruism of humanitarian interventions is used to silence those that criticize the Just War doctrine for its contradictions and hypocrisies.

While military action for the ends of safeguarding human lives in cases of ethnic cleansing and genocide is unarguably an urgency—the freeing of prisoners of the German Nazi concentration camps by the Allies during World War II and the NATO bombing of Serbia to protect Bosnian Muslims from the ethnic cleansing tactics of Serbian paramilitary troops are just two cases in point—there are still, I argue, two problematical issues related to the justifications of violence in the name of 'humanitarian interventions': (1) that such justifications often misuse the 'double-effect' stipulation of the Just War doctrine; and (2) the very selective and subjective nature of the cases that are chosen for humanitarian interventions invalidate the proclaimed 'categorical altruism' of such missions. In addressing the first problematic, which essentially speaks to the contradictions inherent in the stipulation of violence for the ends of humanitarian causes, I quote Steinhoff:

> it is an oversimplification to see the doctrine of double effect only as a *danger* to innocents, for it also allows ... the use of 'wicked things,' for example military violence, in order to *save* innocents (as in the form of humanitarian intervention).[3]

In addressing the second problematic, I quote Walzer, who notes that "humanitarian intervention is justified when it is a response (with reasonable expectations of success) to acts 'that shock the moral conscience of mankind'."[4] The problem with Walzer's assertion is that the notion of 'moral conscience of mankind' completely ignores circumstances where such a unity is exchanged for more immediate selfish interests. Consider, for example, the lack of international humanitarian intervention in the case of the genocide that transpired in Rwanda during 1994.

It is true that the Just War doctrine stipulates that only those wars that have a probability of success should be engaged in, a caution that supposedly also applies to humanitarian interventions. The problem with such a stipulation is that it implies that only wars that can be easily won qualify as 'just' wars, which implies further that war for the ends of 'humanitarian interventions' are necessarily consequentialist in reason. And this is disturbing, even if it substantiates my above noted assertion. This is because many of the cases in urgent need of humanitarian intervention are also complicated cases that do not qualify for easy victory or come with what Walzer calls 'reasonable expectation of success.' While one might defend a lack of a humanitarian intervention in such cases on grounds of the immorality of engaging in an endless war, this stipulation also offers a legal exit for states that do not *want to* engage in much needed humanitarian interventions for reasons of a lack of national interest in such an engagement. So Walzer's assertion above at once validates and nullifies the urgency of humanitarian interventions. And this brings us back to my argument that it is consequentialist reason that forms the bases of all decisions to engage in wars and violence, regardless of what titles are awarded such acts of wars and violence.

Notes

Preface

1 Frederick Weiss, for examples, notes this about his particular interpretation and analysis of Hegel's works: "What is and is not 'essential' in the philosophy of Hegel may well be a matter of debate among the enlightened savants." See Frederick G. Weiss, *Hegel: The Essential Writings* (New York: Harper Torchbooks, 1974), edited and with an introduction by Frederick G. Weiss; Foreword by J.N. Findley; p. xv.
2 Richard Schmitt, "Phenomenology," *Encyclopedia of Philosophy,* 2nd edition, Donald M. Borchert, editor in chief, New York: Thomson Gale, 2005, p. 284.

Introduction

1 See Appendix I for the meaning of 'essence,' both as it is implied in my analysis in this book and as it is understood and used in philosophical writings.
2 I discuss this assertion in detail in Chapters 2 and 3.
3 The theoretical argument that struggles for recognition are existential and that such struggles are fundamentally moral consequentialist in their justifications is discussed in Chapter 1. For further references to violence justified within other religious contexts, see: Bruce Hoffman, *Inside Terrorism*, New York: Columbia University Press, 2006; Mark Juergensmeyer, *Global Rebellion: Religious Challenges to the Secular State, from Christian Militias to Al Qaeda*, Berkeley: University of California Press, 2008; Robert Pape, *Dying to Win: The Strategic Logic of Suicide Terrorism*, New York: Random House, 2005.
4 Many of the authors listed have multiple publications, too many to mention here, and so I have randomly chosen a few to mention. Martha Crenshaw, *Revolutionary Terrorism: The FLN in Algeria, 1954–1962*, Hoover Institution Press, Stanford University, 1978; Augustus Richard Norton, *Amal and the Shi'a: Struggle for the Soul of Lebanon*, Austin: University of Texas Press, 1987, and *Hezbollah*, Princeton, NJ: Princeton University Press, 2007; Hassan Abbas, *Pakistan's Drift into Extremism: Allah, the Army, and America's War on Terror*, New York: M.E. Sharpe, 2005; Assaf Moghadam, "Palestinian Suicide Terrorism in the Second Intifada: Motivations and Organizational Aspects," *Studies in Conflict and Terrorism*, 26, pp. 65–92, 2003; Seyyed Vali Reza Nasr, *The Vanguard of the Islamic Revolution: The Jama'at-i Islami of Pakistan*, Berkeley: University of California Press, 1994; Amal Saad-Ghorayeb, *Hizbu'llah: Politics and Religion*, London: Pluto Press, 2002; Fouad Ajami, *The Vanished Imam: Musa al Sadr and the Shia of Lebanon*, New York: Cornell University Press, 1986; Fawaz A. Gerges, *The Far Enemy: Why Jihad Went Global*, New York: Cambridge University Press, 2005; Ayesha Jalal, *Partisans of Allah: Jihad in South Asia*, Cambridge: Harvard University Press, 2008.

5 Robert Pape, *Dying to Win: The Strategic Logic of Suicide Terrorism*, New York: Random House, 2005, p. 100.

6 Luca Ricolfi, "Palestinians, 1981–2003," *Making Sense of Suicide Missions*, Diego Gambetta, ed., New York: Oxford University Press, 2005, pp. 77–129.

7 Alan B. Krueger, *What makes a Terrorist? Economics and the Roots of Terrorism*, Princeton: Princeton University Press, 2007, p. 50.

8 I have put religious violence in quotation marks since I argue in this book that is a misplaced emphasis; the emphasis, I argue, should be placed instead on the instrumentality of religion. See Chapter 1 and Chapter 4 where I discuss this issue in detail.

9 Richard Bonney, *Jihad: From Quran to bin Laden*, New York: Palgrave Macmillian, 2004; Mark Juergensmeyer, *Terror in the Mind of God: The Global Rise of Religious Violence*, Berkeley, CA: University of California Press, 2003; David Cook, *Understanding Jihad*, Berkeley, CA: University of California Press, 2005.

10 Azmat Abbas, "The Making of a Militant," *The Herald* (Karachi, Pakistan), July 2003, p. 58.

11 See "Men with a Mission," *The Herald* (Karachi, Pakistan), July 2003, pp. 49–56.

12 I have put 'suicide bombings' in quotation marks here as I argue in Chapter 3 that the critical nature of reason in the radical Islamist promotions of self-destruction is not suicidal (in the sense of escaping the drudgery of life) but dialectical and paradoxical.

13 Christoph Reuter, *My Life is a Weapon: A Modern History of Suicide Bombing*, Princeton: Princeton University Press, 2002.

14 Reuter, *My Life is a Weapon.*

15 Mia Bloom, *Dying to Kill,* New York: Columbia University Press, 2005, pp. 2–3.

16 Robert A. Pape. *Dying to Win: The Strategic Logic of Suicide Terrorism*, New York: Random House, 2005.

17 Pape, *Dying to Win*, p. 118.

18 "EU Deplores 'Dangerous' Islam Jibe," *BBC Online,* September 27, 2001; as quoted by Monte Palmer and Princes Palmer, in *Islamic Extremism: Causes, Diversity and Challenges*, New York: Rowman & Littlefield Publishers, Inc., 2008, p. 2. Emphasis added here.

19 Marvin Perry & Howard E. Negrin, editors, *The Theory and Practice of Islamic Terrorism: An Anthology*, New York, NY: Palgrave Macmillan, 2008, p. 10.

20 Marvin Perry & Howard E. Negrin, editors, *The Theory and Practice of Islamic Terrorism: An Anthology*, New York, NY: Palgrave Macmillan, 2008, p. 10.

21 Shmuel Bar, "The religious sources of Islamic terrorism," *Policy Review*, no. 125, June/July 2004, pp. 27–37

22 Mary R. Habeck, "Jihadist Strategies in the War on Terrorism," *The Theory and Practice of Islamic Terrorism: An Anthology*, Marvin Perry & Howard E. Negrin, editors, New York, NY: Palgrave Macmillan, 2008, p. 69.

23 Melanie Phillips, *Londonistan*, New York: Encounter Books, 2006.

24 See Martha Crenshaw's analysis of Raphael Israeli's assertions in "Explaining Suicide Terrorism: A Review Essay," *Security Studies* 16, no. 1, January-March 2007, p. 141. Crenshaw is referring to Raphael Israeli's book *Islamikaze: Manifestations of Islamic Martyrology*, London: Frank Cass, 2003.

25 Bernard Lewis, *The Middle East and the West*, London: Weidenfeld and Nicolson, 1964, p. 137. Emphases added here and not found in the original text. Thus was introduced the term 'clash of civilizations' into both academic and non-academic popular discourse, a term later popularized by Samuel Huntington in his infamous 1993 publication "The Clash of Civilizations?" *Foreign Affairs* 72, Summer 1993: 22–49. This article was later converted into his book *The Clash of Civilizations and the Remaking of the World Order*, New York, NY: Touchstone, 1997.

26 Bernard Lewis, "The Roots of Muslim Rage," *Atlantic Monthly*, September 1990, pp. 47–60.

27 Samuel Huntington, "The Clash of Civilizations?" *Foreign Affairs*, Summer 1993, 72(3), pp. 22–49. See also Huntington, *The Clash of Civilizations and the Remaking of World Order*, New York: Simon & Schuster, 1996.
28 I shall come back to this point later in this Introduction.
29 Joseba Zulaika, *Terrorism: The Self-fulfilling Prophecy*, Chicago: The University of Chicago Press, 2009.
30 Emran Qureshi and Michael A. Sells, "Introduction: Constructing the Muslim Enemy," in *The New Crusades: Constructing the Muslim Enemy*, E. Qureshi & M.A. Sells, eds., New York: Columbia University Press, 2003, p. 4. Emphasis added here and does not appear in the original text.
31 Emran Qureshi & Michael A. Sells, "Introduction: Constructing the Muslim Enemy," in *The New Crusades: Constructing the Muslim Enemy*, E. Qureshi & M.A. Sells, eds., New York: Columbia University Press, 2003, p. 8.
32 'White Man's Burden' originally appeared as a poem written by the English poet Rudyard Kippling in 1899. Some argue that Kippling had intended in this poem a satirical commentary on imperialism, while others argue that Kippling's poem reflected his deeply held Eurocentric views. Whatever the case may be, apologists for Western imperialist have subsequently utilized the phrase to justify imperialism and colonialism as to the benefit of the colonized. This notion is thus decidedly 'orientalist' in essence and vindicates Said's analysis of the mentality and intention of Western imperialists in their incursions to non-Western worlds.
33 Hegel argued that demarcating contrasts were the very bases of struggles for recognition and the explanation of the creation of masters and slaves. I shall discuss this point in more detail in Chapter 1 in this book.
34 See Talal Asad, *On Suicide Bombing*, New York: Columbia University Press, 2007.
35 Asad, *On Suicide Bombing*, pp. 74–76; pp. 84–85.
36 For further distinctions between a broad conceptual analysis and a context-specific causal analysis, see Robert Goodin and Charles Tilly's description of contextual studies in contrast to conceptual studies in *The Oxford Handbook of Contextual Political Analysis*, Robert E. Goodin and Charles Tilly, Eds., New York: Oxford University Press, 2006, p. 7.
37 See Charles W. Mueller's definition of conceptualization in "Conceptualization, Operationalization, and Measurement," in *The SAGE Encyclopedia of Social Science Research Methods*, Michael S. Lewis-Beck, Alan Bryman, Tim Futing Liao, editors, vol. 1, London: SAGE Publications, 2004, p. 162.
38 See Appendix I for a more detailed discussion of the method employed for analysis in this book.
39 Edward Goodwin Ballard introduces the notion of 'reciprocal causality' in defining the meaning of 'dialectic' in *Principles of Interpretation*, Ohio: Ohio University Press, 1983, pp. 180–204. I discuss Ballard's analysis in more detail in Chapter 1 in elaborating the notion of the dialectic.
40 There are, of course, a number of scholars who have challenged the assumption that poverty leads to terrorism—or the so-called poverty–terrorism nexus; see my discussion earlier in this Introduction and the notes related to that discussion. For a solidly quantitative analysis that challenges the poverty–terrorism nexus argument, see Alan B. Krueger, *What Makes a Terrorist: Economics and the Roots of Terrorism*, Princeton, NJ: Princeton University Press, 2007, especially pages 163–176. In this book, Krueger argues that the roots of terrorism are instead a lack of political and civil liberties that leads to alienation and an aggressive rejection of such oppression.
41 I have borrowed this question from the set of questions that form the bases of a multi-author volume edited by Diego Gambetta, *Making Sense of Suicide Mission*, which is dedicated to the study of suicide bombers from the Sri Lankan case to the Japanese Kamikaze case to the suicide bombers of in the radical Islamist case. But while the authors offer compelling data and technical analysis, none are able to adequately

answer the questions they pose at the onset of this book. For the manner in which this question is addressed by authors in Gambetta's edited volume, see *Making Sense of Suicide Mission*, Diego Gambetta, ed., New York: Oxford University Press, 2005.
42 Gambetta, *Making Sense of Suicide Mission.*

1 Struggles for recognition and moral consequentialism

1 I have depicted a conceptual analysis of Islamist extremism in Figure 1.1.
2 It is important to note, as does Walter Kaufmann in his preface to his translation of Nietzsche's *Will-to-Power*, that this document was never published as a book manuscript in Nietzsche's lifetime. Indeed, much of what comprises the Will-to-Power, as a translated manuscript, is but a compilation of the various notes and ideas that Nietzsche jotted on paper, apparently, it is thought, with the intention to at some point publish them in a coherent manuscript. This manuscript was never to be. However, Kaufmann is known to have done an excellent job in maintaining the authenticity of these notes—in terms of their sequence and even in terms of their disjointed nature—in his translation *The Will-to-Power*, New York: Vintage Books, 1968.
3 It should be noted that Hegel's *Phenomenology of Spirit* is largely concerned with the phenomenon of the development of primitive consciousness into self-consciousness (a sense of self, a self-identity for which recognition is sought) and it is only much later in his book that he discusses the phenomenon of *Lordship and Bondage* (or masters and slaves) and only in the context of his characteristic dialectic where over time the slave attains a self-recognition and comes to challenge the master's mastery—where the slave becomes the 'master' and the master the 'slave.' Indeed, some have even argued that an emphasis on the rather controversial and enticing master–slave dialectic is misplaced as it essentially misunderstands Hegel's main aims in the *Phenomenology*—that of a rebuttal to Kant's epistemological arguments (particularly his transcendental idealism) through a meticulously abstract and almost mathematically inspired analysis of consciousness. Be that as it may, none can deny that an analysis of the dynamics of master–slave dialectic does comprise Hegel's analysis in the *Phenomenology* and it is this that I focus on and draw upon in analyzing the nature of reason in radical Islamist rhetoric.
4 See Chapter 5 where I use the example of the US–NATO strategy in Afghanistan to illustrate this point.
5 Later, in Chapter 5, I argue how a lack of understanding of this very existential dynamic on the part of the US–NATO contingencies in Afghanistan (who are at war with the Taliban) is contributing to *losing hearts-and-minds* in Afghanistan and to the victory of the Taliban. Here, I define victory in terms of the absence of the defeat of the Taliban, despite the protracted military engagement of the US–NATO contingents in Afghanistan for over 10 years.
6 The argument that struggles for recognition—defined in the Hegelian sense of a desire for the acknowledgment of the autonomy of the self—are existential appear in varied literature: in studies analyzing the dynamics of slavery, to the paradox of equality in multicultural democracies, to conflicts within societies. For example, Charles Taylor (1994) utilizes the Hegelian notion of desires for recognition to address the question of whether recognition (of one's identity as distinct from the other) can be reconciled with the demands of equality in multicultural democratic societies; see Charles Taylor, *Multiculturalism: Examining the politics of Recognition*, Princeton, NJ: Princeton University Press, 1994. Axel Honneth (1995) utilizes the concept of desires for recognition to analyze the hierarchies within societies wherein a perception of a lack of recognition (on the part of a group) gets linked to a sense of disrespect. Within this context, Honneth shows how this sense of negation leads the group in question to re-definite morality as struggles for recognition

(struggles for respect and acknowledgment); see Axel Honneth, *The Struggle for Recognition: The Moral Grammar of Social Conflicts*, Cambridge, MA: The MIT Press, 1995. I engage Honneth's analysis in more detail in Chapter 4 where I talk about the radical Islamist re-definition of morality in response to their sense of servitude and negation. Patchen Markell (2003) utilizes the recognition-theoretic paradigm to challenge the "equation of recognition with justice"; see Patchen Markell, *Bound by Recognition*, Princeton, NJ: Princeton University Press, 2003; the quoted text is taken from the back cover of Patchen's book. And, in a much celebrated classic scholarship, Frantz Fanon (1963) presented the indigenous Algerian violent struggle against their French colonial masters in terms of the necessity and imperative of a struggle for recognition (the struggle for independence and the rejection of oppression); Frantz Fanon, *The Wretched of the Earth*, Translated from the French by Richard Philcox, with commentary by Jean-Paul Sartre and Homi K. Bhabha, New York: Grove Press, 1963. Later, in more specifically drawing upon Hegel's master–slave dialectic, Fanon (1967) sought to examine the problem of recognition within the context of a hierarchical racial society; see Frantz Fanon, *Black Skin, White Masks*, New York: Grove Press, 1967.

7 In his analysis of struggles for recognition, it should be noted that Hegel does argue that zero-sum and non-reciprocal recognition does ultimately lead to a synthesis of positive-sum and reciprocal recognition over time. However, in this chapter—and in this book—I only engage Hegel's initial notion of struggles for recognition which is based on an assumption of a zero-sum (non-reciprocal) recognition, since I argue that the subsequent creation of masters and slaves, and the fear entailed in the self becoming the slave, sheds critical light on the nature of reason in radical Islamist rhetoric.

8 Honneth, *The Struggle for Recognition*, p. 160. Emphasis added here and does not appear in the original text.

9 Honneth, *The Struggle for Recognition*, pp. 160–161. Emphasis added here and not found in the original text.

10 Honneth, *The Struggle for Recognition*, p. 161. Emphasis added here and does not appear in the original text.

11 This forms the subtitle of Axel Honneth's book *The Struggle for Recognition: The Moral Grammar of Social Conflicts*, Joel Anderson, Trans., Cambridge, Massachusetts: MIT Press, 1995

12 It is important to note here that, at least officially, Nietzsche's work in general has been understood by scholars as necessarily anti-Hegelian. While this may be so in terms of the larger dimensions of Hegel's work—especially those parts of the *Phenomenology of Spirit* that discuss the Holy spirit in the Christian context given Neitzsche's atheistic leanings—it is not necessarily so, I argue, in terms of the implications of Neitzsche's arguments related to his view of notions of morality, in particular, in the context of his notion of 'will-to-power' as the desire for self-assertion which can be understood in terms of the Hegelian desire for recognition. I shall discuss this in more detail later in this chapter.

13 In this way, Nietzsche's view stands in contrast to a Kantian notion of a deontological morality, where notions of morality are understood as 'pure' and reflective of what should be done—out of a sense of duty—regardless of its consequences.

14 Peter Singer, *Hegel: A Very Short Introduction*, Oxford: Oxford University Press, 1983, p. 79. Emphasis added here and does not appear in the original text.

15 Michael Inwood. *A Hegel Dictionary*, Oxford, UK: Blackwell, 1999, p. 246. The emphasis on person is found in Inwood's text.

16 Taken from Jean-Paul Sartre, "The Existence of Others," *Being And Nothingness*, New York: Routledge, 1953, cited in John O'Neill, ed., *Hegel's Dialectic of Desire and Recognition*, New York: State University of New York Press, 1996, p. 88.

17 I shall discuss this notion in more detail later in this chapter.

18 For a discussion of additional questions related to the question of the desire for recognition see Patchen Markell, "Recognition and Redistribution" in *The Oxford Handbook of Political Theory*, John S. Dryzek et al., Eds., UK: Oxford University Press, 2006, pp. 454–456.

19 Inwood, *A Hegel Dictionary*, pp. 245–247.

20 Inwood, *A Hegel Dictionary*, pp. 245–247.

21 Williams, *Hegel's Ethics of Recognition*, p. 60. Emphasis added here and not found in the original text.

22 Solomon, *From Hegel to Existentialism*, p. 243.

23 Pinkard, *Hegel's Phenomenology*, p. 54.

24 Terry Pinkard, *Hegel's Phenomenology: The Sociality of Reason*, New York: Cambridge University Press, 1996, p. 53. Emphasis found in original text except for the emphasis on 'independent.'

25 Pinkard, *Hegel's Phenomenology: The Sociality of Reason*, New York: Cambridge University Press, 1996, p. 59. Emphasis added here and does not appear in the original text.

26 Kojeve, *Introduction to the Reading of Hegel*, p. 46. Emphasis found in the original text.

27 Lauer, S.J. *A Reading of Hegel's Phenomenology of Spirit*, p. 128.

28 Jean Hyppolite, "Self-Consciousness and Life: The Independence of Self-consciousness," in *Hegel's Dialectic of Desire and Recognition: Texts and Commentary*, ed. John O'Neill, Albany: State University of New York Press, 1996, p. 71. See original reference.

29 The assumption of zero-sum struggles for recognition most notably appears in Hegel's *Phenomenology of Spirit*. In his *Jena* manuscripts, Hegel acknowledges that the only possibility of mutual recognition is embodied in a relationship of love between two entities, the discussion of which is beyond the scope of this book.

30 By 'dialectical' I mean related to the dialectic. A dialectic, as we shall see in this section, describes a relationship that is both dynamic and mutually reinforcing *by its very nature* (that is, the mutual reinforcement is not based on consent of the parties involved in a dialectic relationship but reflective of the *relationship*).

31 Edward Goodwin Ballard, *Principles of Interpretation*, Athens, Ohio: Ohio University Press, 1983, p. 185.

32 I've given the example of master and slave as this is the specific kind of dialectic that Hegel talks about and that I engage in this book.

33 Edward Goodwin Ballard, *Principles of Interpretation*, Athens, Ohio: Ohio University Press, 1983, pp. 185–187.

34 Robert R. Williams, *Recognition: Fichte and Hegel on the Other*, New York: State University of New York Press, 1992, p. 179. Emphasis found in the original text.

35 See the Preface of this book where I introduced Edward Said's *Orientalism* in order to shed light on the nature of the Euro-centric, neo-conservative assessments of the Muslim world in general, and of their explanations of Islamist extremism in particular.

36 R.M. Hare's discussion of 'slavery' in his book *Essays on Political Morality*, New York: Oxford University Press, 1998, p. 150.

37 See R.M. Hare's discussion of 'slavery' in his book *Essays on Political Morality*, New York: Oxford University Press, 1998, p. 150. Emphasis found in the original text.

38 Hare, *Essays on Political Morality*, p. 150. Emphasis found in the original text.

39 Hare, *Essays on Political Morality*, p. 150. Emphasis found in the original text.

40 Kojeve, *Introduction to the Reading of Hegel*, p. 47. Emphasis added here.

41 John O'Neill, "Introduction: A Dialectical Genealogy of Self, Society, and Culture in and after Hegel," in *Hegel's Dialectic of Desire and Recognition*, ed. John O'Neill, pp. 1–25.

42 Pinkard, *Hegel's Phenomenology*, p. 61. Emphasis added here and not found in the original text.

43 Jean-Jacques Rousseau, *The Social Contract and Discourse on the Origins of Inequality*, ed. Lester Crocker, New York: Washington Square Press, 1971, p. 7.

44 Jean Hyppolite, "Self-Consciousness and Life: The Independence of Self-consciousness," in *Hegel's Dialectics of Desire and Recognition: Texts and Commentary*, John O'Neill, ed., Albany, NY: State University of New York Press, 1996, p. 81. Emphases added here and do not appear in the original text.

45 William A. Shearson, "The Common Assumptions of Existentialist Philosophy," in *The Development and Meaning of Twentieth-Century Existentialism*, William L. McBride, ed., New York: Garland Publishers, Inc., 1997, p. 288.

46 Robert A. Pape & James K. Feldman, *Cutting the Fuse: The Explosion of Global Suicide Terrorism and How to Stop It*, Chicago: The University of Chicago Press, 2010, p. 11.

47 Pape & Feldman, *Cutting the Fuse*, p. 11.

48 See my review of Pape and Feldman's book in *Perspectives on Terrorism*, Journal of the Terrorism Research Initiative, vol 4(6): www.terrorismanalysts.com/pt/index.php?option=com_rokzine&view=article&id=147

49 Excerpts from Sayyid Qutb's *In The Shade of the Qur'an*, as quoted in *The Sayyid Qutb Reader: Selected Writings on Politics, Religion, and Society*, Albert J. Bergesen, ed., New York: Routledge, 2008, p. 59.

50 Gordon D. Newby, *A Concise Encyclopedia of Islam*, Oxford, UK: Oneworld Publications, 2002, p. 207.

51 Newby, *A Concise Encyclopedia of Islam*, 207.

52 John L. Esposito, *The Oxford Dictionary of Islam*, New York: Oxford University Press, 2003, p. 327. Emphasis added here and not found in the original text.

53 See John Esposito's analysis of the *ummah* in his book *Unholy War: Terror in the Name of Islam*, New York: Oxford University Press, 2002, p. 39.

54 Esposito, *Unholy War*, 39.

55 Indeed, references to the *ummah* in radical Islamist speeches seem quite clearly a reference to a sense of a nation. See for example the speech delivered by Hamas leader Khaled Mash'al at a Damascus mosque in February 2006; archived in *Middle East Media Research Institute* (MEMRI), clip no. 1024, www.memri.org

56 A.H. Nayyar & Ahmed Salim, "The Subtle Subversion: The State of Curricula and Textbooks in Pakistan," published by *Sustainable Development Policy Institute*, as quoted by Amir Mir in his book *The True Face of Jehadis*, Lahore, Pakistan: Mashal Books, 2004, pp. 206–207. Emphasis added here and not found in the original text.

57 A translated version of this entire pamphlet can be found in Johannes J.G. Jansen's book *The Neglected Duty: The Creed of Sadat's Assassins and Islamic Resurgence in the Middle East*, Johannes J.G. Jansen, Trans., New York: Macmillan Publishing Company, 1986, pp. 160–230. I shall return to the analysis of Faraj's *Neglected Duty* in Chapter 4.

58 David Cook, *Understanding Jihad*, Berkeley, California: University of California Press, 2005, pp. 128–131.

59 Azzam, "The Will of Abdallah Yusuf Azzam, Who is Poor unto His Lord," as quoted by Cook, *Understanding Jihad*, Berkeley, California: University of California Press, 2005, p. 130.

60 For an analysis of the utilization of Islam as an effective framing process by leadership of contentious groups in various Muslims states, see Quintan Wiktorowicz, ed. *Islamic Activism: A Social Movement Theory Approach*, Indiana: Indiana University Press, 2004.

61 The radical Islamist definitions of 'morality' are discussed in Chapter 3. For now, I have placed the term in quotations marks to emphasize the very subjective meaning and understanding of the term morality in this context.

62 *Hizbullah* was primarily a grassroots Islamist extremist group until it recreated itself in the 1990s and contested parliamentary elections and won seats in the parliament in 1992 and 1996. See Amal Saad-Ghorayeb, *Hizbu'llah: Politics and Religion*, London: Pluto Press, 2002, pp. 1–15, 69–88.

63 Saad-Ghorayeb, *Hizbu'llah*, pp. 69–88.

64 Naim Qassem, *Hizbullah: The Story from Within*, Dalia Khalil, Trans., Lebanon: Saqi, 2010, p. 311. Emphasis added here.

65 Saad-Ghorayeb, *Hizbu'llah, p.* 72.

66 Amir Mir, *The True Face of Jehadis, p.* 116.

67 Excepts from the speech delivered by *Hamas* leader Khaled Mash'al at a Damascus mosque, February 3, 2006, archived in the *Middle East Media Research Institute* (MEMRI), available at www.memri.org.

68 Amir Mir, *The True Face of Jehadis, p.* 143. Emphasis added here and does not appear in the original text.

69 Taken from Ayman al-Zawahiri, "Knight Under the Prophet's Banner," (December 2, 2001), part 11, at www.fas.org, and quoted by Robert Pape in *Dying to Win: The Strategic Logic of Suicide Terrorism*, New York: Random House, 2005, p. 122.

70 Mir, *The True Face of Jehadis*, p. 213. Emphasis added here and not found in the original text.

71 Hizbullah's definition of its identity, as outlined in an "Open Letter addressed to the downtrodden in Lebanon *and* the World." Text of the "Open Letter" appears in Augustus Richard Norton, *Amal and the Shi'a: Struggle for the Soul of Lebanon*, Austin: University of Texas Press, 1987, pp. 168–169. Emphasis added here and not found in the original text.

72 Muhammad Amir Rana, *A to Z of Jehadi Organizations in Pakistan,* translated by Saba Ansari, Lahore, Pakistan: Mashal Books, 2004, p. 252.

73 Omar Saeed Shaikh, "I'm committed to Mulla Omar as the leader of all Mujahideen today," interview conducted by Massoud Ansari, in *Newsline* (Lahore, Pakistan), April 2005, p. 44.

74 Azmat Abbas, "The Making of a Militant," *The Herald*, Karachi, Pakistan, July 2003, p. 58.

75 Abbas, "The Making of a Militant," p. 57.

76 Abbas, "The Making of a Militant," p. 58.

77 I have devoted the next two chapters—Chapters 2 and 3—to a detailed analysis of the radical Islamist explanations of violence. The analysis of the radical Islamist justifications of violence can be found in Chapter 4.

78 I am not implying here a cultural relativity but a circumstantial relativity. In other words, by noting that morality depends on different perspectives I am suggesting that morality depends on perceptions of reality or, more accurately, the perceptions of urgency that are implied in the understanding of reality.

79 Yuval Ginbar, *Why not Torture Terrorists? Moral, Practical, and Legal Aspects of the "Ticking Bomb" Justification for Torture*, UK: Oxford University Press, 2008, p. 17.

80 Howard Caygill notes, "the categorical imperative … declares an action to be necessary 'without reference to any purpose' [or end]." Caygill, *A Kant Dictionary, p.* 100. The reference to 'GMM' made by Caygill is a reference to Kant's *Grounding for the Metaphysics of Morals*, 1785.

81 Samuel Scheffler, ed. *Consequentialism and its Critics*, Oxford Readings in Philosophy, New York: Oxford University Press, 1988, 1.

82 Henry Allison, *Kant's Theory of Freedom*, UK: Cambridge University Press, 1990, pp. 184; 203–204.

83 F. Nietzsche, *Beyond Good and Evil* [1886], Walter Kaufmann, Trans., New York: Vintage, 1996, p. 109.

84 I use the term 'banal' in the sense that Hannah Arendt used it in her analysis of Eichmann's personality in *Eichmann in Jerusalem: A Report on the Banality of Evil.*

Banality to Arendt meant the human tendency to think uncritically, to uncritically accept what is given to them. A component of banality, argued Arendt, was the fear of challenging the norms, the status quo; so banal individuals were 'ordinary' in the sense that 'banality' was ubiquitous. In this way, the 'banality of evil' was the tendency toward evil based on an uncritical acceptance of norms and orders, even when the latter included the justifications for brutality. Thus, by 'banal acceptance' I mean an uncritical acceptance of given notions of morality.

85 See pages 33–36 where I discuss this in detail.

86 This, according to Nietzsche, also becomes a disguise for lack of creativity, laziness, and fear of change. See my analysis of Nietzsche's notion of morality on pages 36–43.

87 'Violence as Morality' is of course the title of Chapter 4.

88 See Honneth, *The Struggle for Recognition*, p. 160.

89 Honneth, *The Struggle for Recognition*, p. 161.

90 Honneth, *The Struggle for Recognition*, p. 162.

91 Hare, *Essays on Political Morality*, p. 22.

92 Hare, *Essays on Political Morality*, pp. 21–23.

93 Hare, *Essays on Political Morality*, p. 26 for points (1) and (3) and p. 27 for point (4). Emphasis found in original text. I shall leave aside in this chapter the discussion of this last speculative condition as its analysis is beyond the scope of this chapter and this book, and I shall focus instead only on the first three conditions.

94 Axel Honneth, *The Struggle for Recognition: The Moral Grammar of Social Conflicts*, Cambridge, Massachusetts: MIT Press, 1995. I discuss Honneth's argument in more detail later in this chapter in arguing its relevance in understanding the radical Islamist notions of morality.

95 Honneth, *The Struggle for Recognition*, p. 163.

96 For Nietzsche's references to 'Christian morality' see Maudemarie Clark, "Introduction," in *Friedrich Nietzsche: On the Genealogy of Morality," A Polemic*, Maudemarie Clark & Alan J. Swensen, Trans., Indianapolis: Hackett Publishing Company, Inc., 1998, p. xx. Here Clark notes the following: "At the end of *Genealogy*, he [Nietzsche] associates the perishing of morality with the overcoming of 'Christianity *as morality*' (GM 111:27). And in explaining why he chose to call himself an 'immoralist,' he writes: 'What defines me, what sets me apart from the rest of humanity is that I *uncovered Christian morality* [emphasis on Christian morality has been added here and does not appear in Clark's text]" (xx). In other places, Nietzsche criticizes Christian morality in the following terms: "Christian morality— the most malicious form of the will to lie"; as quoted by Keith Ansell-Pearson in *An Introduction to Nietzsche as Political Thinker*, UK: Cambridge University Press, 1999, p. 20.

97 See Maudemarie Clark, "Introduction," in *Friedrich Nietzsche: On the Genealogy of Morality," A Polemic*, Maudemarie Clark and Alan J. Swensen, Trans., Indianapolis: Hackett Publishing Company, Inc., 1998, p. xvi. These claims are understood as meaning that Nietzsche supported an anarchical society, or a radically nihilists society with no set standards of rights and wrongs; as Clark notes later in the text "it is difficult to believe that this [the gradual perishing of morality] might be a 'hopeful' event" (xvi). But, as we shall see in my analysis in this section, these views reflect only a common—and popular, I might add—misunderstanding of Nietzsche's critique of morality. For example, by perishing of morality he meant the perishing of Christianity as morality, that is, the perishing of the uncritical view that all that is framed in the context of Christianity is categorically and deontologically moral. This, as we shall see in this section, is consistent with his view that *all* morality is consequentialist in nature and to claim otherwise is either to be naïve or to have nefarious intentions justifying your actions—and manipulating the masses— under the guise of 'morality' or moral actions.

98 See Richard Schacht's analysis of Nietzsche's philosophy and the popular ways in which he has been understood (or, I would argue, misunderstood) in "Friedrich Wilhelm Nietzsche," *The Cambridge Dictionary of Philosophy*, 2nd Edition, ed. Robert Audi, New York: Cambridge University Press, 2006, p. 614.

99 Richard Schacht's analysis of Nietzsche's philosophy and the popular ways in which he has been understood (or, I would argue, misunderstood) in "Friedrich Wilhelm Nietzsche," *The Cambridge Dictionary of Philosophy*, 2nd Edition, ed. Robert Audi, New York: Cambridge University Press, 2006, p. 614.

100 See Brain Leiter's analysis of Nietzsche's critique of morality which he categories in terms of the 'catalogue approach' (that understands his critique of morality in terms of his rejection of the normative nature of morality), the 'origins approach' (that understands his critique of morality in terms of his frustration that morality is rarely understood, as it should be, in terms of a means to an end), and the 'universality approach' (that understands his critique of morality in terms of his rejection of the presumption in notions of morality of one fits all); see Leiter, *Nietzsche on Morality*, UK: Routledge, 2003, pp. 74–77.

101 Notes written by Nietzsche between November 1887-March 1888, as part of his *Critique of Religion*, and as translated by Walter Kaufmann & R.J. Hollingdale, in *Friedrich Nietzsche, The Will to Power*, Walter Kaufmann, Ed., New York: Vintage Books, 1968, pp. 114–115.

102 Emphasis added here, but quotation marks and exclamation marks are as found in notes written by Nietzsche during November 1887 and March 1888, as part of his *Critique of Religion*, and as translated by Walter Kaufmann & R.J. Hollingdale, in *Friedrich Nietzsche, The Will to Power*, Walter Kaufmann, Ed., New York: Vintage Books, 1968, p. 117.

103 Emphasis on 'knew' and exclamation mark are as found in notes written by Nietzsche during Spring–Fall 1887 (other emphases are added here), as part of his *Critique of Religion*, and as translated by Walter Kaufmann & R.J. Hollingdale, in *Friedrich Nietzsche, The Will to Power*, Walter Kaufmann, Ed., New York: Vintage Books, 1968, p. 118.

104 All emphases (in italics) are added here and do not appear in the notes written by Nietzsche during Spring–Fall 1887, as part of his *Critique of Religion*, and as translated by Walter Kaufmann & R.J. Hollingdale, in *Friedrich Nietzsche, The Will to Power*, Walter Kaufmann, Ed., New York: Vintage Books, 1968, p. 121.

105 This can also be seen as implied in Keith Ansell-Pearson's analysis of Neitzsche's understanding of morality, namely that it serves numerous functions, an understanding that stands in contrast to a deontological understanding of morality as serving only the prescriptive function of forwarding some static notions of 'right' versus 'wrong.' See *An Introduction to Nietzsche as Political Thinker*, Cambridge: Cambridge University Press, 1999, p. 124.

106 Keith Ansell-Pearson's analysis of Nietzsche's critique of morality in *An Introduction to Nietzsche as Political Thinker*, Cambridge: Cambridge University Press, 1999, p. 123. Emphasis added here.

107 See Keith Ansell-Pearson's analysis of Nietzsche's critique of morality in *An Introduction to Nietzsche as Political Thinker*, Cambridge: Cambridge University Press, 1999, p. 123.

108 R.M. Hare, *Moral Thinking: Its levels, Method and Point*, Oxford: Oxford University Press, 1981.

109 Such uncritical thinkers can also be understood in light of Hannah Arendt's notion of the 'banal' individual, an individual that is either too uncritical or too afraid to challenge whatever social, political or moral stipulations that are handed to him or her (regardless of the consequences to the self or society). See Hannah Arendt, *Eichmann in Jerusalem: A Report on the Banality of Evil*, NY: Penguin Books, 2006, special edition with an introduction by Amos Elon; pp. 135–150. For an excellent

analysis of Arendt's notion of banality, see Elisabeth Young-Bruehl's analysis of Arendt's notion of banality in *Why Arendt Matters*, New Haven: Yale University Press, 2006, pp. 1–29.

110 Walter Kaufmann and R.J. Hollingdale, *Friedrich Nietzsche, The Will to Power*, Walter Kaufmann, Ed., New York: Vintage Books, 1968.

111 For those that challenge the importance of the notion of will-to-power in Nietzsche's overall arguments, see Brain Leiter, *Nietzsche on Morality*, New York: Routledge, 2003, p. 142. For those who criticize Nietzsche's notion of the will-to-power for its lack of clarity and its ambiguous nature, see Arthur C. Danto, *Nietzsche as Philosopher*, Columbia Classics in Philosophy, New York: Columbia University Press, 2005, p. 196. For those who argue for the critical centrality of the notion of will-to-power in understanding Nietzsche's philosophy, see Walter Kaufmann (editor & co-translator with R.J. Hollingdale), *Friedrich Nietzsche: The Will-to-Power*, New York: Vintage Books, 1968.

112 Arthur C. Danto disagrees with this interpretation of the will-to-power, but then goes on to analyze this notion in ways that only substantiate my interpretation that will-to-power is indeed the will to self-assertion (or the desire and pursuit of self-assertion), as we shall see later in this section. For Danto's analysis, see *Nietzsche as Philosopher*, Columbia Classics in Philosophy, New York: Columbia University Press, 2005, pp. 196–210.

113 See Brian Leiter's analysis of Nietzsche's will-to-power, which he conducts with reference to Schacht's (1983) analysis and Nietzsche's *The Will-to-Power* (1067) in *Nietzsche on Morality*, New York: Routledge, 2003, p. 139.

114 Alphonso Lingis begins his analysis of Nietzsche's will-to-power by asking what it means when Nietzsche says that "life is will-to-power" (37) and offers an analysis of the notion that substantiates my interpretation that the will-to-power is essentially a will for self-assertion, as we shall see later in this section. See Alphonso Lingis, "The Will-to-Power," in *The New Nietzsche*, David B. Allison, Ed., Cambridge, Massachusetts: MIT Press, 1985, p. 37.

115 Lingis, "The Will-to-Power," in *The New Nietzsche*, p. 38.

116 Lingis, "The Will-to-Power," in *The New Nietzsche*, p. 40.

117 Lingis, "The Will-to-Power," in *The New Nietzsche*, p. 40. Emphasis added here.

118 In its epistemological sense, Nietzsche is known for his view on *perspectivism,* that is, all that is known is based on perspectives; there is therefore no unmediated knowledge, or the thing in itself. To Nietzsche, everything, including knowledge and 'facts,' is a matter of interpretation. See for example Maria Baghramian's analysis of Nietzsche's perspectivism in *Relativism*, New York: Routledge, 2005, pp. 75–82; the discussion of Neitzsche's epistemological views is beyond the scope of this section.

119 Lingis, "The Will-to-Power," in *The New Nietzsche*, p. 41.

120 Lingis, "The Will-to-Power," in *The New Nietzsche*, p. 41.

121 Nietzsche, from his *Genealogy of Morality*, as quoted by Lingis, "The Will-to-Power," in *The New Nietzsche*, p. 45. Emphasis found in the original text.

122 Arthur C. Danto, *Nietzsche as Philosopher*, Columbia Classics in Philosophy, New York: Columbia University Press, 2005, p. 197.

123 For a comparison of Nietzsche with Darwin, see Danto, *Nietzsche as Philosopher*, p. 205.

124 Danto, *Nietzsche as Philosopher*, p. 205.

125 Danto, *Nietzsche as Philosopher*, p. 209.

126 Maudemarie Clark, "Introduction," in *Friedrich Nietzsche: On the Genealogy of Morality, A Polemic*, Maudemarie Clark & Alan J. Swensen, Trans., Indianapolis: Hackett Publishing Company, Inc., 1998, p. xx. Emphases added here and do not appear in the original text.

127 Clark, "Introduction," in *Friedrich Nietzsche: On the Genealogy of Morality, A Polemic*, p. xvi.

2 Recognition through violence

1 This reason, beyond its Hegelian dialectical nature, is also Morgenthauian. Hans Morgenthau is known to have argued that 'real' power need only imply the *threat* of the use of force, not necessarily the actual use of force. This implies that *excessive* and *disproportionate* use of force is reflective of weakness, not power.

2 See Chapter 1 where I introduced the notion of the dialectic as it specifically implied in Hegel's master–slave dialectic.

3 See Chapter 1 where I introduce the notion of self-recognition as implied within Hegel's master–slave dialectic as both its feature and its consequence.

4 At the time of this writing (2006), the fate of Iraq vis-à-vis a full-scale civil war was still undetermined. Radical Sunni orchestrated massacres of Shi'ites, counter Shi'i violent reactions, and talks of the American administration of a gradual phase-out of its military presence in Iraq only point to a relative 'calm' before the real storm; here 'storm' may be defined as an unbridled civil war which comprises not only of Sunni–Shi'i sectarian cleansing, if you may, but also the possible post-US withdrawal radical Sunni efforts at the ethnic cleansing of the contending Kurdish population (which, while Sunni, is not Arab and is thus the other in the eyes of the radical Sunnis, whose objection to the December 2005 American-initiated Iraqi national elections and the subsequent proportionally represented Iraq national congress was the significant change in the balance of power to their disadvantage). For an excellent analysis and informed forecast of post-2003 Iraq see the numerous writings and commentaries of Vali Reza Nasr, a specialist in the Sunni-Shi'i divides in Pakistan, Shi'i revivalism in Iran, and the Sunni-Shi'i violence in post-2003 Iraq.

5 Muhammad Amir Rana, *A to Z of Jehadi Organizations in Pakistan*, pp. 192–203.

6 Amir Rana, *A to Z of Jehadi Organizations in Pakistan*, p. 209.

7 Amir Mir, "Unholy Crusade," *Newsline,* Lahore, Pakistan, October 1999, p. 69.

8 Amir Rana, *A to Z of Jehadi Organizations in Pakistan*, p. 204.

9 Amir Rana, *A to Z of Jehadi Organizations in Pakistan*, p. 225.

10 Amir Rana, *A to Z of Jehadi Organizations in Pakistan*, p. 405.

11 Deposed as result of the American military occupation of Iraq that started in March 2003.

12 Williams, *Hegel's Ethics of Recognition*, p. 60. Emphasis added here and not found in the original text.

13 Pinkard, *Hegel's Phenomenology*, p. 59,

14 Pinkard, *Hegel's Phenomenology*, p. 54.

15 Kojeve, *Introduction to the Reading of Hegel*, p. 41. Emphasis found in the original text.

16 Kojeve, *Introduction to the Reading of Hegel*, p. 43.

17 Kojeve, *Introduction to the Reading of Hegel*, p. 41. Emphasis found in the original text.

18 Mir, *The True Face of Jehadis*, p. 213. Emphasis added here and not found in the original text. The question mark at the end of the title has been deleted here but appears in the original text.

19 Mir, *The True Face of Jehadis*, p. 212. Emphasis added here and not found in the original text.

20 This is a small excerpt of a long speech delivered by bin Laden to *al-Jazeera's* Kabul bureau on November 3, 2001 in which he also makes references to the Palestinian situation, the Sudan, Somalia and more. Quoted in Bruce Lawrence, ed. *Messages to the World: The Statements of Osama bin Laden*, James Howarth, Trans., London: Verso, 2005, pp. 135–137.

21 Kojeve, "Desire and Work in the Master and Slave," p. 56.

22 Quoted in Muhammad Amir Rana, *A-Z of Jehadi Organizations in Pakistan*, Lahore, Pakistan: Mashal Books, 2004, p. 40. Emphasis added here and not found in original text.

23 Quoted in text by Muhammad Amir Rana, *A to Z of Jehadi Organizations in Pakistan*, p. 436. Emphasis added here and not found in the original text.

24 See the earlier subsections 'Masters and Slaves: The Alternative to Death' and 'Recognition: A Life-and-Death Struggle' in this chapter.

25 Amir Mir, *The True Face of Jehadis*, p. 132.

26 Amir Mir, *The True Face of Jehadis*, p. 133. Emphasis added here and not found in the original text.

27 Amir Mir, *The True Face of Jehadis*, p. 133.

28 Excerpt taken from Center for Islamic Studies and Research, an organization affiliated with al-Qaeda, "The East Riyadh Operation and Our War with the United States and its Agents," August 1, 2003; www.cybcity.com/newss, translated by Foreign Broadcast Information Service, and as quoted by Robert A. Pape, *Dying to Win: The Strategic Logic of Suicide Terrorism*, New York: Random House, 2005, p. 118. Emphasis added here and not found in the original text.

29 There have been to date some six attempts on President Musharraf's life. Assassination attempts were carried out on March 23, 2002, December 6, 2002, March 23, 2003, April 26, 2003, December 14, 2003, December 25, 2003. See Zaffar Abbas' report of the assassination attempts in "What Happened?," *The Herald*, Karachi, Pakistan, June 2005, pp. 71–75.

30 Amir Mir, *The True Face of Jehadis*, p. 114.

31 Amir Mir, *The True Face of Jehadis*, p. 128.

32 Abu Musab al-Zarqawi was radical Sunni Islamist know, amongst other things, for his creation of al-Tawhid wal-Jihad in the 1990s and for his part in mobilizing suicide attacks within American-occupied Iraq and the beheadings of captives in Iraq. He was also known for his vehement anti-Shia stand and the organization of terrorist attacks against Shias in Iraq as well as his allegiance to Osama bin-Laden. Zarqawi was killed in Iraq in June 2006 by US targeted bombs.

33 An excerpt from Al-Zarqawi's January 2006 audiocassette circulated on radical Islamist websites, achieved in *Middle East Media Research Institute* (MEMRI); http://memri.org/bin/opener.cgi?Page=archieves&ID=IA28406 Emphasis added here and does not appear in the MEMRI archives; however the parenthetical notes are those of MEMRI.

34 An excerpt from Al-Zarqawi's January 2006 audiocassette circulated on radical Islamist websites, achieved in *Middle East Media Research Institute* (MEMRI); http://memri.org/bin/opener.cgi?Page=archieves&ID=IA28406 Emphasis added here and does not appear in the MEMRI archives.

35 An excerpt from Al-Zarqawi's January 2006 audiocassette circulated on radical Islamist websites, achieved in *Middle East Media Research Institute* (MEMRI); http://memri.org/bin/opener.cgi?Page=archieves&ID=IA28406 Emphasis added here and does not appear in the MEMRI achieves.

36 An excerpt from Al-Zarqawi's January 2006 audiocassette circulated on radical Islamist websites, achieved in *Middle East Media Research Institute* (MEMRI); http://memri.org/bin/opener.cgi?Page=archieves&ID=IA28406

37 Excerpts from the open letter written by bin Laden, as posted on the Internet on October 6, 2002; documented in Bruce Lawrence, ed. *Messages to the World: The Statements of Osama bin Laden*, James Howarth, Trans., London: Verso, 2005, pp. 162–164. Emphasis added here and not found in the original text.

38 Hizbullah's "Open Letter addressed to the downtrodden in Lebanon *and* the World." Text of the "Open Letter" appears in Augustus Richard Norton, *Amal and the Shi'a: Struggle for the Soul of Lebanon*, Austin: University of Texas Press, 1987, p. 170. Emphasis added here and not found in the original text.

39 An excerpt from the declaration of creation of the *World Islamic Front*, February 23, 1998; documented in Bruce Lawrence, ed. *Messages to the World: The Statements of Osama bin Laden*, James Howarth, Trans., London: Verso, 2005, pp. 59–60.

40 An excerpt from Al-Zarqawi's January 2006 audiocassette circulated on radical Islamist websites, achieved in *Middle East Media Research Institute* (MEMRI); http:// memri.org/bin/opener.cgi?Page=archieves&ID=IA28406 Emphasis added here and not found in the original text, however, parenthetical information is as found in the MEMRI achieves.

41 An excerpt from Al-Zarqawi's January 2006 audiocassette circulated on radical Islamist websites, achieved in *Middle East Media Research Institute* (MEMRI); http:// memri.org/bin/opener.cgi?Page=archieves&ID=IA28406 Emphasis added here and not found in the original.

42 It is critical to understand here that the Kojeveian sense of 'prestige' has no economic connotation; so prestige does not refer to economic prestige, the kind one claim from the accumulation of wealth.

43 Kojeve, *Introduction to the Reading of Hegel*, p. 41. Emphasis added here and not found in the original text.

44 An excerpt from Al-Zarqawi's January 2006 audiocassette circulated on radical Islamist websites, achieved in *Middle East Media Research Institute* (MEMRI); http:// memri.org/bin/opener.cgi?Page=archieves&ID=IA28406

45 Interviews conducted by Nasra Hassan of members of *Hamas* and *Islamic Jihad*; see "An Arsenal of Believers: Talking to the Human Bombs," *The New Yorker*, November 19, 2001, p. 41. Emphasis added here and not found in the original text.

46 Muhammad Amir Rana, *A to Z of Jehadi Organizations in Pakistan*, p. 103.

47 Quoted in Muhammad Amir Rana, *A-Z of Jehadi Organizations in Pakistan*, Lahore, Pakistan: Mashal Books, 2004, p. 39. Emphasis added here and not found in original text.

48 Excerpts from Masood Azir's interview conducted by the *South Asia Tribune*, August 24, 2003, as quoted in Amir Mir, *The True Face of Jehadis*, p. 79. Emphasis on 'will' and 'Jihad' added here and does not appear in the original text.

49 Amir Mir, *The True Face of Jehadis*, p. 106. Emphasis added here and does not appear in the original text.

50 Amir Mir, *The True Face of Jehadis*, p. 106. Emphasis added here and does not appear in the original text.

51 Quoted in Oliver and Steinberg, *The Road to Martyrs' Square*, p. 99.

52 This represents my interpretation of the anthem and not that of Oliver or Steinberg.

53 Excerpts from Osama bin Laden's speech as delivered on *Al-Jazeera* TV, January 19, 2006, archived in Middle East Media Research Institute (MEMRI), clip no. 1002, available at www.memri.org

54 Amir Mir, *The True Face of Jehadis*, p. 144. Emphasis added here and does not appear in the original text.

55 Hizbullah's explanation of its motives, as outlined in an "Open Letter addressed to the downtrodden in Lebanon *and* the World." Text of the "Open Letter" appears in Augustus Richard Norton, *Amal and the Shi'a: Struggle for the Soul of Lebanon*, Austin: University of Texas Press, 1987, p. 170. Emphasis added here and not found in the original text.

56 Hizbullah's explanation of use of violence as the last available alternative, outlined in an "Open Letter addressed to the downtrodden in Lebanon *and* the World." Text of the "Open Letter" appears in Norton, *Amal and the Shi'a*, p. 171. Emphasis added here and not found in the original text.

57 Blackburn, *Oxford Dictionary of Philosophy*, p. 169.

58 Amir Rana, *A to Z of Jehadi Organizations in Pakistan*, p. 413.

59 Quoted in text by Amir Rana, *A to Z of Jehadi Organizations in Pakistan*, p. 414. Emphasis added here and not found in original text.

60 Amir Rana, *A to Z of Jehadi Organizations in Pakistan*, p. 415.

61 An excerpt from Al-Zarqawi's January 2006 audiocassette circulated on radical Islamist websites, achieved in *Middle East Media Research Institute* (MEMRI); http:// memri.org/bin/opener.cgi?Page=archieves&ID=IA28406

62 Sebastian Smith, *Allah's Mountains: The Battle for Chechnya*, New York: Tauris Parke paperbacks, 2006, p. 125. Emphasis added here.

63 Excerpts from the speech delivered by Iranian President Mahmoud Ahmadinejad to an audience of hundreds of people in Bushehr on February 1, 2006; archived on *Middle East Media Institute* (MEMRI), clip no. 1019, available at www.memri.org, February 1, 2006. This speech was made in response to the American military response threats as implied in the American warnings to the Islamic Republic of Iran to halt its nuclear research.

64 Amir Mir, *The True Face of Jehadis*, Lahore, Pakistan: Mashal Books, 2004, p. 211.

65 Mir, *The True Face of Jehadis*, p. 79. Emphasis on 'independent' added here and not found in the original text.

66 Excerpts from an interview conducted by CNN's Peter Arnett with Osama bin Laden near Jalalabad in March 1997, as quoted in Bruce Lawrence, *Messages to the World: The Statements of Osama bin Laden*, London: Verso, 2005, pp. 50–51.

67 Quote taken from Pinkard, *Hegel's Phenomenology*, p. 61.

68 All the above excerpts are taken from the report entitled "Egyptian Muslim Brotherhood MPs: The Koran Encourages Terrorism; 'Bin Laden, Al-Zawahiri and Al-Zarqawi are not Terrorists in the Sense Accepted by Some," in *The Middle East Media Research Institute* (MEMRI), March 10, 2006; http://memri.org/bin/opener.cgi?Page=archives&ID=SP111006 The clarifications in parenthesis are not mine but those of MEMRI but the emphasis (italics) are mine and not those of MEMRI.

69 Excerpts of an interview conducted of Iraqi cleric Sheik Ahmad al-Kubeisi on Saudi TV channel *al-Risala* TV on March 15, 2006; archived in *Middle East Media Research Institute* (MEMRI), www.memritv.org/search.asp?ACT=S9&P1=1075 Except for the parenthetical reference to 'shells,' all parenthetical references have been added here by myself and do not appear in the MEMRI achieves.

70 An excerpt from Al-Zarqawi's January 2006 audiocassette circulated on radical Islamist websites, achieved in *Middle East Media Research Institute* (MEMRI); http://memri.org/bin/opener.cgi?Page=archieves&ID=IA28406 Emphasis added here and not found in the original text, however, parenthetical information is as found in the MEMRI achieves.

71 See "Lieberman Suggests Adopting Russian Tactics," *Kavkaz Center* (a Chechen run independent online news source for issues related to the Chechen struggle), November 9, 2006, www.kavkazcenter.com/eng/content/2006/11/09/6324.shtml.

72 An interview of *Abdul-Halim Sadulayev*, Chechen Republic of Ichkeria (CRI) President, conducted by *Jamestown Foundation*, July 9, 2006, www.kavkazcenter.com/eng/content/2006/07/09/4929.shtml

73 The *Kavkaz* Center is a private Chechen news agency that claims independence from any state or government structures, even that of the Chechen government. Although the news agency reports on world news, news regarding the *ummah* in general, its main aim is to report what it calls 'real events' and 'truthful information' regarding in the Caucasus and Russia, especially the 'facts' of Russian genocide against the 'Chechen Mujahideen.' See 'About Us' on the *Kavkaz* Center website: www.kavkaz-center.com

74 "6 'Israeli' Terrorists Killed in East Lebanon," August 19, 2006, www.kavkazcenter.com/eng/content/2006/08/19/5337.shtml

75 "Kremlin Loses its Grip on a Dying Empire," May 25, 2006, www.kavkazcenter.com/eng/content/2006/05/25/4704_print.html

76 "10 Russian Invaders Gunned Down in Chechnya," November 6, 2006, www.kavkaz-center.com/eng/content/2006/11/06/6284.shtml

77 "War on Terror: 3 US Terrorists on Trail in Vietnam," November 10, 2006, www.kavkazcenter.com/eng/content/2006/11/10/6352.shtml

78 Zaidi, "Back to the Drawing Board," *The Herald*, Karachi, Pakistan, September 2003, p. 64.

79 Mir, *The True Face of Jehadis*, p. 113. Emphasis added here and not found in the original text.
80 Excerpts from the speech given by Khaled Mash'al in a Damascus Mosque and as aired on *al-Jazeera* TV on February 3, 2006; archived in *Middle East Media Research Institute* (MEMRI), clip no. 1024, available at www.memri.org February 3, 2006. Emphasis added here.
81 Excerpts from Ayman Al-Zawahiri's video on *al-Jazeera* TV, aired on January 30, 2006; archived in *Middle East Media Research Institute* (MEMRI), clip no. 1082, February 1, 2006, available at www.memri.org. Emphasis added here.
82 William A. Shearson, "The Common Assumptions of Existentialist Philosophy," *The Development and Meaning of Twentieth-Century Existentialism*, William L. McBride, ed., New York: Garland Publishers, Inc., 1997, p. 288. Emphasis added here and does not appear in the original text.
83 An except from an interview conducted by Christoph Reuter of a Palestinian man in Gaza in 2001 as found in his book *My Life is a Weapon*, p. 86.
84 Excerpts from the speech given by Khaled Mash'al in a Damascus Mosque and as aired on *al-Jazeera* TV on February 3, 2006; archived in *Middle East Media Research Institute* (MEMRI), clip no. 1024, available at www.memri.org. Emphasis added here.
85 Taken from "Bin Laden's Sermon," *Middle East Media Research Institute* (MEMRI), March 5, 2003, www.memri.org, quoted by Pape in his book *Dying to Win*, p. 123. Emphasis added here and does not appear in the original text.
86 This excerpt from Fathi Shikaki's book *Jihad fis sabil Allah* (Jihad in the path of God) was originally cited in Christoph Reuter, *My Life is a Weapon*, p. 97.

3 Self-transcendent recognition

1 Daniel Brown, "Martyrdom in the Sunni Revivalist Thought," *Sacrificing the Self: Perspectives on Martyrdom and Religion*, Margaret Cormack, ed., Oxford: Oxford University Press, 2002, p. 113. Emphasis added here.
2 See the Introduction where I have listed a number of paradoxes that I hope to read-dress through the analysis in this book.
3 Brown, "Martyrdom in the Sunni Revivalist Thought," *Sacrificing the Self*, p. 113. Emphasis added here.
4 For the quoted reference see Shmuel Bar, "The Religious Sources of Islamic terrorism," *Policy Review*, no. 125, June/July 2004, pp. 27–37. Such views find their bases in the works of Bernard Lewis, Samuel Huntington, and Michael Walzer, works that reinforce the arguments forwarded in the clash-of-civilizations paradigm and that fit in the broader category of Western neo-conservative school of thought. See David Cook for an analysis of Jewish martyrdom (pp. 5–7) and Christian martyrdom (pp. 8–11) in his book *Martyrdom in Islam*, UK: Cambridge University Press, 2007. See also Marc Brettler for discussion of martyrdom in the Hebrew Bible, (pp. 3–22), Carole Straw for a discussion of Christian martyrdom (pp. 39–57) and Lawrence Fine for a discussion of contemplative death in Jewish Mystical tradition (pp. 92–106), in *Sacrificing the Self: Perspectives on Martyrdom and Religion*, Margaret Cormack, ed., New York: Oxford University Press, 2001.
5 See the Introduction where I introduced these paradoxes as ones that were initially brought to light by the authors in the volume *Making Sense of Suicide Mission*, Diego Gambetta, ed., New York: Oxford University Press, 2005. But, as I noted earlier, these paradoxes were not adequately addressed by the authors that initially brought these paradoxes to light.
6 Mohammed A. Bamyeh, *Of Death and Dominion: The Existential Foundations of Governance*, Evanston, Illinois: Northwestern University Press, 2007, p. 8.
7 See Chapter 1 where I introduce the logic implicit in Hegel's master–slave dialectic.

8 This translation is mine and is based on the remarks of the madrassa teacher in the documentary made by Sharmeen Obaid-Chinoy. The official translation—and, I might add, somewhat inaccurate translation—of what the madrassa teacher said is "someone who sees death as a blessing, then who can defeat him?" See Sharmeen Obaid-Chinoy, *Pakistan: Children of the Taliban*, PBS documentary, funded by The John D. and Catherine MacArthur Foundation, The Skoll Foundation, The William Flora Hewitt Foundation, April 2009.

9 Excerpt of Sheikh Qasim's statement, as cited by Gilles Kepel in his book *Beyond Terror and Martyrdom*, Cambridge, Massachusetts: The Belknap Press of Harvard University Press, 2008, p. 83. Emphasis added here.

10 Sebastian Smith, *Allah's Mountains: The Battle for Chechnya*, New York: Tauris Parke Paperbacks, 2006, p. 156. Emphasis added here.

11 Smith, *Allah's Mountains*, p. 156. Emphasis added here.

12 Mohammed A. Bamyeh, *Of Death and Dominion: The Existential Foundations of Governance*, Evanston, Illinois: Northwestern University Press, 2007.

13 Unless otherwise noted, the references to 'death' in this section are references to the physical death of the self, not the death of self-consciousness as discussed earlier in this chapter.

14 Robert R. Williams, *Recognition: Fichte and Hegel on the Other*, Albany, New York: State University of New York, 1992, pp. 175–180.

15 See Chapter 1 for a basic analysis of Hegel's master–slave dialectic.

16 Robert R. Williams offers a most eloquent analysis of this master–slave dynamics in his book *Hegel's Ethics of Recognition*, Berkeley: University of California Press, 1997. I shall engage Williams arguments later in this chapter.

17 Robert R. Williams, *Recognition: Fichte and Hegel on the Other*, Albany, New York: State University of New York, 1992, p. 175. Emphasis added here.

18 Naim Qassem, *Hizbullah: The Story from Within*, Lebanon: Saqi 2007, pp. 107–108. Emphasis added here .

19 My assertion here stands in contrast to Mia Bloom's assessment that "martyrdom *reinforces* the … *self-image* as an *oppressed people* since this tactic is the *weapon of the weak.*" See Mia Bloom's analysis of motivations of Palestinian suicide bombers, *Dying to Kill: The Allure of Suicide Terror*, New York: Columbia University Press, 2005, p. 36. Emphasis added here and do not appear in the original text.

20 Ali Alfoneh, "Iran's Suicide Brigades," *Middle East Quarterly,* Winter 2007, p. 38.

21 Alfoneh, "Iran's Suicide Brigades," p. 39. Emphasis added here.

22 Inwood, *Hegel Dictionary*, p. 110. The emphasis on 'death' is found in the original text, but the italicized emphasis have been added. For a reference to how freedom in linked to death in Hegelian philosophy, see also Thomas A. Lewis, *Freedom and Tradition in Hegel: Reconsidering Anthropology, Ethics and Religion*, Indiana: University of Notre Dame Press, 2005, p. 70.

23 Excerpt from Hegel's *The Philosophy of History* as quoted by Thomas Lewis in *Freedom and Tradition in Hegel: Reconsidering Anthropology, Ethics and Religion*, Indiana: University of Notre Dame Press, 2005, p. 70. Emphasis added here and does not appear in the original text.

24 Thomas A. Lewis, *Freedom and Tradition in Hegel: Reconsidering Anthropology, Ethics and Religion*, Indiana: University of Notre Dame Press, 2005, p. 70.

25 Pinkard, *Hegel's Phenomenology*, p. 61. Emphasis in italic added here and not found in original text.

26 It should be noted, however, that nowhere does Hegel *sanction* suicide as the *only* possible manifestation of absolute freedom, much less prescribe it as the ideal avenue to absolute freedom.

27 Williams, *Hegel's Ethnics of Recognition*, p. 60. Emphasis added here and not found in original text.

28 Williams, *Hegel's Ethnics of Recognition*, p. 60. Emphasis added here and not found in original text.

29 Quoted in Hala Jaber, "Inside the World of a Palestinian Suicide Bomber," *The Jordan Times*, and cited initially by Nichole Argo, "The Banality of Evil, Understanding Today's Human Bombs," Policy Paper, Preventive Defense Project, Stanford University, 2003, p. 10, cited by Mia Bloom, *Dying to Kill: The Allure of Suicide Terror* (New York: Columbia University Press, 2005), p. 90. Emphasis added here and do not appear in the original text.

30 The last italicized part of the sentence is borrowed from Alan Patten, *Hegel's Idea of Freedom*, p. 130, and it appears in its context in an earlier quoted section.

31 Excerpt from a Hamas leaflet during the First Intifada, translated and cited by David Cook in *Martyrdom in Islam*, p. 144. The parenthetical reference belongs to David Cook but the emphasis is added here and does not appear in Cook's version of the quote.

32 That is, the master maybe deemed as the master based on his superior military capabilities, but not as the master in the 'real' sense, by which I mean in the sense of controlling every action of his slave. And if the master has not absolute control over the slave, then the master has no absolute mastery over the slave.

33 I have italicized 'justifications' and 'explanations' to highlight what I argue is a critical distinction in reason between the two in radical Islamist rhetoric. See the Introduction where I introduce this distinction and Chapter 1 where I elaborate the nature of explanations (Hegelian struggles for recognition) and justifications (moral consequentialist arguments).

34 Mohammed A. Bamyeh, *Of Death and Dominion: The Existential Foundations of Governance*, Evanston, Illinois: Northwestern University Press, 2007.

35 The Epic of Gilgamesh is a classic Mesopotamian mythology of a creature—Gilgamesh—who was two parts god and one part man. Gilgamesh is mythologized as having superhuman strength, a kind of a semi-god. But Gilgamesh falls short of being one of the gods as he is not granted the fortune of immortality by the gods that be.

36 Bamyeh makes a similar argument, see Bamyeh, *Of Death and Dominion*, pp. 7–16.

37 Bamyeh, *Of Death and Dominion*, p. 8. The original text is italicized but I have presented it here without the emphasis.

38 Bamyeh, *Of Death and Dominion*, p. 8.

39 In addition to being presented as empowering for the self as the act of self-destruction negates the master's control over the self, as I noted earlier.

40 The assertion that death of the master, along with the self, is promoted in radical Islamist rhetoric with the logic of equalizing power differentials is mine. However, Reuter's observation, I feel, is relevant as a reinforcement of my assertion.

41 Christoph Reuter, *My Life is a Weapon: A Modern History of Suicide Bombing*, Princeton, NJ: Princeton University Press, 2002, p. 15.

42 Existentialism, as a tradition in philosophy, assumes the commonality of fears and desires in the human existence. So to understand the enemy in existential terms is to acknowledge that the enemy, like the self, is merely a mortal, with fears and desires and vulnerabilities much like the self (even when different in exact nature).

43 This except was originally quoted by David Cook in his book *Martyrdom in Islam*, p. 150. Emphasis is added here and does not appear in the manner in which Cook cites this excerpt. Also, the specific analysis of this excerpt, in the context of the vulnerabilities of the Gilgameshian master is mine and not reflective of Cook's analysis.

44 Nasra Hassan, "An Arsenal of Believers: Talking to the 'Human Bombs'," *The New Yorker*, November 19, 2001, p. 38.

45 Nasra Hassan conducted numerous interviews of Hamas members during 1996–1999. This excerpt is taken from Hassan's report of the outcomes of his interviews. See Hassan, "An Arsenal of Believers: Talking to the 'Human Bombs'," p. 38.

46 Hassan, "An Arsenal of Believers: Talking to the 'Human Bombs'," p. 38.

47 An excerpt from Ayman Al-Zawahiri, "The Choice of Targets and the Importance of Martyrdom Operations," *Knights under the Prophet's Banner*, published in December 2, 2001, as cited in Gilles Kepel & Jean-Pierre Milelli, eds., *Al Qaeda in its Own Words*, Cambridge, Massachusetts: The Belknap Press of Harvard University Press, 2008, p. 203.
48 Quoted in Oliver and Steinberg, *The Road to Martyrs' Square*, p. 81. Emphasis added here.
49 Ali Alfoneh, "Iran's Suicide Brigades," *Middle East Quarterly*, Winter 2007, p. 40. Emphasis added here.
50 Quoted in Oliver and Steinberg, *The Road to Martyrs' Square*, p. 81.
51 This news website was originally cited by Ali Alfoneh in his article "Iran's Suicide Brigades," *Middle East Quarterly*, Winter 2007, p. 40.
52 See Bamyeh's analysis of Hegel's master–slave dialectic in *Of Death and Dominion*, p. 8. Emphasis added here and does not appear in the original text.
53 Mohammed Bamyeh engages in a thought-provoking philosophical analysis of the Gilgameshian master, Leo Tolstoy's *Master and Slave*, and death and dominion in his book *Of Death and Dominion*. See earlier sections in this chapter where I introduce Bamyeh's argument.
54 This children's chant was cited by Anne Marie Oliver and Paul F. Steinberg, *The Road to Martyr's Square: A Journey into the World of the Suicide Bomber*, Oxford: Oxford University Press, 2005, p. 60. Emphasis added here and do not appear in the original text. Of course, reference to martyrdom as desire also has a dialectical logic, as I discussed in Chapter 3.
55 See my analysis of the Islamic notion of the *ummah* in Chapter 1.
56 I have put the word existence in quotation marks since in radical Islamist rhetoric an existence in servitude to the other is not considered a worthy existence and certainly not one that should be guarded (protected from physical death), as I noted earlier in this section.
57 The 'self,' of course, is understood interchangeably as both the individual and the collective (in terms of the larger *ummah* or in terms of the specific ethno-linguistic entity in question). See Chapter 1 where I discuss the meaning of 'self' consciousness in the Islamist context.
58 See Chapter 1 where I discuss this notion in detail.
59 Quentin Lauer, S.J., *A Reading of Hegel's Phenomenology of Spirit*, New York: Fordham University Press, 2002, p. 128.
60 Kojeve, *Introduction to the Reading of Hegel*, p. 46. Emphasis added here and not found in the original text.
61 See my analysis of Hegel's life-and-death struggles for recognition in Chapter 1.
62 Sheikh Muhammad Sayyed Tantawi is the head of Al-Azhar Islamic University. This excerpt was originally recorded in *al-Hayat*, April 8, 1997 and appears in Barry Rubin & Judith Colp Rubin (eds.), *Anti-American Terrorism and the Middle East: Understanding the Violence*, New York: Oxford University Press, 2002, p. 36. Emphasis added here.
63 Fawaz A. Gerges, *The Far Enemy: Why Jihad Went Global*, New York: Cambridge University Press, 2005, p. 160. Emphasis added here.
64 Azzam's last testament, as quoted in Oliver & Steinberg, *The Road to Martyrs' Square*, p. 100.
65 Sebastian Smith, *Allah's Mountains: The Battle for Chechnya*, New York: Tauris Parke paperbacks, 2006, p. 154. Emphasis added here.
66 Smith, *Allah's Mountains*, p. 154. Emphasis added here.
67 This poem is translated by David Cook and quoted in his book *Martyrdom in Islam*, New York: Cambridge University Press, 2007, pp. 161–162. Cook points out that Ghazi al-Qusaybi was the former Saudi ambassador to the United Kingdom. The explanations under parenthesis "()" are David Cook's explanations. The explanations under parenthesis "[]" are my additional explanations.

68 Cook, *Martyrdom in Islam*, p. 162. Other than Cook's analysis, which I have put in quotes here, the rest of the analysis of this poem is mine and not Cook's. Emphases in quotation marks are mine and not found in the original text.

69 Cook emphasizes the significance of "the loss of manhood" which he feels is implied in the poem. While certainly one would have to agree with Cook in terms of the significance of manhood in Arab patriarchal culture, I argue that this is not *the* most significant implication in al-Qusaybi's poem.

70 See, for example, John Calvert, *Sayyid Qutb and the Origins of Radical Islamism*, New York: Columbia University Press, 2010.

71 Sayyid Qutb, from his chapter "A Muslim's Nationality and his Belief" as it appear in his publication *Milestones*, New Delhi, India: Islamic Book Service, 2005, p. 124.

72 This excerpt is translated by David Cook and quoted in his book *Martyrdom in Islam*, p. 141. Emphasis added here. The interpretation of this excerpt is mine and is different from the manner in which Cook interprets this excerpt.

73 Qutb's remarks as originally quoted in Bonney, *Jihad*, p. 221.

74 Here Bonney quotes Qutb from Qutb's book *In the Shade of the Qur'an*, viii, 162. See Bonney, *Jihad*, p. 220. Emphasis added here and not found in the original text.

75 This excerpt is quoted by Mir, *The True Face of Jehadis*, p. 212.

76 Michael Inwood, *A Hegel Dictionary*, UK: Blackwell Publishers, 1999, pp. 312–313. See also a detailed discussion of Hegel's notions of freedom in Alan Patten, *Hegel's Idea of Freedom*, New York: Oxford University Press, 2002.

77 Patten, *Hegel's Idea of Freedom*, p. 130. Except for the last sentence of the quote, all emphases in italics are present in the original text.

78 Patten, *Hegel's Idea of Freedom*, p. 99. Emphasis added here and not found in the original text.

79 Excerpts of interview conducted of al-Qaeda leader Ayman al-Zawahiri, archived in *Middle East Media Research Institute* (MEMRI), clip no. 952, December 7, 2005, www.memri.org.

80 Excerpts from the interview of Osama Hamdan in Lebanon, which aired on January 25, 2006; archived in *Middle East Media Research Institute* (MEMRI), clip no. 1012, January 26, 2006, www.memri.org.

81 Abu-Surur's comments originally quoted in Oliver and Steinberg, *The Road to Martyrs' Square*, p. 120.

82 See the discussion on *Wars of Honor and Prestige* in Chapter 2.

83 This excerpt was originally cited by David Cook in his book *Martyrdom in Islam*, p. 159. However, the analysis of this except is mine and not reflective of Cook's analysis.

84 Excerpt of Sheikh Qasim's statement, as cited by Gilles Kepel in his book *Beyond Terror and Martyrdom*, Cambridge, Massachusetts: The Belknap Press of Harvard University Press, 2008, p. 83.

85 This declaration is produced by the Council of Scholars from the Arabian Peninsula and was originally cited in David Cook's book *Understanding Jihad*, Berkeley, California: California University Press, 2005, p. 230.

86 This excerpt originally appears in Cook, *Understanding Jihad*, p. 143. Except for the word 'iman' and its definition in parenthesis, the italicized emphasis has been added here and was not present in the original text.

87 This slogan is taken from Oliver & Steinberg's *The Road to Martyrs' Square*, p. 61. However, the interpretation are entirely my own and not that of Oliver & Steinberg.

88 Quoted in Christoph Reuter, *My Life is a Weapon*, p. 90.

89 Quoted in Oliver & Steinberg, *The Road to Martyrs' Square*, p. 81.

90 Quoted in Oliver & Steinberg, *The Road to Martyrs' Square*, p. 105.

91 Excerpt from Hegel's *The Philosophy of History*, as quoted in Thomas Lewis' *Freedom and Tradition in Hegel: Reconsidering Anthropology, Ethics and Religion*, Indiana: University of Notre Dame Press, 2005, p. 70. Emphasis added here and does not appear in the original text.

92 Cook, *Martyrdom in Islam*, p. 139.
93 Quoted in Christoph Reuter, *My Life is a Weapon*, p. 115.

4 Violence as morality

1 Islamic theologians have long argued that an interpretation of the Islamic notion of jihad as necessarily violent is a wrong interpretation of the notion of jihad. Amongst a list of numerous such Islamic theologians and scholars, see for example Tariq Ramadan, *Radical Reform: Islamic Ethics and Liberation*, New York: Oxford University Press, 2009.
2 Bruce Lawrence, "Islam at Risk: The Discourse on Islam and Violence," *Islamism: Contested Perspectives on Political Islam*, Richard C. Martin & Abbas Barzegar, eds., Stanford, California: Stanford University Press, 2010, p. 93. Emphasis added here and does not appear in the original text.
3 See Hans-Georg Moeller, *The Moral Fool: A Case for Amorality*, New York: Columbia University Press, 2009.
4 See my analysis of Nietzsche's critique of morality and his assertion of the instrumentality of religion in Chapter 1.
5 See my discussion of Axel Honneth's assertion of the moral grammar of struggles for recognition in Chapter 1.
6 By human condition I mean the tendencies that are argued to be *human, all too human*—if I may borrow here the title of one of Nietzsche's books (1878)—such as the tendency to present all that benefits the self as a 'morality' and everything else (including the similar actions of others) as an 'immorality.' A negative manifestation is then the negative consequences of such a human condition, such as the justifications of violence as a morality.
7 See Chapter 1 where I discuss Neitzsche's critique of Christian morality and his larger critique of religion as morality.
8 See my analysis of Nietzsche's critique of the instrumentality of religion in Chapter 1.
9 As quoted by Craig Calhoun in "Afterword: Religion's Many Powers," in *The Power of Religion in the Public Sphere*, eds. Eduardo Mendieta & Jonathan VanAntwerpen, New York: Columbia University Press, 2011, p. 118.
10 Mark Gregory Pegg argues that the actual goals or consequences for the Christian Crusades the conquest of Jerusalem and the desires for the expansion of Christendom. See Pegg's analysis in his book *A Most Holy War: The Albigensian Crusade and the Battle for Christendom*, New York: Oxford University Press, 2008.
11 Pegg, *A Most Holy War*, p. 188. Emphases have been added here and do not appear in the original text.
12 Pegg, *A Most Holy War*, p. 188.
13 Robert L. Holmes, "Can War Be Morally Justified? The Just War Theory," in *Just War Theory*, ed. Jean Bethke Elshtain, UK: Blackwell, 1992, p. 197.
14 Alan Kramer, *Dynamic of Destruction: Culture and Mass Killing in the First World War*, New York: Oxford University Press, 2007, p. 175. Emphases are added here and do not appear in the original text.
15 Alan Kramer, *Dynamic of Destruction: Culture and Mass Killing in the First World War*, New York: Oxford University Press, 2007, p. 175. Emphases are added here and do not appear in the original text.
16 As quoted by Alan Kramer, *Dynamic of Destruction: Culture and Mass Killing in the First World War*, New York: Oxford University Press, 2007, p. 175. Emphases are added here and do not appear in the original text.
17 Roxanne L. Euben & Muhammad Qasim Zaman, eds. *Princeton Readings in Islamist Thought: Texts and Contexts from al-Banna to Bin Laden*, Princeton, NJ: Princeton University Press, 2009, p. 360.

18 See my analysis of Kant's categorical imperative in Chapter 1.

19 Mark Gregory Pegg, *A Most Holy War: The Albigensian Crusade and the Battle for Christendom*, New York: Oxford University Press, 2008, p. 189.

20 It is not my intention here to offer a genealogy of the Just War doctrine from its Christian historic origins to its contemporary manifestations. For a detailed genealogy of the Just War doctrine, from St. Augustine to Aquinas, from Vitoria to Grotius, along with the various debates related to its contemporary secular version, see the following sources: Alex J. Bellamy, *Just Wars: From Cicero to Iraq*, UK: Polity Press, 2006; Andrew Fiala, *The Just War Myth: The Moral Illusions of War*, New York: Rowman & Littlefield Publishers, Inc., 2008; Jean Bethke Elshtain, ed., *Just War Theory*, UK: Blackwell, 1992.

21 Alex J. Bellamy, *Just Wars: From Cicero to Iraq*, UK: Polity Press, 2006, p. 29.

22 Bellamy, *Just Wars*, p. 29. Emphases added here and do not appear in the original text.

23 See "Augustine, St. (353–430)" in *An Encyclopedia of War and Ethnics*, ed. Donald A. Wells, Connecticut: Greenwood Press, 1996, p. 31.

24 Brien Hallett, "Aquinas, Thomas (1225–1274)," *An Encyclopedia of War and Ethnics*, ed. Donald A. Wells, Connecticut: Greenwood Press, 1996, p. 17.

25 Fergus Kerr, *Thomas Aquinas: A Very Short Introduction*, New York: Oxford University Press, 2009, p. 7.

26 Kerr, *Thomas Aquinas*, p. 7.

27 At the time of the writing of this book in 2010, American forces were still stationed in Iraq despite the shift in the American administration's focus: from the occupation of Iraq to the full-blown occupation of Afghanistan.

28 See the discussion of deontological morality in Chapter 1.

29 Immanuel Kant, *Perpetual Peace and Other Essays*, translated and with introduction by Ted Humphrey, Indianapolis: Hackett Publishing Company, 1983.

30 See Jens Meierhenrich's critical analysis of Kant's notion of perpetual peace in "Perpetual War: A Pragmatic Sketch," *Human Rights Quarterly*, 29 (2007), pp. 631–673.

31 See Alex J. Bellamy's discussion of Aquinas' notion of 'double-effect' in *Just Wars: From Cicero to Iraq*, UK: Polity Press, 2006, pp. 37–40. I shall return to the analysis of this later in this chapter.

32 I shall discuss this point further in Chapter 5.

33 Stipulations of wars as 'just' and 'unjust' are associated with the works of Michael Walzer. See Michael Walzer's delineations of 'just' and 'unjust' wars in *Just and UnJust Wars: A Moral Argument with Historical Illustrations*, New York: Basic Books, 1977; 4th edition 2006.

34 Robert L. Holmes, "Can War be Morally Justified?" in *Just War Theory*, Jean Bethke Elshtain, Ed., Oxford, UK: Blackwell Ltd., 1992, p. 209.

35 I have argued in this book that the essence of violence is struggles for recognition that are always framed in moral terms. It is important to note that while in this book I have been concerned with the essence of Islamist extremism, which I have argued is a Hegelian struggle for recognition of the self as at once distinct and equally significant to the other (and thus as struggles against oppression and negation of the self), struggles for recognition can equally mean struggles for recognition of one's mastery, and thus struggles to assert oneself as in, say, the hegemonic states in the international arena.

36 See Bellamy's discussion of Aquinas in *Just Wars*, p. 38. Emphasis found in the original text.

37 See Bellamy's discussion of Aquinas in *Just Wars*, p. 38. Emphasis found in the original text.

38 I shall address the issue of misguided policies that are a product of misunderstanding the essence of the radical Islamist explanations and the justifications of violence in the next chapter (Chapter 5).

39 In his *De Jure Belli et Pacis,* Hugo Grotius (1583–1645) challenged the unbridled authority of the kings (the sovereigns) to declare wars and offered one of the best known criticism of Europe's holy wars. Alex Bellamy notes that for Grotius, "just cause, right intention and proportionality of ends played a secondary role to right authority and proper declaration." See Bellamy, *Just Wars*, p. 75. See also Bellamy's discussion of Grotius' contributions on pp. 71–76.

40 Uwe Steinhoff, *On the Ethics of War and Terrorism*, Oxford: Oxford University Press, 2007, p. 19.

41 Robert L. Holmes' analysis of legitimate authority in "Can War be Morally Justified?," p. 212.

42 At the time of this writing, the year was 2010, and the war I am referring to started immediately in the aftermath of the September 11, 2001 bombing of the United States by al-Qaeda forces allied with the Taliban in Afghanistan.

43 A.J. Coates, *The Ethnics of War*, Manchester: Manchester University Press, 1997, p. 123, as quoted by Uwe Steinhoff, *On the Ethics of War and Terrorism*, New York: Oxford University Press, 2007, p. 7. Emphasis added here and does not appear in the original text.

44 I address this issue more specifically later in this chapter.

45 Steinhoff, *On the Ethics of War and Terrorism*, p. 12.

46 Janna Thompson, "Terrorism and the Right to Wage War," in *Terrorism and Justice: Moral Argument in a Threatened World*, Tony Coady and Michael O'Keefe, eds., Melbourne: Melbourne University Press, 2002, pp. 87–96 (emphases added here), as quoted by Steinhoff, *On the Ethics of War and Terrorism*, p. 15.

47 Steinhoff, *On the Ethics of War and Terrorism*, p. 15.

48 See Robert L. Holmes' analysis of legitimate authority in "Can War be Morally Justified?,", p. 201.

49 See Hannah Arendt, *Eichmann in Jerusalem: A Report on the Banality of Evil,* New York: Penguin Books, 2006, special edition with an introduction by Amos Elon; pp. 135–150.

50 Arendt, *Eichmann in Jerusalem*, p. 26.

51 Arendt, *Eichmann in Jerusalem*, p. 26.

52 See Elisabeth Young-Bruehl's analysis of Arendt's notion of banality in *Why Arendt Matters*, New Haven: Yale University Press, 2006, pp. 1–29.

53 Gordon D. Newby, *A Concise Encyclopedia of Islam*, Oxford, UK: Oneworld Publications, 2002, p. 135. Kecia Ali and Oliver Leaman point out, "the caliphate became a Sunni institution" after the split occurred between those who considered Ali (Prophet Muhammad's cousin) as the rightful caliph (successor) to the Prophet and those who considered Abu Bakr (who ruled 632–634 and was the Prophet's father-in-law) as the rightful successor. This split eventually culminated into what are now Sunni and Shia schools of thought in Islam. See the entry "Caliphate" in Kecia Ali & Oliver Leaman, *Islam: The Key Concepts*, New York: Routledge, 2008, p. 18.

54 John L. Esposito, *The Oxford Dictionary of Islam*, Oxford: Oxford University Press, 2003, p. 49.

55 Esposito, *The Oxford Dictionary of Islam*, p. 49.

56 Muhammad Abd al-Salam Faraj, *Al-Faridah al-Gha'ibah*, p. 166. Emphasis added here.

57 Muhammad Abd al-Salam Faraj, *Al-Faridah al-Gha'ibah*, p. 167. Emphasis added here.

58 An excerpt from Ayman Al-Zawahiri's *Knights under the Prophet's Banner*, published December 2, 2001, in Kepel & Milelli, eds., *Al Qaeda in its Own Words*, p. 205.

59 Al-Zawahiri's *Knights under the Prophet's Banner*, Kepel & Milelli, eds., p. 205. The parenthetical numbers are the specific pages where the noted references can be found.

60 Gordon Newby notes that even thought the "Mahdi is a figure who is prominently featured in the eschatology of all branches of Islam," "among the Sunni, there is no consistent belief that a rightly guided figure will appear at the last days to restore Islam." See Newby, *A Concise Encyclopedia of Islam*, p. 135.

61 See the discussion of the Mahdi in Newby, *A Concise Encyclopedia of Islam*, p. 135.

62 Esposito, *The Oxford Dictionary of Islam*, p. 185.

63 Esposito, *The Oxford Dictionary of Islam*, p. 185. Emphasis added here.

64 See "Muqtada al-Sadr, Iraqi Leader of the Al-Mahdi Movement, Supports Armed Attacks on U.S. Forces in Iraq," MEMRI, Special Dispatch Series, no. 1883, March 31, 2008.

65 See "Profile: The al-Mahdi Army," *al-Jazeera, at AlJazeera.net,* Sunday, April 20, 2008, http://english.aljazeera.net/news/middleeast/2008/04/2008615165845241319.html

66 Much has been written on the varying interpretations of Islam and Hadith (traditions as reflected of the Prophet's way of life) by Islamic theologians as well as scholars. A discussion of this is both beyond the scope of this chapter as well as irrelevant to the argument.

67 An excerpt from the Charter of the Palestinian Hamas, as cited in Roxanne L. Euben & Muhammad Qasim Zaman, *Princeton Readings in Islamist Thought: Texts and Contexts from al-Banna to Bin Laden*, Princeton, NJ: Princeton University Press, 2009, p. 369. Emphasis is added here.

68 I shall come back to the issue of motivations in the next chapter (Chapter 5) where I discuss epistemological assumptions and logical deduction in order to shed light on the possible nature of the motivations of individuals that voluntarily join extremist groups.

69 The reference to this can be found in Euben & Qasim Zaman, *Princeton Readings in Islamist Thought*, p. 356.

70 Pegg, *A Most Holy War*, p. 189.

71 See Alex J. Bellamy's analysis of the contemporary practice of the Just War doctrine in *Just Wars*, pp. 126–128.

72 Philip Gourevitch & Errol Morris, *The Ballad of Abu Ghraib*, previously published as *Standard Operating Procedure*, New York: Penguin Books, 2008, p. 243.

73 Gourevitch & Morris, *The Ballad of Abu Ghraib*, p. 247.

74 Gourevitch & Morris, *The Ballad of Abu Ghraib*, p. 267.

75 'Intentionality,' of course, is one of the classic loopholes in international law since it can never be proven; it therefore tends to become the last resort of legal defense for the legal legitimacy of one's actions.

76 See Alex J. Bellamy for his discussion of Aquinas' assertions regarding double-effect in *Just Wars*, p. 136.

77 Uwe Steinhoff, *On the Ethics of War and Terrorism*, New York: Oxford University Press, 2007, p. 26. Emphasis found in the original text.

78 Muhammad Abd al-Salam Faraj, *Al-Faridah al-Gha'ibah (The Neglected Duty)*, translated by Johannes J.G. Jansen in *The Neglected Duty: The Creed of Sadat's Assassins and Islamic Resurgence in the Middle East*, New York: Macmillan Publishing Company, 1986, p. 199.

79 Brown, "Martyrdom in Sunni Revivalist Thought," p. 112.

80 Muhammad Abd al-Salam Faraj, *Al-Faridah al-Gha'ibah*, p. 200. Emphasis added here.

81 Muhammad Abd al-Salam Faraj, *Al-Faridah al-Gha'ibah*, p. 200. It is interesting to note that the majority consensus amongst Islamic theologians is that the greater jihad is the non-violent struggle for one's soul and it is the lesser jihad that is the violent struggle against the other. Radical Islamist rhetoric reverses the order of this relegation, as we can see in Faraj's assertions. Within the context of the debate over non-violent and violent jihad, Richard Bonney notes that out of the possible 35 references

to *jihad* in the Quran, there are only four references that are "clearly warlike in intention" (28). Indeed, Bonney points out that of the remaining 31 references, 11 are clearly pacific in nature and 20 are open to interpretation, or *ijtihad*, which is one of the central tenants of Islam. See Richard Bonney, *Jihad: From Qur'an to bin Laden*, London: Palgrave Macmillan, 2004, p. 28.

82 The "Al-Faridah al Gha'ibah" is analyzed in detail later in this chapter in the context of what I am arguing is a consequentialist-deontological fusion in radical Islamist reason.

83 See Chapter 1 where I discuss Axel Honneth and his paradigm of the moral grammar of struggles for recognition.

84 Muhammad Abdel Haleem, *Understanding the Qur'an: Themes and Style,* New York: I.B. Tauris, 2005, p. 62.

85 Abdel Haleem, *Understanding the Qur'an*, p. 62.

86 Abdel Haleem, *Understanding the Qur'an*, p. 62.

87 Abdel Haleem, *Understanding the Qur'an*, p. 62.

88 Abdel Haleem, *Understanding the Qur'an*, p. 61.

89 Excerpt from Sayyid Qutb's *In the Shade of the Qur'an*, vol. 8, surah 9, cited in John Calvert's *Sayyid Qutb and the Origins of Radical Islamism*, New York: Columbia University Press, 2010, p. 244. Emphasis added here.

90 Sayyid Qutb, *Milestone*, New Delhi, India: Islamic Book Service, 2005, p. 57 (for the first part of the quote) and p. 59 (for the latter sections of the quote). Emphasis added here.

91 Qutb, *Milestone*, p. 70.

92 Euben & Zaman, eds., *Princeton Readings in Islamist Thought*, p. 358.

93 An excerpt from the Charter of the Palestinian Hamas, cited in Euben & Zaman, eds., *Princeton Readings in Islamist Thought*, p. 367.

94 An excerpt from the Charter of the Palestinian Hamas, cited in Euben & Zaman, eds., *Princeton Readings in Islamist Thought*, pp. 370–371.

95 Sayyid Qutb, *Milestones*, 2nd edition, New Delhi, India: Islamic Book Service, 2005, pp. 87–92.

96 Quoted in Hala Jaber, *Hezbollah*, New York: Columbia University Press, 1997, p. 86.

97 See Chapter 1 where I introduce Kant's deontological argument in the context of Kant's notion of morality.

98 Wood, *Kant's Ethnical Thought*, p. 29.

99 This leads to another critical implication, though one that is not directly relevant to our current discussion, and that is that freedom and desire do *not* contradict each other in the Kantian notions of absolute freedom. This negates Hegel's criticism of Kant's notions of absolute freedom, namely that Kant does not consider the significance of desire in human actions.

100 This children's chant was cited by Anne Marie Oliver and Paul F. Steinberg, in their book *The Road to Martyr's Square: A Journey into the World of the Suicide Bomber,* Oxford: Oxford University Press, 2005, p. 60. Emphasis added here and do not appear in the original text. Of course, reference to martyrdom as desire also has a dialectical logic, as I discussed in Chapter 3 of this book.

101 See Alex J. Bellamy for his discussion of Aquinas' assertions regarding double-effect in *Just Wars*, p. 38.

102 Bellamy, *Just Wars*, p. 54. Emphases added here.

103 Holmes "Can War be Morally Justified?" p. 209.

104 Steinhoff, *On the Ethics of War and Terrorism*, p. 35.

105 Walzer, *Just and Unjust Wars*, p. 264.

106 Walzer, *Just and Unjust Wars*, p. 264.

107 Steinhoff, *On the Ethics of War and Terrorism*, p. 35.

108 Holmes "Can War be Morally Justified?" p. 209.

109 "Attacks from US Aerial Drones," Amnesty International publication, www.eyeson-pakistan.org/c_drone_attacks.html

110 "US drone strikes kill 14 militants in North Waziristan," *Dawn* (Pakistan's most popular English-version daily newspaper), Friday, June 11, 2010. URL:www.dawn.com/wps/wcm/connect/dawn-content-library/dawn/news/pakistan/14-us-drone-strike-kills-four-in-north-waziristan-zj-08

111 "US drone strikes kill 14 militants in North Waziristan," *Dawn* (Pakistan's most popular English-version daily newspaper), Friday, June 11, 2010. URL:www.dawn.com/wps/wcm/connect/dawn-content-library/dawn/news/pakistan/14-us-drone-strike-kills-four-in-north-waziristan-zj-08

112 "Attacks from US Aerial Drones," Amnesty International publication, www.eyeson-pakistan.org/c_drone_attacks.html

113 See Robert L. Holmes discussion of 'objective' and 'subjective' just cause for war in, "Can War be Morally Justified?" p. 201. See also Bellamy's analysis of Francisco de Vitoria's notion of objective and subjective in *Just Wars*, p. 53.

114 See Chapter 1 where I introduce and discuss the notions of consequentialist morality versus a deontological morality.

115 See Chapter 1 for Axel Honneth's analysis of the subjective notions of morality in struggles for recognition. The latter, of course, can very likely lead to violence and brutality especially when such struggles take place in a context of no legal recourses to injustices (actual or perceived) whether at the national or trans-national level.

116 I shall return to this epistemological debate in the next chapter when I analyze the possible nature of the motivations of individuals that voluntarily join Islamist extremist groups.

117 International non-government human rights organizations are an exception and are thus more likely to question the proclaimed objectivity of a war. Amnesty International is a case in point. Amnesty's recent critical assessments of the US Obama Administration's proclamations of fight a Just War that is legally sound according to international law is a case in point.

118 "Attacks from US Aerial Drones," Amnesty International publication, www.eyeson-pakistan.org/c_drone_attacks.html

119 See Bellamy's analysis of Francisco de Vitoria's contributions to the Just War debate, *Just Wars*, p. 52.

120 Bellamy notes that "Vattel's *Le Droit des gens* (1758) provided the most comprehensive post-Grotian reworking of the laws of war ... [that] dominated thinking about laws of war until the twentieth century." See Bellamy, *Just Wars*, p. 79.

121 See Holmes, "Can War be Morally Justified?" p. 202. Alex Bellamy notes that Vattel understood international law "as the science of the rights which exist between Nations or States, and of the obligations corresponding to those rights." See Bellamy, *Just Wars*, p. 79.

122 I shall discuss these two wars in more detail in the next chapter (Chapter 5) when I discuss the flawed policies of the US 'war on terrorism' that I argue are based on a critical misunderstanding of the nature (essence) of Islamist extremism.

123 See Andrew Fiala, *The Just War Myth: The Moral Illusions of War*, New York: Rowman & Littlefield Publishers, Inc., 2008.

124 Reuven Firestone, *Jihad: The Origins of Holy War in Islam*, New York: Oxford University Press, 1999, p. 13.

125 Fazlur Rahman, *Major Themes of the Qur'an*, Chicago: The University of Chicago Press, 2009, p. 63.

126 John L. Esposito, Editor in chief, *The Oxford Dictionary of Islam*, New York: Oxford University Press, 2003, p. 159.

127 Aziz al-Azmeh is a pre-eminent scholar in the Arab and Islamic historical studies. Aziz al-Azmeh is quoted in Firestone, *Jihad*, p. 14.

128 Elaine Scarry, *Rule of Law, Misrule of Men*, Cambridge, MA: The MIT Press, 2010, p. 58.
129 Scarry, *Rule of Law, Misrule of Men*, p. 59.
130 The White House website, www.whitehouse.gov/the-press-office/remarks-president-address-nation-way-forward-afghanistan-and-pakistan. Emphasis added here.
131 Fawaz A. Gerges, *The Far Enemy: Why Jihad Went Global*, New York: Cambridge University Press, 2005, p. 44.
132 Gerges, *The Far Enemy*, p. 44.
133 Quoted in Bonney, *Jihad*, p. 213. Emphasis added here. It is also important to note, as does John L. Esposito, that the writings of the early Islamic revivalists such as Sayyid Abu'l-A'la Mawdudi (1903–1979), Hasan al-Banna (1906–1949) and Sayyid Qutb (1906–1966) were most influential in determining the Islamic discourse in the later part of the twentieth century. See John L. Esposito, *Unholy War: Terror in the Name of Islam*, Oxford: Oxford University Press, 2002, pp. 50–51, 61.
134 Bonney, *Jihad*, p. 213.
135 Brown, "Martyrdom in Sunni Revivalist Thought," p. 110.
136 Bonney, *Jihad*, p. 213. See also Bonney's discussion of the various avenues to martyrdom in the Islamic tradition, pp. 36–37.
137 See statements made by al-Banna as quoted by Bonney in *Jihad*, pp. 213–214.
138 Quoted in Bonney, *Jihad*, p. 214. Emphasis added here and not found in the original text.
139 Sayyid Qutb, *In the Shade of the Qur'an*, as it appear in Albert J. Bergesen, ed., *The Sayyid Qutb Reader: Selected Writings on Politics, Religion, and Society*, New York: Routledge, 2008, pp. 49–50. Emphasis on 'jihad' is found in the original text, but emphasis on the latter part of the sentence is not found in the original text.
140 Qutb, *In the Shade of the Qur'an*, as it appear in Bergesen, *The Sayyid Qutb Reader*, p. 50. Emphasis on 'jihad' is found in the original text.
141 Qutb, *In the Shade of the Qur'an*, as it appear in Bergesen, *The Sayyid Qutb Reader*, p. 50. Emphasis on 'jihad' is found in the original text.
142 'Sittlichkeit' is the Hegelian notion of an ethnical order or moral standards of a society. Hegel argued that Sittlichkeits are temporally variable, and necessarily so.
143 Mawdudi as quoted by Bonney in *Jihad*, p. 200. Emphasis on 'universal revolution' not found in original text.
144 Excerpt from the Palestinian Charter, as cited in Euben & Zaman, *Princeton Readings in Islamist Thought*, p. 368. The parenthetical note is that of the editors and not mine.
145 Excerpt from the Palestinian Charter, as cited in Euben & Zaman, *Princeton Readings in Islamist Thought*, p. 372. The parenthetical note is that of the editors and not mine.
146 An excerpt from an interview with Shaykh Muhammad Husayn Fadallah (1995), as cited in Euban & Zaman, *Princeton Readings in Islamist Thought*, p. 396.
147 Amir Mir, *The True Face of Jehadis*, p. 131. Emphasis added here.
148 Quoted in Reuter, *My Life is a Weapon*, p. 125. Emphasis added here and does not appear in the original text.
149 Shaykh Muhammad al-Ghazali as quoted by Bonney, *Jihad*, p. 29.
150 Mohammed Masood Azhar, *The Virtues of Jihad*, cited in David Cook's *Understanding Jihad*, Berkeley, California: University of California Press, 2005, p. 137. Emphasis added here.
151 Sebastian Smith, *Allah's Mountains: The Battle for Chechnya*, New York: Tauris Parke paperbacks, 2006, p. 191. Emphasis added here.
152 Bellamy, *Just Wars*, p. 75. Emphasis added here.
153 Fergus Kerr, *Thomas Aquinas: A Very Short Introduction*, New York: Oxford University Press, 2009, p. 7. Emphasis added here.

154 Andrew Fiala, *The Just War Myth: The Moral Illusions of War*, New York: Rowman & Littlefield Publishers, Inc., 2008, p. 39.

155 See Robert L. Holmes, "Can War be Morally Justified?" in *Just War Theory*, Jean Bethke Elshtain, Ed., Oxford, UK: Blackwell Ltd., 1992, p. 215.

156 See Holmes, "Can War be Morally Justified?" p. 215.

157 Michael Walzer, *Just and UnJust Wars: A Moral Argument with Historical Illustrations*, 4th edition, New York: Basic Books, 2006, p. 252.

158 Walzer, *Just and UnJust Wars*, p. 255 (for the first quotation) and p. 253 (for the second quotation).

159 Walzer, *Just and UnJust Wars*, p. 264.

160 Walzer, *Just and UnJust Wars*, p. 264.

161 For the quoted text see Walzer, *Just and UnJust Wars*, p. 253.

162 Holmes, "Can War be Morally Justified?" p. 220.

163 Holmes, "Can War be Morally Justified?" p. 220.

164 Holmes, "Can War be Morally Justified?" p. 217.

165 Marshall Sahlins, "Preface," *The Counter-Counterinsurgency Manual,* Network of Concerned Anthropologists, Chicago: Prickly Paradigm Press, 2009, p. iv. Emphasis added here.

166 The officer with whom I had this conversation has demanded anonymity and thus shall remain unnamed here.

167 I shall address the issue of flawed policies based on a misunderstanding of the essence of Islamist extremism in the next chapter.

168 Steinhoff, *On the Ethics of War and Terrorism*, p. 110. Emphasis added here.

169 Bruce Hoffman, as quoted by Steinhoff, *On the Ethics of War and Terrorism*, p. 110.

170 Steinhoff, *On the Ethics of War and Terrorism*, p. 110. Emphasis added here.

171 The sections of the sentences that are in quotation marks here reflect Bruce Hoffman's words, as quoted originally by Steinhoff, *On the Ethics of War and Terrorism*, p. 110.

172 Vicki Divoll, as quoted by Jane Mayer in "The Predator War," *The New Yorker*, October 26, 2009, p. 37.

173 Muhammad Abd al-Salam Faraj, *Al-Faridah al-Gha'ibah*, p. 217.

174 See the previous section in this chapter for the analysis of the clauses and qualifications of the Just War doctrine.

175 Muhammad Abd al-Salam Faraj, *Al-Faridah al-Gha'ibah*, p. 217. Emphasis added here.

176 See Bonney, *Jihad*, p. 298.

177 Naim Qassem, *Hizbullah: The Story from Within*, Dalia Khalil, Trans., Lebanon: Saqi, 2010, p. 297. Emphasis added here.

178 Interview with Osama bin Laden, conducted by Rahimullah Yusufzai, January 1999, transcribed in *Newsline* (Karachi, Pakistan), January 1999, p. 61.

179 Statement made by Qaradawi, as quoted in Reuter, *My Life is a Weapon*, p. 122.

180 Osama bin Laden, interview conducted by Rahimullah Yusufzai, p. 61.

181 Excerpt taken from Center for Islamic Studies and Research, an organization affiliated with al-Qaeda, "The East Riyadh Operation and Our War with the United States and its Agents," August 1, 2003; www.cybcity.com/newss, translated by Foreign Broadcast Information Service, cited in Robert A. Pape's *Dying to Win: The Strategic Logic of Suicide Terrorism*, New York: Random House, 2005, p. 118.

182 Quoted in Reuter, *My Life is a Weapon, p.* 122. Emphasis added here and does not appear in the original text.

5 Essence, motivations, and flawed policies

1 Michael A. Ledeen. "The Advance of Freedom: US Foreign Policy and Democratic Revolution," *Harvard International Review*, Spring 2005, p. 15. Emphases

added here and do not appear in the original text. Ledeen has also served as a special consultant to the US Department of Defense as well as the US Department of State and is the founder of the Jewish Institute for National Security Affairs (JINSA).

2 Of course, the post-2003 US policy of the occupation of Iraq and the post-2001 US–NATO protracted presence in Afghanistan (which, by definition, is an occupation) certainly substantiate the negative perceptions of the 'other' that are portrayed in radical Islamist rhetoric.

3 Sartre argued that freedom must necessarily be a responsibility, and if so, freedom must necessarily be action. See "The Humanism of Existentialism", "Freedom and Responsibility" and "The Desire to be God" in Jean-Paul Sartre, *Essays in Existentialism*, New York: Kensington Publishing Corp., 1993, pp. 31–75.

4 Graham E. Fuller is a former vice chairman of the National Intelligence Council of the CIA and currently an adjunct professor of history at Simon Fraser University in Vancouver. See Fuller's arguments in his article "A World without Islam," *Foreign Policy*, January/February 2008, pp. 46–53.

5 See Thomas Carothers who criticizes the post-2003 US 'democracy promotion' through occupation of Iraq and Afghanistan on similar grounds in *U.S. Democracy Promotion: During and After Bush*, Washington, D.C., Carnegie Endowment for International Peace, 2007. See also the criticism of the notion of 'preventative war' and 'democracy promotion' through occupation by varies authors in the edited volume *American Hegemony: Preventive War, Iraq, and Imposing Democracy*, Demetrios James Careley, Ed., New York: The Academy of Political Science, 2004.

6 Samuel Huntington's assertion as quoted by David Frum, "Samuel Huntington," *Foreign Policy*, March/April 2007, p. 44. Emphasis added here. Frum is resident fellow at the American Enterprise Institute and a columnist at the National Review Online—bibliographical information as listed by *Foreign Policy.*

7 Frum, "Samuel Huntington," p. 44.

8 The pro-democracy youth movements in the Middle East that have come to be understood as the defining turmoil of the year 2011 speak to the rejection of the oppression of the self by one's own government since the movements were exclusively targeted against the indigenous long-standing autocratic governments. In contrast, the anti-American and anti-NATO rhetoric of the Afghani and the Pakistani Taliban in the years of the US–NATO occupation of Afghanistan from 2001 to the present (the year of this writing was 2011) speak to the rejection of the oppression of the self by foreign entities.

9 See Peter Burnell's analysis of the justification of democracy promotion as a foreign policy objective in "Promoting Democracy," *Comparative Politics*, Daniele Caramani, ed., New York: Oxford University Press, 2008, p. 631.

10 For alleged abuse of Afghani detainees at the hands of the Americans in the U.S. Bagram military base in Afghanistan, see the report by Ian Pannell, "Ex-detainees Allege Bagram Abuse," *BBC News*, June 24, 2009.

11 Bruce Hoffman, "Al Qaeda Resurgent," *The Theory and Practice of Islamic Terrorism: An Anthology*, Marvin Perry & Howard E. Negrin, Eds., New York: Palgrave Macmillan, 2008, p. 111.

12 Hoffman, "Al Qaeda Resurgent," p. 111. Emphases added here and do not appear in the original text.

13 See Chapter 4 where I discuss the stipulations regarding 'self-defense' in the internationally accepted Just War doctrine and the manner in which they allow for carte blanche in actions justified in terms of 'self-defense.'

14 Chapters 2 and 3 discuss in detail the notion of the existential reason.

15 See Chapter 1 where I discuss the notion of the dialectic and dialectical relationships in terms of what Ballard terms as 'reciprocal causality.'

16 See R.M. Hare's discussion on terrorism in his *Essays on Political Morality*, Oxford: Clarendon Press, 1998, p. 39. The spelling of 'centered' is instead 'centred' in the original text, and as it thus appears in my text.

17 Epistemology is, of course, a contested subfield of philosophy which focuses on the theory of knowledge. Nonetheless, epistemological assumptions are useful in delineating the motivations of individuals for action. Of course, individuals' motivations are multifaceted and complex. As Martha Crenshaw notes: "Individuals are motivated differently [and thus] ... There is no single pattern," and that "the organization that recruits and directs ... [the individuals] remains the most important agent [for determining motivations]," in "Explaining Suicide Terrorism: A Review Essay," *Security Studies*, 16(1), January–March 2007, p. 157. I contend, however, that epistemological assumptions do shed instructive light on the possible nature of these motivations. More specifically, I argue in this section that it is the *reason in radical Islamist rhetoric* that both determines and shapes the motivations of individuals for violent or self-destructive actions.

18 Epistemological assumptions and logical deductions are quite different from the econometric equations offered by 'rational choice' theorists as calculations and explanations of individuals' motivations. Such econometric equations assume linear relationships that boast of a technical accuracy. But, as Jon Elster notes, such theories falsely present some given equation of rationality as always applicable in the form it is predicted. See Elster, "Motivations and Beliefs in Suicide Missions," in *Making Sense of Suicide Missions*, Diego Gambetta, ed., New York: Oxford University Press, 2005, pp. 257–258.

19 I have placed reality under quotes to emphasize that an understanding of reality is itself a matter of perceptions. I shall come back to the issue of perceptions later in this section when I engage Merleau-Ponty and his contributions to the subject of perceptions.

20 Anil Gupta, *Empiricism and Experience*, New York: Oxford University Press, 2006, p. 224.

21 Fetzer & Almeder, *Glossary of Epistemology, p.* 5.

22 Mary Gregor, ed. *Kant: Groundwork of the Metaphysics of Morals,* Cambridge Texts in the History of Philosophy, UK: Cambridge University Press, 1997, p. ix.

23 Gregor, *Kant*, ix.

24 Gregor, *Kant*, p. viii. The necessary a priori nature of analytical truths is the reason why, argues Gregor, "there are no analytic a posteriori judgments" (ix).

25 James H. Fetzer & Robert F. Almeder, *Glossary of Epistemology/Philosophy of Science*, New York: Paragon House, 1993, p. 5.

26 Gregor, *Kant*, p. ix.

27 Fetzer & Almeder, *Glossary of Epistemology*, p. 6.

28 Fetzer & Almeder, *Glossary of Epistemology*, p. 6.

29 Dicker, *Kant's Theory of Knowledge*, p. 4. Emphasis added here and not found in the original text.

30 Dicker, *Kant's Theory of Knowledge*, p. 4.

31 See my analysis of Gupta's argument earlier in this section where Gupta argues that observations of reality—or experience—need not be our own, it may very well be the observations of those that we trust and whose judgments we consider legitimate. For example, historical narratives as based on the observations of others but that come to form our own knowledge of reality, both present and past.

32 Dicker, *Kant's Theory of Knowledge*, p. 6.

33 For an excellently detailed analysis of Kant's transcendental idealism see Henry E. Allison, *Kant's Transcendental Idealism*, revised and enlarged edition, New Haven: Yale University Press, 2004.

34 J.N. Mohanty, *Phenomenology: Between Essentialism and Transcendental Philosophy*, Evanston, IL: Northwestern University Press, 1997, pp. 52–61.

35　Mohanty, *Phenomenology*, pp. 52–61.

36　Mohanty, *Phenomenology*, p. 52.

37　Mohanty, *Phenomenology*, p. 52. Emphases added here and not appear in the original text.

38　See Allen W. Wood's analysis of Kant's a priori practical principles in *Kant's Ethnical Through*, UK: Cambridge University Press, 1999, p. 56.

39　Dicker, *Kant's Theory of Knowledge*, p. 34. Emphases added here and do not appear in the original text.

40　Dicker, *Kant's Theory of Knowledge*, p. 32. Emphasis added here and not found in the original text.

41　Dicker, *Kant's Theory of Knowledge*, p. 32. Emphasis added here and not found in the original text.

42　Maria Baghramian, *Relativism*, New York: Routledge, 2004, p. 76. Emphasis added here and does not appear in the original text.

43　Notice the emphasis here on 'not always' as there are those voluntary recruits that do fit the stereotypical category. Indeed, there are those scholars who would argue that the poverty–terrorism nexus is the most important explanation for extremism. See the Introduction where I offer a brief overview of contending explanations of Islamist extremism.

44　I shall come back to the notion of 'strategic' versus 'tactical' successes or failures later in this section.

45　'Existential,' as I have noted before, implies characteristics that are common to human existence.

46　See Chapter 1 where I engage both Hegelian and Nietzschean assertions.

47　In this section I have often hyphenated the term counterinsurgency as counter-insurgency to emphasize that this term is meant to mean a counter-offensive and to highlight the irony in the designation of protracted occupations of Iraq or Afghanistan as a 'counter-insurgency' strategy. In places where I have felt that this emphasis was not needed, I have referred to the term simply as 'counterinsurgency' without the hyphenation.

48　See David Kilcullen, *Counterinsurgency*, New York: Oxford University Press, 2010, pp. 17–27.

49　See David Kilcullen, *Counterinsurgency*, New York: Oxford University Press, 2010, pp. 85–105.

50　I have summarized this information based on exposition of the strategy and tactics of counterinsurgency as offered by Mark Moyer and David Kilcullen. See Mark Moyer, *A Question of Command: Counterinsurgency From the Civil War to Iraq*, Foreword by Donald Kagan & Frederick Kagan, New Haven: Yale University Press, 2009; see Kilcullen, *Counterinsurgency*.

51　See Moyar's discussion of this in *A Question of Command*, p. 2. See also Kilcullen's discussion of this in *Counterinsurgency*, p. 42.

52　The reason for my placing of the term counterinsurgency in quotation marks will become apparent later in this section.

53　The US–NATO operations in Afghanistan, more than ten years after the initial reaction to the 2001 attacks, also qualify as the occupation of Afghanistan. This is particularly true with the post-2009 increase in the deployment of the US troops in Afghanistan. I shall come back to this issue in the next subsection.

54　M. Cherif Bassiouni, "Legal Status of US Forces in Iraq From 2003–2008," *Chicago Journal of International Law*, 11(1), p. 3.

55　Cherif Bassiouni, "Legal Status of US Forces in Iraq From 2003–2008," p. 4. Emphasis added here and does not appear in the original text.

56　Information in this sentence, as well as the source for both the quotations can be found in Cherif Bassiouni, "Legal Status of US Forces in Iraq From 2003–2008," p. 4.

57 Thomas Donnelly, as quoted in Cherif Bassiouni, "Legal Status of US Forces in Iraq From 2003–2008," p. 13.

58 The increase in anti-American sentiments in Iraq was born of atrocities committed by American soldiers such as those at the Abu Ghraib prison and the deaths of innocent Iraqi civilians at the hands of US private contractors—such as Blackwater—which the US military had employed and which operated with an impunity characteristic only of those entities that feel themselves above and beyond the law.

59 An interview with Muqtada al-Sadr as quoted in *The Middle East Media Research Institute* (MEMRI), "Muqtada al-Sadr, Iraqi Leader of the al-Mahdi Movement, Supports Armed Attacks on U.S. Forces in Iraq, Says al-Mahdi Army Will Be," Special Dispatch Series no. 1883, MEMRI, March 31, 2009. http://memri.org/bin/printerfriendly/pf.cgi

60 Excerpts from Osama bin Laden's interview on *al-Jazeera*, December 1998, as cited in Gilles Kepel and Jean-Pierre Milelli, *Al Qaeda in its Own Words*, Cambridge: The Belknap Press of Harvard University Press, 2008, p. 59.

61 Sebastian Smith, *Allah's Mountains: The Battle for Chechnya*, New York: Tauris Parke Paperbacks, 2006, p. 240. Emphasis added here.

62 Michael Schwartz, *War without End: The Iraq War in Context*, Chicago: Haymarket Books, 2008, p. 75.

63 Schwartz, *War without End*, pp. 88–100.

64 Schwartz, *War without End*, p. 91.

65 Rahul Mahajan, as cited by Michael Schwartz, *War without End*, pp. 91–92.

66 Michael Schwartz, *War without End*, p. 92.

67 See Chapter 4, where I discuss the subjectivity inherent in the notions of 'right,' 'just,' 'defensive' and so on.

68 Michael Walzer, *Arguing about War,* New Haven: Yale University Press, 2004, p. 163.

69 Walzer, *Arguing about War*, p. 164. See also Robert Pape, "It's the Occupation, Stupid," *Foreign Policy*, October 18, 2010, URL: www.foreignpolicy.com/articles/2010/10/18/it_s_the_occupation_stupid.

70 Kilcullen, *Counterinsurgency*, p. 166.

71 Kilcullen, *Counterinsurgency*, pp. 165–167.

72 Kilcullen, *Counterinsurgency*, p. 165.

73 Kilcullen, *Counterinsurgency*, p. 35.

74 The politics of semantics is important here. What I mean by the latter can perhaps be explained in light of David Kilcullen's explanation of what really happened in Vietnam, that is, whether it is true to say that the United States 'lost' the war in Vietnam. Kilcullen argues that U.S. "counterinsurgency was highly effective at the tactical level. Given the ultimate U.S. defeat in Vietnam, one might expect to see problems in the application of counterinsurgency in the war ... [...] In fact, the opposite is true: counterinsurgency in Vietnam covered a wide range of methods, was well coordinated, and produced excellent overall results." But, Kilcullen argues, the U.S. lost the war in Vietnam because of the "loss of political will [amongst the American electorate]" over a war that had itself become wider and more involved. See Kilcullen, *Counterinsurgency*, pp. 209–210. But since the war in Vietnam was not popularly seen as an 'American counter-insurgency' at the time, and was seen instead as regular war, it seems to me that the politics of using the term 'counter-insurgency' instead of 'counter-terrorism' to refer to the current (2011) American military involvement in Afghanistan is intended to bypass the very resistance to the idea of a 'regular' war in the United Sates. In other words, to the extent that the term 'counter-insurgency' implies a defensive measure, a sort of 'just action' (in the sense of legality—see Chapter 4 where I discuss at length the notion of 'Just War' in all components) against the 'insurgent' (commonly understood as the illegal agent in a war), it seems to me that the recent (as of 2006)

framing of the American military involvements in both Iraq and Afghanistan as a 'counter-insurgency' is motivated by its expected political expediency at home (in the United States) and less by its actual nature as a genuine counterinsurgency, which, as I note in this section, is traditionally (if not by definition) domestic in scope.

75 Reported by Thom Shanker, "Gates Defends Policy on Afghanistan and the Debate that Shaped it," *The New York Times*, Friday, September 24, 2010, A9.

76 I discuss the nature of the 'population-centric' (hearts-and-minds) and 'enemy-centric' (search-and-kill) components of counterinsurgency later in this chapter.

77 Jens Meierhenrich analyzes the Kantian theoretical notion of 'preventative war' for the ends of 'perpetual peace' and concludes that the modern manner in which 'preventative war' is conducted may actually lead to "perpetual war." See Meierhenrich, "Perpetual War: A Pragmatic Sketch," *Human Rights Quarterly*, 29, 2007, pp. 631–673.

78 By 'tactics' and 'strategy' I am referring to the traditional components of a counter-insurgency, namely the 'enemy-centric' component and the 'population-centric' component. I address the nature of these components later in this chapter.

79 For news on General Petraeus' takeover of command in Afghanistan, see Helene Cooper & David Sanger, "Obama Fires Afghan Commander, Citing Need for Unity in the War," *The New York Times*, Thursday, June 24, 2010, A1.

80 Report by Elisabeth Bumiller, "Petraeus Says He'll Review Curbs on U.S. Strikes and Artillery in Afghanistan," *The New York Times*, Wednesday, June 30, 2010. A4.

81 "U.S. Tries to Calm Pakistan's Anger over an Airstrike," *The New York Times*, Thursday, October 7, 2010.

82 As reported by C.J. Chivers, "Warriors Vexed by Rules for War," *The New York Times*, Wednesday, June 23, 2010.

83 Alissa Rubin & Dexter Filkins, "New Mission for Petraeus: Make his Own Plan Work," in *The New York Times*, Thursday, June 24, 2010. A 12.

84 Beyond the countless—if at times somewhat understated—reports on CIA predator drone attacks (those that hit the target intended and those that hit the wrong target) in popular American newspapers, for a detailed discussion of predator drones that outlines the conflicting debates on the matter, see Jane Mayer, "The Predator War: What are the Risks of the C.I.A.'s Covert Drone Program?," *The New Yorker*, October 26, 2009, pp. 36–45. Mayer notes that while predator drone operations were introduced under the G.W. Bush administration, "the Obama Administration has … widened the scope of authorized drone attacks in Afghanistan," p. 42.

85 This, in part, reflects General Petraeus' policy in Iraq where he is credited at debilitating the successful tide of Iraqi anti-American insurgency by "fostering deals with insurgent leaders who had spent the previous four years killing Americans." See report by Alissa Rubin & Dexter Filkins, "New Mission for Petraeus: Make his Own Plan Work," *The New York Times*, Thursday, June 24, 2010. A 12.

86 This was perhaps the trademark of General McChrystal's counterinsurgency strategy in Afghanistan. Right before his dismissal as the head military commander in Afghanistan in June 2010, General McChrystal was noted as saying, "The Russians killed 1 million Afghans, and that didn't work." For this quote, and a report on General McChrystal's softer enemy-centric approach, see C.J. Chivers, "Warriors Vexed by Rules for War," *The New York Times*, Wednesday, June 23, 2010.

87 Even after General McChrystal was replaced by General David Petraeus as head commander of US and allied military operations in Afghanistan June 2010, Petraeus remained committed to McChrystal's policy of 'going soft' on the population. Alissa Rubin and Dexter Filkins reported in a *New York Times* article that General Petraeus "will continue to coax Taliban fighters away from the insurgency with promises of jobs and security." See "New Mission for Petraeus: Make his Own Plan Work," *The New York Times*, Thursday, June 24, 2010.

88 Kilcullen, *Counterinsurgency*, p. 17.
89 For the quoted passages, see report by Dexter Filkins report, "In Afghanistan, as in Iraq, a New Breed of Commander Stepped In," *The New York Times*, Wednesday, June 23, 2010. A10. This, of course, is a point stressed by David Kilcullen in the section of his book devoted to the effective strategies of "Counterinsurgency." Kilcullen notes that "injudicious use of firepower … fuels and perpetuates the insurgency," a point completely ignored under General Petraeus' authorization of increased predator drone strikes in Afghanistan, as I have noted later in this section. For Kilcullen's quoted assertion, see *Counterinsurgency*, p. 30.
90 General Petraeus' U-turn on General McChrystal's softer enemy-centric strategy (of restrictions on airstrikes) might have been a response to reports that violence in Afghanistan was on the rise, and that "the mission to pacify Marja and Kandahar" was "off track"; or, it might have been a response to the realization that the government of President Karzi was deeply corrupt, making it a fickle ally in the war against the Taliban 'insurgents.' See "General's Job is in Doubt After Remarks Exposing Afghan Rifts," *The New York Times*, Wednesday, June 23, 2010, A10. See also a report by Alissa Rubin and Dexter Filkins, "New Mission for Petraeus: Make his Own Plan Work," *The New York Times*, Thursday, June 24, 2010, A12, that suggests these very reasons for the U-turn in General Petraeus' policy. General Petraeus might have thus calculated that, under such conditions, a harsher enemy-centric strategy was needed for the success of the counterinsurgency. However, the policy change might also have been a response to the complaints on the part of American troops in Afghanistan that McChrystal's rather softer enemy-centric stand, by making it hard to call for airstrikes, was putting soldiers' lives at risk. In fact, a US Army colonel said this about General McChrystal's approach: "The troops hate it … Right now we're losing the tactical-level fight in the chase for a strategic victory." See report by C.J. Chivers, "Warriors Vexed by Rules of War," *The New York Times*, Wednesday, June 23, 2010, A11.
91 Kilcullen, *Counterinsurgency*, p. 42.
92 Kilcullen, *Counterinsurgency*, p. 42.
93 Nadia Schadlow, "A False Dichotomy: Critics of the Army's COIN Focus Ignore World and War Realities," *Armed Forces Journal*, September 2010, p. 28.
94 Schwartz, *War without End*, p. 112.
95 Actions of US troops in the 3rd Armored Cavalry Regiment (ACR) as described by Moyar, *A Question of Command*, p. 224.
96 For a critical assessment of the US use of predator drones and the evaluation of the question of whether such methods are extrajudicial and thus illegal according to international law, see Shane Harris, "Are Drone Strikes Murder?" *National Journal*, January 9, 2010, pp. 21–27.
97 See the report by Umer Farooq and Haji Pazir Gul, "Causing a Stir: Tribesmen Launch Dual Challenge to Drone Attacks," *The Herald*, Karachi, Pakistan, February 2011, pp. 25–27.
98 See the report by Faizul Ameer, "Striking Difference," *The Herald*, Karachi, Pakistan, November 2010, pp. 29–30.
99 I have italicized 'informal' to highlight that these alliances were matters of fluid quid-pro-quo assistance relationships and a formal united front against the American occupation forces. These were not formal alliances in the sense of joint federations.
100 Schwartz, *War without End*, p. 109.
101 Thom Shanker and Alissa Rubin, "Quest to Neutralize Afghan Militants is Showing Glimpses of Success, NATO says," *New York Times*, Tuesday, June 29, 2010, A10. Emphasis added here and does not appear in the original text.
102 "US Drone Strikes Kill 14 militants in North Waziristan," *Dawn* (Pakistan's most popular English-version daily newspaper), Friday, 11 Jun, 2010. Emphasis added here and does not appear in the original text, www.dawn.com/wps/wcm/connect/

dawn-content-library/dawn/news/pakistan/14-us-drone-strike-kills-four-in-north-waziristan-zj-08

103 William Dalrymple, "Afghanistan is Going Down," *New Statesman*, June 14, 2010, p. 23. Emphasis added here and does not appear in the original text.

104 Dalrymple, "Afghanistan is going down," p. 25. Emphasis added here and does not appear in the original text.

105 Dalrymple, "Afghanistan is going down," p. 23.

106 Dalrymple, "Afghanistan is going down," p. 24. Emphasis added here.

107 Dalrymple, "Afghanistan is going down," p. 23. Emphasis added here.

108 'Tactical' victory is essentially a military victory, whereas a 'strategic' victory is a political victory in a war. A military (tactical) victory doesn't necessarily mean a political (strategic) victory. And, indeed, winning a tactical victory over a strategic victory is a band-aid (temporary) solution to whatever problem let to the engagement in war in the first place.

109 Andrew Bacevich makes a similar point when he argues that "you can't kill people on Tuesday and negotiate with them on Wednesday." Bacevich is a professor of history and international relations at Boston University. For the quoted text, see Jane Mayer's article, "The Predator War," *The New Yorker*, October 26, 2009, p. 43. Bacevich's comment was in response to the fact of the widening of the use of predator drones under President Obama's Administration and the Senate Foreign Relations Committee findings that the Pentagon's "Join Integrated Prioritized Target List" of "approved terrorist targets" was expanded to include Afghan drug lords and others suspected of sympathy towards al-Qaeda and Taliban (thus, beyond the list of known terrorists). See Mayer, pp. 42–43.

110 For quoted text, see C.J. Chivers, "Warriors Vexed by Rules for War," *The New York Times*, A11, Wednesday, June 23, 2010.

111 Chivers, "Warriors Vexed by Rules of War," A11.

112 Thom Shanker & Alissa Rubin, "Quest to Neutralize Afghan Militants is Showing Glimpses of Success, NATO says," *New York Times*, A10, Tuesday, June 29, 2010,.

113 Shanker & Rubin, "Quest to Neutralize Afghan Militants is Showing Glimpses of Success, NATO says," A10.

114 Shanker & Rubin, "Quest to Neutralize Afghan Militants is Showing Glimpses of Success, NATO says," A10.

115 See my analysis of the internationally accepted justifications of violence and brutality in Chapter 4.

116 Thomas L. Friedman, "What's Second Price?" *New York Times*, Op-Ed, Wednesday, June 23, 2010.

117 Friedman, "What's Second Price?"

Conclusion

1 See Chapter 4 where I discuss this issue in detail. The analysis of the rhetoric of the Christian Crusades in terms of 'salvation' and 'redemptive homicide' can be seen in the work of Mark Gregory Pegg; see Chapter 4 of this book for more details and full citation of Pegg's work.

2 See the assertion made by the BNP to this effect in Kevin Passmore, *Fascism: A Very Short Introduction*, New York: Oxford University Press, 2002, p. 119.

3 Passmore, *Fascism*, p. 121.

4 Here I am drawing upon Hannah Arendt's notion of 'banality' as it originally appeared in her infamous work *Eichmann in Jerusalem: A Report on the Banality of Evil*, New York: Penguin Classics, 2006, with an introduction by Amos Elon. Arendt's banal individual is one who unquestioningly accepts the explanations or justifications offered to him or her because he or she is at once uncritical (analytically

speaking) and afraid (to challenge the mainstream views). See Elisabeth Young-Bruehl's excellent analysis of Arendt's notion of the banal individual in *Why Arendt Matters*, New Haven, CT: Yale University Press, 2006.

5 Melanie Phillips has in fact written a book with that title, see *Londonistan*, New York: Encounter Books, 2006.

6 The *Rashtriya Swayamsevak Sangh* (RSS) is part of the umbrella organization the *Sangh Parivar* which consists of a few dozen other organizations and parties, such as the ultra-nationalist *Bajrang Dal* and the Hindu nationalist *Bharatiya Janata Party* (BJP). See Siddharth Varadarajan, "Chronicle of a Tragedy Foretold," *Gujarat: The Making of a Tragedy*, Siddharth Varadarajan, ed., India: Penguin Books, 2002, p. 3.

7 Varadarajan, "Chronicle of a Tragedy Foretold," p. 7.

8 This narrative has only grown stronger ten years after September 11, 2001, and manifests itself in tabloid newspaper headings such as 'the enemy amongst us' or 'the Muslims next door.'

9 Passmore, *Fascism*, p. 120.

10 Walter Laqueur, *A History of Zionism: From the French Revolution to the Establishment of the State of Israel*, New York: Schocken Books, 2003, p. 445.

11 It is a fact that fascism is almost always defined and understood with reference to Hitler's Germany, or to Mussolini's Italy; see for example Passmore, *Fascism*.

12 For Milton Friedman's assertion, see Alan B. Krueger, *What Makes a Terrorist: Economics and the Roots of Terrorism*, Princeton, New Jersey: Princeton University Press, 2007. For President George W. Bush's references to Islamist extremism in terms of fascism akin to the German Nazi fascists, see President Bush's address to the American Legion National Convention, Salt Lake City, Utah, on August 31, 2006, as cited in Richard Bonney's *False Prophets: The 'Clas of Civilizations' and the Global War on Terror*, UK: Peter Lang, 2008, p. 1. For President Bush's reference to Islamist extremism in terms of 'Islamofascism' see his speech given at the National Endowment for Democracy on October 6, 2005, as cited in Bonney, *False Prophets*, p. 3.

13 Fred Halliday makes a similar point in his analysis of the term 'Islamo-fascism' in his book *Shocked and Awed: A Dictionary of the War on Terror*, Berkeley, University of California Press, 2010, pp. 185–187.

14 See my analysis in Chapters 2 and 3 where I argue that radical Islamists present themselves much as the Hegelian slaves in their rhetoric; that is, they present themselves in terms of their newly awakened self-consciousness (a sense of distinct identity) that deserves recognition not negation. In terms of the classic characteristics of fascism, of which the projection of the supposed superiority of the self is central, see Passmore, *Fascism*, pp. 23–32.

15 See, for example, Marvin Perry and Howard Negrin's assessment to this effect in "Jihadism: Theory and Ideology," *The Theory and Practice of Islamic Terrorism*, Marvin Perry and Howard Negrin, eds., New York: Palgrave, 2008, pp. 7–10.

16 This, of course, should not be understood as an apology for Islamist violence. My statement here is intended instead to highlight the dynamics of any violence—whether radical Islamist or otherwise—which is based on a *perception* (whether real or not) of a causality (an action–reaction rubric) on the part of those that engage in violence.

17 See Chapters 2 and 3 where I discuss this argument in the context of the larger struggles for recognition.

18 See Chapter 5 where I engage epistemological assumptions and the Kantian notion of transcendental idealism to shed light on the possible nature of the motivations of individuals that voluntarily join Islamist extremist groups.

Appendix I: on essence

1 Richard Schmitt, "Phenomenology," *Encyclopedia of Philosophy*, 2nd edition, Donald M. Borchert, Editor in Chief, New York: Thomson Gale, 2005, p. 284.

2 It deserves to be mentioned that the phenomena appropriate for a conceptual analysis can range widely from abstract intangible phenomena such as human consciousness, human fears, and desires to less abstract phenomena with a more tangible existence such as ideological movements, mass brutality, ethnic cleansing, genocide and xeno-phobia (particularly when the latter translates into state policies). Brian Rathbun, for example, conceptualizes the phenomenon of American neoconservatism as a sense of moral superiority which fuels a kind of ultra-nationalism so distinctly a characteristic of *all* American neoconservative camps *regardless* of the changing temporal settings or movement figure-heads. See Brian C. Rathbun, "Does One Right make a Realist? Conservatism, Neoconservatism, and Isolationism in the Foreign Policy Ideology of American Elites," *Political Science Quarterly*, vol. 123, no. 2, Summer 2008, pp. 271–299.

3 Mohanty, *Phenomenology*, p. 89.

4 Mohanty, *Phenomenology*, p. 4.

5 Schmitt, "Phenomenology," p. 286. Emphasis added here and does not appear in the original text.

6 The sociologist Harvey Sacks is most popularly associated with the pioneering of CA, and the linguistics Ruth Wodak and Norman Fairclough—inspired by the works of Jurgen Habermas that formed the ideological bases of CDA, formerly known as *crit-ical linguistics*—are most popularly associated with CDA. For more details on the Habermas-connection in CDA, see Mesfin Awoke Bekalu, "Presupposition in News Discourse," in *Discourse and Society*, vol. 17, no. 2, 2006, p. 12.

7 For an excellent account of the Laclau and Mouffe's discourse theory, *discursive psy-chology*, and detailed study of *critical discourse analysis*, see Marianne Jorgensen & Louise Phillips, *Discourse Analysis as Theory and Method*, London: SAGE Publica-tions, 2002. For a detailed discussion of other forms of DA such as *content analysis, distinctive theory text analysis, objective Hermeneutics, narrative semiotics* as well as a detailed discussion of the two types of CDA see Stefan Titscher, Michael Meyer, Ruth Wodak and Eva Vetter, *Methods of Text and Discourse Analysis*, trans. Bryan Jenner (London: SAGE Publications, 2000).

8 Julia Gillen& Alan Peterson, "Discourse Analysis," in *Research Methods in the Social Sciences*, Bridget Somekh & Cathy Lewin, editors, London: SAGE Publications, 2005, p. 149.

9 Gilbert Weiss & Ruth Wodak, "Introduction: Theory, Interdisciplinarity and Critical Discourse Analysis," in *Critical Discourse Analysis: Theory and Interdisciplinarity*, Gilbert Weiss & Ruth Wodak, Eds., London: Palgrave Macmillan, 2003, p. 13. Emphasis added here and not found in the original text.

10 Norman Fairclough, "Critical Discourse Analysis," *The SAGE Encyclopedia of Social Science Research Methods*, vol. 1, Michael Lewis-Beck, Alan Bryman and Tim Futing Liao, Eds., London: SAGE Publications, 2004, p. 214.

11 Gillen & Peterson, "Discourse Analysis," p. 146. Emphasis present in the original text.

12 Derek Edwards, "Discourse Analysis," in *The SAGE Encyclopedia of Social Science Research Methods*, vol. 1, Michael Lewis-Beck, Alan Bryman, & Tim Futing Liao, Eds., California: SAGE Publications, Inc, 2004, p. 267. Emphasis added here and not found in the original text.

13 For more information on the methods of phenomenology and the detailed classifica-tion of the two types of phenomenological methods—the Direct Approach (phenome-nological sociology) and Indirect Approach (existential phenomenology)—see illustrative tables in Titchen and Hobson, "Phenomenology," pp. 124 and 126.

14 Gillen, "Discourse Analysis," p. 147.

15 Richard Schmitt, "Phenomenology," *Encyclopedia of Philosophy*, 2nd Edition, vol. 7, Donald Borchert, Ed., New York: Thomson Gale, 2006, p. 285.

16 In other words, in focusing on a critical analysis of radical Islamist discourse, I am not negating the importance of causal studies of Islamist extremism. There are, after

all, numerous valuable empirical analyses that have been conducted in search of an understanding of Islamist extremism that emphasize the importance of contexts, especially in terms of cause and effect understanding of Islamist extremism. Proponents of empirical analysis are, of course, by no means limited to the scholars concerned with the studies of Islamist extremism. An excellent survey of the arguments made in favor of empirical, context-specific analyses can be found in *The Oxford Handbook of Contextual Political Analysis*, Robert E. Goodin & Charles Tilly, Eds., New York: Oxford University Press, 2006.

17 It is beyond the scope of this section, and indeed this study, to examine the causes and reasons formulating the specific (context-dependent) goals of Islamist extremist groups. Readers interested in such analysis should refer to the many valuable empirical, case-specific studies conducted of Islamist extremist groups the world over.

18 Quote taken from Anders Strindberg & Mats Warn, "Realities of Resistance: Hizballah, the Palestinian Rejectionists, and al-Qaeda compared," *Journal of Palestine Studies,* vol. xxxiv (3), Spring 2005, p. 35. Emphasis added here and not found in the original text.

19 Exceptions to this are, of course, cases such as post-2003 Iraq where Jihadi Islamist extremist groups operated within the state (intra-state) as their targets existed within the state (all those foreign entities seen as being responsible for the military occupation of Iraq).

Appendix II: virgins in heaven

1 See Muhammad Abdel Haleem's analysis of Paradise in Heaven, in his book *Understanding the Qur'an: Themes and Style*, New York: I.B. Tauris, 2005, p. 99. Incidentally, it should be noted that Muhammad Abdel Haleem bears no relation to me despite the last name being 'Haleem.'

2 Ibid.

3 For Muhammad Abdel Haleem's analysis of Paradise in Heaven, see "Paradise in the Qur'an" in his book *Understanding the Qur'an*, pp. 93–106.

4 See Chapter 3 for an analysis of the nature of reason in the radical Islamist promotion of self-destruction.

5 David Cook, *Martyrdom in Islam*, New York: Cambridge University Press, 2007.

6 Cook, *Martyrdom in Islam*, p. 33.

7 Cook, *Martyrdom in Islam*, p. 33.

8 Cook, *Martyrdom in Islam*, p. 40.

9 Daniel Brown, "Martyrdom in the Sunni Revivalist Thought," *Sacrificing the Self: Perspectives on Martyrdom and Religion*, Margaret Cormack, Ed., Oxford: Oxford University Press, 2002, p. 107.

10 Cook, *Martyrdom in Islam*, p. 47.

11 Brown, "Martyrdom in the Sunni Revivalist Thought," p. 107.

12 Brown, "Martyrdom in the Sunni Revivalist Thought," p. 107. Emphasis added here.

13 See Chapter 1 where I discuss the notion of the *ummah* in relation to the Hegelian notion of 'self-consciousness.'

14 See Chapter 1 where I discuss the collective meaning of the 'self' in Islamist literature and discourse.

15 Brown, "Martyrdom in the Sunni Revivalist Thought,", p. 107.

16 For the analysis of Hegelian struggles for recognition, see Chapters 1, 2 and 3.

Appendix III: humanitarian interventions

1 Dangerous in the sense that human rights atrocities have at times become justified and excused since they were committed under the banner of 'humanitarian intervention,' as we shall see in this subsection.

2 Michael Walzer, *Just and Unjust Wars: A Moral Argument with Historical Illustrations*, Fourth Edition, New York: Basic Books, 2006, p. 101. I have added the emphases here and they do not appear in the original text.
3 Uwe Steinhoff, *On the Ethics of War and Terrorism*, New York: Oxford University Press, 2007, p. 36. Emphasis and quotation marks on wicked things were found in the original text.
4 Walzer, *Just and Unjust Wars*, p. 107.

Bibliography

"10 Russian Invaders Gunned Down in Chechnya," *Kavkaz Center*, an independent Chechen news center, November 6, 2006, www.kavkazcenter.com/eng/content/2006/11/06/6284.shtml

"6 'Israeli' Terrorists Killed in East Lebanon," *Kavkaz Center*, an independent Chechen news center, August 19, 2006, www.kavkazcenter.com/eng/content/2006/08/19/5337.shtml

Abbas, Azmat, "The Making of a Militant," *The Herald*, Karachi, Pakistan, July 2003, p. 58.

Abbas, Hassan, *Pakistan's Drift into Extremism: Allah, the Army, and America's War on Terror*, New York: M.E. Sharpe, 2005.

Abbas, Zaffar, "What Happened?" *The Herald*, Karachi, Pakistan, June 2005, pp. 71–75.

Ajami, Fouad, *The Vanished Imam: Musa al Sadr and the Shia of Lebanon*, N.Y.: Cornell University Press, 1986.

Alfoneh, Ali, "Iran's Suicide Brigades," *Middle East Quarterly*, Winter 2007, pp. 37–44.

Ali, Kecia & Leaman, Oliver, *Islam: The Key Concepts*, New York: Routledge, 2008.

Allison, Henry E., *Kant's Transcendental Idealism*, revised and enlarged edition, New Haven: Yale University Press, 2004.

Allison, Henry, *Kant's Theory of Freedom*, UK: Cambridge University Press, 1990.

al-Qusaybi, Ghazi, *Li-i-shuhada* (For the Martyrs), published in *al-Hayat* (London, New York, Beirut, Jeddah, Dammam, Riyadh), 2002, David Cook, Trans., cited in David Cook's *Martyrdom in Islam*, New York: Cambridge University Press, 2007, pp. 161–162.

al-Zawahiri, Ayman, "Knight Under the Prophet's Banner," part II, December 2, 2001, www.fas.org, cited in Robert Pape, *Dying to Win: The Strategic Logic of Suicide Terrorism,* New York: Random House, 2005, p. 122.

Al-Zawahiri, Ayman, "The Choice of Targets and the Importance of Martyrdom Operations," *Knights under the Prophet's Banner*, December 2, 2001, cited in Gilles Kepel & Jean-Pierre Milelli's, Eds., *Al Qaeda in its Own Words*, Cambridge, Massachusetts: The Belknap Press of Harvard University Press, 2008, p. 203.

Ameer, Faizul, "Striking Difference," *The Herald*, Karachi, Pakistan, November 2010, pp. 29–30.

Amir Mir, *The True Face of Jehadis: Inside Pakistan's Network of Terror*, India: New Delhi, Roli Books, 2006.

Amir Rana, Muhammad, *A to Z of Jehadi Organizations in Pakistan*, Saba Ansari, Trans., Lahore, Pakistan: Marshal Books, 2004.

218   *Bibliography*

Ansell-Pearson, Keith, *An Introduction to Nietzsche as a Political Thinker*, UK: Cambridge University Press, 1999.

Arendt, Hannah, *Eichmann in Jerusalem: A Report on the Banality of Evil,* special edition with an introduction by Amos Elon, NY: Penguin Books, 2006.

Argo, Nichole, "The Banality of Evil, Understanding Today's Human Bombs," Policy Paper, Preventive Defense Project, Stanford University, 2003.

Asad, Talal, *On Suicide Bombing*, New York: Columbia University Press, 2007.

"Attacks from US Aerial Drones," Amnesty International, www.eyesonpakistan.org/c_drone_attacks.html

Azhar, Mohammed Masood, *The Virtues of Jihad*, cited in David Cook's *Understanding Jihad*, Berkeley, California: University of California Press, 2005.

Baghramian, Maria, *Relativism*, New York: Routledge, 2004.

Baghramian, Maria, *Relativism*, New York: Routledge, 2005.

Ballard, Edward Goodwin, *Principles of Interpretation*, Athens, Ohio: Ohio University Press, 1983.

Ballard, Edward Goodwin, *Principles of Interpretation*, Ohio: Ohio University Press, 1983.

Bamyeh, Mohammed A., *Of Death and Dominion: The Existential Foundations of Governance*, Evanston, Illinois: Northwestern University Press, 2007.

Bar, Shmuel, "The Religious Sources of Islamic Terrorism," *Policy Review*, no. 125, June/July 2004, pp. 27–37.

Bassiouni, M. Cherif, "Legal Status of US Forces in Iraq From 2003–2008," *Chicago Journal of International Law*, 11(1), pp. 1–38.

Bellamy, Alex J., *Just Wars: From Cicero to Iraq*, UK: Polity, 2008.

Bergesen, Albert J., Ed., *The Sayyid Qutb Reader: Selected Writings on Politics, Religion, and Society*, New York: Routledge, 2008.

Blackburn, Simon, Ed., *Oxford Dictionary of Philosophy*, New York: Oxford University Press, 1996, p. 169.

Bloom, Mia, *Dying to Kill: The Allure of Suicide Terror*, New York: Columbia University Press, 2005.

Bonney, Richard, *Jihad: From Quran to bin Laden*, New York: Palgrave Macmillian, 2004.

Brown, Daniel, "Martyrdom in the Sunni Revivalist Thought," *Sacrificing the Self: Perspectives on Martyrdom and Religion*, Margaret Cormack, Ed., Oxford: Oxford University Press, 2002.

Bumiller, Elisabeth, "Petraeus Says He'll Review Curbs on U.S. Strikes and Artillery in Afghanistan," *The New York Times*, Wednesday, June 30, 2010. A4.

Burnell, Peter, "Promoting Democracy," *Comparative Politics*, Daniele Caramani, Ed., New York: Oxford University Press, 2008.

Calhoun, Craig, "Afterword: Religion's Many Powers," *The Power of Religion in the Public Sphere*, Eduardo Mendieta & Jonathan VanAntwerpen, Eds., New York: Columbia University Press, 2011.

Calvert, John, *Sayyid Qutb and the Origins of Radical Islamism*, New York: Columbia University Press, 2010.

Careley, Demetrios James, ed., *American Hegemony: Preventive War, Iraq, and Imposing Democracy*, New York: The Academy of Political Science, 2004.

Carothers, Thomas, *U.S. Democracy Promotion: During and After Bush*, Washington, D.C., Carnegie Endowment for International Peace, 2007.

Caygill, Howard, *A Kant Dictionary*, UK: Blackwell Publishers Ltd., 2000.

Chivers, C.J., "Warriors Vexed by Rules for War," *The New York Times*, Wednesday, June 23, 2010.

Clark, Maudemarie, "Introduction," *Friedrich Nietzsche: On the Genealogy of Morality," A Polemic*, Maudemarie Clark & Alan J. Swensen, Trans., Indianapolis: Hackett Publishing Company, Inc., 1998.

Coates, A.J., *The Ethnics of War*, Manchester: Manchester University Press, 1997.

Cook, David, *Martyrdom in Islam*, New York: Cambridge University Press, 2007.

Cook, David, *Understanding Jihad*, Berkeley, California: California University Press, 2005.

Cooper, Helene & Sanger, David, "Obama Fires Afghan Commander, Citing Need for Unity in the War," *The New York Times*, Thursday, June 24, 2010, A1.

Cormack, Margaret, Ed., *Sacrificing the Self: Perspectives on Martyrdom and Religion*, New York: Oxford University Press, 2002.

Crenshaw, Martha, "Explaining Suicide Terrorism: A Review Essay," *Security Studies*, 16(1), January–March 2007, 133–162.

Crenshaw, Martha, *Revolutionary Terrorism: The FLN in Algeria, 1954–1962*, Hoover Institution Press, Stanford University, 1978.

Dalrymple, William, "Afghanistan is going down," *New Statesman*, June 14, 2010.

Danto, Arthur C., *Nietzsche as Philosopher*, Columbia Classics in Philosophy, New York: Columbia University Press, 2005.

Dicker, Georges, *Kant's Theory of Knowledge: An Analytical Introduction*, New York: Oxford University Press, 2004.

Elshtain, Jean Bethke, ed., *Just War Theory*, UK: Blackwell, 1992.

Elster, Jon, "Motivations and Beliefs in Suicide Missions," *Making Sense of Suicide Missions*, Diego Gambetta, Ed., New York: Oxford University Press, 2005.

Esposito, John L., Ed., *The Oxford Dictionary of Islam*, New York: Oxford University Press, 2003.

Esposito, John L., *Unholy War: Terror in the Name of Islam*, Oxford: Oxford University Press, 2002.

Euben, Roxanne L. & Zaman, Muhammad Qasim, eds. *Princeton Readings in Islamist Thought: Texts and Contexts from al-Banna to Bin Laden*, Princeton, NJ: Princeton University Press, 2009.

Fanon, Frantz, *Black Skin, White Masks*, New York: Grove Press, 1967.

Fanon, Frantz, *The Wretched of the Earth*, Richard Philcox, Trans., with commentary by Jean-Paul Sartre & Homi K. Bhabha, New York: Grove Press, 1963.

Faraj, Muhammad Abd al-Salam, *Al-Faridah al-Gha'ibah* (*The Neglected Duty*), Johannes J.G. Jansen, Trans., in *The Neglected Duty: The Creed of Sadat's Assassins and Islamic Resurgence in the Middle East*, New York: Macmillan Publishing Company, 1986.

Farooq, Umer & Gul, Haji Pazir, "Causing a Stir: Tribesmen Launch Dual Challenge to Drone Attacks," *The Herald*, Karachi, Pakistan, February 2011, pp. 25–27.

Fetzer, James H. & Almeder, Robert F., *Glossary of Epistemology/Philosophy of Science*, New York: Paragon House, 1993.

Fiala, Andrew, *The Just War Myth: The Moral Illusions of War*, New York: Rowman & Littlefield Publishers, Inc., 2008.

Filkins, Dexter, "In Afghanistan, as in Iraq, a New Breed of Commander Stepped In," *The New York Times*, Wednesday, June 23, 2010. A10.

Firestone, Reuven, *Jihad: The Origins of Holy War in Islam*, New York: Oxford University Press, 1999.

Friedman, Thomas L., "What's Second Price?" *New York Times*, Op-Ed, Wednesday, June 23, 2010.

Frum, David, "Samuel Huntington," *Foreign Policy*, March/April 2007, p. 44.

Fuller, Graham E., "A World without Islam," *Foreign Policy*, January/February 2008, pp. 46–53.

Gambetta, Diego, Ed., *Making Sense of Suicide Mission*, New York: Oxford University Press, 2005.

"General's Job is in Doubt After Remarks Exposing Afghan Rifts," *The New York Times*, Wednesday, June 23, 2010, A10.

Gerges, Fawaz A., *The Far Enemy: Why Jihad Went Global*, New York: Cambridge University Press, 2005.

Ginbar, Yuval, *Why Not Torture Terrorists? Moral, Practical, and Legal Aspects of the 'Ticking Bomb' Justification for Torture*, UK: Oxford University Press, 2008.

Goodin, Robert and Tilly, Charles, Eds., *The Oxford Handbook of Contextual Political Analysis*, New York: Oxford University Press, 2006.

Gourevitch, Philip & Morris, Errol, *The Ballad of Abu Ghraib*, previously published as *Standard Operating Procedure*, New York: Penguin Books, 2008.

Gregor, Mary, Ed., *Kant: Groundwork of the Metaphysics of Morals*, UK: Cambridge University Press, 1997.

Gupta, Anil, *Empiricism and Experience*, New York: Oxford University Press, 2006.

Habeck, Mary R., "Jihadist Strategies in the War on Terrorism," *The Theory and Practice of Islamic Terrorism: An Anthology*, Marvin Perry & Howard E. Negrin, Eds., New York, NY: Palgrave Macmillan, 2008.

Haleem, Muhammad Abdel, *Understanding the Qur'an: Themes and Style*, New York: I.B. Tauris, 2005.

Hallett, Brien, "Aquinas, Thomas (1225–1274)," *An Encyclopedia of War and Ethnics*, ed. Donald A. Wells, Connecticut: Greenwood Press, 1996, p. 17.

Halliday, Fred, *Shocked and Awed: A Dictionary of the War on Terror*, Berkeley, University of California Press, 2010.

Hare, R.M., *Essays on Political Morality*, New York: Oxford University Press, 1998.

Hare, R.M., *Moral Thinking: Its Levels, Method and Point*, Oxford: Oxford University Press, 1981.

Harris, Shane, "Are Drone Strikes Murder?" *National Journal*, January 9, 2010, pp. 21–27.

Hassan, Nasra, "An Arsenal of Believers: Talking to the 'Human Bombs'," *The New Yorker*, November 19, 2001.

Hoffman, Bruce, "Al Qaeda Resurgent," *The Theory and Practice of Islamic Terrorism, An Anthology*, Marvin Perry and Howard E. Negrin, Eds., New York: Palgrave Macmillan, 2008.

Hoffman, Bruce, *Inside Terrorism*, New York: Columbia University Press, 2006.

Holmes, Robert L., "Can War be Morally Justified?" *Just War Theory*, Jean Bethke Elshtain, Ed., Oxford, UK: Blackwell Ltd., 1992.

Honneth, Axel, *The Struggle for Recognition: The Moral Grammar of Social Conflicts*, Cambridge, MA: The MIT Press, 1995.

Huntington, Samuel, "The Clash of Civilizations?" *Foreign Affairs*, 72, Summer 1993, pp. 22–49.

Huntington, Samuel, *The Clash of Civilizations and the Remaking of the World Order*, New York: Simon & Schuster, 1996.

Hyppolite, Jean, "Self-Consciousness and Life: The Independence of Self-consciousness,"

Hegel's Dialectic of Desire and Recognition: Texts and Commentary, ed. John O'Neill, Albany: State University of New York Press, 1996.

Inwood, Michael, *A Hegel Dictionary*, UK: Blackwell Publishers, 1999.

Israeli, Raphael, *Islamikaze: Manifestations of Islamic Martyrology*, London: Frank Cass, 2003.

Jaber, Hala, *Hezbollah*, New York: Columbia University Press, 1997.

Jalal, Ayesha, *Partisans of Allah: Jihad in South Asia*, Cambridge: Harvard University Press, 2008.

Jamaat-ul-Dawa (formerly *Lashkar-e-Toiba*), "Majjalatul Dawa" monthly newsletter, cited in Amir Mir, *The True Face of Jehadis: Inside Pakistan's Network of Terror*, India: New Delhi, Roli Books, 2006, p. 212.

Juergensmeyer, Mark, *Global Rebellion: Religious Challenges to the Secular State, from Christian Militias to Al Qaeda*, Berkeley: University of California Press, 2008.

Juergensmeyer, Mark, *Terror in the Mind of God: The Global Rise of Religious Violence*, Berkeley, CA: University of California Press, 2003.

Kant, Immanuel, *Perpetual Peace and Other Essays*, Ted Humphrey, Trans., Indianapolis: Hackett Publishing Company, 1983.

Kepel, Gilles and Milelli, Jean-Pierre, *Al Qaeda in its Own Words*, Cambridge: The Belknap Press of Harvard University Press, 2008.

Kepel, Gilles, *Beyond Terror and Martyrdom*, Cambridge, Massachusetts: The Belknap Press of Harvard University Press, 2008.

Kerr, Fergus, *Thomas Aquinas: A Very Short Introduction*, New York: Oxford University Press, 2009.

Kilcullen, David, *Counterinsurgency*, New York: Oxford University Press, 2010, pp. 17–27.

Kojeve, Alexandre, *Introduction to the Reading of Hegel*, Allan Bloom, Ed., James H. Nichols, Trans., New York: Cornell University Press, 1980.

Kramer, Alan, *Dynamic of Destruction: Culture and Mass Killing in the First World War*, New York: Oxford University Press, 2007.

"Kremlin loses its grip on a dying empire," *Kavkaz Center*, an independent Chechen news center, May 25, 2006, www.kavkazcenter.com/eng/content/2006/05/25/4704_print.html

Krueger, Alan B., *What Makes a Terrorist: Economics and the Roots of Terrorism*, Princeton, New Jersey: Princeton University Press, 2007.

Laqueur, Walter, *A History of Zionism: From the French Revolution to the Establishment of the State of Israel*, New York: Schocken Books, 2003.

Lauer, Quentin, S.J., *A Reading of Hegel's Phenomenology of Spirit*, New York: Fordham University Press, 2002.

Lawrence, Bruce, "Islam at Risk: The Discourse on Islam and Violence," *Islamism: Contested Perspectives on Political Islam*, Richard C. Martin & Abbas Barzegar, Eds., Stanford, California: Stanford University Press, 2010.

Lawrence, Bruce, Ed. *Messages to the World: The Statements of Osama bin Laden*, James Howarth, Trans., London: Verso, 2005.

Ledeen, Michael A. "The Advance of Freedom: US Foreign Policy and Democratic Revolution," *Harvard International Review*, Spring 2005, p. 15.

Leiter, Brain, *Nietzsche on Morality*, New York: Routledge, 2003.

Lewis, Bernard, "The Roots of Muslim Rage," *Atlantic Monthly*, September 1990, pp. 47–60.

Lewis, Bernard, *The Middle East and the West*, London: Weidenfeld and Nicolson, 1964.

Lewis, Thomas, *Freedom and Tradition in Hegel: Reconsidering Anthropology, Ethics and Religion*, Indiana: University of Notre Dame Press, 2005.

"Lieberman Suggests Adopting Russian Tactics," *Kavkaz Center*, an independent Chechen news center, November 9, 2006, www.kavkazcenter.com/eng/content/2006/11/09/6324.shtml.

Lingis, Alphonso, "The Will-to-Power," *The New Nietzsche*, David B. Allison, ed., Cambridge, Massachusetts: MIT Press, 1985.

Markell, Patchen, "Recognition and Redistribution," *The Oxford Handbook of Political Theory*, John S. Dryzek Ed., et al., UK: Oxford University Press, 2006.

Markell, Patchen, *Bound by Recognition*, Princeton, NJ: Princeton University Press, 2003.

Mayer, Jane, "The Predator War: What are the Risks of the C.I.A.'s Covert Drone Program?" *The New Yorker*, October 26, 2009, pp. 36–45.

"Men with a Mission," *The Herald*, Karachi, Pakistan, July 2003, pp. 49–56.

Meierhenrich, Jens, "Perpetual War: A Pragmatic Sketch," *Human Rights Quarterly*, 29, 2007, pp. 631–673.

Mir, Amir, "Unholy Crusade," *Newsline*, Karachi, Pakistan, October 1999, p. 69.

Mir, Amir, *The True Face of Jehadis*, Lahore, Pakistan: Mashal Books, 2004.

Moeller, Hans-Georg, *The Moral Fool: A Case for Amorality*, New York: Columbia University Press, 2009.

Moghadam, Assaf, "Palestinian Suicide Terrorism in the Second Intifada: Motivations and Organizational Aspects," *Studies in Conflict & Terrorism*, 26, 2003, pp. 65–92.

Mohanty, Jitendranath, *Phenomenology: Between Essentialism and Transcendental Philosophy*, Evanston: Northwestern University Press, 1997.

Motahhery, Mortaza, *The Martyr*, translated and cited by David Cook, *Martyrdom in Islam*, New York: Cambridge University Press, 2007, p. 141.

Moyer, Mark, *A Question of Command: Counterinsurgency from the Civil War to Iraq*, Foreword by Donald Kagan & Frederick Kagan, New Haven: Yale University Press, 2009.

Mueller, Charles W., "Conceptualization, Operationalization, and Measurement," *The SAGE Encyclopedia of Social Science Research Methods*, Michael S. Lewis-Beck, Alan Bryman, & Tim Futing Liao, Eds., vol. 1, London: SAGE Publications, 2004.

"Muqtada al-Sadr, Iraqi Leader of the Al-Mahdi Movement, Supports Armed Attacks on U.S. Forces in Iraq," *Middle East Media Research Institute* (MEMRI), Special Dispatch Series, no. 1883, March 31, 2008.

Nasr, Seyyed Vali Reza, *The Vanguard of the Islamic Revolution: The Jama'at-i Islami of Pakistan*, Berkeley: University of California Press, 1994.

Nayyar, A.H. & Salim, Ahmed, "The Subtle Subversion: The State of Curricula and Textbooks in Pakistan," *Sustainable Development Policy Institute*, as cited in Amir Mir, *The True Face of Jehadis*, Lahore, Pakistan: Mashal Books, 2004, pp. 206–207.

Newby, Gordon D., *A Concise Encyclopedia of Islam*, Oxford, UK: Oneworld Publications, 2002.

Nietzsche, Friedrich, *Beyond Good and Evil* [1886], Walter Kaufmann, Trans., New York: Vintage, 1996.

Nietzsche, Friedrich, *On the Genealogy of Morality, A Polemic*, Maudemarie Clark & Alan J. Swensen, Trans., Indianapolis: Hackett Publishing Company, Inc., 1998.

Nietzsche, Friedrich, *The Will to Power*, Walter Kaufmann, Trans., Walter Kaufmann & R J. Hollingdale, Eds., New York: Vintage Books, 1968.

Norton, Augustus Richard, *Amal and the Shi'a: Struggle for the Soul of Lebanon*, Austin: University of Texas Press, 1987.

Norton, Augustus Richard, *Amal and the Shi'a: Struggle for the Soul of Lebanon*, Austin: University of Texas Press, 1987.

Norton, Augustus Richard, *Hezbollah*, Princeton, NJ: Princeton University Press, 2007.

O'Neill, John, Ed., *Hegel's Dialectic of Desire and Recognition*, New York: State University of New York Press, 1996.

Obaid-Chinoy, Sharmeen, *Pakistan: Children of the Taliban*, PBS documentary, funded by The John D. and Catherine MacArthur Foundation, The Skoll Foundation, The William Flora Hewitt Foundation, April 2009.

Oliver, Anne Marie & Steinberg, Paul F., *The Road to Martyr's Square: A Journey into the World of the Suicide Bomber*, Oxford: Oxford University Press, 2005.

Palmer, Monte and Palmer, Princes, *Islamic Extremism: Causes, Diversity and Challenges*, New York: Rowman & Littlefield Publishers, Inc., 2008.

Pannell, Ian, "Ex-detainees Allege Bagram Abuse," *BBC News*, June 24, 2009.

Pape, Robert A, *Dying to Win: The Strategic Logic of Suicide Terrorism*, New York: Random House, 2005.

Pape, Robert A. and Feldman, James K., *Cutting the Fuse: The Explosion of Global Suicide Terrorism and How to Stop It*, Chicago: The University of Chicago Press, 2010.

Pape, Robert, "It's the Occupation, Stupid," *Foreign Policy*, October 18, 2010, URL: www.foreignpolicy.com/articles/2010/10/18/it_s_the_occupation_stupid

Passmore, Kevin, *Fascism: A Very Short Introduction*, New York: Oxford University Press, 2002.

Patten, Alan, *Hegel's Idea of Freedom*, New York: Oxford University Press, 2002.

Pegg, Mark Gregory, *A Most Holy War: The Albigensian Crusade and the Battle for Christendom*, New York: Oxford University Press, 2008.

Perry, Marvin & Negrin, Howard E., Eds., *The Theory and Practice of Islamic Terrorism: An Anthology*, New York, NY: Palgrave Macmillan, 2008.

Phillips, Melanie, *Londonistan*, New York: Encounter Books, 2006.

Pinkard, Terry, *Hegel's Phenomenology: The Sociality of Reason*, New York: Cambridge University Press, 1996.

"Profile: The al-Mahdi Army," *al-Jazeera*, April 20, 2008, http://english.aljazeera.net/news/middleeast/2008/04/2008615165845241319.html

Qassem, Naim, *Hizbullah: The Story from Within*, Dalia Khalil, Trans., Lebanon: Saqi, 2010.

Qureshi, Emran & Sells, Michael A., "Introduction: Constructing the Muslim Enemy," *The New Crusades: Constructing the Muslim Enemy*, E. Qureshi & M.A. Sells, Eds., New York: Columbia University Press, 2003.

Qutb, Sayyid, *In the Shade of the Qur'an*, Vol. 8, Surah 9, cited in John Calvert's *Sayyid Qutb and the Origins of Radical Islamism*, New York: Columbia University Press, 2010, p. 244

Qutb, Sayyid, *Milestones*, New Delhi, India: Islamic Book Service, 2005.

Qutb, Seyyed, *Ma'alim fi al-tariq* (Signposts along the Way), cited in David Cook's *Martyrdom in Islam*, New York: Cambridge University Press, 2007, p. 139.

Rahman, Fazlur, *Major Themes of the Qur'an*, Chicago: University of Chicago Press, 2009.

Ramadan, Tariq, *Radical Reform: Islamic Ethics and Liberation*, New York: Oxford University Press, 2009.

Rana, Muhammad Amir, *A-Z of Jehadi Organizations in Pakistan*, Lahore, Pakistan: Mashal Books, 2004.

Reuter, Christoph, *My Life is a Weapon: A Modern History of Suicide Bombing*, Princeton, NJ: Princeton University Press, 2002.

Ricolfi, Luca, "Palestinians, 1981–2003," *Making Sense of Suicide Missions*, Diego Gambetta, ed., New York: Oxford University Press, 2005, pp. 77–129.

Rousseau, Jean-Jacques, *The Social Contract and Discourse on the Origins of Inequality*, Lester Crocker, Ed., New York: Washington Square Press, 1971.

Rubin, Alissa & Filkins, Dexter, "New Mission for Petraeus: Make his Own Plan Work," *The New York Times*, Thursday, June 24, 2010. A 12.

Rubin, Barry and Rubin, Judith Colp, Eds., *Anti-American Terrorism and the Middle East: Understanding the Violence*, New York: Oxford University Press, 2002.

Saad-Ghorayeb, Amal, *Hizbu'llah: Politics and Religion*, London: Pluto Press, 2002.

Saad-Ghorayeb, Amal, *Hizbu'llah: Politics and Religion*, London: Pluto Press, 2002.

Saeed Shaikh, Omar, "I'm Committed to Mulla Omar as the Leader of all Mujahideen Today," interview conducted by Massoud Ansari, *Newsline*, Karachi, Pakistan, April 2005, p. 44.

Sahlins, Marshall, "Preface," *The Counter-Counterinsurgency Manual*, Network of Concerned Anthropologists, Chicago: Prickly Paradigm Press, 2009.

Sartre, Jean-Paul. *Being and Nothingness: An Essay on Phenomenological Ontology*, Hazel E. Barnes, Trans., UK: Routledge, 2003.

Scarry, Elaine, *Rule of Law, Misrule of Men*, Cambridge, MA: The MIT Press, 2010.

Schacht, Richard, "Friedrich Wilhelm Nietzsche," *The Cambridge Dictionary of Philosophy*, 2nd Edition, Robert Audi, Ed., New York: Cambridge University Press, 2006.

Schadlow, Nadia, "A False Dichotomy: Critics of the Army's COIN Focus Ignore World and War Realities," *Armed Forces Journal*, September 2010, www.armedforcesjournal.com/2010/09/4707126

Scheffler, Samuel, ed. *Consequentialism and its Critics*, Oxford Readings in Philosophy, New York: Oxford University Press, 1988.

Schwartz, Michael, *War without End: The Iraq War in Context*, Chicago: Haymarket Books, 2008.

Shanker, Thom and Rubin, Alissa, "Quest to Neutralize Afghan Militants is Showing Glimpses of Success, NATO says," *New York Times*, Tuesday, June 29, 2010, A10.

Shanker, Thom, "Gates Defends Policy on Afghanistan and the Debate that Shaped it," *The New York Times,* Friday, September 24, 2010, A9.

Shearson, William A., "The Common Assumptions of Existentialist Philosophy," *The Development and Meaning of Twentieth-Century Existentialism*, William L. McBride, Ed., New York: Garland Publishers, Inc., 1997.

Shikaki, Fathi, *Jihad fis sabil Allah* (Jihad in the path of God), as cited by Christoph Reuter, *My Life is a Weapon: A Modern History of Suicide Bombing*, Princeton, NJ: Princeton University Press, 2002, p. 97.

Singer, Peter, *Hegel: A Very Short Introduction*, Oxford: Oxford University Press, 1983.

Smith, Sebastian, *Allah's Mountains: The Battle for Chechnya*, New York: Tauris Parke Paperbacks, 2006.

Solomon, Robert C., *From Hegel to Existentialism*, Oxford: Oxford University Press, 1987.

Steinhoff, Uwe, *On the Ethics of War and Terrorism*, Oxford: Oxford University Press, 2007.

Taylor, Charles, *Multiculturalism: Examining the Politics of Recognition*, Princeton, NJ: Princeton University Press, 1994.

Thomas L. Friedman, "What's Second Price?" *The New York Times*, Op-Ed, Wednesday, June 23, 2010.

Thompson, Janna, "Terrorism and the Right to Wage War," *Terrorism and Justice: Moral Argument in a Threatened World*, Tony Coady and Michael O'Keefe, Eds., Melbourne: Melbourne University Press, 2002.

"U.S. Tries to Calm Pakistan's Anger over an Airstrike," *The New York Times*, Thursday, October 7, 2010.

"US Drone Strikes Kill 14 Militants in North Waziristan," *Dawn* (Pakistan's most popular English daily newspaper), Friday, June, 11, 2010.

Varadarajan, Siddharth, "Chronicle of a Tragedy Foretold," *Gujarat: The Making of a Tragedy*, Siddharth Varadarajan, ed., India: Penguin Books, 2002.

Walzer, Michael, *Arguing about War*, New Haven: Yale University Press, 2004.

Walzer, Michael, *Just and UnJust Wars: A Moral Argument with Historical Illustrations*, New York: Basic Books, 1977; 4th edition 2006.

"War on Terror: 3 US Terrorists on Trail in Vietnam," *Kavkaz Center*, an independent Chechen news center, November 10, 2006, www.kavkazcenter.com/eng/content/2006/11/10/6352.shtml

Wells, Donald A., Ed., *An Encyclopedia of War and Ethnics*, Connecticut: Greenwood Press, 1996.

Wiktorowicz, Quintan, Ed. *Islamic Activism: A Social Movement Theory Approach*, Indiana: Indiana University Press, 2004.

Williams, Robert R., *Hegel's Ethics of Recognition*, Berkeley: University of California Press, 1997.

Williams, Robert R., *Recognition: Fichte and Hegel on the Other*, New York: State University of New York Press, 1992.

Wood, Allen W., *Kant's Ethnical Thought*, UK: Cambridge University Press, 1999.

www.dawn.com/wps/wcm/connect/dawn-content-library/dawn/news/pakistan/14-us-drone-strike-kills-four-in-north-waziristan-zj-08

Young-Bruehl, Elisabeth, *Why Arendt Matters*, New Haven: Yale University Press, 2006.

Zaidi, "Back to the Drawing Board," *The Herald*, Karachi, Pakistan, September 2003, p. 64.

Zulaika, Joseba, *Terrorism: The Self-Fulfilling Prophecy*, Chicago: University of Chicago Press, 2009.

Charters, declarations, statements, open letters, interviews

Abu-Surur, A videotaped last testament of a Palestinian suicide bomber, cited in Anne Marie Oliver & Paul F. Steinberg's *The Road to Martyr's Square: A Journey into the World of the Suicide Bomber*, Oxford: Oxford University Press, 2005, p. 120.

An anthem of the Palestinian *Hamas*, cited in Anne Marie Oliver & Paul F. Steinberg's *The Road to Martyr's Square: A Journey into the World of the Suicide Bomber*, Oxford: Oxford University Press, 2005, p. 99.

Azzam, Abdullah, A videotaped last testament of a Palestinian suicide bomber, cited in Anne Marie Oliver and Paul F. Steinberg's *The Road to Martyr's Square: A Journey into the World of the Suicide Bomber*, Oxford: Oxford University Press, 2005, p. 100.

Charter of the Palestinian *Hamas*, cited in Roxanne L. Euben & Muhammad Qasim Zaman, *Princeton Readings in Islamist Thought: Texts and Contexts from al-Banna to Bin Laden*, Princeton, NJ: Princeton University Press, 2009, p. 369.

Excerpts from a speech delivered by *Hamas* leader Khaled Mash'al at a Damascus mosque, aired on *al-Jazeera* TV, February 3, 2006, archived in *Middle East Media Research Institute* (MEMRI), clip no. 1024, available at www.memri.org

Excerpts from a speech delivered by Iranian President Mahmoud Ahmadinejad in Bushehr on February 1, 2006, archived in the *Middle East Media Institute* (MEMRI), clip no. 1019, available at www.memri.org, February 1, 2006.

Excerpts from Al-Zarqawi's audiocassette, January 2006, achieved in *Middle East Media Research Institute* (MEMRI); http://memri.org/bin/opener.cgi?Page=archieves&ID =IA28406

Excerpts from Ayman Al-Zawahiri's video, as seen in *al-Jazeera* TV, January 30, 2006, archived in *Middle East Media Research Institute* (MEMRI), clip no. 1082, February 1, 2006, available at www.memri.org.

Excerpts from Osama bin Laden's speech as delivered on *al-Jazeera* TV, January 19, 2006, archived in *Middle East Media Research Institute* (MEMRI), clip no. 1002, available at www.memri.org.

Hizbullah, "Open Letter to the Downtrodden in Lebanon and the World," cited in Augustus Richard Norton's *Amal and the Shi'a: Struggle for the Soul of Lebanon*, Austin: University of Texas Press, 1987, p. 170.

Interview of Abdul-Halim Sadulayev, Chechen Republic of Ichkeria (CRI) President, conducted by *Jamestown Foundation*, archived in *Kavkaz Center*, an independent Chechen news center, July 9, 2006, www.kavkazcenter.com/eng/content/2006/07/09/ 4929.shtml

Interview of al-Qaeda leader Ayman al-Zawahiri, archived in *Middle East Media Research Institute* (MEMRI), clip no. 952, December 7, 2005, available at www. memri.org.

Interview of *Hamas* and *Islamic Jihad* members, conducted by Nasra Hassan, cited in Nasra Hassan's "An Arsenal of Believers: Talking to the Human Bombs," *The New Yorker*, November 19, 2001, www.newyorker.com/archive/2001/11/19/011119fa_ FACT1

Interview of Iraqi cleric Sheik Ahmad al-Kubeisi on Saudi TV channel *al-Risala*, March 15, 2006, archived in *Middle East Media Research Institute* (MEMRI), www.memritv. org/search.asp?ACT=S9&P1=1075

Interview of Masood Azir, conducted by the *South Asia Tribune*, August 24, 2003, cited in Amir Mir's, *The True Face of Jehadis: Inside Pakistan's Network of Terror*, India: New Delhi, Roli Books, 2006,

Interview of Muqtada al-Sadr, cited in *The Middle East Media Research Institute* (MEMRI), "Muqtada al-Sadr, Iraqi Leader of the al-Mahdi Movement, Supports Armed Attacks on U.S. Forces in Iraq, Says al-Mahhdi Army Will Be," Special Dispatch Series no. 1883, *Middle East Media Research Institute* (MEMRI), March 31, 2009. http://memri.org/bin/printerfriendly/pf.cgi

Interview of Osama bin Laden with *al-Jazeera*, November 3, 2001, cited in Bruce Lawrence, Ed. *Messages to the World: The Statements of Osama bin Laden*, James Howarth, Trans., London: Verso, 2005, pp. 135–137.

Interview of Osama bin Laden, conducted by CNN's Peter Arnett, Jalalabad, March 1997, cited in Bruce Lawrence's *Messages to the World: The Statements of Osama bin Laden*, James Howarth, Trans., Bruce Lawrence, Ed., London: Verso, 2005, pp. 50–51.

Interview of Osama bin Laden, conducted by Rahimullah Yusufzai, January 1999, transcribed in *Newsline*, January 1999, p. 61.

Interview of Osama Hamdan in Lebanon, aired on January 25, 2006; archived in *Middle East Media Research Institute* (MEMRI), clip no. 1012, January 26, 2006, available at www.memri.org.

Osama bin Laden's open letter to the world, October 6, 2002, cited in Bruce Lawrence's *Messages to the World: The statements of Osama bin Laden,* James Howarth, Trans., Bruce Lawrence, Ed., London: Verso, 2005, pp. 162–164.

"The East Riyadh Operation and Our War with the United States and its Agents," a declaration of the *al-Qaeda* affiliated *Center for Islamic Studies and Research*, August 1, 2003; www.cybcity.com/newss, translated by Foreign Broadcast Information Service, cited in Robert A. Pape's *Dying to Win: The Strategic Logic of Suicide Terrorism*, New York: Random House, 2005, p. 118.

"The Islamic Ruling on the Permissibility of Martyrdom Operations," a declaration of the *Council of Scholars from the Arabian Peninsula*, cited in David Cook's *Understanding Jihad*, Berkeley, California: California University Press, 2005, p. 230.

"The Koran Encourages Terrorism; Bin Laden, Al-Zawahiri and Al-Zarqawi are not Terrorists in the Sense Accepted by Some," a statement forwarded by Egyptian Muslim Brotherhood, achieved in *The Middle East Media Research Institute* (MEMRI), March 10, 2006; http://memri.org/bin/opener.cgi?Page=archives&ID=SP111006

World Islamic Front, Declaration, February 23, 1998, cited in Bruce Lawrence's *Messages to the World: The Statements of Osama bin Laden,* James Howarth, Trans., Bruce Lawrence, Ed., London: Verso, 2005, pp. 59–60.

Index

Page numbers in *italics* denote tables, those in **bold** denote figures.